Mastering Criminal Law

Carolina Academic Press Mastering Series

Russell Weaver, Series Editor

Mastering Administrative Law
William R. Andersen

Mastering Alternative Dispute Resolution
Kelly M. Feeley, James A. Sheehan

Mastering American Indian Law
Angelique Townsend EagleWoman, Stacy L. Leeds

Mastering Appellate Advocacy and Process
Donna C. Looper, George W. Kuney

Mastering Art Law
Herbert Lazerow

Mastering Bankruptcy
George W. Kuney

Mastering Civil Procedure 2d e
David Charles Hricik

Mastering Constitutional Law 2d e
John C. Knechtle, Christopher J. Roederer

Mastering Contract Law
Irma S. Russell, Barbara K. Bucholtz

Mastering Corporate Tax
Reginald Mombrun, Gail Levin Richmond, Felicia Branch

Mastering Corporations and Other Business Entities 2d e
Lee Harris

Mastering Criminal Law 2d e
Ellen S. Podgor, Peter J. Henning, Neil P. Cohen

Mastering Criminal Procedure, Volume 1: The Investigative Stage 2d e
Peter J. Henning, Andrew Taslitz, Margaret L. Paris,
Cynthia E. Jones, Ellen S. Podgor

Mastering Criminal Procedure, Volume 2: The Adjudicatory Stage 2d e
Peter J. Henning, Andrew Taslitz, Margaret L. Paris,
Cynthia E. Jones, Ellen S. Podgor

Mastering Elder Law 2d e
Ralph C. Brashier

Mastering Employment Discrimination Law
Paul M. Secunda, Jeffrey M. Hirsch

Mastering Evidence
Ronald W. Eades

Mastering Family Law
Janet Leach Richards

Mastering Income Tax
Christopher M. Pietruszkiewicz, Gail Levin Richmond

Mastering Intellectual Property
George W. Kuney, Donna C. Looper

Mastering Labor Law
Paul M. Secunda, Anne Marie Lofaso, Joseph E. Slater, Jeffrey M. Hirsch

Mastering Legal Analysis and Communication
David T. Ritchie

Mastering Legal Analysis and Drafting
George W. Kuney, Donna C. Looper

Mastering Negotiable Instruments (UCC Articles 3 and 4)
and Other Payment Systems
Michael D. Floyd

Mastering Partnership Taxation
Stuart Lazar

Mastering Products Liability
Ronald W. Eades

Mastering Professional Responsibility 2d e
Grace M. Giesel

Mastering Property Law
Darryl C. Wilson, Cynthia H. DeBose

Mastering Secured Transactions (UCC Article 9) 2d e
Richard H. Nowka

Mastering Statutory Interpretation 2d e
Linda D. Jellum

Mastering Tort Law
Russell L. Weaver, Edward C. Martin, Andrew R. Klein,
Paul J. Zwier II, Ronald W. Eades, John H. Bauman

Mastering Trademark and Unfair Competition Law
Lars S. Smith, Llewellyn Joseph Gibbons

Mastering Criminal Law

SECOND EDITION

Ellen S. Podgor
GARY R. TROMBLEY FAMILY WHITE-COLLAR CRIME RESEARCH PROFESSOR
PROFESSOR OF LAW
STETSON UNIVERSITY COLLEGE OF LAW

Peter J. Henning
PROFESSOR OF LAW
WAYNE STATE UNIVERSITY LAW SCHOOL

Neil P. Cohen
RETIRED DISTINGUISHED SERVICE PROFESSOR &
W.P. TOMS PROFESSOR OF LAW
UNIVERSITY OF TENNESSEE COLLEGE OF LAW

CAROLINA ACADEMIC PRESS
Durham, North Carolina

Library of Congress Cataloging-in-Publication Data

Podgor, Ellen S., 1952- author.
Mastering criminal law / Ellen S. Podgor, Peter J. Henning, and Neil P. Cohen. -- Second Edition.
    pages cm. -- (Carolina Academic Press Mastering Series)
Includes bibliographical references and index.
ISBN 978-1-61163-549-2
1. Criminal law--United States. 2. Criminal law. I. Henning, Peter J., author. II. Cohen, Neil P., author. III. Title.

KF9219.P63 2015
345.73--dc23

2015006498

Carolina Academic Press
700 Kent Street
Durham, NC 27701
Telephone (919) 489-7486
Fax (919) 493-5668
www.cap-press.com

Printed in the United States of America

Yetta & Ben
(esp)

&

Philip, Thomas, Edward, and Nancy
(pjh)

&

First Edition
Ella Florence Cohen and Molly Mae Cohen —
welcome to a family that loves you dearly and
a Papa who can't wait to hear your jokes

Second Edition
Charley Cohen—
the newest member of a family that has your back forever
(npc)

Contents

Series Editor's Foreword

The Carolina Academic Press Mastering Series is designed to provide you with a tool that will enable you to easily and efficiently "master" the substance and content of law school courses. Throughout the series, the focus is on quality writing that makes legal concepts understandable. As a result, the series is designed to be easy to read and is not unduly cluttered with footnotes or cites to secondary sources.

In order to facilitate student mastery of topics, the Mastering Series includes a number of pedagogical features designed to improve learning and retention. At the beginning of each chapter, you will find a "Roadmap" that tells you about the chapter and provides you with a sense of the material that you will cover. A "Checkpoint" at the end of each chapter encourages you to stop and review the key concepts, reiterating what you have learned. Throughout the book, key terms are explained and emphasized. Finally, a "Master Checklist" at the end of each book reinforces what you have learned and helps you identify any areas that need review or further study.

We hope that you will enjoy studying with, and learning from, the Mastering Series.

Russell L. Weaver
Professor of Law & Distinguished University Scholar
University of Louisville, Louis D. Brandeis School of Law

Preface

It is not easy to capture all of criminal law in one relatively small book. With different state statutes, and also a federal system, it is difficult to include all of the nuances in the law. The Model Penal Code has exerted a substantial influence on the development of state statutes, despite it not being adopted in complete form by any jurisdiction. This book covers the major points that are discussed in many criminal law courses. It is intended to provide an overview of this important subject, as opposed to a resolution of a specific problem or case. The authors hope that this book will offer students an easier road in comprehending the subject area of criminal law.

There are many to thank, including Brooklyn Law School, Florida State University College of Law, Santa Clara University Law School, Stetson University College of Law, Wayne State University Law School, and Deans Jocelyn Benson, Christopher M. Pietruszkiewicz, Don Polden, Dana Brakman Reiser, Larry Solan, and Joan Wexler.

Ellen S. Podgor
Peter J. Henning
Neil P. Cohen
January, 2015

Mastering Criminal Law

Chapter 1

Introduction to Criminal Law

Roadmap

- What is criminal law?
- Distinguishing crimes from civil liability
- The basic elements of a crime
- Classification of crimes
- Sources of criminal law
- Role of the common law
- Jurisdiction for criminal acts
- Players in the criminal justice system
- The process of a criminal case

A. Introduction

Identifying conduct as a crime is one of the most important acts that society performs. Unlike injuries caused by acts or omissions that might support a private claim for damages or an injunction, attaching the label *crime* to a person's conduct means that the government can impose a legislatively-prescribed punishment, which can include the loss of certain liberties, incarceration, monetary penalties, and—for certain offenses—the loss of life. What does the label "crime" mean? Professor Henry Hart summarized it when he wrote that "[i]t is conduct which, if duly shown to have taken place, will incur a formal and solemn pronouncement of the moral condemnation of the community." Henry M. Hart, Jr., *The Aims of the Criminal Law*, 23 L. & CONTEMP. PROBS. 401 (1958).

There are two important points to notice about this description. First, the conduct must be "duly shown" to have occurred, which means it must have been determined by a trier of fact, such as a jury, to have occurred beyond a reasonable doubt and that it violates the law. This means there was a criminal *conviction.* Second, the criminal law invokes, at least in part, the morality of the community imposing the punishment, so that the label should not apply randomly or inconsistently.

There are thousands of criminal statutes at the state and local level, and estimates of as many as 40,000 federal provisions that could be applied in a criminal prosecution. Learning the details of such a broad array of laws is impossible. No law student (or lawyer) is expected to master even a fraction of the criminal laws on the books. There are, however, certain unifying aspects to all these criminal laws such that each can be analyzed, for the most part, using the same basic tools.

B. Distinguished from Civil Claims

Since the criminal and civil systems have so many similarities, it is easy to miss the significant differences between the two approaches. Nevertheless, there are distinctions that should be understood.

1. Harmful Conduct

Both criminal and tort law deal with actions deemed sufficiently harmful to merit government involvement in the creation of a remedy for the misconduct. Not surprisingly, the two systems are not mutually exclusive. Frequently, conduct deemed a crime is also a tort. For example, if D gets angry and hits V over the head with a tire iron, D has committed the crime of battery and also the tort of battery. D may face charges in a criminal court and a civil suit in the appropriate forum.

The conduct selected as a tort or crime is the product of a policy decision that the public interest is furthered by extending the civil or criminal laws to cover it. For example, lying to a friend about your social activities has not been made criminal, but lying to a police officer investigating a crime may be criminalized in some jurisdictions.

Today, the content of the criminal law is ordinarily determined by the legislature, while the reach of tort law may be the product of judicial decisions using a common law approach or legislative enactments defining tort liability.

2. Underlying Purpose

A primary purpose of the criminal law is to inflict *punishment* on people who violate its prohibitions. Ordinarily this means that the person is deemed *morally blameworthy* for his or her criminal conduct. The civil tort system, on the other hand, is basically designed to *compensate* people who were harmed by others. These fundamental differences are reflected in the remedies provided by the two approaches.

3. The Victim

In a tort case, the victim is the person or entity harmed. If victorious, he or she is entitled to compensation for the harm. While it is true that there are civil proceedings that may result in confinement of an individual suffering from a mental illness, or restrictions placed on the freedom of a sexual predator, those are not labeled as punishments even though the person's liberty is affected. For the most part, a private civil action is limited to monetary or injunctive relief. Only the parties to the action have a stake in its outcome, even in cases that involve thousands of claimants.

In a criminal case, however, the victim is considered to be the sovereign or other government unit, not the individual who was actually injured by the defendant. Indeed, the victim is usually not even considered to be a party to the criminal proceeding.

4. Remedies

Since punishment is a fundamental underpinning of the criminal justice system, the sanctions include incarceration and the like. For torts, the goal of compensating the victim ordinarily results in a money judgment designed to "make the victim whole." For example, assume that T, a trustee, steals money from the trust that he or she oversees. If T is caught and prosecuted criminally, the punishment for T's embezzlement may be a prison term plus a significant fine. If T is sued civilly by the people who created the trust, the court may order T to pay the victims the amount of money T took from the trust.

Sometimes a court may order the defendant who loses a civil or criminal case to pay a substantial sum. Although to the defendant it may not matter much whether the court order is the product of a civil or criminal matter since he or she is forced to pay money in both situations, there are significant differences. The money in the civil judgment is paid to the victim to compensate for the loss. If the money in the criminal case is paid as a *fine*, it goes to the government prosecuting the case, not to the actual victim. The difference is consistent with the view that the victim in the civil case is the individual or entity that directly suffered harm, while the victim in the criminal case is the government.

The boundaries between civil and criminal law become murky in a few situations. Often the criminal defendant is ordered to pay *restitution* to the victim to compensate for the harm. Similarly, occasionally the defendant in the civil case is ordered to pay *punitive damages*, which are designed to punish the defendant for especially serious misconduct.

5. Names of Parties

The differences between the civil and criminal system are reflected in the name (or style) of the case. In a civil case the names of the two parties are usually represented in the style of the case. Thus, *Smith v. Jones* often indicates that Smith is the plaintiff and Jones is the defendant. *United States v. Jones* indicates that the United States government is the plaintiff suing Jones, the defendant, in the civil matter.

A criminal case is similar. Since the government is, in theory at least, the victim, it is the equivalent of the plaintiff and its identity is included in the style of the case. For example, in a criminal case the first party listed may be the "United States" (for a federal prosecution) or "People," "Commonwealth," or "State" (for a state or local prosecution). The second named party is the accused. Thus, *State v. Jones* may be the style of a state criminal case in which Jones is prosecuted for robbery, while *United States v. Jones* would be a federal prosecution.

6. Procedures

One important effect of designating a proceeding as criminal is that certain *procedural protections* will apply that are not available in a civil action. While the law of criminal procedure is, for the most part, not directly relevant to the study of the criminal law and is beyond the scope of this book, there are certain fundamental aspects that need to be considered in understanding how the law of crimes operates.

Perhaps the most important procedural protection for a defendant is the *due process* right to the *presumption of innocence*. This requires the government to prove the defendant's guilt *beyond a reasonable doubt* (See Chapter 7). No such presumption exists in civil cases where the usual standard of proof is *preponderance of the evidence*, a much lower threshold than that used in criminal matters.

The criminal accused is entitled to many other rights not accorded the defendant in a civil case. The Bill of Rights, for example, grants many protections to the accused in a criminal case, but has no direct application in civil litigation. For example, only in a criminal case is the defendant guaranteed the Sixth Amendment's right to appointed counsel and the Eighth Amendment's prohibition of cruel and unusual punishment.

C. Elements of a Crime

A legislature desiring to make certain conduct criminal will enact a statute describing the conduct with particularity. This description establishes the *elements* that the government must prove to establish a person's guilt for that crime. In enacting the criminal statute, legislators should choose their words carefully so that it covers only the activities that the legislature wants to make criminal.

There are five types of elements in criminal statutes. Although all five are not always present in the same statute, an understanding of the categories will greatly assist in sorting out the exact meaning of a criminal law.

1. *Actus Reus*

A fundamental element in a criminal statute is the *actus reus,* which is the physical act (or omission) criminalized in the particular statute. For example, a homicide statute punishes people who commit the *actus reus* of "killing," arson criminalizes "setting fire to" a building, and larceny bans "taking and carrying away" someone else's personal property.

An *actus reus* may be present in one of two manners and is discussed extensively in Chapter 4. First, an *actus reus* occurs if the defendant undertakes a *voluntary act* covered by the criminal law. This would embrace the hired assassin who shoots the victim because the killer was paid to do so. The killer's action would satisfy the element in a murder law that made criminal the act of "killing" someone.

The second variety of *actus reus* is a *failure to act when there was a legal duty to do so,* called an *omission.* For example, a mother who allows her child to starve to death may be deemed to have committed the *actus reus* of "killing" her child. The mother failed to perform her legal duty to take reasonable care of the child and that breach of duty caused the child's death.

2. *Mens Rea*

While the *actus reus* is a critical part of criminal statutes, the *mens rea* or mental culpability requirement is at least equally as important. Criminal laws routinely limit liability to those who perform an act with a specified mental state. As discussed more fully in Chapter 5, the mental state is described in countless ways in American criminal laws. For example, homicide laws may punish a killing that is committed with "malice aforethought," "with the intent to kill," "recklessly," "with criminal negligence" or "negligently," "knowingly," or "willfully, deliberately, and with premeditation."

Mens rea elements allow the legislature to fine-tune its criminal laws by extending criminal liability only to people who fall into very specific categories. These categories are often used to determine the gravity of punishment. For example, someone who kills intentionally is punished more severely than someone who kills through criminal negligence.

Mens rea is also used to reflect the criminal law's focus on punishing those who are *morally blameworthy*. For example, if a person mistakenly takes someone else's umbrella, believing it was his or hers, the person is not guilty of a theft offense because the crime requires the defendant to have taken the item "with the intent to deprive the owner of it." It is simply an honest mistake, and does not merit punishment. By way of contrast, if someone took that same umbrella knowing that it belonged to another person and intending to sell it, the thief would violate the theft law because he or she intended to deprive the owner of the property.

Some criminal laws are *strict liability* offenses, meaning they do not have a *mens rea* element. Ordinarily these are minor offenses, such as speeding, but may be more serous ones, such as certain crimes punishing environmental harm or food and drug safety violations.

3. Circumstances

A third element in many criminal laws is one or more *circumstances*, which are facts that limit the reach of the provision. For example, a state assault statute may punish those who inflict serious bodily injury on a "child under age ten." The age of the victim is a circumstance that, like other elements, the government must prove beyond a reasonable doubt.

In selecting the circumstances in a criminal statute, the legislature narrows the scope of that law. Returning to the above example, if the legislature had used the age "eighteen" rather than "ten" in defining who could be the victim of the assault, the statute would be applied quite differently, perhaps now covering high-school fights and some gang-related activities.

4. Harm

Some criminal statutes include a particular *harm* as an element. The harm is viewed as a social harm that merits punishment when caused in a particular situation. A good example is the various homicide crimes that require the government to prove that the defendant killed someone. This means that there must have been a death, which is the harm embraced in the homicide law. Similarly, the crime of arson requires that a building be set on fire, a battery may mandate that someone suffer bodily injury, and an embezzlement statute may extend only to those who acquire money from the victim.

5. Causation

If a criminal statute includes harm as an element, it also includes the element of *causation*, which links the *actus reus* and the harm. In general, causation requires the prosecution to prove that the defendant's *actus reus* led to the harm prohibited in the statute. For example, in a homicide case the state must prove that the defendant's actions caused the death of the victim. Causation is discussed more fully in Chapter 6.

6. An Illustration

To illustrate the elements of a crime, assume that the jurisdiction has enacted a gang assault crime similar to the New York provision, N.Y. Penal Law § 120.06:

> A person is guilty of gang assault in the second degree when, with intent to cause physical injury to another person and when aided by two or more other persons actually present, he causes serious physical injury to such person or to a third person.

This statute contains all five types of elements. The *actus reus* is the conduct that causes serious physical injury. The *mens rea* is the "intent to cause physical injury to another person. "The circumstance is "aided by two or more other persons actually present." The harm is causing "serious physical injury to such person or to a third person." Causation is specifically mentioned: "he causes serious physical injury."

Although this provision incorporates all five types of elements, many statutes do not. It is common for a criminal statute to contain no element involving a harm or causation, such as a statute punishing the possession of cocaine. Other statutes may lack a *mens rea*. Note also that one element in a criminal statute may be both a circumstance and a harm. The exact category of an element does not matter. The important point is to understand the various types of elements and how to spot them in a criminal statute.

Each element must be proven by the prosecution beyond a reasonable doubt, which may be difficult in some cases. For example, in the gang assault statute it may be hard for the government to establish that two other people actually aided the defendant. What if they were just present and provided moral support, but did not render any actual assistance? Would this prove beyond a reasonable doubt that they were "aiding" the person who caused the serious physical injury?

D. Constitutional Limits

There are *constitutional* limits on the power of a legislature to enact criminal laws. Many, including vagueness, *Ex Post Facto*, and Bills of Attainder are discussed in Chapter 3. The First Amendment and Equal Protection are discussed below.

1. First Amendment

One of the clearest examples of a constitutional limit is the First Amendment, which provides that "Congress shall make no law . . . abridging the freedom of speech." A law contravening that proscription would be declared unenforceable and no one could be prosecuted for violating it. For example, a statute that barred all public demonstrations on an issue or prohibited chanting a particular slogan would run afoul of the First Amendment and be struck down.

2. Equal Protection

Similarly, the Equal Protection Clause of the Fourteenth Amendment would not allow a legislature to single out a particular group for punishment based on their race or sex, although the fact that a law has a disproportionate impact on a particular group usually is not a basis to invalidate a prosecution for violating the provision. An illustration of an equal protection violation would be a statute that punished women who battered men but did not punish men who battered women.

E. Classification of Crimes

1. Felony and Misdemeanor

Systems of criminal law routinely place crimes in various categories. The categories may be important for determining the punishment and procedures used in the case.

The English common law, discussed in more detail below, divided offenses into *felonies* and *misdemeanors*. This classification was based on the punishment that could be inflicted on a defendant upon conviction for a particular type of offense. Felonies were punished by death and misdemeanors were sanctioned by lesser penalties, such as imprisonment, forfeiture of land, whipping, fines, or forced manual labor.

The English terminology continues today in the United States, with the distinction between the different types of offenses still based in large part on the statutory penalty that may be imposed for a violation. The most common dividing line in American jurisdictions is that all crimes with a potential prison sentence of a year or more are categorized as felonies, while those with imprisonment of less than a year are misdemeanors.

2. Degrees of Crimes

Many modern jurisdictions today divide their felonies and misdemeanors into various *degrees*. For example, a state may have five degrees of felonies and three degrees of misdemeanors. The purpose of this classification system is to grade crimes for purposes of punishment. For example, a Class 1 felony may include such grave crimes as aggravated robbery and rape. It may carry a punishment of a prison sentence of twenty years to life. A Class 5 felony, on the other hand, would include less serious violations, such as small thefts and perhaps assaults not involving serious injury or a deadly weapon. A Class 5 felony could be punished by a maximum of two years in jail.

3. *Malum in Se* and *Malum Prohibitum*

Another traditional classification of crimes categorizes them as *malum in se*, which means wrongful in itself, or *malum prohibitum*, which is wrongful based on violating a legislative or administrative provision. Crimes that are *malum in se* may be described as involving *moral turpitude*, meaning that the offender has engaged in a breach of a social norm. The common law felonies, which include murder, rape, robbery, burglary, arson, and mayhem, were viewed as *malum in se* because the conduct was clearly against social norms.

In the modern era, a number of record-keeping, environmental, tax, and other regulatory offenses come under the label of *malum prohibitum*. They are so categorized because the legislature enacted them as a means to ensure the integrity of the administrative state and require adherence to its regulations, but the conduct is not viewed as involving serious moral wrongdoing in itself.

While today it ordinarily does not matter whether a crime is classified as a *malum in se* or a *malum prohibitum*, in one area the distinction may be important. The general rule is that only a *malum prohibitum* crime can be a strict liability offense, which is an offense that does not require proof of the defendant's mental state.

4. Moral Turpitude

In certain contexts, it matters whether a crime is one involving *moral turpitude*. Some licenses, for example, may be denied people convicted of a crime involving moral turpitude. Case law in the jurisdiction will determine which crimes are so classified. In addition, immigration law provides that a person may be deported or barred from naturalization for being convicted of a crime involving moral turpitude.

5. Effect of Classification of Crimes

The classification of a crime as a felony or misdemeanor, or some other category, can be very important in the case. It will affect the upper and lower limits of the authorized sentence and may also affect which sentencing alternatives are available. Thus, in many jurisdictions a person convicted of one of the top classes of felonies is ineligible for probation.

It may also affect which court has jurisdiction over the matter. Many states have lower-level courts of limited jurisdiction that are only allowed to hear certain types of minor offenses, usually misdemeanors, while a higher-level trial court hears felony cases.

Another way the classification is significant stems from offenses in which a prior felony conviction is an attendant circumstance of the offense. For example, the federal "felon-in-possession" law, 18 U.S.C. § 922(g)(1), makes it a crime for a person convicted of a crime punishable by imprisonment for a term exceeding one year to possess a firearm. This restriction does not apply to someone with only a misdemeanor record.

Under immigration law, a person convicted of a felony or aggravated felony may be deported or barred from naturalization, while someone with a misdemeanor conviction may not suffer this extreme hardship. The precise definition of these terms is quite significant and is determined by federal case law.

A felony conviction may also result in collateral civil consequences involving the loss of certain rights, such as the opportunity to hold elected or appointed office or to serve on a jury, and, in some states, the right to vote or obtain certain licenses. Often, misdemeanor convictions do not trigger these disabilities.

6. Administrative Sanctions

Not all violations of a law involve a criminal prosecution. Many states classify traffic violations and other minor misconduct as *civil infractions* that permit the payment of a fine without involvement in any further legal proceeding.

Many regulatory regimes, particularly at the federal level, allow administrative agencies to pursue *civil enforcement actions* against individuals and companies for violating the law. These administrative proceedings can result in the imposition of civil monetary penalties, injunctions from future violations, license revocation, and bans on future involvement in an industry or profession.

For example, while insider trading can be prosecuted as a criminal offense, the Securities and Exchange Commission, a federal administrative agency, brings most cases as civil actions to obtain disgorgement of the ill-gotten profits and a penalty, but with no criminal prosecution involved. These civil cases usually settle without an admission of a violation, unlike a criminal conviction that usually requires an acknowledgement of guilt.

F. Sources of Criminal Law

While today most criminal laws are statutory, the common law is still important both as a source of criminal laws in some jurisdictions and as a guide to interpreting statutes in all jurisdictions. Other less obvious sources also provide criminal laws that are applied in American courts to various degrees.

1. Common Law

a. Historical Status

Today statutes are the foundation for the criminal law, but its historical roots in the *common law* are very important for understanding the terminology used in many statutes and the types of defenses that may be available in a particular prosecution. The common law developed in England in the Middle Ages as judges recognized that certain conduct should be subject to criminal sanctions, the most extreme being death. Courts accommodated this concern by creating specifically defined offenses, such as larceny and arson. These *common law crimes* were recognized through a series of judicial decisions that served as *precedents* for future applications and development of the law. This slow process allowed the courts to both create crimes and adapt them as new situations and unexpected results arose.

The best illustration is the common law crime of larceny, originally defined by the courts as the *taking and carrying away of the personal property of another with intent to deprive the owner of it permanently*. When novel situations arose that were not technically covered by existing precedent, the courts expanded the reach of common law larceny by enlarging certain definitions. The evolution of theft law is discussed in Chapter 11.

The common law also divided crimes into the two basic categories of felonies and misdemeanors. The punishment for felonies such as murder, rape, and burglary was death, with lesser punishments for misdemeanors.

b. Relevance Today

The common law is still important in many areas of criminal law. First, although most jurisdictions no longer recognize these offenses without a corresponding statute, a few states still prosecute *common law crimes* when those offenses are not inconsistent with statutes. Courts, including those in states in which the legislature has abolished common law crimes, may also recognize *common law defenses* and rely on the common law to determine their scope. An example is insanity, which some jurisdictions accept as a defense but do not define by statute. Instead, the courts use the common law definition.

Second, some jurisdictions have statutes that generally define a crime but leave the detailed meaning to the common law precedents. People interested in the precise elements of a crime must search judicial precedents. In Michigan, for example, the legislature has defined murder in general terms but courts use common law decisions for more precise definitions of the statutory terms. *People v. Kevorkian*, 527 N.W.2d 714 (Mich. 1994).

Third, the common law is often an important tool of *statutory construction* to determine the meaning of the elements of a statutory crime. The Supreme Court stated that, as a general rule, "where a federal criminal statute uses a common-law term of established meaning without otherwise defining it, the general practice is to give that term its common-law meaning." *United States v. Turley*, 352 U.S. 407 (1957).

2. Statutes

The criminal law today is almost completely statutory, which means that the legislature plays the primary role in determining what types of conduct can be labeled as crimes. The legislature creates a crime when it concludes that there is an aspect of *wrongfulness*, that the person's acts are not socially beneficial, and that there is a general consensus that the conduct should be actively discouraged.

The legislature's pre-eminent role in defining crimes and defenses is relatively new in America. Both before and after the American Revolution, the states retained and developed the common law by adapting it to the particular circumstances present in the United States. During the nineteenth century, the legislatures began to enact statutes creating or refining crimes, a movement that culminated in the twentieth century with the adoption of extensive criminal codes designed to *supplant the common law.*

Today many state statutes and federal law specifically repudiate common law crimes and only permit prosecutions for violations of specific provisions of the state's criminal code. For example, the Pennsylvania statute states, "No conduct constitutes a crime unless it is a crime under this title or another statute of this Commonwealth." *18 Pa. C.S.A. § 107(b)*.

A few states permit prosecution of a statutory offense or a common law crime arising out of the same course of conduct so long as the legislature has not abolished the common law crime. For example, the adoption of a kidnapping statute does not affect the common law crime of false imprisonment in those states that have not prohibited prosecution of common law crimes. It is quite uncommon for a state court to create a new common law crime, and the breadth of state criminal codes means that the *statutes are the primary source of the criminal law.*

3. Administrative Crimes

In addition to particular crimes adopted by the legislature, the growth of the large administrative state has spawned a significant array of regulatory codes that govern a wide swath of daily life. Violation of an administrative provision may result in a civil enforcement action, and can even lead to criminal charges when the legislature has authorized criminal penalties for violation of the administrative regulations.

For example, under the federal securities laws, a defendant who "willfully violates any ... rule or regulation" issued pursuant to those laws can be subject to a criminal prosecution, which means that a large volume of administrative provisions can result in a criminal conviction and even a prison sentence.

4. Other Sources

While virtually all crimes today are the product of statutes, the common law, and administrative regulations, there are several other sources that arise occasionally. *International criminal law* is typically not enforced in American courts, although some statutes in the United States are enacted because of international treaties. For example, the United States enacted explicit statutes prohibiting the crime of torture following its ratification of the Torture Convention. 18 U.S.C. § 2340 et. seq. Additionally, courts will sometimes reference international principles in interpreting U.S. statutes.

On Indian reservations and some other areas under Indian auspices, *tribal law* defines certain crimes. The general area of criminal law on Indian reservations and related property is quite complex and varies depending on the precise legal status of the area. In the most general terms, tribal laws are enacted by the tribal council and approved by the Secretary of the Interior. Some trials for less serious offenses are conducted by tribal courts.

Another source of criminal law is the Military Code of Justice for crimes involving armed forces personnel or property. These offenses are tried in military courts and operate under their own rules of procedure.

5. Model Penal Code

One of the most important penal codes is not in fact a law itself but a model for state legislation. The *Model Penal Code*, adopted in 1962 by the American Law Institute, has been quite influential in many states, leading to significant changes and revisions to criminal codes. Even in jurisdictions that have not adopted it, its principles and commentary on the criminal law have been influential on judicial interpretation of criminal statutes and the scope of defenses. For example, the Model Penal Code provides a structure for the *mens rea* element of offenses that has been widely adopted by state legislatures in modernizing their criminal codes. Some courts in jurisdictions that have not enacted statutes based on the Model Penal Code have also used the its definitions in interpreting the meaning of *mens rea* elements in their criminal laws.

The primary reason for studying the Model Penal Code, despite the fact that no state has adopted it *in toto*, is because of the comprehensiveness of its provisions. The Model Penal Code provides a foundation for understanding how the basic principles of the criminal law can be applied consistently across the spectrum of state statutes and judicial precedents.

Nevertheless, in jurisdictions that have not adopted any of the Model Penal Code's provisions, the Code may be irrelevant to virtually all issues that arise for the criminal law practitioner. In a jurisdiction that has adopted some of the Code's provisions, a lawyer is well advised to consider the Code's extensive commentary in interpreting and advocating the meaning of those Code-based laws.

G. Jurisdiction

In the United States, there are two levels of government that may be authorized to pursue criminal charges: the federal government and each of the fifty states (plus the District of Columbia and Puerto Rico). States in turn may delegate a portion of their authority to local bodies, such as counties or municipalities. Each level of government has authority to punish criminal conduct that comes within its *jurisdiction*, which involves two aspects: first, the *power to enact a statute* designating conduct as criminal, and second, the *authority to prosecute a person* in that government's courts and impose punishment for a violation.

1. Federal

Under the United States Constitution, the federal government has a limited power to regulate and punish conduct, and every federal statute must be based on a specific grant of authority to the Congress, such as the Commerce Clause. Because the federal government is one of limited power, the states retain the broad *police power* recognized as inhering in all sovereign nations to adopt regulations "to define the criminal law and to protect the health, safety, and welfare of their citizens." *Gonzales v. Raich*, 545 U.S. 1 (2005). The federal government has the equivalent of the police power of the states to legislate on property it owns or administers, including military installations outside the United States. The same authority applies to conduct occurring within the "admiralty and maritime jurisdiction," including ships and aircraft from the United States even if the crime occurs in another country.

2. Territorial

The second issue related to jurisdiction is the authority of a nation (or state) to impose its laws on a particular defendant in a criminal prosecution in its courts. There are different grounds on which a government can assert jurisdiction to apply laws to an individual defendant for conduct that may have violated one of its statutes. The fundamental basis for criminal jurisdiction is based on the *territoriality principle*, which specifies that conduct within the confines of a state or nation is subject to its criminal (and civil) laws. This was the basis for jurisdiction under the common law in England and has been recognized in the United States.

Today, criminal conduct that occurs outside the country's territorial boundaries is often prosecuted when it *affects* the United States. For example, a key stroke on a computer releasing a computer virus by someone in another country, who has never been inside the United States, may result in the individual being prosecuted in this country because of the harm caused to domestic businesses or individuals.

H. Participants in the Criminal Justice System

There are a number of different individuals involved in a criminal investigation and prosecution. Of course, the key person is the defendant, who has certain rights guaranteed by the Constitution during both a police investigation and any subsequent prosecution for an offense. It is the defendant who will suffer the consequences of a determination of guilt, and so it is this person who can challenge the decisions made during the process. Therefore, judicial opinions refer to the "defendant" offering an argument or motion, even though lawyers do the actual work in large part. There are many other key participants in the system.

1. Investigators

All levels of government have, or contract for, law enforcement officers whose duty is to ensure public safety and investigate crimes. For example, there are state police officers, Federal Bureau of Investigation (FBI) agents, and local police who investigate alleged criminal conduct within their jurisdiction. As public officials, they are subject to the constraints imposed by the Constitution, such as the requirement of probable cause to obtain a search warrant or providing specified warnings before beginning an interrogation.

Investigators also may appear as witnesses at trial and assist the prosecutor in preparing for the trial. Because of their familiarity with the details of the case, some investigators, such as the lead detective, may even sit at the prosecution's table during the trial and advise the prosecutor about documents and other matters relevant to the case.

Defense lawyers may also use investigators. Often public funds are available to hire investigators for indigent defendants, if they can convince a judge of the need to retain an investigator. Some law firms and public defender offices have their own investigators on staff.

2. Prosecutors

Prosecutors may become involved in an investigation before a person is charged with a crime, such as when there is a need for a warrant to search property. Once a person is arrested and charged with a crime, the prosecutor's office assumes responsibility for the case from the police and makes decisions as to what charges (if any) will be pursued, what evidence will be presented at trial, whether to enter into a plea bargain, how to try the case, and what recommendation to make for an appropriate sentence if there is a conviction. Prosecutors have almost unreviewable discretion, absent evidence of improper discrimination, regarding whether or not to prosecute a case and what charges will be prosecuted.

Prosecutors are viewed as "ministers of justice" in addition to their role as an advocate on behalf of the government. This means they have an ethical obligation to seek justice rather than just vengeance.

3. Defense Counsel

The Sixth Amendment provides that "[i]n all criminal prosecutions, the accused shall enjoy the right ... to have the Assistance of Counsel for his defence." As interpreted by the Supreme Court, the government must provide a defendant with counsel if he or she cannot afford to retain a lawyer in any felony prosecution and in misdemeanor cases in which a term of imprisonment is imposed. State laws often expand the right to counsel even further, extending it to all felony and serious misdemeanor cases irrespective of the actual punishment.

The defense lawyer is crucial to the system because counsel is the primary voice for the defendant from the time charges are filed through the appeal of a conviction, ensuring that the prosecution is fair and that the law is followed. Accordingly, the Sixth Amendment guarantee has been interpreted as providing that both appointed and retained counsel must provide *effective assistance* to a defendant. A determination that counsel was ineffective can result in a reversal of a conviction even though the government did nothing to affect the representation of the defendant.

4. Judges

Both the defendant and the government are entitled to a fair and disinterested judge. This means that the judge should not be involved in a case if biased for or against a party. To ensure impartiality, the law even says a judge should not participate in a case if there is the *appearance* of any partiality or interest in the matter.

While the judge is viewed as a neutral referee, the court has a significant interest in ensuring that the trial proceed expeditiously and that the evidence introduced meets the requirements for admissibility under the relevant evidence and procedure rules. If there is a conviction, it will be the judge's responsibility to impose an appropriate punishment on the defendant, subject to legislative limitations such as minimum and maximum sentences.

5. Jury Trial

The trial jury, sometimes known as a "petit" jury, is a group of citizens selected to decide whether the government's evidence establishes the defendant's guilt beyond a reasonable doubt. The Sixth Amendment provides that a defendant in a prosecution for any crime in which a prison sentence of more than six months is authorized has the right to "an impartial jury of the State and district wherein the crime shall have been committed." Many state laws expand the right to a jury to any felony or serious misdemeanor.

Despite the constitutional guarantee, in actuality a jury trial—or even a bench trial on the merits of the case—occurs in relatively few cases. The vast majority of criminal cases end in a plea bargain, in which the government and defendant agree that the defendant will enter a guilty plea to certain charges. In such cases the defendant waives the right to have both a trial and a jury.

For those few cases that proceed to trial, it is the jury that decides the facts, based on its review of the evidence and credibility of witnesses, and then applies the law to those facts to determine whether the defendant is guilty. If a jury returns a "not guilty" verdict on a charge, under the Double Jeopardy Clause the defendant cannot be retried in that jurisdiction for the same crime, nor can the government appeal even if the verdict was erroneous. Because a "not guilty" verdict is unreviewable, juries have the power to *nullify the law*, *i.e.* refuse to apply the law in a manner consistent with its factual determination that would otherwise lead to a guilty verdict.

6. Victims

In the analysis of the criminal law, victims are probably the least discussed group, although they feel the direct effects of the misconduct. Through a nationwide *victim's rights movement*, there has been a push to grant victims greater participation in the criminal justice process. Advocates for victims' rights have been successful in having statutes and court rules promulgated in many jurisdictions. These laws give victims many rights to participate in the prosecution that they did not have in the past. A common illustration is a law giving victims the right to be notified of the status of the case and the times and dates of court proceedings. Another example is that many jurisdictions now give the victim the right to remain in the courtroom during the entire trial. This is a change from evidence rules barring the victim, like any other witness, from hearing the testimony of other witnesses.

Victims' rights provisions frequently also allow victims (or their surrogates) to provide *victim impact* information for the court to use in determining the appropriate sentence. Sometimes these laws specifically give the victim the right to appear in person and testify at the sentencing hearing.

Although victims have increased rights during various court proceedings, victim's rights laws usually do not give them the right to participate directly in the plea bargaining process. Many prosecutors, however, routinely advise the victim about ongoing plea discussions and get the victim's input before agreeing on a sentence.

7. Probation Office

The probation office, which may operate under a different name, prepares a *presentence report* on the defendant after a conviction, regardless of whether by jury verdict or guilty plea. Except for minor offenses, sentencing usually takes place in a proceeding separate from the trial on the defendant's guilt. At the sentencing hearing the judge considers the presentence report. This report contains information about the background of the defendant, prior arrests and convictions, work and family history, and other information that is gathered in a separate investigation. Often, statements from victims are included to inform the court of the effect of a crime, such as the amount of loss or physical damage from the conduct.

Unlike a trial, in which the jury may only consider admissible evidence, a presentence report can relate information about the defendant as a person. Since the rules of evidence usually do not apply at sentencing (or at least do so only in a watered-down fashion where some otherwise inadmissible evidence is permitted), the presentence report may include hearsay and perhaps unverified statements or information that would not be admissible at trial.

I. The Process of a Criminal Case

1. Prosecutorial Discretion

For complex crimes, a unit within the prosecutor's office may become involved in a case at an early stage, often before any individuals have been identified as potential defendants, and undertake the task of gathering and analyzing evidence to ascertain the perpetrator. The prosecutor's office makes, or approves, the decision to file particular charges, usually without outside review under an exercise of *prosecutorial discretion* granted to the executive branch of government. Courts rarely intervene in the exercise of this discretion, citing concerns about separation of powers between the executive and judicial branches of government. Courts do step in, however, when the discretion is abused in violation of the Equal Protection or Due Process Clauses.

2. Complaint or Information

After the police arrest a person and complete an investigation, or at least gather the basic evidence identifying the perpetrator(s), the person will be charged with a crime by a document called a *complaint* or *information*. These describe basic facts about the offense.

A complaint is drafted by a *complainant* who may be the victim, a police officer, or a prosecutor. It is given under oath. Sometimes the prosecutor must sign the complaint for it to be valid. This procedure allows the prosecutor to screen out complaints filed by angry or vindictive individuals on flimsy or nonexistent grounds.

If an information (which is prepared and signed by the prosecutor) is used, it must be based on a conclusion that there is *probable cause* to believe that the defendant committed the crime. That standard means that the prosecutor found sufficient evidence to reasonably believe the defendant committed the crime.

3. Preliminary Hearing

For a defendant charged by complaint or information, courts in many jurisdictions will conduct a *preliminary hearing* to make an independent determination of whether there is probable cause that the defendant committed the offense. The preliminary hearing is adversarial; defense counsel and a prosecutor represent the two sides. There is no jury and the case is heard by a single judge or magistrate.

The issue is whether there is probable cause to believe a crime was committed and the defendant was the perpetrator. The preliminary hearing is far less formal than a trial. For example, in many locales, the rules of evidence do not apply or apply in a watered-down fashion.

In some jurisdictions, if the court finds probable cause at the preliminary hearing, the case is *bound over* to the grand jury. The defendant may waive a preliminary hearing and have the case submitted directly to the grand jury. This may occur to speed up the process if the defendant is incarcerated pending the trial.

4. Grand Jury

Some jurisdictions allow the prosecutor to proceed directly to the grand jury to charge a defendant with a crime. Like the determination at a preliminary hearing, the grand jury decides whether there is probable cause to believe the defendant committed the crime. If the grand jury finds probable cause, it approves an *indictment* as recommended and drafted by the prosecutor's office.

The grand jury is comprised of a group of citizens. Its proceedings can be characterized as non-adversarial, informal, and secretive. The prosecutor serves as legal advisor for the grand jury. No judge is present during the grand jury's proceedings and defense counsel is usually not permitted inside the grand jury room. The rules of evidence ordinarily do not apply, meaning the grand jury is routinely presented with hearsay evidence and even evidence obtained in violation of the Constitution. Often the only witness is the investigating police officer who tells the grand jurors about the evidence. If the grand jury returns an indictment, the case will proceed to trial or result in a guilty plea or other disposition.

5. Arraignment

After the complaint is filed or the grand jury votes to indict, the usual procedure is that the defendant will be *arraigned*. An arraignment is an administrative hearing where the defendant is formally apprised of the charges, invited to enter a plea, and, if a "not guilty" plea is entered, the court sets a trial date, perhaps many months in the future.

6. Motion Practice

A *motion* is a formal request for a court to issue an order on a particular topic. In criminal cases most motions are filed before trial. Typical pretrial motions seek rulings on such matters as the exclusion of evidence (*e.g.*, *Miranda* and the exclusionary rule) and obtaining materials through discovery. A critically important set of motions may seek dismissal of the charges for insufficient evidence, failure to charge a crime, statute of limitations, or double jeopardy.

If one side files a motion, the other side may file a response indicating why the motion should be denied. Usually courts will hold a *motion hearing* before trial to hear arguments, examine evidence, and issue rulings on the various motions. The court's decision on a motion may shape the trial strategy and often will encourage one or both sides to enter serious plea negotiations to resolve the case. For example, this could occur if the defendant filed a motion to suppress certain prosecution evidence and the court ruled against the motion and in favor of admitting the proof. Faced with the prospect of a jury that will hear the adverse evidence, the defense may be more receptive to avoiding a trial and entering a plea agreement.

7. Plea Bargain

The government and the defendant—usually through counsel—can agree to a *plea bargain* under which a defendant will plead guilty to certain charges, often in exchange for a lower sentence than would be imposed if the case went to trial and a conviction resulted. Plea bargains are so widespread that it is not unusual for them to be used to resolve over ninety percent of felony cases.

If the two sides agree on a plea deal, the agreement will require the defendant to waive the right to trial and proceed immediately to sentencing. The government may demand as a condition of the plea bargain that the defendant cooperate in its investigation by identifying other wrongdoers against whom the defendant will testify if the government initiates or continues other prosecutions.

8. Trial Rights

The criminal accused has a host of rights at trial. Though these important issues are beyond the scope of this book, a few merit brief mention. A defendant is entitled to a *lawyer* if incarceration is ordered. Moreover, the accused may have a *jury trial* if he or she can be incarcerated for more than six months for the offense. A defendant can waive a jury trial if the prosecution agrees, in which case the judge hears the case as the trier of fact. For most minor offenses, the court will decide the case without use of a jury.

At trial, the defendant has the constitutional right *to testify*, but the Fifth Amendment's privilege against self-incrimination prohibits the government from calling the defendant as a witness and forcing him or her to testify. Moreover, if a defendant does not testify, the prosecutor may not comment directly or indirectly on the defendant's decision.

9. Jury Instructions

At the end of a jury trial, the judge will give *instructions* to the jury that include a statement of the law relevant to the determination of guilt. The jury instructions usually originate with counsel for both parties who suggest to the judge what they view as appropriate statements of the law, although many courts rely on model jury instructions that can be tailored to a particular case. Ultimately, the judge decides what to tell the jury in the instructions, and they are often a source of claimed error on appeal after a conviction. Among other things, the jury instruction will contain a description of the elements of the crime and of any applicable defenses.

The jury must decide whether the proof establishes these elements beyond a reasonable doubt. The jury may also be instructed to consider whether any defenses, such as insanity or self defense, have been established.

10. Double Jeopardy

Under the *Double Jeopardy* Clause, a defendant may not be put "twice in jeopardy" for the same offense. If a person is found "not guilty" of a charge, then the prosecution may not pursue that charge in a second proceeding, regardless of the strength of its evidence. An important exception to this rule is the *Dual Sovereignty Doctrine*, which permits a different state or the federal government to prosecute a person for the same crime so long as that second state or federal government has jurisdiction over the offense. For example, Terry Nichols was tried by both federal and Oklahoma courts for the deaths that occurred in connection with the Oklahoma City bombing in 1996. The double jeopardy protection is the source of the jury's power to nullify the law because its not guilty verdict is unreviewable.

11. Appeal

If the defendant is found guilty, then he or she can appeal any errors in the trial (*e.g.*, improper jury instructions, insufficient evidence, etc.) and the sentence to a higher court for further review. A defendant must demonstrate a *legal error* in the trial or pre-trial procedure if the person seeks to have the conviction overturned. An appeal based on *insufficient evidence* questions whether the government presented enough evidence of the defendant's guilt at trial such that a *reasonable juror* could find the defendant guilty beyond a reasonable doubt. Appellate courts often state that their role is not to second-guess the jury's factual determinations or assessments of the credibility of witnesses, which are based on viewing their demeanor that is not conveyed by a written transcript. If a defendant is acquitted, under principles of double jeopardy the government cannot appeal, even if there was a legal error that contributed to the verdict.

Many criminal appeals raise questions about the jury instructions, in particular whether the court gave an improper definition of the crime or the scope of the conduct that comes within the statutory prohibition. A defendant can also appeal a conviction on the ground that *evidence was improperly admitted* under the evidence rules, or whether the court *excluded the defendant from presenting evidence* relevant to the case that might have affected the jury's determination of guilt. A defendant can also raise a *constitutional challenge* to the statute he or she was convicted of violating, or argue that conduct by the judge or prosecutor violated a constitutional right, such as the right to confront witnesses or the prohibition on prosecutorial comment on the defendant's decision not to testify.

12. Remedy

The usual *remedy* for a legal error at trial that substantially affected the outcome is a *new trial.* However, if the appellate court finds that the government failed to introduce sufficient evidence of guilt, then a "not guilty" verdict must be entered.

Despite the prevalence of appeals in criminal cases, relatively few are actually successful. Even if there was a statutory or constitutional violation during trial, most of those are reviewed on appeal under the *harmless error* standard, which permits an appellate court to uphold a conviction if it determines that there was sufficient evidence of guilt and the error did not affect the outcome.

The government cannot appeal a "not guilty" verdict returned by a jury, but if a court dismisses a charge before trial, or grants a judgment of acquittal after the jury returns a guilty verdict, then the government is allowed to appeal. The government also can appeal sentencing issues, although a jury decision not to impose a death sentence cannot be reviewed.

Checkpoints

- A crime is a label for conduct that incurs "a formal and solemn pronouncement of the moral condemnation of the community."

- Although criminal law and private civil claims may overlap, the criminal law involves governmental action seeking to punish the defendant for violating a social norm.

- The criminal law is now largely statutory, although its roots are in the common law and many offenses reflect the influence of common law crimes.

- A criminal law defines the type of conduct and, in most cases, the intent of the actor that must be proven for a determination that the person is guilty of violating the provision.

- The elements of a crime are the constituent parts of the offense that the government must prove beyond a reasonable doubt.

- There are limits on what a legislature can designate as criminal, and the statute must be sufficiently clear to give adequate warning of what conduct is prohibited.

- Crimes can be divided into different categories, the two most prominent being felony/misdemeanor and *malum in se/malum prohibitum.*

- Most states limit prosecutions to violations of statutes and do not recognize common law crimes, but the common law remains important for interpreting the language and scope of criminal laws.

- The Model Penal Code provides a systematic treatment of the criminal law that has been influential in the interpretation of statutes.

- The principal participants in the criminal justice system, in addition to the defendant, are: investigators, prosecutors, defense counsel, the judge, the jury, and probation officers.

- A defendant and the government can agree to a plea bargain that results in a guilty plea to specified charges without a trial, which is how most criminal cases are resolved.

- In a jury trial, the judge provides instructions on the law to the jury, which is responsible for applying the law to the facts to decide whether the government has proven the defendant's guilt beyond a reasonable doubt.

- If a defendant is convicted, he or she can appeal and seek to overturn the guilty verdict by demonstrating legal errors in the trial that substantially affected the outcome.

Chapter 2

Interpretation and Constitutionality

Roadmap

- How to interpret statutes generally
- Using the common law to interpret criminal statutes
- Unique interpretation principles that apply to criminal law statutes
- Constitutional constraints placed upon Congress in drafting statutes

---

A. General Rules of Statutory Interpretation

1. Generally

As criminal law is statutory in nature, the process of interpreting these statutes is important. Merely reading the language of a statute, however, may not provide sufficient guidance to courts when they apply a statute to a specific factual scenario. A variety of interpretative principles have developed to assist in this regard. Equally important are constitutional constraints that place restraints on legislatures to protect rights afforded to criminal defendants, rights that cannot be infringed upon by government legislation.

In interpreting a statute, courts typically start with the text itself, looking at the *plain meaning* of the words used. This is the clearest indication of what the legislators intended when they passed the statute. If the statute has terms that cannot be determined solely from the text, then courts will examine the *legislative history* of the statute to try to discern the intent of the legislature when the law was passed. Courts also look at *precedent*, as prior caselaw offers judicial opinions that have previously examined the statute. Finally, courts also consider the *policy considerations* behind the statute. They will look at what motivated the legislature to pass the law and what purpose the legislature had when the legislation was initially considered.

2. Plain Meaning

In interpreting a statute, courts start with the text of the provision by looking at its plain meaning and applying a common sense interpretation to the words used. Sometimes courts will resort to dictionaries to determine how to interpret a term within a statute. Thus, it is common to see references to *Webster's Dictionary* or *Black's Law Dictionary* when a court is trying to find the common meaning of a term used in a statute. For example, in deciding how to interpret the term "carries a firearm" in a criminal statute, the Court looked to many dictionaries in deciding that "the word 'carry' includes the carrying of a firearm in a vehicle." *Muscarello v. United States*, 524 U.S. 125 (1998). Courts also refer to rules of grammar and look at punctuation in interpreting statutes.

The statute is examined as a whole. Thus, in interpreting a statute, courts try to find a meaning that can be applied to the entire subject matter. A statute's title can also be helpful. For example, although the term "murder" may not be used in the statute that speaks to the "unlawful killing of a human being by malice aforethought," the use of the term "murder" in the title provides a clear indication of the conduct envisioned to be covered under the statute.

3. Legislative Intent

As legislatures enact the statutes, courts are left with the task of trying to discern the meaning intended by the drafters. Determining the legislative intent may be accomplished by looking to the history surrounding the passage of the statute. There may be discussion at hearings, committee reports, or floor debates that can provide guidance as to what the legislature intended to accomplish by passing the statute.

In addition to these legislative materials, courts can also examine changes in the law to identify the meaning of the words in a statute. For example, a statute may initially have the terms "knowingly and intentionally" as an element of a crime. When the legislature modifies the statute by deleting the word "intentionally" from the statute, it indicates to courts that the legislature no longer requires prosecutors prove "intentionally" for this crime. Proof of knowledge alone will suffice.

It can also be helpful to see how the same term is used in other statutes passed by the legislature. For example, if a carjacking statute requires a "felonious taking" of a motor vehicle, and the term "felonious taking" is also used in the state's robbery statute, a court may decide that the term should have the same meaning in both statutes and look to how it is defined in the robbery statute to determine how it should be applied in the carjacking statute.

Some words, however, may have different meanings depending on the statute in which they are used. For example, courts have held that the term "willfully" is a word of many meanings and may be interpreted differently when used in a tax statute than when used in a firearm statute.

4. *Ejusdem Generis*

When general language follows specific terms in a statute, the rule of *ejusdem generis* limits the general language to the specific categories listed. For example, a statute that prohibited possession of a dagger, blackjack, pistol, and other deadly or dangerous weapons, would not include a flare gun designed as an emergency signaling device.

5. *Expressio Unius Est Exclusio Alterius*

This principle means that "the expression of one thing is the exclusion of another." For example, a statute passed by a legislature that expressly prohibits the exportation of drugs but makes no mention of importation, means that the legislature's expression of exportation limits the scope of the statute only to exportation and does not extend the statute to importation of drugs.

6. Precedent

When a court interprets a statute for the first time, it is called a case of *first impression*. Most often, however, prior courts have looked at the same terms in the statute and interpreted these terms. The *precedent* produced by these prior cases is heavily relied upon by courts in the same jurisdiction. When a higher court has spoken on the issue in question, this is considered controlling precedent and lower courts are bound to follow the ruling of the superior jurisdiction. In some cases, such as when a court does not have precedent within the controlling jurisdiction, precedent from another jurisdiction with a similar statute may be examined.

7. Policy Considerations

Courts interpret statutes to reflect the policy rationale of the legislature. Thus, if Congress passes a statute to combat terrorist activity, courts will interpret the statute to include activities that might be within the realm of terrorism even though the specific activity might not have been included by Congress in the statute. In *Bond v. United States*, 134 S. Ct. 2077 (2014), the

Supreme Court rejected the government's use of the Chemical Weapons Convention Implementation Act of 1998 (18 U.S.C. §229) in a case involving a simple assault by a woman who placed chemicals on the car door, mailbox and door knob of her husband's lover hoping that she would "touch the chemicals and develop an uncomfortable rash." The Court held that "the global need to prevent chemical warfare does not require the Federal Government to reach into the kitchen cupboard, or to treat a local assault with a chemical irritant as the deployment of a chemical weapon."

8. Textual v. Dynamic Approach

Judges do not always have a consistent approach to statutory interpretation. Some prefer to use a strict textual approach relying heavily on the language used in the statute. Others take a more dynamic approach looking at extrinsic factors in interpreting the words used in a statute. This can sometimes account for a majority and dissent in cases that require the interpretation of a statute.

B. Interpreting Criminal Laws

1. Common Law

The United States law to a large extent comes from England. The body of law that developed from the judicial decisions of England and later statutes forms the common law in the United States. Although there is no single book that compiles the common law, and oftentimes it has an amorphous nature to it, courts regularly refer to the common law for guidance in interpreting criminal statutes as common law crimes often serve as the basis for statutory crimes. Unless a statute states otherwise, courts will often rely on the common law when interpreting the meaning of statutory terms. For example, the federal perjury statute does not explicitly require testimony from two witnesses to prove that a person lied under oath. Courts, however, have followed the common law "two-witness rule" that requires proof by two different witnesses or items of evidence to serve as sufficient corroboration in a perjury prosecution.

Many states model their statutes after the common law. For example, at common law murder was an unlawful killing done with "malice aforethought." Some states will use these explicit common law words in their statute. Others, still using a common law approach, will designate murder into degrees, having murder in the first degree as killings committed "willfully, deliberately, and with premeditation." In interpreting these common law statutes, courts will often look to the precedent developed in the common law.

2. Model Penal Code

As noted in Chapter 1, the *Model Penal Code* (MPC), adopted by the American Law Institute (ALI) in 1962, serves as a guide to states in passing criminal statutes. Though provided as a model statute, it has not been adopted in its entirety by any jurisdiction. States that have adopted MPC provisions have a number of resources to use in interpreting its language as the ALI provided both Explanatory Notes and Comments as guidance. These Explanatory Notes and Comments discuss the rationale for various terms used in the MPC. The Comments also analyze state statutes and cases that are instructive in interpreting the MPC.

The Model Penal Code also includes some general rules for interpreting its provisions. For example, it states that an underlying purpose governing the definition of an offense is "to give fair warning of the nature of the conduct declared to constitute an offense." *Model Penal Code § 1.02.* The MPC also indicates that, in general, when the law defining an offense provides a *mens rea* element, that element applies to all the material elements of the offense, unless the statute indicates to the contrary. *Model Penal Code § 2.02.*

C. Specific Rules Applicable to Criminal Law Interpretation

1. Rule of Lenity

The *rule of lenity*, sometimes called the *rule of strict construction*, applies to criminal statutes that do not have a clear meaning or are subject to more than one possible constitutional meaning. The rule requires that the statute be interpreted narrowly to favor the accused. The policy rationale here is to make certain that the accused has fair notice of the crime. Another rationale is that the state, which enacted the unclear statute and has a duty to ensure that its criminal laws are reasonably understandable, should not benefit from its poor drafting. If a statute is subject to two possible meanings, then the benefit is given to the accused to minimize arbitrary enforcement by the prosecution. For example, in defining the word "property" for the mail fraud statute, the Court decided that a video poker license would not be considered property. As the term in the statute was ambiguous, the Court selected the definition most favorable to the accused. *Cleveland v. United States*, 531 U.S. 12 (2000). Some jurisdictions codify the rule of lenity, such as Florida which provides for strict construction of statutes and states that "when the language is susceptible of differing constructions, it shall be construed most favorably to the accused." *Fla. St. § 750.021*.

Other jurisdictions may specify when another test, called the *rule of fair import*, may apply. This rule encourages interpreting a statute to further the general purposes of the statute. For example, a New York statute provides that criminal laws "must be construed according to the fair import of their terms to promote justice and effect the objects of the law." *N.Y. Penal Law § 5.00*.

2. Extraterritorial Application

The place of the crime normally determines the place of prosecution. Although extraterritorial prosecutions may be permitted when the conduct affects the United States or a state, there is a presumption against extraterritorial application when interpreting a statute. For example, a statute that prohibits individuals who have been convicted in *any court* from possessing a firearm, will be interpreted to include only U.S. courts absent congressional language that explicitly allows foreign courts to also be covered by the statute. *Small v. United States*, 544 U.S. 385 (2005).

D. Constitutional Constraints

1. Generally

The United States Constitution, as well as specific Constitutions of a state, place constraints on the legislature in their adoption of statutes. These principles, sometimes called principles of legality, serve to make certain that individuals are properly advised of what conduct will be subject to punishment so that this conduct can be avoided. Legislators must therefore write clear statutes. There is also a need to make certain that police and prosecutors, who have enormous discretion in arresting and charging defendants, remain within the constitutional mandates when applying the law.

2. Vagueness

A statute cannot be so "vague that men of common intelligence must necessarily guess at its meaning and differ as to its application." *Connally v. General Construction Co.*, 269 U.S. 385 (1926). A vague statute violates the Due Process Clause of the U.S. Constitution. Courts require clear statutes (1) to allow people to arrange their conduct so as to steer clear of unlawful acts, (2) to prevent arbitrary and discriminatory enforcement of laws by police officers, judges and juries, and (3) to avoid limiting individual freedom of speech and expression. Thus a California loitering statute that required people to provide "credible and reliable" identification when stopped by the police was held unconstitutional, as it failed to specify clearly what constituted "credible and reliable" identification and left it to police to decide the scope of the statute on a "moment to moment judgment." Statutes cannot "confer[ ] on police a virtually unrestrained power to arrest and charge persons with a violation." *Kolander v. Lawson*, 461 U.S. 352 (1983). Likewise, a loitering statute that infringed on the "freedom to loiter for innocent purposes," would infringe on a fundamental "liberty" interest protected by the Due Process Clause of the Fourteenth Amendment to the U.S. Constitution. *Morales v. City of Chicago*, 527 U.S. 41 (1999).

3. Federalism

The federal government can only pass legislation that is within the exercise of its constitutional powers. Most typically federal criminal legislation comes from the Commerce Clause or the taxing powers of the Constitution. Thus, when Congress passes a criminal law that encompasses conduct that is traditionally a state concern, federalism concerns may be raised. For example, the Supreme Court invalidated the Gun-Free School Zones Act, which made it a federal crime to have a firearm within one thousand feet of school, because the activity was strictly a state concern and that "neither the actors nor their conduct" had a "commercial character," thus exceeding Congress' powers under the Commerce Clause. *United States v. Lopez*, 514 U.S. 549 (1995).

Likewise, the Court reversed a federal arson conviction, finding that the federal arson statute did not cover the arson of an owner-occupied dwelling that was "used for everyday family living." The Court found that the federal statute "covers only property currently used in commerce or in an activity affecting commerce." *Jones v. United States*, 529 U.S. 848 (2000).

4. Right to Privacy

Criminal statutes cannot violate the right to privacy guaranteed by the Due Process Clause of the Fourteenth Amendment. For example, the Court invalidated a Texas statute that was exclusively focused on same-sex sodomy that was applied to a consensual act within the privacy of a home. *Lawrence v. Texas*, 539 U.S. 558 (2003).

5. Cruel and Unusual Punishment

The Eighth Amendment of the U.S. Constitution prohibits "cruel and unusual punishments." In reality there is no explicit list of punishments that are deemed "cruel and unusual." This constitutional provision is discussed in more detail in Chapter 3.

6. *Ex Post Facto*

The Constitution prohibits ex post facto laws. *U.S. Constitution*, Art. 1, §§ 9, 10. This provision means that a defendant cannot be punished for a crime that was not a statutory offense at the time he or she committed the act. The fact that the legislature later makes this activity criminal will not allow for its prosecution under the new law. For example, if A puts a virus into a computer system, and at the time A did this act the state where A was located did not have a law prohibiting this activity, that particular state cannot prosecute A for a crime, even if legislators later pass a statute making this conduct criminal.

In the same vein, an accused cannot be punished for an aggravated crime that increases the crime or penalty from that which existed at the time the accused committed the criminal activity. Punishment is limited to what is contained in the statute at the time of the act. The rationale behind this constitutional mandate is that the general public should be placed on notice of what is considered criminal. The policy rationale here is that one could refrain from committing the activity if he or she knows in advance that the activity will result in a criminal prosecution and possible punishment.

7. Bill of Attainder

The Constitution prohibits laws that punish without first having a trial. *U.S. Constitution*, Art. I, §§ 9,10. Thus, legislation that designates a person as a criminal without first affording the individual a trial and without the person first being convicted by a judge or jury is not allowed.

Checkpoints

- In interpreting a statute one starts with the plain meaning of the statute.

- Courts seek to interpret a statute in accordance with the legislative intent and to discern this intent they look at legislative history and policy considerations used by the legislature when they passed the statute.

- As criminal law comes from the common law, common law precedent is often used to interpret a criminal statute.

- When a criminal statute has two possible meanings and neither of these interpretations renders the statute unconstitutional, the Rule of Lenity provides for an interpretation that favors the accused.

- Some jurisdictions also use a Rule of Fair Import that interprets words in a statute according to their "fair meaning" consistent with the goals of the criminal law.

- The U.S. Constitution requires that statutes be clear and that they provide sufficient notice of what will be punished.

- Federal statutes must be premised upon a constitutional power and federalism concerns are raised when the statute encompasses conduct that is traditionally a state concern.

- Criminal statutes cannot infringe on constitutional rights of privacy and the punishment cannot be "cruel and unusual."

- Under the *Ex Post Facto* Clause, only conduct occurring after the passage of a criminal statute can be punished, and under the Bill of Attainder provision, the Constitution requires that statutes provide individuals the right to a trial and conviction prior to the imposition of punishment.

Chapter 3

Sentencing

A. Sentencing: In General

One hallmark of the criminal justice system is that the accused, once convicted, is *punished* for the crime. Punishment refers to state-imposed sanctions for being convicted of violating the criminal law. Common forms of punishment are fines, incarceration, probation, and even the death penalty. By way of contrast, punishment does not include the many unpleasant collateral consequences that may accompany a criminal conviction but are not the direct product of government action. While a private employer may fire an employee because of the latter's criminal conviction, the job loss is technically not considered punishment because it is not imposed by the government.

This chapter presents an overview of the American sentencing system. It addresses theories of punishment and constitutional limits on sentencing, then turns to the structure of sentencing law. This includes various models and options as well as the many actors who play a role in sentencing and the procedures used in the American system of assigning sanctions for criminal behavior.

B. Theories of Punishment

Though often sentencing decisions become so routine that it is quite predictable that a particular judge will put a first-time shoplifter on probation or send an armed robber to prison for ten years, sentencing should be based on fundamental theoretical principles. Traditional American sentencing rules ordinarily identify four basic theories that, in whole or part, guide sentencing decisions in individual cases. Other theories have also been advanced.

Theories of punishment may be divided into two categories: *utilitarian* and *deontological*. Utilitarian theories (sometimes called *consequentialist* theories) are designed to accomplish a good purpose, such as rehabilitating a criminal's crime-prone values or frightening him or her into foregoing criminal activity. Deontological theories view sanctions as serving intrinsic or morality-based justice, irrespective of the practical impact of the sentence. Retribution, for example, fits this second category.

1. Rehabilitation

A mainstay of sentencing theory is *rehabilitation*, which means that the sentence should be designed to turn the defendant into a person with law-abiding values and behavior. Ideally, rehabilitative sentences should be individualized for each offender, identifying the causes of the offender's criminal behavior and making the necessary changes to "cure" those causes. Often characterized as based on the "medical model" involving an "illness" and curative action, typical rehabilitative sentences would require counseling for defendants guilty of domestic assault, sex abuse of minors, or drug-related behavior.

Critics of rehabilitative sentencing argue that it gives too much discretion to judges and others who, though lacking in adequate training and evidence-based approaches, and sometimes bearing substantial biases, decide what the defendant's problem is and what is needed to rectify it. This could result in unfair discrimination against certain individuals or groups. The opponents also note that sometimes rehabilitative sentences are too lenient when compared with the gravity of the offense. Finally, the wisdom of rehabilitation-based sentences is challenged by studies casting doubt on whether such sentences are actually successful in altering a criminal offender's values and behavior.

2. Retribution

A popular theory of sentencing is *retribution*, which holds that a criminal deserves punishment for violating the law. Sometimes referred to as *just deserts*, this theory posits that a person who commits a crime should be punished in order to be fair to the victim, others who have been punished for the same crime, and even to the offender who, as a human being, deserves to be held accountable for his or her actions.

Retribution not only holds that a person should be punished, but it also places limits on what that punishment should be. Loosely reflecting the values behind "an eye for an eye," this theory says that the punishment should be proportionate to the gravity of the crime. This formulation is a two-edged sword, setting a measure for both the minimum and maximum punishment given an offender. At the bottom, retribution provides that the punishment should not be too lenient when measured against the gravity of the offense. At the other end, it should also not be too severe when measured against the gravity of the crime. Thus, retributivists would argue that sentencing a person guilty of a torture-murder to one year in prison is disproportionate considering the seriousness of the crime. Similarly, sentencing a first-time shoplifter to twenty years in prison is too severe, being disproportionate to the gravity of a relatively minor crime.

Some critics of retribution argue that it is based on primitive notions of vengeance and should not be part of a civilized nation's jurisprudence. Other scholars argue that retribution should set the upper and lower parameters of a potential sentence, but theories such as rehabilitation and incapacitation should be used to fashion the exact sentence.

3. Deterrence

Deterrence is a theory that is based on the premise that people will refrain from criminal activity because of fear of getting caught and punished. There are two types of deterrent. *Special deterrence* involves punishing the actor in order to deter that actor from future criminal activity. *General deterrence* is designed to deter people in general by punishing the criminal actor. For example, if a drunk driver is given a month-long jail sentence, that sanction may be considered to be a special deterrent to induce in the defendant an unwillingness to reoffend because of a fear that he or she could suffer an unpleasant loss of liberty. The jail term may also serve as a general deterrent if it convinces other people that they should not drive while drunk because they, too, may suffer a significant jail sentence if apprehended.

Critics of deterrence theory point out the lack of reliable information that changes in sentences actually affect deterrent levels. For example, they note that social science research has not confirmed that increasing an authorized sentence from five to ten years will increase the deterrent value of that sentence. These theorists posit that the likelihood and fear of apprehension, rather than the scale of the punishment, are actually the most important factors in making sanctions a deterrent.

4. Incapacitation

Incapacitation seeks to reduce future crime by making it difficult or impossible for the defendant to reoffend during the period of the sanction. In essence, it "gets the criminal off the streets" so that society is protected for at least a period of time. The death penalty is the ultimate incapacitative sentence. Incarceration also prevents the defendant from directly committing a crime against the non-prison population as long as the defendant is behind bars. A recent trend in sentencing, called *Three Strikes You're Out*, is another example of incapacitation since it increases substantially the sanction for a third (or sometimes just a repeat) conviction. A good illustration is that in some jurisdictions a person convicted of a third violent felony may receive a sentence of life imprisonment as an habitual or three-strikes offender. A primary purpose of this severe sanction is to incapacitate an offender who has demonstrated a propensity to commit crimes and is deemed likely to reoffend in the future.

Incapacitation requires a prediction of future dangerousness and a sanction that protects society during that dangerous period. Some theorists argue for *selective incapacitation*, which means that incapacitation should be applied to those offenders with a very high likelihood of reoffending. Ordinarily, this means the defendant has a lengthy record of previous criminal activity and will get an especially long sentence since the past extensive record is deemed an indication of substantial future criminality.

Critics of incapacitation argue that it gives too much discretion to those who assign sentences and that it is based on a false assumption that these decision makers can predict which offenders need to be incapacitated and how long that incapacitation should last. The net result, the critics argue, is that some people are incarcerated needlessly for incapacitative reasons since they were never (or are no longer) a threat to society.

5. Education (or Expressive Sanctioning)

Some penologists argue that criminal sanctions are important because they help *educate* the public about the values of society. By punishing a person for drunk driving, for example, society condemns that behavior and clearly conveys the message that it is not tolerable. The total package of criminal sanctions provides citizens with a general sense of what conduct is permissible and what is forbidden.

6. Restitution

While restitution is ordinarily not considered a separate theory of punishment and is utilized in conjunction with one of the four traditional sanctions, it is an important sentencing goal. Restitution requires the offender to "make the victim whole" by compensating the victim for the loss. Ordinarily, restitution involves a court-ordered payment of money to compensate for such costs as the victim's medical expenses, property damage, and even lost wages caused by the crime. For example, if the defendant commits a carjacking in which the victim suffers injury and the car is wrecked, restitution may require the defendant to pay the cost of the victim's hospital and related expenses, repairing or replacing the car, replacing lost wages, and even paying for mental health treatment to deal with the trauma of the carjacking. While a large restitution may be ordered, in many cases the actual payment the victim receives is quite small because of the defendant's inability to pay.

7. Restorative Justice

Restorative justice is an increasingly popular theory that maintains the criminal justice system should attempt to restore social relationships between the victim and the offender. When possible, both sides should work together in resolving how to deal with the victim's loss and the defendant's conduct. Used most frequently for minor offenses, the defendant's sanction may be the product of a mediation session or at least substantial input from the victim and the defendant. For example, assuming a willing victim and a cooperative defendant, if the defendant gets drunk and vandalizes a person's house, under restorative justice the defendant and the victim would meet and discuss the incident. Perhaps the defendant would agree to repair the damage, hear from the victim how disturbing the vandalism was, apologize to the victim, join an alcohol treatment program, and mow the victim's lawn or perform community service for three months. The victim would agree to the prosecutor dropping the charges if the defendant complied with the program. Perhaps the defendant and victim would even meet a few times during that period to discuss the situation.

While restorative justice may be successful in some cases, in many others it is not appropriate. If the victim refuses to participate or the defendant is unwilling to go through the process with an accepting attitude, the efforts may fail or even be harmful. Victims may feel or actually be threatened while in the defendant's presence. Some critics also note that the restorative sanction may be inappropriately lenient considering that the crime is a harm to society (which may not be represented during the negotiations), not just the individual actors.

C. Constitutional Limits on Sentences

The United States Constitution places limits on sentences, though these limits rarely matter in individual cases since sentencing procedures are routinely deemed to satisfy constitutional standards. A comprehensive view of the subject is beyond the scope of this book, but a few of the more important issues are discussed.

1. Equal Protection

Sentencing issues may engender equal protection challenges. The Equal Protection Clause may be violated if a judge or legislature uses race or gender as the basis for assigning a sentence. A sentence that, without any rational basis, reflects disparate treatment of similarly situated defendants may also violate equal protection. Not surprisingly, there are very few cases finding an equal protection violation since virtually all sentencing classifications and decisions are held to be based on a rational classification system. For example, a federal appellate court held that a mandatory sentence for using a firearm to commit a crime of violence is rationally related to the purpose of reducing violent crime by incapacitating and deterring those likely to commit violent crimes and does not violate equal protection or due process rights.

2. Cruel and Unusual Punishment

The Eighth Amendment bars the infliction of cruel and unusual punishments. One way a sentence would violate this principle is if it is exceptionally cruel. The most obvious illustration would be a sentence requiring that a defendant be subjected to torture. The less obvious version of cruel and unusual punishment is *proportionality* between the severity of the crime and the sentence. Although the United States Supreme Court has been sharply divided on the issue, there seems to be agreement that at the least the Eighth Amendment bars a sentence that is *grossly disproportionate* or "excessive" when the offender and the crime are taken into consideration. The measuring stick is the "evolving standards of decency that mark the progress of a maturing society." *Trop v. Dulles*, 356 U.S. 86 (1958). A sentence of thirty years incarceration for possessing one marijuana cigarette may be so extreme as to constitute cruel and unusual punishment.

For example, in *Ewing v. California*, 538 U.S. 11 (2003), the defendant stole three golf clubs worth about $1200 and was convicted of felony grand theft. Because of four previous felony convictions, under California's "Three Strikes" law the defendant was sentenced to 25 years to life for the golf club theft. He argued that the lengthy sentence was cruel and unusual punishment for a relatively minor crime. A seriously fractured Supreme Court upheld the sentence. Justice O'Connor, representing the views of three Justices, found the sentence was not grossly disproportionate to the crime because of the defendant's felonious past. Justices Scalia and Thomas concurred on the theory that the Eighth Amendment does not guarantee proportionality or even protect against grossly disproportionate sentences. Justice Breyer's dissent, speaking for four members, opined that the sentence at issue was grossly disproportionate to the offense.

Another illustrative case is *Miller v. Alabama*, 567 U.S. _____ (2012), where the Supreme Court held that a mandatory sentence of life without parole for offenders under age eighteen at the time of their crimes violates the Cruel and Unusual Punishment Clause. This provision, according to *Miller*, bans sentences that mismatch the culpability of a class of offenders (such as minors) and the severity of a penalty. Minors, unlike adults, have diminished culpability, more impetuosity and less maturity, but also have greater chance for reform.

Some state courts rely on their state constitution's Cruel and Unusual Punishment Clause to invalidate a sanction. *E.g., People v. Bullock*, 485 N.W.2d 866 (Mich. 1992) (state cruel and unusual punishment guarantee violated by life without parole sentence for defendant convicted of possessing more than 650 grams of cocaine mixture).

3. Sentencing Models

American sentencing schemes follow several models.

a. Determinate and Indeterminate

Some jurisdictions use *indeterminate sentencing*, which means the defendant is given a sentence within a range, such as 2–5 years. The parole board or an equivalent body decides when the defendant will be released after serving two years, or less for a good prison record. The defendant must be freed after five years. The board may base its release decision on such factors as the gravity of the initial crime, the prisoner's institutional record, the views of the victim and others, and the extent of prison overcrowding.

Scholars have been especially critical of the indeterminate model. They argue that it gives too much discretion to the parole board, allows discrimination on the basis of impermissible factors such as race, affluence, or gender, and provides the defendant with too much uncertainty since he or she does not know, at the time the sentence is imposed or even during the period of incarceration, when the prison term will end.

A *determinate sentencing* approach gives the defendant much more specific information. The sentence is for a set number of months or years, such as "three years in prison" or "one year on probation." If the jurisdiction in the prior example uses parole, the offender sentenced to three years in prison may be released after serving two years and then be on parole for the remaining year.

b. Sentencing Guidelines

Concerns about *too much discretion* and *disparity* in sentencing led many jurisdictions to adopt *sentencing guidelines*. Sentencing guidelines represent an effort to give more predictability to sentencing decisions. A state, often through a *sentencing commission*, prepares a set of guidelines that judges must (or may) follow in assigning sentences. The commission may be comprised of a group of people from various backgrounds, often appointed by the governor or other political figures.

Ordinarily, the commission produces a set of guidelines that are presented in the form of a two-dimensional grid. The two variables are (1) the gravity of the offense, often expressed in a category such as "Level 6" or "Class 2," and (2) the defendant's prior history. For instance, a state's guidelines may provide that a defendant convicted of a Class 4 felony who has two prior convictions should receive a determinate sentence between 3–5 years. The judge has the discretion to select a specific sentence within that range, such as four years in prison.

The judge may have to give reasons for the sentence. Often the jurisdiction will have a list of aggravating and mitigating factors that the court should use in determining the precise sentence within the applicable range. Frequently the court is also given the discretion to go above the maximum grid sentence (5 years) or below the minimum grid term (3 years), but will have to give reasons on the record for this *departure*.

The most complicated set of guidelines is the *Federal Sentencing Guidelines* adopted by Congress and effective in 1987. Because of judicial decisions, the federal guidelines are advisory rather than mandatory, meaning federal judges have discretion whether to follow them. It uses the two dimensional concept of sentence severity and the defendant's criminal history, but involves a detailed analysis to assess the exact *offense severity* level and the defendant's *criminal history*. The offense severity level is determined by giving or taking points for a number of specific factors included in the guidelines. For example, a federal offender ordinarily gets the offense severity level reduced by two points if he or she *accepts responsibility* for the crime and would get a two level increase if deemed to have obstructed justice during the prosecution of the case.

D. Actors in the Assignment of Sentences

Many people play an important role in the sentencing system in America. Some of their involvement escapes public attention while the roles held by others are the product of local rules or customs, sometimes subjected to intense political scrutiny.

1. Legislature

While no American legislature assigns criminal sentences in an individual case, it does set the parameters of sentences by enacting the sentencing laws that judges and others in the system must follow. For example, the legislature usually places limits on the judge's discretion, such as by providing a minimum and maximum possible sanction (for example, 2–5 years), a minimum sanction (not less than 2 years), a maximum sentence (not more than 5 years), or guidelines that greatly restrict the judge's range of choices.

2. Judge

The trial judge is ordinarily considered the most important actor in assigning sentences. While to some extent this is true, in actuality the issue is more complex. In non-capital cases, the trial judge has the ultimate responsibility for selecting a sentence, but, as discussed below, may have to rely on the jury if certain facts must be determined in order to assign the sentence. Thus, a judge is the person who would assign a robbery defendant a five-year prison sentence. In capital cases, ordinarily the jury decides whether the defendant will be given the death penalty or a lesser punishment, such as life (or life without parole) in prison. But even in capital cases when the jury decides to impose the death penalty, the judge is usually given the power to overrule the jury's decision and give the defendant a non-capital sentence.

Though the trial judge does have the authority to impose sentence, that authority may be severely constrained. In addition, since most convictions are the result of guilty pleas, discussed in more detail below, the judge's importance in the typical plea-bargained case is minimal. Trial courts routinely approve the sentence agreed on by the defendant and prosecutor during plea negotiations.

3. Jury

The American jury used to play a direct role in sentencing, but over time *jury sentencing* was replaced by *judge sentencing*. The change stemmed from concerns that jurors were too inexperienced to impose sentences that were consistent with those given by other juries in the same jurisdiction. Critics also alleged that juries may be biased against certain groups or individuals and that judges could be more trusted to be fair to everyone.

The trend toward judge sentencing was somewhat reversed when the Supreme Court decided in *Apprendi v. New Jersey*, 530 U.S. 466 (2000), that the Sixth Amendment right to a jury trial, combined with due process, requires greater jury participation in sentencing. The defendant in *Apprendi* pled guilty to a number of weapons-related crimes carrying a maximum sentence of twenty years. Under New Jersey's hate crime law, however, the court could increase (or "enhance") the maximum to thirty years if the judge found that one of the offenses was motivated by "a purpose to intimidate" a person or group of people on the basis of race or other impermissible reasons (color, gender, handicap, religion, sexual orientation or ethnicity). The court could not enhance the sentence without making a factual finding of purposeful racial bias. After a hearing, the judge found by a preponderance of evidence that the defendant's conduct was racially motivated and imposed the enhanced sentence. The defendant argued that the jury, not judge, was required to make the racial motivation factual determination by the higher standard of proof beyond a reasonable doubt. The Supreme Court agreed, holding that under due process and the Sixth Amendment the jury must decide facts that expose the defendant to a sentence that is greater than that authorized by the guilty verdict alone.

Apprendi created great uncertainty since in many jurisdictions it was not clear what had to be submitted to a jury and what could be decided by the judge alone. In *Blakely v. Washington*, 542 U.S. 296 (2004), the defendant pled guilty to kidnapping his wife and faced a maximum sentence of 53 months. However, as authorized by Washington sentencing law, the judge found that the defendant had acted with "deliberate cruelty" (qualifying defendant for an "exceptional sentence" involving an upward departure from the normal sentencing guideline range) and sentenced him to 90 months in prison. Relying on *Apprendi*, the defendant argued that the deliberate cruelty finding should have been made by a jury rather than the judge alone. The Supreme Court found the argument persuasive, citing *Apprendi* for the proposition that "other than the fact of a prior conviction, any fact that increased the penalty for a crime beyond the prescribed statutory maximum must be submitted to a jury, and proved beyond a reasonable doubt." *Blakely* interpreted this language as meaning that the "statutory maximum" refers to the maximum sentence the judge may impose solely on the basis of the facts reflected in the jury verdict. Since the finding of "deliberate cruelty" was not inherent in the finding of guilt, the jury should have been given the task of deciding whether the defendant's acts involved deliberate cruelty. A subsequent decision expanded *Blakely* to require a jury finding of facts that increase the mandatory minimum penalty. *Alleyne v. United States*, 133 S. Ct. 2151 (2013).

After *Blakely,* states scrambled to make their sentencing schemes consistent with the new constitutional requirements. There were several options. Some jurisdictions chose to follow *Apprendi* literally and submit the additional facts to a jury in a second proceeding after the initial jury determination of guilt. Another possibility was to have the jury decide the sentencing facts at the same time it decided guilt or innocence. This possible solution was heavily criticized since it would expose the jury to evidence that was relevant only to sentencing but would be inadmissible as irrelevant or too prejudicial in the assessment of guilt. The third possibility was to refashion the sentencing scheme to give the court much more discretion. *Apprendi* had made it clear that the Constitution permitted a sentencing system that gave the court the discretion to impose a sentence within the maximum range authorized for the jury verdict, even if the court would have to make some additional factual determinations before imposing the actual sentence.

This principle was implemented in *United States v. Booker*, 543 U.S. 220 (2005), when the Court held that the Federal Sentencing Guidelines were constitutional if construed as recommendations the trial judge *may* follow rather than edicts the court *must* follow. The *Booker* decision means that sentences determined by the Guidelines' calculations are simply advisory, but the judge has the discretion to ignore those limits and sentence up to the statutory maximum. Since this may be done without any additional fact finding, the system complies with the defendant's Sixth Amendment right to a jury trial.

4. Prosecutor

The prosecutor plays perhaps the most significant role in assigning a sentence in an individual case. Most defendants (90% or even more in some locales) plead guilty and enter a plea agreement which sets the sentence the defendant will receive. Virtually all judges encourage guilty pleas and routinely accept the deal, and then sentence the defendant in accordance with it. These practices create a system in which the prosecutor essentially decides the actual sentence in the case. When the district attorney agrees to recommend a three-year prison term for a robbery if the defendant enters a guilty plea, and if both the defendant and the court accept the arrangement, it is fair to say that the prosecutor was primarily responsible for setting the punishment. Had he or she agreed to a two- or four-year term, the resulting sentence would likely not have been three years.

5. Victim

While technically the victim in a criminal case is not even a party to the criminal proceeding, often the victim plays a role — sometimes significant — in the sentencing process. Informally, many district attorneys will consult with the victim before agreeing to accept a particular sentence as part of a plea deal. Moreover, in an increasing number of states the victim's rights movement has led to court rules or statutes mandating a greater role in sentencing for victims. It is not unusual for the victim to have the right to testify in person or in writing at the sentencing hearing. The victim may simply relate the facts of the crime (especially if there were no trial) and how it affected the victim and others, such as the victim's family, but may also express a preference for or against a particular sentence. For example, a rape victim may ask the court to impose a harsh sentence and not consider granting probation. A domestic violence victim, on the other hand, may have reconciled with the defendant and may request a lenient sentence that will allow the defendant to rejoin the family.

E. Sentencing Procedures

1. Guilty Plea

One of the truisms of American sentencing is that a large percentage of cases (sometimes 90% or more) end in a guilty plea where the defendant and prosecutor agree on a sentence or a sentence recommendation and the court accepts the deal. This means that the guilty plea process actually represents the primary mode for determining punishment for crimes.

The process is straightforward and similar in most locales. The defense lawyer and prosecutor engage in discussions about a possible plea. Either may initiate the conversation. After a discussion about the case, one side may suggest a possible resolution. For example, in exchange for a guilty plea, the prosecutor offers to drop or reduce one or more charges or to agree on a particular sentence or at least not to oppose a sentence (such as probation). Sometimes the deal is for a specific punishment, such as three years in prison, or to recommend a specific sentence with the understanding the court may reject the proposed sentence and impose a more or less rigorous one. The proposed deal may be quite detailed, even embracing specific probation conditions, such as the payment of a certain sum as restitution.

Criminal procedure rules, such as Federal Rule of Criminal Procedure 11, provide detailed guidance about the plea proceeding before a judge. In general terms, the procedures recognize that a guilty plea involves the waiver of many constitutional rights and are designed to ensure that the plea is both a voluntary and knowing waiver of those rights. The proceeding is to be on the record to provide proof that the correct procedures are followed. First, the court informs the defendant of—and ensures the defendant understands—the many rights that the criminal accused has and that will be waived if he or she pleads. Then the plea deal is disclosed to the court if it was not already provided in advance. Finally, the court assures itself that the plea is voluntary and that there is a factual basis for it. The court then accepts or rejects the deal and sentences the defendant accordingly.

Routinely, a judge accepts the agreed disposition. In those rare cases where the court does not, the defendant may be permitted to withdraw the plea and go to trial.

2. Sentencing Hearing

In cases where the defendant pleads guilty or is convicted in a jury or nonjury trial, the judge may set a later date for a *sentencing hearing*. At this hearing, the defense lawyer represents the defendant and the prosecutor represents the government. Usually the prosecutor goes first, introducing proof relevant to the sentencing decision. The defense may cross examine government witnesses and present its own evidence.

The defendant is accorded the right of *allocution*, which means the opportunity to address the court on issues pertinent to the sentence. Since the government will be permitted to cross-examine the defendant if he or she chooses to testify, often the accused will elect not to allocute to avoid being cross-examined. In some states the accused makes his or her statement to the court without being subject to cross-examination.

The rules of evidence may or may not apply at the sentencing hearing, depending on the particular jurisdiction. In addition, the court may be presented with a *presentence report* prepared by a probation or other court officer. This document can include background information about the defendant and details of the crime, plus information from various other sources such as the victim, mental health professionals who treated the defendant, and previous employers or others who know the defendant personally. In many, though not all, jurisdictions, the defendant is permitted to review the presentence report before the sentencing hearing, though sometimes confidential information may be excised from the version given to the defendant.

After considering the evidence from the trial, the sentencing hearing, and other data, the court then imposes a sentence. As noted above, recent constitutional developments may mandate that the jury decide certain factual questions that could increase the sentence beyond what would be permitted if sentencing were premised solely on the basis of the jury verdict of guilt.

F. Sentencing Options

In every jurisdiction, there are a number of sentencing options available to the judge. The precise range and details vary from jurisdiction to jurisdiction, but in general terms are as follows:

1. Diversion

A popular option used in minor cases and for first-time offenders is *diversion*, which usually means that the court gives the defendant a set of specific conditions to meet and, upon compliance, is diverted from the criminal justice system. The conditions, often the product of a plea bargain between the defense lawyer and the prosecutor, may include remaining arrest-free for a set period of time; attending counseling, substance abuse or anger management classes; maintaining employment; passing regular drug screens; and paying various court costs and making restitution to the victim. If the defendant abides by these conditions, after a certain period of time he or she returns to court and the criminal charges are dismissed. This means the defendant has no criminal record and avoids incarceration. On the other hand, if the defendant does not satisfy the agreed-on conditions, the defendant is returned to court to face trial for the original charges.

2. Financial: Fines, Restitution, and Court and Similar Costs

Crime may be quite expensive. A frequent criminal sanction is a court order requiring the defendant to pay money to various entities.

a. Fine

Often the defendant must pay a *fine*, which is a financial penalty payable to the state. Statutes set the amount of permissible fines for each particular offense, such as "a fine of no more than $1000." Sometimes the fine is based on the amount of gain from the criminal activity.

b. Restitution

Another financial penalty is *restitution* paid to the victim and designed to compensate the victim for the loss caused by the crime. In many ways, restitution resembles a civil cause of action conducted as part of the criminal proceeding. Often restitution is included as a condition of probation, but it may be a separate order issued with the conviction. In federal law, it is technically not a sentence, but a separate order authorized (and sometimes mandated) by a separate statute. It usually compensates the victim for such out of pocket losses as property damage, medical and related expenses, and even lost wages engendered by the crime. The amount of restitution is agreed on by the defendant and state or is determined by the court after a hearing on the issue. Restitution may be heavily contested, as when the two sides disagree on the value of property destroyed during the crime.

While restitution does resemble a tort action, there are many differences. The amount of restitution is determined by the court, while tort damages may be assessed by a jury. Moreover, many defenses (such as last clear chance and comparative fault) may be unavailable in the criminal case but could be raised in a tort case. Finally, often the plaintiff in a tort case must pay his or her lawyer's fees, but the prosecutor represents the victim's interests in obtaining restitution through the criminal process.

c. Court and Related Costs

Though it is debatable whether *court and related costs* are technically considered as part of the defendant's punishment, it is clear that they are taken seriously by many jurisdictions and may amount to a considerable sum. Frequently, the defendant is ordered to pay such costs as a condition of probation, which may mean the court could order the defendant to be incarcerated for nonpayment under certain circumstances.

d. Ability to Pay

The Supreme Court has held that the Due Process and Equal Protection Clauses place limits on the consequences of nonpayment of fines, restitution, and court costs. In general terms, a defendant may not be incarcerated for nonpayment of such financial obligations if he or she is simply unable to do so despite good faith efforts to get the money. The accused may be imprisoned, however, if the nonpayment was willful. *Bearden v. Georgia*, 461 U.S. 660 (1983).

3. Probation

One of the most popular criminal sentences is *probation*. The defendant may be sentenced to a jail or prison term, but incarceration is *suspended* and the defendant is placed on probation for a specific period (such as three years) and ordered to comply with a set of *conditions* during this *probation term*.

In theory at least, the list of probation conditions is tailored to the individual needs of each offender, but in reality often the defendant is simply given a *standard list of probation conditions*. Perhaps 10–15 in number, these traditionally include such terms as serving a short term in jail, supporting dependents, maintaining employment, attending counseling and/or regular sessions with a probation officer, paying restitution and other financial obligations, abstaining from all alcohol (or sometimes from the excessive use of alcohol), obeying the law, reporting arrests to the probation officer, avoiding contact with stated persons (such as the crime victim), and not leaving the geographical area without the written permission of the court or probation officer.

If the defendant satisfies the release conditions while on probation, he or she returns to court and the sentence is deemed to have been satisfied. If the defendant violates one or more of the terms of release, the court may hold a *probation revocation hearing* and, if the violation is proven, send the defendant to prison for all or part of the original prison term. At this hearing the defendant is accorded defense counsel. The prosecutor may introduce proof that the violation occurred and defense counsel may counter with proof that it did not or may simply argue that the violation was minimal or excusable and should not result in a revocation. The court then decides whether to revoke probation and send the defendant to jail or prison for the original or a shorter term.

4. Community Service

A rather recent sanction for minor crimes is to order the defendant to perform a specific number of hours of *community service*. The tasks vary considerably, including such public service acts as picking up trash along roads, painting a community center, or building a playground. When, as often occurs, community service is included as a probation condition, the defendant who fails to satisfy the community service order may be sent to court for a probation revocation hearing where the judge may alter the conditions of release or even order the defendant to serve a prison or jail term.

5. House Arrest and Electronic Monitoring

A distinct trend in criminal sanctions is for the court to order the defendant to *house arrest* for a specific period of time, such as one year. During this time the defendant must remain in a particular home all day, although the court may allow the defendant to leave the house to go to work or church or medical and other necessary appointments. Often the defendant will wear a wristlet or anklet that automatically sends a signal to a computer if the defendant strays from the assigned location. The computer then sends a telephone message to probation authorities who may make a house visit to check on the probationer's whereabouts.

6. Halfway House

In lieu of prison or near the end of a prison term, some jurisdictions allow a defendant to serve the sentence in a *halfway house* where the defendant is required to live for a period of time with a small number of other offenders in the same situation. During the work day, the defendant may be permitted to go to a job site, but must return to the halfway house at the end of the work day. The halfway house is staffed by people who monitor the defendant's behavior. A defendant who violates halfway house rules may be sent to a more secure environment, even without a court or other hearing.

7. Incarceration

An obvious criminal sanction is *incarceration* in which the defendant is sentenced to jail or prison for a set period of time. The facilities vary considerably from a small local jail to a huge state prison with thousands of inmates. The term of incarceration may be reduced for *good time* and various other credits given an inmate for satisfactory activities or simply for not getting in trouble. These credits may reduce the sentence considerably, sometimes as much as by half or even more. In most American jurisdictions, as discussed below, the defendant will be eligible for *parole* and may be released well before completion of the prison term.

G. Death Penalty

1. Background: Before *Furman*

The death penalty is the ultimate sanction in criminal law. Over two-thirds of American jurisdictions authorize capital punishment for the most serious homicides, yet the death penalty is still a controversial issue in both political and legal arenas.

The death penalty was specifically recognized in the United States Constitution. For example, the Fifth Amendment requires a grand jury indictment before a person may be "held to answer for a capital" crime in federal courts and the Due Process Clause bars depriving someone "of life" without first according the person "due process of law." These provisions were in accordance with both popular sentiment and state law, resulting in the frequent use of the death penalty throughout United States history.

2. *Furman v. Georgia*

In 1972, the United States Supreme Court entered the ongoing debate over capital punishment by holding that the death penalty, as administered, violated the guarantee against cruel and unusual punishment of the Eighth Amendment. *Furman v. Georgia*, 408 U.S. 238 (1972). The five-Justice majority could agree only on a short paragraph that concluded: "[T]he imposition and carrying out of the death penalty in these cases constitutes cruel and unusual punishment in violation of the Eighth and Fourteenth Amendments." Since each of the nine Justices wrote a separate opinion expressing his individual reasoning, there was no consensus on why the death penalty was unconstitutional and what, if anything, could be done to restore it as a viable sanction.

Two Justices (Brennan and Marshall) in the *Furman* majority argued that death itself is an unconstitutional penalty, while three majority Justices seemed to suggest that the death penalty *per se* does not violate the Eighth Amendment but as applied in the cases at bar was so arbitrary and unstructured that it constituted cruel and unusual punishment. Justice Stewart, one of the three, eloquently expressed this concern about a penalty that is so "wantonly and freakishly imposed" when he noted in an often-quoted statement: "These death sentences are cruel and unusual in the same way that being struck by lighting is cruel and unusual." The four dissenters argued that the death penalty did not violate the Eighth Amendment and had long been a constitutional facet of American criminal law. Chief Justice Burger's *Furman* dissent, for example, noted: "In the 181 years since the enactment of the Eighth Amendment, not a single decision of this Court has cast the slightest doubt on the constitutionality of capital punishment."

One consequence of *Furman* was that in the 1970s over 600 death row inmates throughout the country had their sentences commuted and the death penalty statutes of 40 states were deemed unconstitutional. The political reaction to *Furman* was strong and in many states there were concerted legislative efforts to enact new criminal laws designed to restore capital punishment by meeting the majority's concerns in *Furman*. Supporters were quick to note that a change in the vote of even one of the Justices in the *Furman* majority would lead to a reversal of the Court's ban on the death penalty.

Considering that three Justices in the *Furman* majority expressed concerns about the lack of standards in selecting those offenders who may be sentenced to death, states took two approaches in adopting new laws. Some enacted a *mandatory death penalty* so that every person guilty of a particular heinous type of murder was given the death penalty. The decision maker had no discretion. The other approach was to add specific standards to limit discretion in death penalty cases. These jurisdictions also created appellate structures to review death penalties. Both approaches attempted to reduce the arbitrariness condemned in *Furman*.

3. Post-*Furman* Supreme Court Developments

When these new death penalty laws were applied to crimes committed after 1972 and resulted in a death sentence, defense counsel appealed the sentence to the Supreme Court which, in 1976, again faced the issue of the constitutionality of the ultimate sanction. In *Gregg v. Georgia*, 428 U.S. 153 (1976), a majority of the Court reversed *Furman* and upheld the death penalty as applied under Georgia law. The Court also upheld new statutes in Florida and Texas. The Court noted that the death penalty had long been a part of American criminal law and was thought by legislators to serve both deterrent and retributive functions. The *Gregg* Court noted that legislators, not judges, are entrusted with decisions about what policy values are valid and should be the basis for their sentencing laws. The primary reason *Gregg* upheld the state capital statutes is that each of these jurisdictions created procedures that replaced the extensive discretion permitted under the old statutes. The new laws provided far more focused approaches that limited discretion by giving the decision maker much more specific guidance in deciding which offenders merited the death penalty.

The approved procedures did not eliminate all discretion. Indeed, the Supreme Court has held that there must be some discretion in the death decision so that statutes imposing *mandatory* death penalties were struck down. In *Woodson v. North Carolina*, 428 U.S. 280 (1976), the Court held: "[W]e believe that in capital cases the fundamental respect for humanity underlying the Eighth Amendment requires consideration of the character and record of the individual offender and the circumstances of the particular offense as a constitutionally indispensable part of the process of inflicting the penalty of death."

The capital statutes that were upheld gave the decision maker some guidance but not so much that all discretion was removed.

4. Limits on Death Penalty

a. Type of Crime

Historically, the death penalty in England and the United States was authorized for a vast array of felonies. In *Coker v. Georgia*, 433 U.S. 584 (1977), the Supreme Court restricted the death penalty by holding that it was a disproportionate penalty for the crime of rape of an adult woman. The Court reasoned that relatively few American jurisdictions permitted the death penalty for adult rape and that the harm caused by rape, though severe, was not sufficiently grave to merit the ultimate penalty. The latter argument seemed to suggest that the death penalty was disproportionate to any offense other than murder. Though the death penalty for treason has had a long history, the Supreme Court has not yet indicated whether it would violate the Cruel and Unusual Punishment Clause based on the logic of *Coker*. Moreover, states have enacted statutes imposing the death penalty for serious crimes other than murder or treason, but the Supreme Court has not revisited the issue in recent years.

b. Defendants

i. Worst of the Worst; Accomplices

Based on the fact that the Eighth Amendment's proportionality requirement serves to limit the death penalty to the "worst of the worst," those acting with extreme moral culpability, the Supreme Court has recognized several categories of murderers that may not be executed because the offenders lack something that puts them in the category of serious offenders who merit the law's most severe penalty. For example, sometimes two or more people are involved in committing a homicide. The quest for proportionality requires some differentiation among the actors in the felony. The Supreme Court has permitted the death penalty for accomplices in a felony murder, but has said they must be "major participants" and must have acted with "reckless indifference to human life." *Tison v. Arizona*, 481 U.S. 137 (1987). Note that defendants may satisfy this test even though they lacked an intent to kill.

ii. Minors

Another proportionality-based limit is the age of the defendant. The Supreme Court has held that it is cruel and unusual punishment to execute defendants who were under age 18 at the time of the crime. *Roper v. Simons*, 543 U.S. 551

(2005). Minors who commit crimes, the Court reasoned, are not as morally reprehensible as adults committing the same acts because the juveniles lack maturity, are more susceptible to negative influences and outside pressures, and have not yet found their character.

iii. Mental Status

A related limit addresses the defendant's mental status. Note that these cases focus on limits on *execution*, not on criminal conviction. In a series of cases the Court has overturned the execution of defendants who, though competent to stand trial, are insane or mentally incompetent. *Ford v. Wainwright*, 477 U.S. 399 (1986). The Court explained the decision by citing two rationales, either of which would trigger the Eighth Amendment's protection: "to protect the condemned from fear and pain without comfort of understanding, or to protect the dignity of society itself from the barbarity of exacting mindless vengeance."

Similarly, the Court has barred execution of some persons with "intellectual disability" (formerly referred to by the Court as "mental retardation"). *Hall v. Florida*, 134 S.Ct. 1986 (2014). *See also Atkins v. Virginia*, 536 U.S. 304 (2002). The *Hall* opinion explained this result as appropriate because executing such people would serve no penological purpose, would violate the person's "inherent dignity as a human being," would not deter anyone with an intellectual disability who has limited ability to learn from experience, and would ill-serve retribution because of the defendant's reduced "moral culpability." The Court also noted that executing the intellectual disabled would challenge the integrity of the trial process because these defendants are more likely to be poor witnesses and to give false confessions.

Whether a person's intellectual disability is so extreme as to bar execution is to be decided in a flexible manner. No particular IQ test or score or factor is dispositive. Rather, the defendant may introduce additional evidence, including expert testimony and other information that bear on an ability to understand and process information, communicate, abstract from mistakes, learn from experience, control impulses, engage in logical reasoning, and understand the reactions of others.

5. Death Penalty Procedures

a. Bifurcation

Before the defendant is given the death penalty, ordinarily the same jury participates in *two hearings*, often referred to as *bifurcated hearings*. The first ascertains guilt or innocence. If the defendant is found guilty, he or she then faces a second hearing called the *sentencing hearing*. At the sentencing or second hearing, new proof may be offered by both sides, though either may simply rely on the evidence already presented at the earlier guilt hearing.

b. Aggravating and Mitigating Circumstances

Recall that several Justices in *Furman* were concerned that the death penalty was assigned in an arbitrary fashion. To add structure and limits to this decision, states enacted new death penalty laws that contain lists of both aggravating and mitigating factors that the jury must consider. Though there are considerable variations among the jurisdictions, historically the penalty of death (as opposed to lesser penalties such as life without parole or life imprisonment) is only authorized if the trier of fact finds one or more *aggravating circumstances* and then, after considering the *mitigating factors*, decides that the case merits death.

Aggravating circumstances are typically a closed list of perhaps 10–15 factors that are deemed to increase the gravity of the murder. These typically include such facts as the particular nature or identity of the victim (a person of particular vulnerability because of age or health, or a law enforcement officer or judge killed while on the job), the defendant's status (on bail, probation, or parole or a prison inmate at the time of the killing), especially cruel method of killing (torture, involving extreme pain), the defendant's motivation (for remuneration, sexual gratification, racial hatred), and the number of victims (killed two or more people in same episode).

The list of mitigating factors is open-ended, usually involving a list of 10–15 factors plus a broad one authorizing the jury to consider any other fact about the crime or the offender that could cause the jury to reject the penalty of death. *Lockett v. Ohio*, 438 U.S. 586 (1978). Typical mitigating factors include the defendant's age or history of mental illness, relatively minor role in the killing, and even good behavior while in jail or prison awaiting trial. Since the defendant may introduce any other fact in mitigation, often defense proof may include the defendant's mother or wife or child who pleads for the defendant's life. The defendant may also testify about why he or she should not be executed.

c. Role of Trial Judge and Jury

The death penalty is routinely assessed by a jury rather than the judge. Often state law does permit the judge to reverse the jury's decision to impose the death penalty and, instead, sentence the defendant to life or life without parole. And the defendant may waive the jury and have the sentence decided by the court alone.

d. Role of Victim

As part of nationwide efforts to give the victim a larger role in the criminal justice system, many jurisdictions give the victim's family an opportunity to make a *victim's impact statement* to the jury during the sentencing hearing. Though some critics argue that this introduces irrelevant information and substantially increases the arbitrariness of the death penalty decision, the Supreme Court upheld this practice. *Payne v. Tennessee*, 501 U.S. 808 (1991). The Court found it appropriate for the jury in assessing whether to impose the death penalty to consider the harm the defendant caused.

e. Appellate Review

One feature of the post-*Furman* capital laws is the provision of extensive appellate review of the sentence. In state courts, often the appeal of a death sentence to the state's highest court is *automatic*, though many locales give the defendant the option of waiving the appeal if certain procedures are followed that ensure the defendant is competent, has received adequate advice, and the waiver is voluntary and knowing. Federal *habeas corpus* and related procedures are also used in capital cases to bring challenges based on violations of the United States Constitution. The combination of state and federal appellate options ordinarily means that capital cases take years to get resolved as each of the courts spends months or even years addressing the grave issues before it.

6. Continuing Debate

Though the death penalty in general has become accepted as part of American constitutional law, it still engenders significant debate. Proponents argue that it serves legitimate retributive, incapacitative, and general deterrent purposes. Opponents reject it as "bloodthirsty" and inappropriate retribution in a civilized society. They also deny its effect as a general deterrent and claim it provides too much incapacitation, removing from society people who over time would not be a threat to public safety. Moreover, critics of the death penalty note that it discriminates against the poor who too often get inferior legal representation in capital cases. Another argument against this sanction is that it is race-based, assigning the death penalty in some cases based on the race of the defendant and/or the victim. Finally, opponents note that on occasion innocent people have been sentenced to death, an irreversible punishment that cannot be rectified once the truth about their innocence becomes known.

H. Parole and Supervised Release

In most jurisdictions, a defendant given a prison sentence may be released early on *parole* or, as an altered version of it is called in the federal system, *supervised release*. Typically, a defendant receiving a prison term is eligible for parole after serving twenty to sixty-five percent of the sentence. Before the parole eligibility date, the defendant will meet with the *parole board* or an equivalent body or hearing panel. The parole board, often comprised of a diverse group of people appointed by the governor or other political agency, may consist of three to ten members who meet as a whole or in smaller panels.

At the parole release hearing the prisoner may be represented by counsel, but usually is not. The board assesses the defendant's prison record, the details of the case, and other information about the defendant's background and physical and mental status, then decides whether to release the defendant in the coming months or to deny parole at that time, perhaps reviewing the case in another year or two. In many locales the victim is entitled to be notified of the parole release hearing and to provide the board with pertinent information. There may be witnesses who testify at the hearing, including the victim or the victim's representatives.

The parole board's decision may be subject to appeal in court, though this occurs rarely and usually results in the board's decision being upheld.

Like probation, the parolee must report regularly to a *parole officer*, who may also serve as a probation officer for other offenders. Once on parole, the defendant may be subject to a list of 10–15 parole conditions, virtually identical to conditions given to people put on probation. These include such routine provisions as not violating the law, meeting regularly with the parole officer, attending counseling, holding a job, supporting dependents, remaining drug and alcohol free, and abiding by more specific conditions individualized for this particular parolee.

A defendant who violates parole may face a *parole revocation* hearing before the parole board or a hearing panel of the board, or occasionally before a court, that decides whether to *revoke parole* and return the offender to prison to serve the remainder (or a shorter portion) of the original prison term. Once reincarcerated, the defendant may become parole eligible again after the passage of some period of incarceration.

A few American jurisdictions, including the federal government, have abolished parole in an effort to serve *truth in sentencing* and to reduce the amount of discretion exercised over the offender's plight. In these jurisdictions, the defendant serves virtually all of the prison term with a slight reduction (perhaps ten to twenty percent) for satisfactory prison behavior. Upon release from prison, the defendant may be subject to parole-like terms for a short period of time and be under the supervision of a parole officer. Revocations may be handled by a court or board.

I. Executive Clemency

People convicted of crimes routinely may seek *executive clemency* to be relieved of some or all of the consequences of the conviction. The President of the United States (for people with federal convictions) and state Governors (for state convictions) are given the authority under the relevant constitution to override a criminal conviction in their jurisdiction and grant relief. Though *executive clemency*, sometimes called *pardon* or *commutation of sentence*, is given rarely, it may be based on a determination that the defendant was actually not guilty of the crime, has been completely rehabilitated, the judicial proceedings were so seriously tainted that there are profound concerns about their legitimacy, or on humanitarian grounds, such as the defendant is terminally ill or needs to be available to take care of a seriously ill relative.

The executive may decide to grant a *full pardon*, exonerating the defendant entirely, or a *reprieve*, which reduces the gravity of the punishment. For example, a governor may grant a reprieve of a death row inmate and reduce the sentence from death to life without parole. The executive's decision may be exempt or virtually exempt from judicial and legislative review.

Checkpoints

- The primary theories of punishment are rehabilitation, retribution, deterrence (both general and specific), and incapacitation.

- Restorative justice is designed to restore the victim while effectuating a relationship between the criminal and the victim.

- The primary Constitutional limits on sentencing are equal protection and the guarantee against cruel and unusual punishment.

- Sentencing systems may be determinate or indeterminate.

- Sentencing guidelines are now widely accepted as a way to minimize discretion and make sentences more predictable.

- Sentences are affected by legislators, judges, the jury, the victim, and especially the prosecutor.

- Since most sentences are determined by negotiations that lead to a guilty plea, the prosecutor plays a major role in the actual sentence that is imposed.

Checkpoints *cont.*

- At a sentencing hearing, the accused is entitled to counsel, to present evidence, to cross-examine adverse witnesses, and to speak (allocution).

- Sentencing options include diversion, various financial penalties (fines, restitution, and court and related costs), probation, community service, house arrest, halfway house, and incarceration.

- The Supreme Court rejected the death penalty in 1972 as cruel and unusual punishment (*Furman*), but restored it in 1976 (*Gregg*).

- The Court has limited the death penalty to certain crimes (homicide) and bars execution of defendants who are under age 18 at the time of the crime or are insane or mentally incompetent, or are intellectually disabled.

- States ordinarily use death penalty procedures that provide a list of aggravating and mitigating factors for the jury to consider.

- Many prisoners are released on parole, which subjects them to supervision by a parole officer and obligates them to follow a set of parole conditions.

- The Governor or President may grant executive clemency (sometimes called pardons) that can reduce the gravity of criminal punishment or even exonerate the accused.

Chapter 4

Actus Reus

A. *Actus Reus*, Voluntary Acts, and Omissions: In General

Anglo-American criminal law has long recognized that it is wrong to punish for thoughts alone. Action or the equivalent of some kind is needed as well. Moreover, any such action or inaction should be voluntary, the product of the actor's will.

Several reasons are given for this fundamental principle. First, involuntary acts may be deemed to lack the moral blameworthiness that is the hallmark of the criminal law. People should be punished for bad choices rather than simply for acts that cause harm. Second, it is argued that only voluntary acts may be deterred, making it useless to punish involuntary behavior. And even those who believe in retribution (sometimes called revenge) to justify criminal punishment often conclude that it is inappropriate to exact revenge on someone who acts involuntarily. Moreover, punishing for thoughts alone would criminalize most of us who occasionally allow our base nature to emerge in our thoughts and it would be virtually impossible to prove the content of our thoughts when there is no physical manifestation of our mental processes. Thus, there is a danger that by punishing for what one could do in the future, the law may permit dangerous intrusion into people's lives and may convict those who never actually posed a threat of harm.

This general approach has produced the concept of *actus reus*, a legal term encompassing, in general terms, the conduct (or lack of conduct) required for liability under the criminal law. More specifically for this chapter, the *actus reus* principle is that the criminal law will reach only voluntary acts or omissions to act when there was a duty to do so.

American courts routinely apply the common law concept of *actus reus*, even in the absence of a statute on point. Many modern statutes, however, mirror the Model Penal Code and specifically provide that the concept of *actus reus* is part of the jurisdiction's criminal law.

B. Voluntary Act

In most cases, criminal liability stems from an act rather than an omission. Thus, an arsonist sets fire to a building, a thief takes property, and a murderer stabs the victim. For our purposes, an act can be defined as a movement of part of the body. Thus, the killer commits an act when stabbing the victim and the purse snatcher does an act in grabbing the victim's purse.

An act alone, however, does not satisfy the *actus reus* requirement. It must also be a *voluntary act*. The Model Penal Code characterizes it as "conduct that is within the control of the actor." MPC § 2.01 comment. This means the act is the product of the actor's will. The actor could have chosen to refrain from doing the act. By way of contrast, an involuntary act, which does not constitute an *actus reus*, is not an act that the defendant chose to do. Common examples include crimes committed while in a convulsion, sleepwalking, or possibly even in a hypnotic state. It also includes acts physically beyond the actor's control, such as when Hiker X pushes Hiker Y into Hiker Z, who falls off a mountain and is killed. Hiker Y would be deemed to lack an *actus reus* even though he or she actually caused Hiker Z's death when Y's body crashed into Hiker Z.

Other illustrative cases where an involuntary act was found include a man, convicted of being drunk on a public highway, who had been arrested in his home and carried onto a public highway by police. There is a disagreement among the states about whether there is a voluntary act when a man arrested and brought in handcuffs to a jail and then found in possession of drugs or a weapon can be charged with bringing a forbidden object into the facility.

Case law has expanded the concept of voluntary act to behavior committed earlier in a sequence of events. In a classic case, a man who knew he was subject to epileptic seizures nevertheless drove a car, then had a seizure and crashed his car into other people. *People v. Decina*, 138 N.E.2d 799 (N.Y. Ct. App.

1956). The court held that the defendant committed a voluntary act when he drove a car knowing of the danger of his seizures. This pre-collision act satisfied the *actus reus* requirement when he later had the seizure while driving. The Model Penal Code explains this as requiring a voluntary act during the "entire course of conduct," not necessarily at the moment of the harm. MPC § 2.01 comment. Accordingly, he was subject to liability for criminally negligent homicide.

C. Omission to Act When There Was a Legal Duty to Act

Sometimes criminal liability stems from an omission—a failure to act—rather than an action. Examples include failing to file an income tax form or to take required precautions to prevent environmental contamination. Such liability could even extend to homicide, as when a parent fails to feed a child and is charged with negligent homicide for the child's death.

1. Requirement of a Duty to Act

When an omission is the *actus reus*, the law provides that there must have been an *omission which breached a duty to act under circumstances where the defendant was capable of performing the act*. In other words, the only omissions that engender criminal liability are those that are in violation of a legal duty to act. Absent this duty to act, the failure to perform the action does not create criminal liability.

2. No General Legal Duty to Aid

The duty to act must be a *legal* duty, not merely a moral duty. Some facet of the legal system must impose the duty. In general terms, there is no general legal duty to aid another person, even if one could do so safely. Thus, an Olympic swimmer who is walking in the park and sees a day-old baby drowning in a one inch puddle of water has no legal duty to rescue the child. Similarly, a classic case held that a man whose occasional sexual partner took a lethal overdose of morphine while at his house, had no legal duty of care or protection. *People v. Beardsley,* 113 N.W. 1128 (Mich. 1907). In a few American jurisdictions, however, statutes or ordinances do impose a general duty of assistance, but the penalties for violation are very minor and the rescuer is given some relief from civil liability for the rescue attempt.

3. Sources of Duty to Aid

When there is a legal duty to act, it stems from the common law, contract, or statutes.

a. Common Law Duty

The common law has long imposed a number of duties. Often these obligations are based on a particular relationship, including the duty of a parent to care for a child, a spouse to care for a spouse, an employer to care for employees, and the captain of a ship to care for the sailors and passengers on the ship. Similarly, common law may impose on a landowner the duty to provide reasonably safe premises for people who are invited to come on the land. Some situations produce differing results among the jurisdictions. For example, live-in boyfriends who assume a parental role are sometimes, but not always, classified as having the same duty of care as parents.

The common law duty may also arise from someone who undertakes to provide care, even without a duty to do so, and is given a duty to follow through with assistance once it is begun. For example, a passenger riding a bus is seated next to an elderly person who falls over, yelling, "I'm having a heart attack again." If the passenger begins CPR, a common law duty arises for that person to continue rendering aid. He or she would violate this duty by discontinuing CPR after a few minutes because, though the CPR is reviving the elderly person, the passenger feared the CPR would cause the passenger to sweat and be unattractive for a dinner date starting in a few minutes.

The common law also imposes a duty on someone who causes a peril. The person must act to remove the peril or alleviate the harm. Thus, the driver of a car who accidentally hits a pedestrian may have a duty to assist the pedestrian. The common law also may embrace a requirement to prevent someone else from harming the person protected by the duty. For example, a father may be held criminally responsible for failing to prevent the mother from abusing the child.

b. Contractual Duty

A duty may also be created by contract. For example, a person may sign a contract requiring a security company to protect a visiting dignitary, an extended care facility to care for a seriously ill parent, or an environmental control company to clean up a dangerous dump site. The breach of that contract could lead to criminal liability for the party that breached the contract in a way causing a harm. For example, if the environmental company did not clean up the dump site and someone died as a result of the contamination, the company could face criminal liability for negligent homicide for violating its contractual duty.

c. Statutory Duty

The third source of a duty is statutes. In many areas of life a legislative body has determined that the failure to act breeds criminal liability. As noted above, failure to file an income tax return is a good example. Another is a teacher or doctor's failure to notify authorities about suspected child abuse. Some jurisdictions even require that a statute, not common law, impose the duty to act.

4. Awareness of Duty

Though there may be a legal duty to act, sometimes the person with that duty is unaware of the responsibility. For example, a mother has a duty to care for her children, but case law exempts her if she does not know of the relevant facts—that she is the mother of the child or that the child needs care. On the other hand, she is not excused from the duty if she does not know that, as a mother, she has a legal duty to care for her child. The law does not require knowledge of the law in order for the law to impose a duty of care.

5. Reasonable Limits on What Action Is Required

When the law imposes a duty to act, it does not require the impossible. If a person is unable to satisfy the legal duty, the criminal law will not impose liability for breach of that duty. For example, if a mother suffers an unexpected stroke and becomes unable to feed her child, she will not be held responsible for that failure, even if the baby starves to death. In essence, her omission would be involuntary and would not constitute an *actus reus*.

6. Causation

When a person is charged with a crime by omission and the offense requires a particular harm, such as death or serious physical injury, it must also be established that the omission caused the harm. For example, assume a parent waits several days to take a very ill child to the emergency room. If the child would have died anyway from an irreversible fatal disease, irrespective of the parent's neglect, the parent is not criminally responsible for the death by omission.

D. Special Issue: Possession

Actus reus embraces both acts and omissions, but is has a rather special application in possession crimes. It is common for the criminal law to punish the possession of certain items, such as pornography, illegal drugs, and weapons. Possession may be *actual* or *constructive*. Actual possession is when a person has actual physical control over an item. A person has actual possession of this wallet in his or her pocket or in a purse of briefcase. Constructive possession, a legal fiction, is when there is no actual control but the person nevertheless has "dominion and control" or at least the power to get dominion and control over the property. For example, a person has constructive possession over property in his or her house, car or storage locker, or in the basement of a friend who is holding the property for the constructive possessor. The constructive possessor must have at least knowledge of the presence of the item and some degree of control over it.

Ordinarily in these possession cases *actus reus* is not an issue because the offender is quite aware of the drugs in the glove compartment or the pornography in the bedroom. But what if he or she does not know that the item is in the car or bedroom? Though there may be physical possession, can it be said to be a voluntary act or omission satisfying the *actus reus* requirement? Criminal law answers the question by holding that possession must be knowing and not accidental.

The theory is that if the defendant knows that he or she has cocaine in a coat pocket, the possession is a voluntary act punishable as an *actus reus*. Section 2.01(4) of the Model Penal Code is quite specific about possession as *actus reus*, providing that possession is an act "if the possessor knowingly procured or received the thing possessed or was aware of his [or her] control" of the item "for a sufficient [time] to have been able to terminate [the] possession." On the other hand, mere presence where an item is located is not enough to establish possession of the item. *State v. Kimbrell*, 362 S.E.2d 630 (S.C. 1987).

E. Special Issue: Vicarious Liability

Another complex *actus reus* issue arises with vicarious liability. As a general rule, criminal law punishes people for their own *actus reus*. But in a few situations, a criminal statute punishes one person for the acts of another. For example, an employer may be made criminally responsible for the illegal acts of an employee if a statute so provides. Accordingly, a company president could be prosecuted for environmental violations committed by an employee. A defendant may also be held liable for the acts of another if the person is used as an innocent instrumentality to engage in the conduct at the defendant's behest but without knowledge that it is a crime.

F. Common Law and Model Penal Code Compared

The common law and Model Penal Code approaches to *actus reus* are similar. The common law rule is simple: a crime must include either a voluntary act or an omission when there is a duty to act. Section 2.01 of the Model Penal Code restates that principle with considerable more detail. It also indicates what are not voluntary acts as a matter of law: a reflex, convulsion, movement during unconsciousness or sleep, conduct during hypnosis or while from hypnotic suggestion, or any other bodily movement not the product of the actor's effort or determination. The Code also provides specifically that possession is an act "if the possessor knowingly procured or received the thing possessed or was aware of his [or her] control" of the item "for a sufficient [time] to have been able to terminate [the] possession." *Model Penal Code § 2.01(4).*

G. Status Crimes: *Robinson* and *Powell*

Virtually all crimes punish doing something the legislature has forbidden. One category of offenses is different, however, and presents unique *actus reus* issues. Some legislative bodies have criminalized a person's *status*. For example, a law punishing someone for being a vagrant may be seen as punishing for a status rather than an act.

In the leading case, *Robinson v. California*, 370 U.S. 660 (1962), the Supreme Court considered the constitutionality of a California statute that made it a crime to "be addicted to the use of narcotics." While conceding that the legislature may protect the public welfare and punish the manufacture, sale, or possession of illegal drugs, the Court found that the California "addicted" statute violated the Eighth Amendment's ban on Cruel and Unusual Punishment. Noting that the defendant could be found guilty under this statute even though he never touched a narcotic in California or did any misbehavior there, the *Robinson* Court concluded that "in the light of contemporary human knowledge" an illness, such as being a leper or mentally ill or afflicted with a venereal disease or a narcotic addict, cannot be made criminal. A state may still deal with such issues by non-criminal means.

After *Robinson* there was much speculation about whether the law could criminalize conduct that was the direct product of an illness. After all, the argument went, if a state may not make having the illness a crime, how could it criminalize acts that occur only because of that illness? For example, could a kleptomaniac be convicted of theft if the crime were the direct product of the mental illness? A general answer was provided a few years later in *Powell v. Texas*, 392 U.S. 514 (1968), where an alcoholic was convicted of public intoxication. The defendant argued that he was being punished for his status in violation of *Robinson* and the Eighth Amendment. The Supreme Court disagreed, upholding the conviction on the theory that the defendant was being punished for an *act* (being drunk in public) rather than the status of being an alcoholic. However, the Court indicated that the case would be different if there were convincing proof that the defendant had an irresistible compulsion to drink and to be drunk in public, such that he could not be deterred from public intoxication.

Checkpoints

- Anglo-American law requires an *actus reus* for each crime.

- An *actus reus* is either a voluntary act or an omission when there was a duty to act.

- A voluntary act is the product of the actor's will. A reflex is not a voluntary act.

- An omission is an *actus reus* only when it violated a duty to act, which could be imposed by the common law or statutes.

- Possession is an *actus reus* if the actor knows that he or she has possession.

- The Eighth Amendment bars punishing someone for a status, such as being a narcotic addict, but does not ban criminalizing an act that may result from a status, such as being drunk in public.

Chapter 5

Mens Rea

Roadmap

- The meaning of *mens rea*
- The rationale(s) for including *mens rea* as a crime element
- How the prosecution proves *mens rea*
- How the Model Penal Code construes *mens rea* elements
- The four Model Penal Code *mens rea* formulations and how are they similar and dissimilar
- The definition and use of strict liability crimes
- Ignorance or mistake about a fact or law as a defense to a crime

---

A. Introduction

1. Definition

Mens rea is one of the defining concepts of Anglo-American criminal law. Ordinarily translated as "guilty mind" or "evil mind," it expresses the traditional notion that criminal law applies to those whose mental processes make them morally blameworthy for their acts. In modern criminal law, the concept of *mens rea* is far more expansive than it was many years ago. In general terms, today *mens rea* refers to the mental state needed for criminal liability. There are a host of different terms within statutes that are considered *mens rea* terms. Examples include statutes that require the accused to act with one or more of the following *mens rea* elements: wilfully, knowingly, intentionally, purposefully, feloniously, or recklessly.

2. Role of *Mens Rea*

Mens rea allows those who define crimes and defenses to fine tune their product to reach only a certain category of offenders. Thus, the use of a particular *mens rea* element is a policy judgment reflecting a decision about the type of offender to be eligible for criminal sanctions. For example, a statute that applies to those who "intentionally pollute" a water reservoir will embrace far fewer people than one that applies to those who "negligently pollute" it.

Similarly, *mens rea* allows legislators to sort offenders on the basis of moral culpability. For example, assume that D kills V. The homicide statute punishes those who "intentionally kill" by a prison sentence of 30 years to life, but punishes those who "negligently kill" by a term of no more than five years. In this context *mens rea* is used to allocate punishment to reflect notions of moral culpability that one who kills intentionally is more morally blameworthy than a person who kills carelessly.

Another rationale for *mens rea* is that it would be useless to punish someone who acted with a "clean" mind. Such people, it is argued, are not dangerous and do not need to be deterred or rehabilitated. A counter-argument is that punishing such people may nevertheless deter others who have an "evil mind" and, in any event, may induce all people in a certain situation to be more careful in their actions.

3. Proof of *Mens Rea*

As with any crime element, the prosecution must prove *mens rea* beyond a reasonable doubt. This may be a daunting task since it often requires the prosecutor to convince the jury what was going on in the defendant's mind at the time of the crime. Judges ease this decision, on occasion, by instructing the jury that intent may be inferred from circumstances.

Sometimes the mental processes are proved by the defendant's own words in a confession to police. Even more frequently, the government uses circumstantial evidence to convince the jury that the necessary *mens rea* is present. For example, if the defendant is charged with intentional homicide, the government may prove the killing was intentional by introducing circumstantial evidence that the defendant hated the victim because the victim had cheated the defendant at a card game, that the defendant had threatened to "get even," and that the defendant had been seen right before the shooting with a gun pointed at the victim's head.

4. Role of Motive

Motive — the reason the defendant acted — is often circumstantial evidence of *mens rea,* especially of intent, but motive is not the same as intent. Motive itself is virtually never an element to be proven. For example, if the defendant hated the victim, this fact is some evidence that the defendant killed this victim intentionally rather than accidentally. Similarly, if the victim were a total stranger and the defendant had no motive to kill the victim, the lack of motive may be circumstantial evidence that the homicide was accidental rather than intentional.

The same is true if the defendant had a different motive than indirectly required by the criminal statute. If defendant were charged with "activating an explosive device with the intent to kill an on-duty judge," defendant would not be guilty if his reason (motive) for causing the explosion was to kill the judge's law clerk. The motive would negate the specific intent in the statute.

A few statutes make motive itself an element of the crime. These include laws punishing so-called hate crimes, which involve acts committed because of a person's religious, racial or ethnic characteristics. The prosecution must prove that the defendant was motivated by the fact that the victim possessed one of the racial or other attributes.

B. Construction of *Mens Rea* Elements

Most modern criminal statutes contain one or more *mens rea* elements. For example, a homicide statute could punish those who "intentionally kill." The *mens rea* in this illustration is that the prosecution must prove that the defendant *intended* to kill. An accidental killing would not suffice.

1. Precise *Mens Rea* Often Unclear

While many statutes are clear in the meaning of the mental element, some are not, for several reasons. First, some mental elements simply are not defined in the statute. This is especially likely for older statutes which leave to the courts the task of defining words such as "maliciously" or "deliberately."

Second, some statutes are written so that it is difficult to decide what element(s) the mental component covers. Consider a statute that punishes someone who "knowingly releases" a specific chemical "in a navigable stream." Obviously the *mens rea* is "knowingly," but the statute is not clear what the defendant must know in order to be guilty. Must the defendant (1) "knowingly release" a chemical regardless of the defendant's knowledge of whether the forbidden chemical is present, or (2) knowingly release a chemical that the defendant knows is the particular chemical, or (3) knowingly release a chemical that the defendant knows is the particular chemical and into a stream that the defendant knows is a "navigable stream"? The issue is one of statutory interpretation to determine what elements of the crime the defendant must know. The issue is frequently framed: "Does the *mens rea* apply only to some elements or to all of them?"

2. Model Penal Code Rules of Construction

Many jurisdictions answer this question by applying the usual methods of statutory interpretation, including seeking the legislative intent and applying such rules as strict construction against the government. The Model Penal Code goes further and provides two rules to assist in resolving the application of mental elements. Section 2.02(4) indicates that a culpability state (purposely, knowingly, recklessly, or with criminal negligence) in a criminal statute applies "to all the material elements of the offense, unless a contrary purpose plainly appears." A "material element" is one that does not relate exclusively to the statute of limitations (the date of the offense) or jurisdiction or venue (such as the county where the crime occurred). Rather it includes the conduct, attendant circumstances and result described in the criminal statute. *MPC § 1.13(9), (10).* This means most elements are "material" and the statute's mens rea applies to them all.

This means that a mental element, such as knowingly, modifies every single material element unless the statute or legislative history plainly indicates that this is not the case. A "material element" may involve the nature of the forbidden conduct, the attendant circumstances, or the result of the conduct. *MPC § 2.02 comment.* Taking the pollution example above, the MPC formulation would most likely mean that the third interpretation is correct: the defendant must knowingly release a chemical that the defendant knows is the particular one described in the statute and the release must be in a stream the defendant knows is a navigable one.

The MPC also adds a second rule of construction. As discussed below, the MPC has a strong preference against strict liability crimes (those having no *mens rea*). Accordingly, Section 2.02(3) states that when a statute does not provide a *mens rea* for a particular element, the *mens rea* of purposely, knowingly, or recklessly is applicable by default to that element. Strict liability, in general, is reserved for the most minor infractions, called *violations* and carrying no prison term.

C. Varieties of *Mens Rea*

Virtually all criminal statutes include at least one — and sometimes several — mental elements. These varied considerably since often each statute was passed by a legislature with little regard for any system of categorizing or defining the *mens rea*. This is still true today in many locales. It is not uncommon to find criminal statutes in a single jurisdiction using many *mens rea* elements, sometimes in curious or even incomprehensible combinations. For example, current criminal statutes include the following mental formulations: willfully and maliciously sets fire to; knowingly and willfully with intent to defraud; with specific intent to destroy an ethnic group; wilful, deliberate, malicious, and premeditated killing; good faith; reckless disregard in controlling a dog; and loiter in a public place with intent to commit prostitution.

The issue can be even more complicated since in two rare situations, discussed below, courts will add a *mens rea* element to a statute that does not have one in it. The first is when it is held that due process requires a statute to have a particular *mens rea* element. The second is when courts find that the legislature intended for a statute to have a certain *mens rea* element even when the statute itself, as passed by the legislature, did not contain that particular element.

1. Model Penal Code's Revolutionary Formulation

Perhaps the most significant contribution of the Model Penal Code is its realization that American *mens rea* formulations needed significant reconceptualization since they included a dazzling array of mental elements, many of which were undefined and some downright misleading. A classic example is the traditional view that murder (unlike manslaughter) required the defendant to act with "malice aforethought," which was not defined by statute and which case law determined did not necessarily require either malice or aforethought.

The MPC's bold solution was to reduce the total number of mental elements (called "culpability") to four, and to define each one. The four mental elements are: purposely, knowingly, recklessly, and with criminal negligence. Each is defined and discussed in the succeeding sections. The MPC also authorizes strict liability (where there is no *mens rea* element) for minor infractions that carry no prison time, but rejects strict liability for almost all other offenses.

The four MPC culpability states are defined in descending order from most morally blameworthy (purposely) to less morally blameworthy (knowingly, recklessly) to the least morally blameworthy (with criminal negligence). Moreover, § 2.02(5) has adopted the concept of *downward inclusiveness*, which means that when one of the four is present, automatically so are the ones below but not those above. Thus, the government is free to prove that the defendant's *mens rea* was more serious than that required for conviction. For example, if the defendant is charged with a crime requiring recklessness and the government proves that D acted knowingly, the government has automatically established that D acted recklessly and with criminal negligence, but it has not established that the D acted purposely.

2. General/Specific Criminal Intent

At common law, the two levels of intent were: general and specific. Historically, some crimes were interpreted as requiring *general criminal intent*. Though no modern criminal code uses this term and it has been condemned as meaningless by virtually every commentator, vestiges of it have survived and the term is still used in some traditional American jurisdictions. The precise definition of general criminal intent is difficult since there is no statutory definition and courts have used various terms to describe it. Often it is described as requiring that the defendant intended to perform the physical act (though not to intend the result or to violate the law) proscribed by the statute. Sometimes general criminal intent is found in a statute that uses the word "intent" in the context of intending to do the act proscribed by the applicable statute. For example, in many locales the crime of assault requires general criminal intent because the defendant must intend to do an act and that act must actually cause physical harm to another person, irrespective of the actor's intent to cause such harm.

Courts sometimes refer to the *mens rea* of a crime as requiring proof of a *specific intent*, a term that is undefined in the common law. It is often understood to mean that a defendant must have a particular state of mind in relation to the offense conduct, such as a conscious object to cause a result or with a purpose to engage in the illegal conduct. Example of common law specific intent crimes are larceny, in which the *mens rea* is to deprive another permanently of property, and burglary, which requires proof of the defendant's purpose to engage in a felony once inside a home. The importance of distinguishing between a general intent and specific intent crime comes into play when examining whether a defense can be used. It can also apply when deciding whether to allow a mistake claim.

D. Intentionally (Purposely, With Intent To, Sometimes Willfully)

American jurisdictions, as well as the Model Penal Code, routinely include *intentionally* or some variety of it as a *mens rea* element which, of course, the government must prove beyond a reasonable doubt. Since this element requires a finding that the defendant personally (as opposed to a reasonable person) had the necessary *mens rea*, it is the prototypical *subjective* element which looks inside the actor's head to determine what he or she was thinking at a particular time.

The exact words for this element vary considerably among the crimes and among the jurisdictions. Sometimes it is phrased in specific terms, such as "with intent to defraud" or "with the intent to injure." Other statutes may simply prescribe elements that must be done "intentionally." Ordinarily this mental element requires the actor to intend to cause the harm condemned in the statute, such as intentionally kill, destroy, mislead, or burn.

While most jurisdictions use the term "intentionally," some, including the Model Penal Code, use "purposely" to articulate this *mens rea*. Another version is "with a design to." Some jurisdictions may even use different words for this concept in different criminal statutes.

1. Intentionally and Knowingly

Although the MPC distinguishes between the mental states of "purposely" and "knowingly," case law under more general statutes occasionally does not. Some cases find a person acted "intentionally" or "purposely" if he or she wanted the result to occur or were simply aware that it was very likely to occur. The latter "awareness" approach merges the concepts of intent and knowledge into a single mens rea element.

a. Willfully

The *mens rea* "willfully" (or "willful") appears in many statutes but poses significant interpretive problems. Sometimes it is read the same as "intentional," requiring purposeful conduct. Other times "willfully" means simply that the act must have been the product of the defendant's volition or will. This meaning may be the same as the mental component of *actus reus*, which requires a voluntary act.

Other courts define "willfully" with a meaning dependent on the context. Thus, a criminal law prohibiting the "willful violation" of a particular statute was read as requiring knowledge of the statute's requirements and a specific intent to violate the law. This reading is an exception to the general rule that ignorance of the law is no excuse. Other interpretations of "willfully" indicate the act must be done with a bad or evil purpose. Finally, the Model Penal Code provides that the element "willfully" is satisfied when a person acts knowingly. *MPC § 2.02(8)*. It would also be satisfied if the person acted purposely.

b. Definition

The definition of the intentionally/purposely culpability elements ordinarily focuses on the actor's conscious decision to do a particular act for a particular purpose. Thus, a statute could punish someone who "intentionally killed," embracing a defendant who pointed a gun at a victim and pulled the trigger for the purpose of killing the victim.

Sometimes, however, the statute requires intentional or willful conduct but does not require a particular purpose. For example, a statute may apply to a person who "willfully discharges a firearm in a grossly negligent manner." The *mens rea* requires a voluntary decision to discharge the firearm but does not mandate a particular purpose behind the act.

c. Model Penal Code Definition

Model Penal Code § 2.02(2)(a) uses the term "purposely" to describe the highest *mens rea* element. It distinguishes between acting purposely with regard to conduct or result, and with regard to circumstances. For conduct or result, a defendant acts purposely when the defendant's "conscious object" is to engage in the conduct of that nature or to cause that result. Circumstances are another matter since it makes little sense to think of one acting "purposely" with regard to circumstances. The MPC handles this linguistic dilemma by defining purposely as if it were "knowingly" in this context. Thus, under § 2.02(2)(a) a defendant acts purposely with regard to circumstances when the defendant is aware of the existence of the circumstances or at least believes or hopes that the circumstances exist.

For example, assume that D is hired to kill V. D decides to shoot V when V is camping alone in a remote part of a state park. D does so and is charged with violating a statute that makes it an aggravated form of murder "purposely to kill someone in a state park." Assume that the word "purposely" applies to every element of the crime. Since D shot V in order to kill V, D would be found to have purposely killed V under the MPC. "Killing" is both conduct and result and D's conscious objective was to do both. Similarly, D purposely killed "in a state park" since the location of the homicide is a circumstance of which D was aware at the time of the homicide.

2. Transferred Intent (or Bad Shot Doctrine)

Sometimes the defendant intends to inflict a particular harm on one victim but ends up inflicting it on a different one. For example, the defendant could shoot a rifle at Victim A but miss Victim A and mistakenly kill Victim B who stood next to Victim A. The defendant clearly intended to kill A and could be held for intentional homicide had the shot been true. But can the defendant be convicted of intentional homicide for Victim B's death? Note that the defendant never intended to shoot B; the only intent was to shoot Victim A. In such cases, under the doctrine of *transferred intent*, a doctrine applicable in both tort and criminal law, the defendant is held responsible for the death of Victim B as if the defendant had intended to kill Victim B.

There is no need to apply the doctrine of transferred intent in the misidentification cases. If defendant wants to kill Smith and shoots at a person the defendant believes is Smith, the defendant is liable for intentional homicide even if the defendant is mistaken and the homicide victim is Jones rather than Smith. Defendant has harmed the very person he or she intended to shoot. The doctrine of transferred intent also does not apply if a statute explicitly precludes its being used.

Note that the harm that occurs must be of the same type as the harm intended; the only difference is the identity of the victim. Returning to the hypothetical above, while defendant would be guilty of intentional homicide for Victim B's death, the doctrine of transferred intent would not make defendant liable for an assault (intentionally causing fear) of a bystander who was near defendant and became frightened by the loud noise that was produced when defendant shot the rifle at Victim A. Defendant never intended to cause fear; the intent was to kill another person.

A related issue is raised by a statute making it an especially serious crime to intentionally kill (or injure) a member of a specific identified group of people, such as a police or correctional officer or teacher who is working at his or her job. Assume D shoots at Victim A, intending to kill A, but misses and kills

Victim B, an on-duty police officer. Ordinarily the doctrine of transferred intent would make D liable for the intentional killing of Victim B, but not for the more serious offense of intentionally killing a working law enforcement officer. D never intended to kill the officer.

3. Proof of Intent: Motive

As noted above, intent is routinely proven by circumstantial evidence. The defendant's *motive* in doing the act may be critical evidence in assessing whether the defendant had the necessary intent, though motive itself is rarely an element of a crime.

4. Proof of Intent: Presumptions

Another approach to proving intent involves the use of *presumptions*. A presumption is a rule of law that authorizes a trier of fact to find that Fact B is established if Fact A is proven. For example, a traditional presumption authorizes a jury instruction that a person of sound mind intends the natural and probable consequences of his or her actions. Thus, if D points a gun at V and pulls the trigger, this presumption would allow the jury to find that D intended to kill V since D is deemed to have intended the natural and probable consequences of D's actions (pointing the gun at V and pulling the trigger). If D is charged with intentional homicide for V's death, the presumption would significantly aid the prosecution in its burden of proving that D intended to kill V.

In *Francis v. Franklin*, 471 U.S. 307 (1985), the Supreme Court struck down the above presumption because, even though the presumption could be rebutted by defense proof, it could be interpreted by jurors as relieving the government of the burden of proving the killing was intentional. Jurors could simply find that the defendant fired a gun at the victim, then from that finding rely on the presumption to conclude that the defendant intended to kill the victim. This outcome violated the due process requirement that the government prove — and the jury find — each element beyond a reasonable doubt, including proof of intent. It also suffered from the vice of possibly shifting the burden of persuasion to the defendant if the presumption allows the jury to find Fact B simply from proof of Fact A without any other proof of Fact B. Once the government proves Fact A, according to *Francis*, the jury could read the presumption as shifting the burden of persuasion to the defendant to disprove the existence of Fact B.

Francis does not mean that the above presumption, and similar ones making proof of intent easier, are no longer part of American criminal law. Rather, the Supreme Court has made it clear that such "presumptions" may be constitutional if they inform the jury that the "presumption" is merely an inference which the jury may or may not follow. Thus, the jury would be told that it could, but is not required to, find that the element of "intent" is proven by facts showing that the defendant fired a gun at the victim. The notion that a person intends the natural and probable consequences of his or her behavior is just one factor that the jury could use in assessing whether the defendant had the requisite *mens rea*.

E. Knowingly

Another common *mens rea* element requires the defendant to act with some type of knowledge. Sometimes the requirement is quite specific in stating what the defendant must know. The two issues surrounding this mental element are what must the defendant know and how certain must that knowledge be.

1. What Must Be Known

A criminal statute containing a "knowledge" element ordinarily indicates what must be known. An example is a crime of assaulting a school employee when the defendant knows of the victim's employment status. On occasion the knowledge element even reaches beyond what the defendant actually knew and extends to what the defendant *should have known*. For example, a statute punishes assault of an on-duty prison guard when the defendant knows or should know that the victim (1) is a prison guard (2) who is on duty at the time of the assault.

As we saw in the discussion of intent, on occasion statutes are unclear about what the defendant must have known since the *mens rea* could be read as applying only to the element immediately following the word "know" or could extend to many other elements as well. For example, imagine a statute that punished someone for "knowingly delivering more than an ounce of marijuana." What must the government prove in order to convict a defendant of this crime? Must the defendant simply know that he or she delivered a substance, or must the defendant also know that the quantity exceeded an ounce and that the substance was marijuana? Model Penal Code § 2.02 (4) solves this by providing that the word "knowledge" applies to all material elements, unless a contrary purpose plainly appears. As discussed more fully above, the MPC defines "material" to cover elements that relate to the harm or evil, incident to conduct, to be prevented by the law defining the offense. *MPC § 1.13(1)*. Elements are not material if they relate only to the statute of limitations (the date of the crime) or jurisdiction or venue (the location of the crime).

2. How Certain is Knowledge: Model Penal Code Definition

Though statutes routinely require proof that the defendant had knowledge of something, how certain does the defendant have to be to have that knowledge? What if the defendant merely *believes* the fact to be true, or is 90% certain it is so? Does knowledge require absolute or almost absolute certainty?

Many common law decisions held that a person has knowledge when he or she is aware of a fact or believes it to be true (and it is, in fact, true). No effort is made to quantify the degree of certainty needed to "know" a particular fact. Model Penal Code § 2.02(7) answers this important question by specifying that a person has "knowledge" of a particular fact if the person "is aware of a high probability of its existence." Absolute certainty is not required. This interpretation of "knowledge" supports the concept of deliberate indifference described below. On the other hand, the MPC further notes that in those unusual cases where the defendant is aware of a high probability of a fact but actually believes that the fact does not exist despite the high probability that it does exist, the defendant does not have knowledge of the fact's existence. For example, assume that D cut a major artery in V's neck and is charged with knowingly killing V. If D were aware that cutting this particular artery would create a high probability of death but believed that V had an unusual clotting capacity and therefore would not die, the MPC would permit a finding that the defendant did not "knowingly" kill by cutting the artery.

The MPC § 2.02(2)(b) also defines "knowingly" slightly differently for acts and circumstances than it does for results. For acts and circumstances, the defendant satisfies "knowingly" if he or she is "aware that his conduct is of that nature or that such circumstances exist." As noted above, this means that the defendant is aware of a high probability that the fact exists. For example, if D is charged with "knowingly making a counterfeit certificate of deposit," the MPC definition of knowingly is satisfied if D is aware that (1) the item D made looks like a certificate of deposit and (2) is not an authentic one. D need not know that the law prohibits this conduct.

For a result element, the MPC provides that a person acts knowingly with regard to a result when the defendant is "aware that it is practically certain that" his or her "conduct will cause such a result." Again, absolute certainty is not necessary, but the "practically certain" standard surely requires a rather high degree of confidence that the result is likely to occur. For example, if D shoots V in the head five times, D will surely be held to have "knowingly" caused V's death even though D thought there was a slight possibility that V would survive the head wounds. A jury would likely find that D, though perhaps not 100% certain, was nevertheless aware that it was practically certain that D's actions would cause V's death.

3. Deliberate Indifference (or Willful Blindness or the Ostrich Instruction)

Sometimes people try to avoid criminal liability by intentionally remaining ignorant of certain facts. For example, a pawn shop owner, who buys an authentic gold Rolex watch for $100 and knows that it is worth at least $2,000, may try to avoid liability for receiving stolen property (which requires knowledge that the property was stolen) by structuring the transaction in a way that does not reveal the fact that the property had been stolen. This ploy would allow the pawn shop owner to defend against a receiving stolen property charge by proving that he or she had no idea whether the property had been stolen, found on the street, inherited, the subject of a gift, etc.

To counter what has been called the "deliberate indifference" or "willful blindness," many jurisdictions authorize a trial judge to give a jury instruction dealing specifically with the issue. Named an "ostrich" or a *Jewell* instruction (after *Jewell v. United States*, 532 F.2d 697 (9th Cir. 1976)), a jury may be instructed that the government can prove beyond a reasonable doubt that the defendant had knowledge of a fact if, even though not actually aware of that fact, the defendant was aware of a high probability that the fact existed and the ignorance about the fact was due to a conscious effort to disregard information about that fact with a "conscious purpose to avoid learning the truth." A number of courts using this instruction do so sparingly and only when there are facts in the record suggesting deliberate indifference rather than mere negligence about gathering the information. These courts are legitimately concerned that the defendant will be convicted of a crime requiring knowledge when he or she actually lacked that knowledge. They also note that the deliberate indifference instruction actually revises the definition of knowledge to something like "should have been aware under the circumstances."

In *Global-Tech Appliances, Inc. et al, v. SEB S.A.*, 131 S.Ct. 2060 (2011), the Supreme Court examined willful blindness in the criminal law, in the context of a patent infringement case and held that "[w]hile the Court of Appeals articulate the doctrine of willful blindness in slightly different ways, all appear to agree on two basic requirements: (1)the defendant must subjectively believe that there is a high probability that a fact exists and (2) the defendant must take deliberate actions to avoid learning of that fact." The Court stated that "[w]e think these requirements give willful blindness an appropriately limited scope that surpasses recklessness and negligence."

F. Recklessly

The *mens rea* element, *recklessly,* may well be the one with the most disagreement in meaning. In some locales it simply refers to gross negligence. Often terms like "depraved heart" or an "indifference to the value of human life" are used to describe the serious degree of carelessness required for someone to act recklessly. The vagueness of this concept may make it difficult to distinguish from "criminal negligence," described below. Indeed, in some locales the effort may be fruitless since the terms "recklessness" and "criminal negligence" are used as synonyms for the same degree of carelessness.

Many American jurisdictions with modern criminal laws adopt the approach of the Model Penal Code, which includes both objective and subjective components in its definition of recklessness. The *subjective prong* of recklessness under MPC § 2.02(2)(c) requires that the defendant personally ignore a known risk. Thus, under the MPC a person acts recklessly when he or she "consciously disregards a substantial and unjustifiable risk that the material element exists or will result from the conduct." The government must prove beyond a reasonable doubt that the defendant (1) recognized that his or her behavior presented a risk, (2) was aware of facts that made the risk substantial and unjustifiable (irrespective of whether the defendant even thought about whether the risk was "substantial" or justified), and (3) nevertheless went ahead despite this knowledge. In other words, recklessness under the MPC involves "conscious risk creation." *MPC§ 2.02 comment.*

The *objective prong* of recklessness under MPC describes the nature of the risk that the defendant consciously ignored. The risk must be characterized as "substantial" and "unjustifiable," neither of which is defined. In assessing whether a risk is "substantial," the degree of harm is a key factor. A risk of death is substantial while a risk of a slight inconvenience may not be. Moreover, the likelihood of the harm is also important. A one-in-a-hundred risk of death may be substantial but a one-in-five-billion chance may be insubstantial.

Whether a risk is "unjustifiable" requires an assessment of why it was taken. If the product of medically necessary life-endangering surgery, it may be justifiable. On the other hand, if the risk was taken for fun, it may be unjustifiable under the circumstances.

Because of the important factual differences in each case, the jury is given considerable leeway in deciding these issues. The MPC provides that the jury should measure whether the risk was substantial and unjustifiable by asking whether its disregard "involves a gross deviation from the standard of care that a law abiding person would observe in the actors situation." Note that the perspective is the "actor's situation" which views the world from the actor's perceptions at the time and looks at the circumstances known to the actor. *MPC § 2.02(c).*

G. Criminal Negligence

It is common for American jurisdictions to impose criminal liability for those whose negligent acts cause a harm. Negligent homicide is a common illustration. Ordinarily, criminal negligence is an entirely objective standard, focusing on the choices that a reasonable person should have made under the circumstances. In other words, punishing someone for causing a result by criminally negligent behavior involves sanctioning a person for creating a risk of harm by failing to act as a reasonable person would have acted.

1. Rationale

Many commentators are critical of imposing criminal liability for negligence, reasoning that the criminal law should require more moral blameworthiness than mere carelessness. They argue that the careless person does not need punishment because he or she cannot be deterred and, in a retributive sense, does not merit punishment. The counter argument is that punishing for carelessness may make people more careful and that causing harm, such as death, is deserving of criminal sanctions irrespective of the actor's lack of an "evil mind." The latter argument may note that the defendant who is insensitive to the interests of other people, but has enough information about a situation to have acted differently, has exhibited a variety of moral blameworthiness that can legitimately be punished.

2. Definition

Jurisdictions differ in their approach to considering the individual characteristics of the actor when assessing whether he or she acted with criminal negligence. Often the person's physical status is considered, such as whether the defendant suffered from seizures or was deaf. The issue would be whether a reasonable person who suffered regular seizures late at night would drive a car during the period when seizures were most likely.

The precise definition of criminal negligence varies considerably among the jurisdictions. Some jurisdictions define negligence in criminal cases the same as it is defined in civil cases: a deviation from the standard of care of a reasonable person.

In most American jurisdictions, however, negligence for criminal liability is more egregious carelessness than that required for civil liability. Terms such as "gross negligence" or "criminal negligence" or "willful and wanton conduct" may be used to express the extra degree of carelessness needed for criminal liability. The reason for requiring this extra degree of carelessness (over that required for tort liability) is that the criminal law attempts to punish people who are morally blameworthy, not just negligent.

3. Model Penal Code Definition

Model Penal Code § 2.02(2)(d) adopts the usual view that negligence sufficient for criminal liability should be more egregious than for ordinary tort liability. Thus, under the MPC a person acts negligently when he or she "should be aware of a substantial and unjustifiable risk that the material element exists or will result from" his or her conduct. The disregard of the risk must be a gross deviation from the standard of care that a reasonable person would observe in the defendant's situation.

The perspective is that of the actor to some extent. In assessing whether the conduct satisfied the "gross deviation" standard, the jury looks at the circumstances that the actor perceived as well as the nature and purpose of the actor's conduct.

It should be noted that the "gross deviation" standard for criminal negligence under the MPC is the same as it uses for recklessness. Thus, while the risk is the same, the primary difference between recklessness and criminal negligence under the MPC is subjective awareness of the risk. For recklessness, MPC § 2.02(2)(c) provides that the defendant must have been aware and consciously ignored the risk, while for criminal negligence the defendant was not aware of the risk but should have been so aware.

H. Strict Liability

While most criminal laws involve some sort of *mens rea* element, there is a category that does not. Called *strict liability* offenses, these crimes simply do not contain a *mens rea*. The elements include an *actus reus* and perhaps circumstances and even harm, but the defendant's *mens rea* is not ordinarily an issue. An example is speeding, where the offense is exceeding the speed limit and it is irrelevant whether the defendant did so intentionally or negligently.

Strict liability crimes tend to be minor, often misdemeanors and are often disfavored. Indeed the Supreme Court has noted that the existence of mens rea in a criminal statute is the rule rather than the exception. Frequently, strict liability crimes are called "public welfare" crimes because they aim at protecting the public health or safety. The Supreme Court has upheld strict liability crimes against constitutional attack, though *Lambert v. California*, discussed below, invalidated a particular variety of such offenses.

When a statute contains no *mens rea* element, often courts will accept it as a strict liability crime. However, on occasion, courts will look at the common law and other sources and conclude that the legislature meant to include a *mens rea* element. The classic case is *Morissette v. United States*, 342 U.S. 246 (1952), where the defendant, a junk dealer, took rusting shell cases from a government practice bombing range. The defendant thought the shells were abandoned. The Supreme Court noted that traditionally common law theft crimes required proof of mens rea (intent to steal). Considering the common law origins of the statute barring the knowing conversion of government property, the *Morissette* Court held that this meant that Congress wanted proof that the defendant had criminal intent when he took the government assets. Thus, his mistaken belief that the shell casings were abandoned could be a defense to the conversion charge.

This same approach was taken in *Staples v. United States*, 511 U.S. 600 (1994), where the Supreme Court, as in *Morissette*, added a *mens rea* element to a criminal statute that appeared to be strict liability. Defendant was charged with the federal crime of unlawful possession of an unregistered machine gun. Defendant maintained he did not register the weapon because he did not know it was a machine gun, defined as capable of automatic firing. The Supreme Court held that while the statute appeared to be strict liability, Congress intended for the statute to require the offender knew the weapon was capable of automatic fire. The Court looked at the nature of the statute and the character of the items regulated by it, noting that guns "in general" do not put their owner on notice that they stand in "responsible relation to a public danger." The Court found that Congress did not intend to place on gun owners the onus of assessing whether their weapon had been modified to function as a machine gun. The Court in *Staples* also reasoned that the severe penalty also indicated Congress did not intend to eliminate a *mens rea* element. According to the *Staples* Court, there is no "precise line" for distinguishing between strict liability and other crimes that require a mental element. But if Congress meant the former when the crime carries a substantial penalty, as here, its should clearly indicate its intent to impose strict liability.

The opposite result is represented by another classic case, *United States v. Balint*, 258 U.S. 250 (1922), involving the sale of opium without a written form issued by the Commissioner of Internal Revenue. The defendant claimed he did not know the drugs were prohibited. The Supreme Court held that Congress intended for the statute to be strict liability, even though the defendant is "ignorant of the noxious character of what he sells," in order to "stimulate proper care" and adequate records in a situation where negligence may be dangerous, such as with the sale of diseased food or poison.

A third important case is *United States v. Dotterweich*, 320 U.S. 277 (1943), where the defendant was charged with delivering misbranded and adulterated drugs in interstate commerce. Even though the defendant did not directly participate in the shipments, the Supreme Court held the statute created a strict vicarious liability offense in order to regulate a public danger by putting the burden on a person in a responsible relation to the danger. A spirited dissent argued that in Anglo-Saxon jurisprudence, guilt is personal and should not be placed on a person who has no evil intention or consciousness of wrongdoing. Absent clear legislative mandate, the *Dotterweich* dissent maintained, a statue should not be interpreted as imposing strict liability.

1. Rationale for Strict Liability Crimes

The rationale for strict liability crimes is that punishing for conduct alone makes the target actors more careful in their behavior as they strive to evade criminal liability. Arguments such as "I did not know my factory was leaking contaminants into the river" or "I didn't mean to pollute the stream" provide no defense to a strict liability crime. The actor must take extra precautions since he or she will be liable for the consequences of actions, irrespective of the presence or absence of intent, knowledge, recklessness, or criminal negligence.

2. Model Penal Code

Many commentators argue that the criminal law should not impose strict liability because doing so permits criminal conviction without moral blameworthiness. These advocates suggest that civil liability may be appropriate in such cases but the person who acts without any *mens rea* is not the kind of person who deserves punishment.

The Model Penal Code essentially adopts this approach and rejects strict liability except for the most minor offenses. Section 2.02(1) states that a person is not guilty of a criminal offense unless he or she acts purposely, knowingly, recklessly, or negligently. Moreover, if the criminal statute imposes criminal liability without including a *mens rea*, MPC§ 2.02(3) states that recklessly (which is also established by proof the defendant acted knowingly or intentionally) is by default included as an element.

I. Vicarious and Corporate Liability

1. Vicarious Liability

As discussed in Chapter 4, there are some circumstances in the criminal law that permit a person (often including a business entity) to be held liable for the acts of another person with whom there is a relationship. Called *vicarious liability*, the most common situation involves an employer, usually a corporation or other business organization, that is charged with a crime for the conduct of one of its employees acting in the course of business.

In civil tort law, this is known as *respondeat superior* liability and may require an employer to pay the damages caused by an employee acting in the course of his or her employment. Criminal liability is similar. For example, a statute making it a crime to sell alcohol to a minor ordinarily is interpreted as meaning that a bar or liquor store could be held criminally liable for such a sale even though it is done by an employee, who may be acting contrary to express rules against such conduct.

Vicarious liability is sometimes confused with strict liability, but there are differences. An important distinction is that the party vicariously liable need not personally engage in any acts that comprise the offense; the acts of the subordinate person are attributed to the person vicariously liable for those acts. But the person vicariously liable may, depending on the applicable criminal statute, still have to have the *mens rea* required by the statute. For strict liability, on the other hand, the defendant ordinarily will have engaged in the criminal conduct forbidden by the statute, but there need be no proof that there was any *mens rea* in the occurrence. Some criminal statutes combine vicarious and strict liability, holding one person liable for the actions of another, with no requirement of proof of any *mens rea* by either party.

2. Corporate Liability

a. Historical Development

Corporations were not subject to criminal liability under the common law because they were viewed as incapable of forming the requisite intent to commit a crime. Over time this rule changed to allow corporations to be convicted of a crime. The early development of corporate criminal liability involved regulatory offenses based on acts of omission. Because these were strict liability crimes requiring no *mens rea*, and the defendant assessed only a fine, corporations came to be viewed as subject to criminal liability.

The most significant expansion of corporate criminal liability occurred when the Supreme Court held in *New York Central & Hudson R.R. Co. v. United States*, 212 U.S. 481 (1909), a case involving illegal rebates on sugar shipments, that a corporation could be held liable for any crime by imputing the intent of the employee to the organization. The Court stated that in "[a]pplying the principle governing civil liability, we go only a step farther in holding that the act of the agent, while exercising the authority delegated to him to make rates for transportation, may be controlled, in the interest of public policy, by imputing his act to his employer and imposing penalties upon the corporation for which he is acting in the premises." The Court rejected the claim that due process required proof of the corporation's own intent and not merely the intent of the employee. Courts have extended the notion of corporate intent to include the *collective knowledge* of all employees, so that even if no individual is guilty of the offense the corporation can be convicted of a crime based on an aggregation of its employees' intent.

b. Model Penal Code Comparison

Model Penal Code § 2.07 takes a more restrictive view on corporate criminal liability. A corporation can be prosecuted only if the applicable statute "plainly states" that a company is liable for a violation and its employee's conduct was "within the scope of his office or employment" and the employee was "acting in behalf of the corporation." If the violation involves an omission by the corporation, the omitted act must have been one the corporation was required to perform. A corporation can also be prosecuted if the employee's conduct was "authorized, requested, commanded, performed or recklessly tolerated by the board of directors or by a high managerial agent acting on behalf of the corporation within the scope of" the agent's job. A high managerial agent is an officer whose duties are such that the agent's conduct "may fairly be assumed to represent the policy of the corporation." It should be noted that under the MPC there is a defense for criminal acts (but not omissions) if the high managerial agent with supervisory responsibility over the subject matter employed "due diligence" to prevent the commission of the crime. The MPC does not address vicarious liability.

J. Ignorance and Mistake

1. Mistake or Ignorance Negates *Mens Rea*

Sometimes a person is mistaken or ignorant about a fact or the law. For example, a nearsighted hunter might believe that he or she is shooting a deer when really the object behind a bush is a person. This ignorance or mistake could be a defense to a subsequent criminal charge if it negates (sometimes called "negatives") the mental element of a crime. Thus, the hunter would not be guilty of intentional homicide even if the human victim died since the defendant never intended to kill a person. What this means, of course, is that the state cannot meet its burden of proving that the defendant had the necessary *mens rea* for the crime. Of course, the sight-challenged hunter may be guilty of reckless or negligent homicide, crimes that punish harm caused by carelessness rather than intent.

Another example is *People v. Navarro*, 160 Cal. Rptr. 692 (L.A. Super. Ct. 1979), where the defendant was charged with theft of wooden beams from a construction site. He maintained he thought they were abandoned and the owner did not object to their being taken. The court held that if the jury believed this, the defendant had a valid mistake of fact defense to the theft offense which required an intent to steal the property. Defendant's good faith belief in the abandoned status of the property, even if unreasonable, negated the intent to steal required to convict him.

A minority of jurisdictions limit this mistake defense by requiring that the mistake be *reasonable* before it may be used to negate a *mens rea* element. The MPC contains no such restriction. To some scholars, the rule requiring the mistake be reasonable is unwise since it does not account for the fact that if the defendant lacks the necessary *mens rea* for any reason, including an unreasonable mistake, he or she should not be guilty since a key element of the crime is absent.

The difference is illustrated by a crime that requires proof the defendant (1) knowingly possessed a pistol (2) knowing it to be loaded. Assume that the defendant carried a pistol he or she thought was unloaded but in reality was loaded. If the mistake in the lethality of the weapon was unreasonable, in those jurisdictions permitting a defense only for a "reasonable" mistake, the unreasonable error could bar the defendant from even arguing that the mistake negated the *mens rea* requiring proof of knowledge the gun was loaded. On the other hand, in a jurisdiction, like the MPC, that allows any mistake to negate the knowing *mens rea*, whether the defendant's error was reasonable or unreasonable would not prevent a defense based on the mistake.

2. Not Negativing *Mens Rea* — General Intent Crimes

As noted above, some crimes are deemed to contain a general criminal intent, which in essence simply requires the actor to intend to do the act prohibited by the criminal law. For example, often statutory rape is considered a general intent crime that punishes someone who has sexual relations with a person under a certain age. Ordinarily, a mistake of fact about the victim's age does not qualify as a defense in general intent cases, though in some jurisdictions an honest and reasonable mistake as to age of the victim is a viable defense.

3. Ignorance of Illegality

If the mistaken belief is that the actor's conduct does not violate the criminal law, ordinarily the error will not affect liability since belief or knowledge of violating the law is rarely an element of a crime and therefore is not negated by the mistake. Thus, there is truth in the aphorism that ignorance of the law is no excuse. The basis for this principle is the common law view that every person is presumed to know the law.

On occasion, however, a statute actually includes a mental element mandating knowledge of illegality, an intent to violate a legal duty, or a particular legal status. In these cases a mistake about the law may provide a defense to the *mens rea* element. For example, if the crime is "knowing violation of an official duty," the defendant's mistake about the scope of his or her official duties may constitute a defense for a failure to perform those duties. Similarly, for the crime of trespass, defined as entering property with knowledge that one is not privileged to do so, the defendant's mistaken belief that the property was owned by an uncle who had given the defendant permission to enter it will be a valid defense to a trespass charge. Another illustration is a person who put her key in a car and drove it away while believing that she still owned the car. If, unknown to the driver, the car had been sold to someone else, the driver would not be guilty of larceny of the car because she did not intend to deprive the owner of it permanently. Her mistake about a legal relationship—ownership of the car—would provide a mistake defense.

Two Supreme Court cases with the *mens rea* "willfully" illustrate that in some unusual situations ignorance of the law is an excuse. In *Ratzlaf v. United States*, 510 U.S. 135 (1994), the defendant had broken a large cash transaction into smaller ones below the $10,000 amount that triggered the bank's legal obligation to report the transaction to federal authorities. Charged with "willfully violating" the rule requiring banks to report large cash transactions, the defendant argued he was not guilty because though he knew he was trying to avoid the $10,000 reporting rules, he did not know his actions of structuring transactions to fall below the $10,000 threshold were unlawful. The Supreme Court accepted this defense, interpreting the applicable statute as requiring proof that the defendant acted with knowledge that his or her conduct was unlawful.

Another illustration is provided by federal tax law that makes it a crime "willfully" to attempt to evade a tax or "willfully" to fail to file a mandatory tax return. *Cheek v. United States*, 498 U.S. 192 (1991). The Supreme Court interpreted this *mens rea* as requiring a voluntary, intentional violation of a known legal duty. This means that liability under this statute depends on proof that the defendant knew of the duty imposed by law and voluntarily and intentionally violated that duty. The Court also stated that the defendant had a defense if he believed he had no such duty, even if the belief was unreasonable. In an unusual twist, the defendant maintained that the complexity of the tax law was responsible for his misunderstanding about his duty to file.

4. Crime as Facts or Law Thought to Be

In some jurisdictions that follow MPC § 2.04(2) the rule is qualified by another one that provides the mistaken actor may still be convicted of whatever crime would have occurred had the facts been as the actor believed them to be. Thus, in a jurisdiction that punished forcible sodomy more severely than consensual sodomy, if D thought he was committing consensual sodomy but D was mistaken and the victim had not consented, D may not be guilty of forcible sodomy but could be convicted of the less serious crime of consensual sodomy.

5. *Lambert v. California*

The United States Supreme Court found a constitutional "ignorance of law" defense in the classic case of *Lambert v. California*, 355 U.S. 225 (1957). A Los Angeles ordinance required certain convicted offenders who were in Los Angeles for more than five days to register with the police. The *Lambert* defendant, a felon who had lived in Los Angeles for seven years but had never registered, was convicted of violating the ordinance. The Supreme Court held that her conviction violated the due process requirement of notice because she had no actual knowledge of the duty to register and there was no proof that there was the possibility of such knowledge. The Court stressed that the crime punished passive conduct (failure to register). Justice Frankfurter wrote a spirited dissent that argued the statute was constitutional, noting the widespread acceptance of laws punishing people who had no awareness of what the law required or that they were doing something wrong. Subsequent case law has virtually ignored *Lambert*, refusing to follow it because in the particular case there was actual or likely knowledge of the law in question, or simply by limiting *Lambert* to punishment for passive conduct.

6. Law Not Accessible

On rare occasions a law is in force but has not been made sufficiently available to inform those subject to it. A number of jurisdictions, lead by MPC § 2.04(3), provide a defense when someone believes that his or her conduct is not a crime and the statute enacting the defense has not been published or otherwise made reasonably available before the conduct in question. This defense has strong due process roots but also recognizes that in such cases punishment would be both unfair and ineffective.

7. Reliance Upon Official Statement

Sometimes a person will make sincere, reasonable efforts to find out what the law requires and then acts in a law-aiding manner consistent with the information, but then is caught in the trap of violating the law because the legal information was inaccurate. For example, someone may take a course of action in reliance on an intermediate appellate court's decision that is subsequently reversed by the state's supreme court.

Some jurisdictions hold that liability under these circumstances is unfair and does not reflect the kind of moral blameworthiness that the criminal law should punish. It has even been held to violate due process. Accordingly, these jurisdictions, following Model Penal Code § 2.04(3), specifically make it a defense to criminal liability that the defendant honestly believed his or her actions were not criminal because of a good faith, reasonable reliance on an erroneous official statement of the law in a statute or similar enactment, judicial decision, administrative order, or official interpretation of law by a public officer charged with interpreting, administering, or enforcing the law in question.

Note that this defense does not allow a person to rely on many people whose advice is sought and taken routinely, such as employees of gun stores, members of the clergy, or well-informed friends. Note further that the MPC version requires the reliance to be "reasonable," which is an objective standard. Some jurisdictions reject the reasonableness limitation and simply permit a defense for an actual, good faith reliance, even if unreasonable.

As an example of this defense, a snowmobile driver, charged with speeding, successfully defended by showing that a state agency's pamphlet about snowboarding rules failed to indicate that a general speed limit, described in the pamphlet, could be altered, without signs, by particular speeding rules for the location. Similarly, a judge at sentencing seemed to tell the defendant that he was barred from possessing a handgun only while being on probation, but state law prohibited the defendant from ever having a firearm. After completing probation the offender acquired a firearm and was then prosecuted under state law for illegal possession of a firearm. A state court overturned the conviction since the defendant had, in good faith, relied on the sentencing judge's erroneous representations about state law.

8. Reliance Upon Advice of Private Lawyer

While reliance on an official statement may be a defense in some locales, reliance on the advice of a private lawyer is virtually never recognized as a defense. Model Penal Code § 2.04, which specifically provides a defense for certain reliances, does not indicate that good faith reliance on a private lawyer's legal advice is sufficient to exclude liability. The concern is that the client and lawyer will collude to permit a violation of the criminal law.

In some situations, however, a defendant may offer a defense that he or she acted in accordance with the advice of an attorney and therefore lacked the *mens rea* required for the particular crime. The fact of consulting with an attorney could be proof of the person's good faith, which can be a defense to a specific intent crime, such as one involving an intent to defraud or making false statements. For example, if D is charged with "willfully evading payment of a tax" and if D had consulted a lawyer who advised D that D owed no taxes on the particular transaction, D may use the advice of counsel to defend against proof that D "willfully" evaded payment.

In order to establish an advice of counsel "mistake defense," a jurisdiction may mandate that the defendant must establish that, before taking the action that allegedly violated the law, the defendant in good faith sought the advice of an attorney considered competent for the purpose of securing legal counsel about the lawfulness of his or her possible future conduct. In obtaining the legal advice, the person must have made a full and accurate report of all material facts to the attorney, and then acted strictly in accordance with the advice of the lawyer. A crucial element of the defense is the defendant secured the advice on the lawfulness of possible future conduct and not about a course of action already commenced.

Checkpoints

- *Mens rea*, meaning "guilty mind," allows the criminal law to reach people who possess sufficient moral blameworthiness to merit criminal sanctions and it permits the legislature to fine-tune criminal laws so they apply only to actors with a specified mental state.

- The prosecution, which must prove *mens rea* beyond a reasonable doubt, ordinarily does so by circumstantial evidence.

- Motive itself is rarely a mental element, but may be powerful circumstantial evidence of *mens rea*, especially intent.

- The Model Penal Code generally applies the *mens rea* requirement in a criminal statute to each element of that statute.

- The Model Penal Code disfavors strict liability crimes and contains a default rule that makes recklessness the default *mens rea* when a criminal statute contains no *mens rea* element.

- While traditional criminal laws used a variety of *mens rea* elements, the Model Penal Code uses four: purposely, knowingly, recklessly, and with criminal negligence.

- General criminal intent, a term most authorities argue should be discarded, has many meanings, though often it means simply that the actor intended to perform the physical act condemned in the criminal statute.

- "Intentionally" (or "purposely" or sometimes "wilfully") ordinarily means the actor consciously chose to do a certain act or cause a specific result. For circumstances, this *mens rea* element means the actor was aware of the circumstances.

- "Knowingly" means the defendant was aware of a high probability that a fact existed or that it was practically certain that a particular result would occur.

- "Recklessly," though subject to many definitions, contains both subjective and objective components. Under the MPC it means the actor consciously disregarded a substantial and unjustifiable risk and this was a gross deviation from the standard of care of a reasonable person.

- "Criminal negligence" is an objective test that, under the MPC, asks whether the defendant should have been aware of a risk and the failure to perceive the risk was a gross deviation from the standard of care of a reasonable person.

- Strict liability crimes contain no *mens rea* and are ordinarily minor crimes.

- Ignorance or mistake about a fact or the law may negate the *mens rea* of a crime.

- In some jurisdictions, a person's good faith reliance on an official statement of the law by a court or public official is a defense if the statement was wrong and the person relying on it violated a criminal law.

- Reliance on the advice of counsel may provide a defense if it negates a *mens rea*.

Chapter 6

Causation

A. Overview and Policy Basis

If X is to be responsible for homicide for V's death, X must *cause* that death, as causation is defined by the criminal law. The defendant is not accountable for that result unless his or her *actus reus* caused that result. Causation is an issue when a crime requires a harm or result, as is the case for homicide (the victim must be killed), arson (a building must be set on fire), and some varieties of assault (someone must suffer serious bodily injury). If a crime requires proof of a result, causation links that result with the defendant's actions. In other words, causation connects the defendant's *actus reus* with the harmful result. Causation is not an issue for crimes that do not require any actual injury, such as reckless endangerment, which punishes conduct that puts someone at risk of harm but does not require any actual harm.

1. Policy Basis

The rationale for requiring proof of causation in a criminal case is obvious: it is unfair to punish a person for a result that he or she did not cause. Sometimes this common sense observation is attributed to the theory of retribution, which holds that a person should only be punished when and to the extent that punishment is deserved in a moral sense. Punishment is only deserved if the defendant has personal responsibility for the harm that the criminal law sanctions.

2. Proof Issues

Causation, like any element, must be proven by the government beyond a reasonable doubt. In criminal law, causation arises most frequently in homicide cases. The usual issue is what caused the death. Sometimes the answer is clear, and ordinarily the prosecution proves the cause of death by expert testimony. The pathologist who performed an autopsy on the victim is a typical prosecution witness on the issue. The defense may counter with its own expert testimony on causation.

B. Two Varieties: "But For" and Proximate Cause

In assessing whether X has caused V's death and therefore may be criminally responsible for it, American jurisdictions ordinarily ask two questions: was X the "but for" cause as well as the *proximate cause* of V's death? These two tests, discussed in more detail in the next two sections, address very different concerns. The former asks whether the laws of science and logic support the proposition that the death would not have happened when it happened without X's actions. If "but for" causation is present, the next step is to ask the proximate cause question: Would it be fair to hold X criminally responsible for this result?

C. "But For" or "Actual" or "Cause-in-Fact" Causation

The first issue in assessing causation is whether the defendant's acts actually played a role in producing the harm. Called by various names such as "but for cause," "actual cause," "factual cause," "*sine qua non* cause," or "cause-in-fact," this facet of causation relies on the laws of science and logic in deciding whether the harm would have happened without the defendant's actions.

It must be stressed that "but for" cause has a common sense dimension that places obvious and sensible limits on how far this concept of causation is extended. Many "causes" are simply ignored in assessing criminal liability, though technically they could be deemed to satisfy "but for" causation. For example, assume that D kills V by sneaking rat poison into V's coffee. Of course D's actions satisfy "but for" causation since D placed the poison in the coffee, V drank the coffee, and then died from the poison. But there are other actors as well without whom V would not have perished. Had D not been born, V would not have died from this poison, but no one would hold D's mother or father responsible for the homicide. (Of course the parents would also escape liability since they had no relevant *mens rea*.) These remote factors are sometimes called "conditions" and are not considered part of the actual cause.

"But for" causation has several other important dimensions. First, it can exclude someone from criminal liability if he or she is not a "but for" cause. On the other hand, "but for" causation, alone, will generally not make the person the legal cause of a harm since that determination also requires a finding that the person is the proximate cause of the harm, as discussed below.

Second, there may be more than one "but for" cause of a result. For example, two hired killers each could shoot the victim in the heart at about the same time with each bullet capable of causing immediate death. Both could be guilty of murder even though it would be impossible to say which bullet actually entered the body before the other.

1. Acceleration of Death

Another dimension of "but for" causation is that it is satisfied if the defendant accelerates the death of someone who would have died without the defendant's actions. Thus, if X poisons V who would likely die within a few minutes from the poison, but Z, acting independently, then sneaks into the room and kills V by shooting V in the heart, Z would be the "but for" cause of V's death because Z hastened the death. In some jurisdictions X would not be considered to be the cause of V's death (but may be guilty of attempted murder; X could be guilty of the murder if X and Z acted in concert, as discussed elsewhere). In other jurisdictions, *both* Z and X would be deemed to have caused V's death and each could be convicted of homicide.

Liability for *accelerating* a death must be distinguished from *aggravating* a harm. The latter simply makes pain or other harm more severe, but it does not make death occur sooner. Liability for accelerating a death applies only to conduct that causes the victim to die at an earlier date than would be the case without the harmful conduct.

2. More Than One Cause: Substantial Factor

Sometimes a person dies from a combination of actions. In a number of jurisdictions "but for" causation is established when the defendant's conduct was a "substantial" or a "substantial and material" or even a "contributing" factor in the resulting harm. It need not be the sole factor. Under this approach there could easily be several people, each acting independently, responsible for a result if each was a substantial factor in bringing it about. Conversely, people with minimal involvement would be excluded in a jurisdiction that required the actor to have been a substantial factor in the outcome.

Note that the substantial factor approach can be viewed as a modification of traditional "but for" causation. No individual actor's conduct may be sufficient to satisfy but for causation, but each is a substantial factor in the harm collectively caused. An example would be two people who, acting independently, each stab a drug dealer they both despise. The victim dies from the trauma of both wounds, but would have survived had only one of the stabbings occurred.

3. Concurrent Causes

There is a highly unusual fact pattern where two (or more) acts cause the same harm and both are deemed adequate "but for" causes for criminal prosecution though in fact there is no proof beyond a reasonable doubt that either was the actual "but for" cause of the harm. This occurs in two situations. First, when the two causes occur at the same time and each is sufficient by itself to bring about the result that occurred, each actor is liable for the result. Thus, if A and B, acting independently, each pour a cup of rat poison into a glass and force V to drink it, both A and B will be held to "cause" V's death if the amount of poison each contributed was sufficient in itself to cause V's death. (Of course, the same result is possible if A and B are deemed accomplices or co-conspirators who are each held responsible for their collective criminal activities; these issues are discussed in Chapters 13 and 16.) The same result if V dies from a drug overdose and an autopsy reveals that V's body contained a lethal dose of both cocaine and heroin. D, who independently supplied the heroin, may satisfy "but for" causation for the death even though the source of the cocaine is unknown and the expert witnesses cannot say which of the two deadly drugs actually killed V.

The second situation is when neither cause is sufficient in itself to bring about the harm, but in combination the two causes are adequate. In the example above, if A and B each supplied a small amount of rat poison that, alone, would not have killed V, but the combined amount of the two doses was lethal, both A and B would satisfy "but for" causation for the ensuing homicide. Note, here neither A nor B alone would satisfy but for cause, however, collectively both of them do. This conclusion produces a change in the usual approach to but for causation.

4. Omission to Act as a Cause

As noted in the discussion of *actus reus* in Chapter 3, sometimes criminal law imposes liability for an omission to act when the failure to act violated a legal duty to take action. Thus, a mother who did not feed her infant child may be found liable for reckless or negligent homicide if the child dies from hunger. The mother has a legal duty to provide necessaries for her offspring.

The doctrine of causation applies to omissions as it does to commissions. If the nonaction satisfies "but for" and proximate causation, the person whose failure to act caused the harm may be criminally responsible for that harm.

D. Proximate Cause

Even though a person is the "but for" cause of an injury, criminal law ordinarily does not impose liability unless the defendant is also the "proximate cause" (sometimes called "legal cause"). Proximate cause engenders an important policy decision about the proper reach of the criminal law. Often proximate or legal cause asks the fundamental question whether it is fair to hold the defendant responsible for a harm for which the defendant is the "but for" cause. In many jurisdictions a key question is whether the harm that occurred was intended or foreseeable at the time of the act.

Proximate cause cases arise in a number of specific contexts and may produce different results in different jurisdictions or with slightly different fact patterns. Often courts look at a number of factors in determining whether it would be fair to extend liability in a particular situation. Indeed, it can be argued persuasively that there is no single common law rule of proximate cause, but rather a set of rules applied in different ways by different jurisdictions. Moreover, since the issue of proximate cause may be decided by a jury rather than the judge, it is not surprising that the results may vary considerably from case to case as jurors apply the causation rules in ways that reflect the particular values of the individuals deciding that case.

A classic illustration is provided by the drag racing cases. A and B agree to race their cars on a public street. During the race, A loses control and dies when her car hits a telephone pole. Should B be held to have caused A's death and be guilty of reckless homicide? Most cases hold it fair to hold B responsible. *But see Velazquez v. State*, 561 So.2d 347 (Fla. Dist. Ct. App. 1990)(though B satisfies "but for" causation, it would be unfair to hold B proximately caused A's death because A killed himself by his own volitional reckless driving).

Case law, however, has produced some situations where proximate cause results have evolved into patterns.

1. Very Minor or Remote Effect

Sometimes a defendant commits a crime that puts in motion a series of events producing a much graver harm. For example, assume that D makes a harassing five-minute telephone call to V. After the call, V hangs up the phone, leaves the building to drive home, but V's car is struck by a train as the car goes through a railroad crossing. The train engineer was drunk. Although it is true that D is a "but for" cause of the accident since D's call delayed V's trip over the railroad tracks, which had no train traffic for six hours before the fatal accident, D's involvement in the event would be viewed as so minor or remote that D would not be held criminally responsible for V's death. In other words, D would not be deemed to be the proximate cause of the harm. The drunk train engineer, on the other hand, would be found to be the cause of the death and possibly responsible for reckless or criminally negligent homicide.

2. Different Victim Than Intended

Sometimes the defendant intends to inflict a particular harm on one victim but ends up inflicting it on a different one. For example, D shoots a rifle at A but misses A and mistakenly kills B who stood next to A. In such cases, under the doctrine of transferred intent, discussed in Chapter 5, D is held responsible for the death of B as if D had intended to kill B.

3. Unexpected Result from Negligence or Recklessness

Just as intentional crimes use the concept of transferred intent to extend liability for an intended harm, for negligent or reckless crimes the doctrines of "transferred negligence" and "transferred recklessness" sometimes are used for the same purpose. Thus, if D is reckless or negligent toward X but instead harms V, D would be viewed as having been negligent toward V just as D was negligent or reckless toward X. Model Penal Code § 2.03(3) provides that for a reckless or negligent crime, if the actual and probable result differs only in that a different person is injured, the actor is deemed to have been negligent or reckless with regard to the actual victim.

4. Multiple Causes: Dependent and Independent Intervening Causes

Sometimes there is more than one "but for" cause, raising the issue of who should be held criminally responsible for the ultimate result. The additional causal agent may be the victim, a third person, or the forces of nature. For example, assume that D shoots V in the head; V is rushed to the hospital for emergency brain surgery, where E (V's worst enemy) sneaks into the operating room and stabs V to death. Assume that V would have died in a matter of hours from D's bullets, despite heroic medical measures. Who is responsible for the murder? In some jurisdictions, the stabber, E, may be viewed as an *intervening cause* — someone (other than the defendant) who satisfies the "but for" test of causation and could possibly be held for the murder. Ordinarily the intervening cause occurs *after* the defendant's actions. Criminal liability may depend on whether the intervening cause is deemed to be *independent* or *dependent*.

It should be noted that though courts sometimes resolve cases on the basis of whether the intervening cause is dependent or independent, in close cases these terms give little guidance on which category a particular intervening cause is in. They provide only general criteria rather than helpful descriptions.

a. Independent Intervening Cause

An independent intervening cause is so unrelated to the defendant's own causal actions that it would be unfair to hold the defendant criminally responsible for the result. Thus, an independent intervening cause may mean that one or more people who satisfy the "but for" cause test are relieved of criminal responsibility for the harm because they do not satisfy the "proximate cause" prong of causation.

In general, an independent intervening cause was neither intended nor foreseeable when the defendant acted, or, under the unusual circumstances of the case, it would be unfair to extend criminal liability. Thus, if the intervening cause involved intentional conduct or gross negligence by a third person, or the forces of nature (sometimes referred to as an "act of God") where no human cause is involved, many courts would hold that the action was an independent intervening cause. For example, D stabs V who is then rushed to the hospital and dies a week later from a brain tumor that had not been diagnosed until V entered the hospital after the stabbing. The tumor would be an independent intervening cause of death. In general terms, an actor, such as D the stabber, is not responsible for a result that is the product of an intervening independent (sometimes called *superceding*) cause of death.

b. Dependent Intervening Cause

On the other hand, a dependent intervening cause is one that occurs as the result of the first cause. In general terms, ordinarily a criminal defendant is not relieved of responsibility for a result that is caused by a dependent intervening cause if the dependent intervening cause was reasonably foreseeable or intended or, in some locales, closely or sufficiently related to the defendant's conduct to make it fair to hold the defendant responsible for the result.

For example, assume that D sets fire to an old warehouse building in order to collect insurance on it. The fire kills (1) a homeless person sleeping in the building, (2) an employee who rushed into the burning building to save business records, and (3) a firefighter responding to the blaze. Though one could argue that each of the three victims is an independent cause of his or her own death and therefore D should not be responsible for homicide, case law holds that D is responsible for all three deaths. The three victims' conduct would be classified as dependent intervening causes, resulting from D's setting the fire. Each was a foreseeable result of setting fire to the building.

i. Poor Medical Care

Case law provides a number of repeated situations raising the issue of what is a dependent intervening cause. Thus, when medical care is made necessary because of the defendant's action, if the medical care is delivered negligently and causes harm, the defendant is ordinarily held responsible for the outcome because the careless medical attention is deemed a dependent intervening cause that was reasonably foreseeable. For example, assume that D stabs V, who dies a few days later after emergency surgery by a surgeon who mistakenly used equipment that had not been sterilized and resulted in a deadly infection that quickly killed V. The surgeon would likely be considered a dependent cause of V's death because the surgeon operated on V only because D had stabbed V.

Medical malpractice is considered to be a foreseeable risk from an act that sends a victim to the care of a physician. However, if the degree of medical malpractice is severe, perhaps constituting gross recklessness, some cases hold that the seriously flawed medical care was so bad that it was not foreseeable, making it an independent intervening cause and relieving the defendant of responsibility for the harm caused by the inadequate treatment. In such cases, the defense will argue that the negligence was "gross" (thus relieving the defendant of responsibility) while the prosecution will argue it was "ordinary" negligence that was foreseeable and does not spare the defendant of responsibility for the harm.

ii. Pre-Existing Medical Condition

If a victim suffers harm because of a pre-existing medical condition, ordinarily the defendant is held accountable for that harm since the medical condition is reasonably foreseeable. The pre-existing condition is considered to be a dependent intervening cause. This issue arises most frequently in the context of a felony-murder prosecution when, for example, the victim of an armed robbery, who had been treated for years for a serious heart ailment, suffers a terminal heart attack during the crime. Expert testimony established that the stress of the robbery likely triggered the mortal heart attack.

iii. Harm by Third Person

An interesting set of cases raises the issue of the defendant's liability for harm inflicted by someone else. Most of these cases arise in the context of the felony murder doctrine where a defendant is involved in a felony and someone is killed during that crime. Is the defendant liable for that death? For example, assume that A and B rob a small market with their guns pointed at the clerk. Assume also that there is a gunfight and A is shot and killed by (1) the store clerk, (2) a customer, (3) the store's armed guard, (4) or a police officer who happened to be on patrol in the neighborhood and saw the robbers enter the store. Many, though not all, cases hold that B can be prosecuted for A's death because it was reasonably foreseeable that there could be a shoot out and someone would get killed. Other jurisdictions reject this view and hold that B is only responsible for the actions of people with whom B is in an agency-type relationship. Under this view, B would not be deemed to have "caused" A's death since none of the four hypothetical killers would be considered B's agent. The same array of results if Police Officer X accidentally shoots Police Officer V during the ensuing shootout.

In all of these situations most authorities hold that the killer (clerk, customer, guard, police officer) was a dependent intervening cause whose actions were reasonably foreseeable. Some cases, however, refuse to extend liability if the shooting was lawful, such as when Police Officer X shot A during a gunfight after the robbery. These cases maintain that B, the co-felon, is not responsible for a homicide (such as that by Officer X) that did not violate any criminal law because the officer, who was the direct cause of A's death, committed no crime.

iv. Victim's Own Actions

A variation on this scenario involves a negligent homicide case where the victim was struck by defendant's speeding car, taken to the hospital, placed on a ventilator to breathe, then died after being removed from the ventilator at the victim's request. The victim did not want to suffer the permanent breathing problems that were the likely result of the accident. The same issue arises if the victim commits suicide because of the effects of the defendant's conduct. The careless driver would probably be found to have caused the victim's death. Even though the victim made the decision to remove the life-saving breathing machine or to commit suicide, the resulting death would be attributed to the defendant since the process could be deemed "foreseeable" despite its rareness. In other words, there was a dependent intervening cause that did not relieve the defendant of responsibility for causing the death.

E. Model Penal Code and Common Law Compared

The Model Penal Code § 2.03 and the common law apply both the "but for" and proximate cause tests of causation. MPC § 2.03(1)(a) states the "but for" test concisely: conduct is the cause of a result when "it is an antecedent but for which the result in question would not have occurred." Causation is not present absent a "but for" connection under either the MPC or common law.

The MPC does not use the term "proximate cause." Instead, it defines when the causation element is satisfied once "but for" causation is found. In other words, "but for" causation *alone* does not satisfy the MPC's requirement that D's conduct "cause" V's harm. Rather, the MPC provides rules for when, assuming "but for" cause is present, the defendant's *actus reus* can be deemed sufficient to hold that the defendant's conduct "caused" the result so that the defendant may be held criminally responsible for that result. This approach ties together the concepts of causation and blameworthiness, while rejecting the idea that a physical relationship between act and result is the sole criterion.

1. Different Actual Result

The MPC creates different proximate cause rules depending on whether the *mens rea* for the crime is purposely or knowingly, on the one hand, or recklessly or negligently on the other. As a general rule, subject to two exceptions discussed below, there is no proximate cause if the actual result is not within the purpose (crime requires purposely causing the result) or contemplation (crime requires knowingly causing the result) of the actor or the actual result is not within the risk of which the actor is aware (recklessly causing the result) or should have been aware (causing the result through criminal negligence).

Thus, under the MPC if the defendant commits a robbery and the victim is frightened, suffers a heart attack and dies, the defendant is not guilty of intentional or knowing homicide because the actual result (the death) was not within the purpose or contemplation of the robber. In other words, by definition the defendant did not intentionally or knowingly "cause" the death, according to the MPC's definition of proximate cause. However, if this same robber is charged with criminally negligent homicide for the death, it is possible that causation would be found because the victim's death by heart attack could be considered a risk of which the defendant-robber should have been aware.

There are two exceptions to the above rule. Under MPC § 2.03 there is proximate cause in cases where the result differs only in respect that a different person or property is injured. Thus, the MPC recognizes liability under the doctrines of transferred intent, knowledge, recklessness, or criminal negligence. For instance, if X intentionally or negligently shoots at Y but misses and kills V, the MPC would hold that X proximately caused V's death under the rubric of transferred intent or transferred criminal negligence.

The second exception—meaning there is proximate cause—occurs when the harm the defendant intended or contemplated (acting knowingly), or the harm risked recklessly, or negligently was more serious than that which actually occurred. Thus, if R intended to kill V by shooting V in the heart but missed and accidentally shot V in the arm, R would have proximately caused V's arm wound because the harm intended (death) was more serious than that actually caused. R could be convicted of intentional battery for intentionally causing the wound even though R never intended merely to wound V.

2. Same Actual Result

Similarly, under the MPC there is also proximate cause if the actual result involves the same kind of injury or harm intended (crimes requiring purposely causing a result), contemplated (knowingly causing a result), or likely to occur (recklessly or with criminal negligence causing a result). But in these situations where the same kind of injury or harm is involved, the MPC grants an exception—meaning there is no proximate cause—if the actual result is too far removed or accidental to have a bearing on the actor's liability or the gravity of the offense. Recognizing that the resolution of this issue raises serious policy questions about how a jurisdiction chooses to hold its citizens accountable, the MPC specifically permits jurisdictions to add the word "just" before the word "bearing," providing juries with even more discretion in assessing criminal responsibility in such unusual situations.

This imprecise test gives the trier of fact the opportunity to apply philosophical notions of fairness and individual responsibility in deciding whether to hold the defendant accountable criminally for the harm the defendant brought about. An example would be a hired assassin who took the victim into a back alley to commit the murder. Just before the assassin pulled the trigger, a safe burglar in an upper floor office threw a safe out the window and the safe fell on the murder victim's head, killing him or her instantly. Under the MPC the defendant may satisfy "but for" causation by placing the victim in the spot where the safe fell, but the proximate cause prong would present the jury with the question whether the actual result is too far removed or accidental to have a just bearing on the assassin's liability for intentional murder.

3. Special Rule for Strict Liability

The common law does not appear to have any special rule for causation in strict liability crimes, but the MPC does. Section 2.03(4) states that for strict liability crimes, the harm described in the statute is "caused" by the defendant only if the "actual result is a probable consequence of the actor's conduct."

Checkpoints

- Causation is an element of a crime when a result, such as death, is an element.
- Causation links the *actus reus* and the result.
- Causation often requires the government to prove both "but for" and proximate cause.
- "But for" causation assesses whether the result would have occurred had the defendant not committed the *actus reus*.
- Two or more causes are concurrent causes, each deemed adequate for criminal liability for causing the harm, if each alone is sufficient to have caused the harm or if neither alone would have caused it but both in combination were sufficient to bring about the harm.
- Proximate or legal cause is present when there is more than one cause but it is fair to hold the defendant accountable for the ultimate result.
- Proximate cause is present if the second cause is a dependent intervening cause.
- Proximate cause is absent if the second cause is an independent intervening cause.
- The Model Penal Code requires both "but for" and satisfaction of one or more other rules for criminal liability, but does not use the term "proximate cause."

Checkpoints *cont.*

- Under the Model Penal Code, if the actual result differs from the result intended (*mens rea* of purposely) or contemplated (knowingly) or is not within the risk the defendant ignored (recklessness) or should have been aware of (criminal negligence), there is no causation for that actual result.

- Under the Model Penal Code, if the actual result is the same as that intended, contemplated, or risked, there is no causation for that result if that result is too far removed or accidental to have a bearing on the actor's liability or the gravity of the offense.

- For strict liability crimes, the Model Penal Code finds causation only if the actual result is a probable consequence of the actor's conduct.

Chapter 7

Burden of Proof

Roadmap

- The distinctions between burden of production, burden of persuasion, burden of proof, and standard of proof

- The meaning and rationale for requiring proof "beyond a reasonable doubt" in criminal cases

- The options available to a state in assigning the burdens of production and persuasion and the standard of proof for elements of a crime, defenses, and factual findings in sentencing

- Differences in, and validity of, mandatory and rebuttable presumptions and permissive inferences

A. Terminology: Different Burdens

At the heart of the criminal justice process is the concept of burden of proof, which refers to which party (prosecution or defense) has the responsibility of producing a sufficient quantity of evidence. Burden of proof actually has three dimensions: standard of proof, burden of production, and burden of persuasion. Often these three interrelated concepts are grouped together under the rubric "burden of proof."

1. Standard of Proof

The *standard of proof* refers to the degree of certainty that must be established. Ordinarily in criminal cases, the prosecution must prove each element of the crime *beyond a reasonable doubt*, a particularly high standard. States are free to assign that or a lower standard of proof for defenses. Thus, the defendant may have to establish a defense beyond a reasonable doubt, by clear and convincing evidence, by a preponderance of evidence, or simply by a *prima facie* case.

2. Burden of Production

The *burden of production* (or *burden of going forward*) indicates which party initially must produce at least some evidence on a specific issue in order to make that issue one to be considered in the case. Sometimes this is called establishing a *prima facie* case. For the elements of a crime, the prosecution has the burden of production. It must introduce proof of each element of the crime. Ordinarily the defendant has the burden of production for defenses. For example, unless the defendant produces some evidence that the defendant was criminally insane at the time of the crime, the defense of insanity is not an issue in the case.

3. Burden of Persuasion

The *burden of persuasion* refers to which party is assigned the task of convincing the trier of fact that a particular fact exists. The party who has the burden of production usually also bears the burden of persuasion. The burden of persuasion is most relevant after the burden of production has been satisfied and the issue is now "ripe" for consideration by the trier of fact. Federal constitutional law mandates that the prosecution has the burden of persuasion for each element of the crime. *Sandstrom v. Montana*, 442 U.S. 510 (1979). The defense ordinarily, though not always, is given the job of persuading the trier of fact about facts underlying a defense, though some states place the burden on the prosecution of persuading the jury that a defense is not present.

B. Overview of Parties' Burdens

1. Elements of a Crime

Unifying these three aspects of burden of proof produces the rule for crime elements that the prosecution has the burden of (1) production (introducing evidence of the existence of each element), and (2) persuasion (convincing the trier of fact), (3) that the evidence is sufficient to prove each element of the crime beyond a reasonable doubt.

2. Defenses

For defenses, states may assign both the standard of proof and the burdens of production and persuasion as they see fit. For example, for an insanity defense, a state could give the defendant the burden of production (introducing evidence that the defendant was insane), set the standard of proof at the preponderance-of-evidence level, and assign the burden of persuasion to the defense to convince the trier of fact by a preponderance of evidence that the defendant was criminally insane. Or the state may create a structure where the burden shifts. For example, the defendant must introduce some evidence of insanity (burden of production), then the burden of persuasion shifts to the prosecution to persuade the jury, perhaps by a preponderance of evidence, that the defendant was not insane at the time of the crime.

C. Prosecution Must Prove Each Element Beyond a Reasonable Doubt

1. Due Process Requirement of Prosecution's Burden

An axiom of criminal law is that the prosecution must prove each element of the crime beyond a reasonable doubt. This means that the prosecution has both the burdens of production and persuasion on each element, subject to a few exceptions (such as the prosecution may be permitted to prove venue—location of the crime within the court's territorial jurisdiction—by a preponderance of the evidence). The source of this fundamental principle is the Due Process Clause in the Fifth and Fourteenth Amendments to the United States Constitution.

In the leading case, *In re Winship*, 397 U.S. 358 (1970), the Court observed that the reasonable doubt standard is important for many reasons. One is because the accused has an immense stake since he or she may lose liberty as well as face public stigma if convicted. Another rationale is that this long-recognized standard was essential as "a prime instrument for reducing the risk of convictions resting on factual error" and "provides concrete substance for the presumption of innocence—that bedrock 'axiomatic and elementary' principle whose 'enforcement lies at the foundation of the administration of our criminal law.'" The Court further noted that the high standard is indispensable to impress on the trier of fact the necessity of reaching a subjective state of certitude of the facts in issue. It also helps ensure that the moral force of the criminal law is not diluted by a process that leaves people in doubt whether an innocent person was convicted of a crime.

2. Definition of Reasonable Doubt

The precise meaning of the key phrase "reasonable doubt" has been the subject of countless discussions and seemingly conflicting opinions. While the

Supreme Court has held that trial judges must instruct jurors on the reasonable doubt standard, the Court also stated that the Constitution does not require any particular form for this instruction. The Court even held that no definition is needed. The only agreement is that there should be no mathematical facet of the instruction, such as the jury must be convinced of guilt to ninety percent certainty. The test is qualitative, not quantitative.

The Supreme Court has provided minimal—and sometimes conflicting— guidance to trial courts. One simple description is "a subjective state of near certitude" of the accused's guilt. *Jackson v. Virginia*, 443 U.S. 307 (1979). However, the Court noted that a trial judge's suggestion that reasonable doubt equates to a "grave uncertainty" or an "actual substantial doubt" sets too high a bar. *Cage v. Louisiana*, 498 U.S. 39 (1990). On the other hand, it approved a jury instruction that "a reasonable doubt is an actual and substantial doubt … as distinguished from a doubt arising from mere possibility, from bare imagination, or from fanciful conjecture." *Victor v. Nebraska*, 511 U.S. 1 (1994). Similarly, it approved jury instructions to the effect that a reasonable doubt is present when the evidence leaves the minds of the jurors in the condition that they cannot say they feel an abiding conviction, to a moral certainty, of the truth of the charge.

3. Venue, Jurisdiction, and Statute of Limitations

A criminal case may be dismissed unless (1) the trial court has jurisdiction, (2) the case is in the proper venue, and (3) the case is not barred by the statute of limitations. While it may appear that each of these is an element that the prosecution must prove beyond a reasonable doubt, statutes and case law vary considerably among the jurisdictions and often soften the burden of proof for each of these.

a. Venue and Jurisdiction

Model Penal Code § 1.12 and a number of states provide that venue and jurisdiction are elements that the prosecution must prove beyond a reasonable doubt. Other states require the prosecution to establish these elements by a preponderance of the evidence. A few use a lower standard, such as "reasonably be inferred." Since in some states neither jurisdiction nor venue is an element of the crime, the issue may be waived if not raised by the defense. If raised, the prosecution has the burden of establishing it by the applicable standard of proof.

b. Statute of Limitations

Jurisdictions routinely impose a statute of limitations for most crimes, re-quiring that the prosecution commence a specified time after the crime. For example, a jurisdiction may establish a ten-year statute of limitations for a par-ticular category of felony. Since the statute of limitations is not mandated by the Constitution but rather is considered an "act of grace" by the jurisdiction, states vary considerably in their treatment of the burden of proof.

A minority treat the statute of limitations as if it were an element of the crime, requiring the state to shoulder both the burden of production and the burden of persuasion, and by setting the standard of proof beyond a reason-able doubt. Some states even make the statute of limitations a jurisdictional issue that cannot be waived and can be raised at any time. Many other jurisdictions reject the view that the statutes of limitation are jurisdictional and require no more than that the indictment, information, or other charging instrument state that the crime occurred within the permissible period.

The statute of limitations is then treated as a defense and the defendant has the burden of production to establish some evidence that the crime was barred by the statute of limitations. Once the defense meets the burden of production about a statute of limitations violation, states take one of two ap-proaches. A minority rule keeps the burden of persuasion on the defense to prove by a preponderance of evidence that the prosecution was not timely. In many other locales, once the defendant has satisfied the burden of pro-duction to provide some basis that the crime was time barred, the burden then shifts to the prosecution to prove by a preponderance of evidence or even beyond a reasonable doubt that the prosecution commenced before the statute of limitations had run. A defendant's failure to raise the issue is deemed a waiver or forfeiture of it.

D. Flexibility in Burden of Proof of Defenses

1. Flexibility Among Jurisdictions

While the prosecution has the burdens of production and persuasion for each element of a crime, the rules for the various burdens are far more flexi-ble for defenses. In general terms, legislatures are free to assign the various burdens and standards of proof for defenses. Thus, a state often will place the burdens of production and persuasion on the defendant for various defenses. It may also specify that the burden must be met by anything from a prepon-derance of the evidence to proof beyond a reasonable doubt.

The Supreme Court raised the issue of the proper burden for defenses in *Mullaney v. Wilbur*, 421 U.S. 684 (1975), when it interpreted Maine's homicide law as requiring the state to prove malice aforethought beyond a reasonable doubt but struck down the rule that once the state proved this, the defendant could escape a murder conviction by proving that he killed in the heat of passion. The Supreme Court held that since malice aforethought only existed in the absence of heat of passion under Maine law, the state had to prove both malice aforethought and the absence of heat of passion. Maine could not impose on the defendant the burden of proving heat of passion, since absence of heat of passion, through malice aforethought, was an element of the crime of murder. In other words, the state may not shift the burden of proof to the defendant to prove a defense when that defense negates an element of the crime. *Smith v. United States*, 133 S.Ct. 714 (2013)(statute of limitations defense may be allocated to defendant because it does not controvert any element of the crime).

A few years later, the Supreme Court further explained the distinction in *Patterson v. New York*, 432 U.S. 197 (1977), where it upheld New York's murder laws which made it second degree murder to intentionally cause a death. New York also provided a defense to murder, which would then reduce the offense to the lesser crime of manslaughter, if the defendant could prove by a preponderance of evidence the affirmative defense of extreme emotional disturbance. The Supreme Court upheld placing this burden on the defendant; due process only mandated that the prosecution prove each element beyond a reasonable doubt. It did not prescribe the burdens or standard of proof for defenses raised by the defendant which do not negate a crime element. Other decisions have upheld placing on the defendant the burden of proving insanity and self-defense.

2. Defenses, Affirmative Defenses, and Exceptions

Many jurisdictions categorize their defenses into "defenses" and "affirmative defenses." Some add a third category: "exceptions." Under this model, for the category of "defenses," often the defendant has the burden of production, then the burden of persuasion shifts to the prosecution to disprove the existence of the defense. For affirmative defenses, ordinarily the defendant has both the burdens of production and persuasion. The statute relating the elements of each defense indicates whether that particular one is a "defense" or an "affirmative defense." For example, in Arkansas the defendant has the burden of production for both "defenses" and "affirmative defenses." After the defendant meets this burden of production, for a "defense" the burden of persuasion shifts to the prosecution to disprove the existence of the "defense" beyond a reasonable doubt. If the defense is deemed an "affirmative defense," however, the defendant also bears the burden of persuasion by a preponderance of evidence. *Ark. Code Ann. § 5.1-111.*

In states specifically recognizing the category of "exceptions," the statute defining the crime establishes one or more exceptions to liability. For example, a state may ban possession of controlled substances or certain weapons but provide an exception for people who have lawful authority to possess the item. In general, the state ordinarily need not disprove the exception; the burden is on the defendant to prove that he or she comes within the exception. For example, in Tennessee a defendant relying on an exception must prove it by a preponderance of the evidence. *Tenn. Code Ann. § 39-11-202.* This allocation of the burden of persuasion is permissible since the absence of the exception is not deemed to be an element of the crime. The exception is treated as a defense. Another approach, used rarely, provides that the defendant bears the burden of production for the exception, then the burden of persuasion shifts to the prosecution to establish that the defendant is not covered by the exception. An even rarer view, treating the exception as an element of the crime, requires the prosecution to negate the exception in the indictment and then to prove beyond a reasonable doubt that the defendant does not fall within the exception. *Tex. Pen. Code Ann. § 32.02.*

3. Defenses that Negate a *Mens Rea* Element

One category of "defenses" bears special mention. Sometimes the defendant offers proof that he or she did not have a particular *mens rea* because of a mistake or other reason. In such cases, the usual rule is that the defendant has the burden of production to establish the mistake, but has no further burden. Consistent with due process, the prosecution still has the burden of persuading the trier of fact, beyond a reasonable doubt, of the existence of the element. The defendant's proof of mistake or other reason is some evidence that the trier of fact will use in deciding whether the prosecution met its burden and standard of proof.

E. Sentencing

In general terms, in recent years factual findings relating to the sentence, as opposed to guilt, were made by the judge. In *Apprendi v. New Jersey,* 530 U.S. 466 (2000), however, the United States Supreme Court significantly altered the traditional model. Resolving a case where the defendant was given an enhanced sentence because the judge found that the crime was racially motivated and therefore a hate crime, the Supreme Court held that for sentencing purposes any fact, other than the fact of a prior conviction, had to be submitted to a jury and found beyond a reasonable doubt if that fact increased the penalty beyond a statutory maximum sentence.

The Court further explained this in *Blakely v. Washington*, 542 U.S. 296 (2004), involving sentencing guidelines, which mandated a sentence of 49–53 months but permitted the court, without jury involvement, to increase that sentence if aggravating facts justified an exceptional sentence. The Supreme Court overturned the trial court's ruling that the sentence should be enhanced to 90 months because the crime was committed with "deliberate cruelty." The Supreme Court held that the issue whether the crime involved "deliberate cruelty" should have been submitted to the jury where the standard of proof should have been beyond a reasonable doubt.

United States v. Booker, 543 U.S. 220 (2005), further refined the issue and recognized that courts, not juries, may decide facts affecting the sentence as long as the resolution does not produce a sentence that exceeds the statutory maximum. If the sentencing system gives the sentencing judge the discretion, but does not require it, to set a particular sentence, the facts underlying that decision need not be submitted to a jury; the judge alone may decide them.

F. Model Penal Code

Model Penal Code § 1.12 establishes three rules which have been adopted by many states. First, consistent with due process, the prosecution must prove each element of the crime beyond a reasonable doubt. Second, the category of "defenses" requires the defendant to prove by a preponderance of evidence each component of the defense. Third, for "affirmative defenses" the defendant must present some evidence (i.e., present a *prima facie* case) supporting the defense, then the burden shifts to the prosecution to disprove the existence of that affirmative defense. Ordinarily a defense is distinguished from an affirmative defense by specific language in the applicable rule. For example, the MPC says that ignorance or mistake is a defense, while self-defense, protection of third persons, and insanity are affirmative defenses.

G. Presumptions

Sometimes statutes or case law create a presumption that eases the prosecution's burden of proving a fact, usually the mental element required for an offense. For example, in some jurisdictions, possession of stolen items (called the "predicate fact") created a presumption that the possessor knew the items had been stolen (called the "presumed fact"), making it easier for the prosecution to prove the *mens rea* of the crime of receiving stolen property (which requires the defendant to know the items had been stolen).

The problem with these presumptions is that they conflict with the due process requirement that the prosecution has the burden of proving each element beyond a reasonable doubt, the rule that juries (unless waived) are solely responsible for finding the presence or absence of crime elements, and with the presumption of innocence. In the receiving stolen property hypothetical above, the prosecution's burden of persuasion may be greatly reduced since proof of possession may be used to prove knowledge, even absent any other proof that the defendant knew the property had been stolen.

It should be noted that a presumption that favors *the accused* is not barred by due process. For example, it is universally held that each defendant is presumed innocent. The prosecution may overcome this only by proving guilt beyond a reasonable doubt.

1. Conclusive and Rebuttable Presumptions

In a number of cases that are not always consistent, the United States Supreme Court has faced the issue of the validity of presumptions in criminal cases. In *Frances v. Franklin*, 471 U.S. 307 (1965), the Court considered two widely-adopted presumptions. First, acts of a person of sound mind and discretion are presumed to be the product of the person's will, but the presumption may be rebutted. Second, a person of sound mind is presumed to intend the natural and probable consequences of his or her actions but the presumption may be rebutted. The defendant in *Franklin* claimed the homicide was an accident, but the jury, using the presumption above, found him guilty of intentional homicide. The Supreme Court overturned the conviction.

The Court held that both conclusive (jury must find presumed fact once prosecution proves "predicate" fact) and rebuttable (requires the jury to find the presumed element unless the defendant persuades the jury that this finding is unwarranted) presumptions violate due process because they relieve the prosecution of its burden of persuasion of the presumed element of the offense. Thus, presumptions, proving or helping prove an element of a crime, that are conclusive or otherwise shift the burden of persuasion to the defendant are unconstitutional. They conflict with the presumption of innocence and invade the jury's factfinding function.

An illustrative case, *Sandstrom v. Montana*, 442 U.S. 510 (1979), involved a Montana presumption that a person intends the ordinary consequences of his or her voluntary acts. Charged with intentional homicide, the defendant successfully argued that this presumption shifted the burden of persuasion on the issue of whether he killed with the necessary intent. The Supreme Court agreed, finding that the presumption could have been read by the jurors as either a conclusive presumption (they *must* find he killed intentionally if they find he killed the victim by a voluntary act) or a rebuttable one (once they find he killed the victim by a voluntary act the burden of persuasion shifts to the defense to prove that he did not kill intentionally). The former essentially relieved the prosecution of the burden of persuasion on intent since all it had to prove was that the defendant killed by a voluntary act; it did not have to offer any proof at all on intent. The elimination of the need for the prosecution to offer any proof at all on the *mens rea* of intent, an element of the crime, violated due process. The latter presumption was struck down as relieving the prosecution of the burden of persuasion on intent once it proved a voluntary killing. Under the latter presumption, once the prosecution proved a killing by a voluntary act, the burden of persuasion shifted to the defense to prove that he lacked intent even though he killed by means of a voluntary act. This shifting of the burden of persuasion violated due process.

2. Permissive Inference (or Permissive Presumption)

While the *Franklin* Court struck down both permissive and rebuttable presumptions, it held that a *permissive inference* is constitutional since it permits the jury to draw a particular conclusion (the presumed fact) from a proven fact, but does not require the jury to do so and does not shift the burden of persuasion on this inferred issue. The state still must convince the jury that the inferred fact exists beyond a reasonable doubt. The inference simply tells the jurors that they may, but do not have to, use this inference to assist them in deciding whether the prosecution proved the inferred element beyond a reasonable doubt.

Whether a presumption or inference has been used is determined by assessing the jury instructions. According to the Supreme Court, "courts should ask whether the specific instruction, both alone and in the context of the overall charge, could have been understood to reasonable jurors to require them to find the presumed fact if the state proves certain predicate facts." *Carella v. California*, 491 U.S. 263, 265 (1989).

Rules apparently creating a mandatory or rebuttable presumption are routinely interpreted as being only a permissive inference that the jury may use as some evidence in assessing whether the prosecution has met is obligation to persuade the jury beyond a reasonable doubt that a particular element is present. It should be noted that some courts use the term "permissive presumption" when referring to a "permissive inference." This terminology is not important, however, as long as the jury is clearly instructed that the permissive presumption simply permits juries to infer a fact if the jurors elect to do so.

Such inferences, though permissible in general, are limited by the rule that there must be a rational connection between the facts proved and the ultimate fact that may be inferred from the facts that were established. This means that the latter must more likely than not flow from the former. *County Court of Ulster County v. Allen*, 442 U.S. 140 (1979). Often courts express the test as one of common sense and logic. For example, if a state recognized a permissive inference that knowledge that a substance was heroin could be inferred from possession of heroin, the inference may be upheld since it is more likely than not that someone in possession of heroin knows the nature of the drug he or she possesses. The prosecution could use the inference as some evidence in support of its burden of persuasion that the defendant knew the substance was heroin. On the other hand, a permissive inference that someone in possession of cocaine knows that it was imported from Thailand would be struck down since it is not more likely than not that the possessor knew the origins of the drug.

Checkpoints

- Burden of proof includes the standard of proof (degree of certainty, such as beyond a reasonable doubt), burden of persuasion (must convince trier of fact that standard of proof is satisfied), and burden of production (introducing sufficient proof to put a matter in issue).

- Due process mandates the prosecution to prove each element of the crime beyond a reasonable doubt.

- Due process gives states great leeway in deciding the standard of proof and burdens of production and persuasion for defenses in criminal cases.

- In sentencing, the jury must make certain factual findings beyond a reasonable doubt if those findings will establish a sentence beyond the maximum required or presumed, unless the court has discretion whether to impose the additional sentence.

- Mandatory presumptions, even if rebuttable, may violate due process if they remove the prosecution's burden of persuasion on an element of a crime, but rebuttable inferences are constitutional, since they do not change the burden of persuasion.

Chapter 8

Homicide and Related Crimes

Roadmap

- The definitions of "born alive" and of "death"
- The consequence of death a year and a day after the fatal blow
- The role and meaning of malice aforethought
- The structure of the traditional homicide model of homicide
- The impact and limits of the felony murder and misdemeanor manslaughter rules
- The meaning of wilful, deliberate, and premeditated
- The elements of second degree murder
- The meaning and importance of "depraved heart" murder
- The elements of voluntary manslaughter
- The elements of involuntary manslaughter
- The structure of homicide under the Model Penal Code
- The crimes of suicide and assisting suicide
- Vehicular homicide and its relation to depraved heart and criminally negligent homicide

---

A. Homicide and Related Crimes: In General

American law, understandably, treats killing a human being as a very serious offense under most circumstances. Some killings, though, are not crimes, as when a person kills another in self defense or a soldier kills an enemy soldier in combat. In technical terms, this means that criminal homicide is a killing without legal justification or excuse and committed in a manner that violates the jurisdiction's homicide laws. Both justification and excuse are discussed in later chapters on defenses in criminal cases. For the remainder of this chapter, it is assumed that the killing lacks either justification or excuse.

127

American homicide law has a long history with strong common law roots. Traditional American law is ordinarily attributed to early Pennsylvania statutes that were later adopted by most states. The Model Penal Code presents a much simpler, more modern approach that has been followed in general terms, though not specifically, in many jurisdictions with revised penal codes. While American jurisdictions differ markedly in their homicide laws, virtually all have their roots in the traditional American or Model Penal Code provisions. If you understand these two approaches, you can understand any American homicide statute.

Looking at the two versions of homicide law from a broad perspective, there are many similarities. Both punish intentional, reckless, and negligent homicides. Both also provide lesser punishment for people who kill rashly in a highly emotional state. On the other hand, they differ markedly in their approach to homicides that occur during the commission of a misdemeanor or felony, in the degree of precision in their description of the elements in the various homicide crimes, and in their use of definitions.

The traditional American and Model Penal Code approaches to homicide are supplemented by several other crimes that cover the taking of life. Vehicular manslaughter is a crime in most jurisdictions that punishes someone who kills by means of a motorized vehicle. While suicide is not a crime, assisting or causing a suicide is an offense in most American jurisdictions.

B. Object of Homicide

American homicide law is rather specific in its application to the unborn. While killing a baby or an adult clearly satisfies homicide law, the matter is far more complicated if the victim has not yet been born.

1. Both Killer and Victim Must Be Human Beings

The traditional American view is that homicide requires the killer and the victim be different human beings. Thus, it is not homicide if either the killer or victim is an animal, unless the animal is used as a weapon by a human being. Similarly, suicide is not homicide since the killer and victim are the same person.

2. Traditional View: Victim Must Have Been Born Alive

Serious legal questions are presented when the fatal blow is inflicted to a fetus. Many older American homicide laws provided that the victim of criminal homicide must be a *reasonable creature in being*. This and similar terms were interpreted to mean that the victim must be a human being who is *born alive.* *Model Penal Code § 210.0(1)* ("human being" is a person who "has been born and is alive").

Under this model which requires the victim to be born alive, D does not commit a homicide by assaulting a pregnant woman who does not die but, because of D's blow, delivers a stillborn child. D would be guilty of the infant's homicide, however, if the child survived long enough to be born alive but died one second later from D's pre-birth assault. Similarly, D would be responsible if the blow caused the child to be born alive quite prematurely, but death, caused by D's acts, followed immediately after the birth.

The meaning of "born alive" has changed over time and has differed slightly among the jurisdictions. Early on—and still in many states—the homicide victim had to have become separate from the mother and the umbilical cord must have been severed, meaning the child had its own circulation system. This rule also required that the child must have breathed.

Some jurisdictions are less strict, rejecting the born alive rule. They find a homicide when the victim dies after the birth process has begun, even if the umbilical cord were not severed when the child passed away during the birth process. *People v. Chavez,* 176 P.2d 92 (Cal. App. 1947).

3. Pre-Birth Killings: Modern Laws

Many American jurisdictions have revised their definition of homicide to include the killing of an unborn fetus. Often these laws reflect an effort to eliminate or at least reduce the incidence of abortions. One approach is to add a separate homicide crime that specifically covers the killing of a fetus. *§ 720 Ill. Comp. Stat. Ann. 5/9-1.2* (crime of intentional homicide of unborn child). Sometimes this is called feticide.

Another approach is to expand liability for existing homicide crimes to very early in the human development cycle, such as by applying to the killing of a "human embryo or fetus." *Idaho Code Stat. Ann. § 18-4001*; *Cal. Penal Code § 187* (murder is the unlawful killing of a human being or fetus); *Ky. Rev. Stat. § 507A.010(c)*("unborn child' means a member of the species homo sapiens in utero from conception onward"); *Ariz. Rev. Stat. § 13-1102* ("unborn child in the womb at any stage of its development"); *§ 720 Ill. Comp. Stat. Ann. 5/9-1.2* (unborn child means any individual of the human species from fertilization until birth).

Some jurisdictions punish the killing of the fetus exactly the same as if the mother had died. *Fla. Stat. Ann. § 782.09.* If the mother also dies, in these jurisdictions the killer may face homicide charges for both deaths.

A few jurisdictions punish partial birth abortions in which the fetus is intentionally killed during the birth process. There may be a statutory exception when the partial birth abortion is performed to save the life of the mother. *Fla. Stat. Ann. § 782.34.*

Because of the constitutional guarantees surrounding a mother's right to abortion, the various laws criminalizing the killing of a fetus cannot violate the mother's constitutional rights and many of the statutes specifically so state. *Ariz. Rev. Stat. § 13-1104* (defense to murder of unborn child is that the defendant was performing an abortion with appropriate consent or was performing medical treatment on the pregnant mother or the unborn child); *Cal. Penal Code § 187* (a defense to murder is that the defendant killed a fetus during a lawful abortion). Some jurisdictions specifically exempt the mother from liability for the unborn child's death.

C. Definition of Death

1. Traditional View: Natural Heartbeat and Breathing

It is obvious and accurate to say that the victim of a homicide must be killed, which means "dead" in everyday parlance. Thus, one cannot be guilty of homicide if the victim were already dead when the defendant shot or stabbed the corpse.

While it is also a truism that the life or death status of the victim is rarely a serious issue, the meaning of death has become a matter of concern and undergone significant change in recent years as the result of technological innovations. The traditional common law approach was that a person was dead, and hence could be the object of a homicide, if the natural heartbeat (circulatory function) and breathing (respiratory function) had irreversibly stopped. Of course the killing was homicide even if the victim would have died eventually or even very soon had the defendant not inflicted the fatal blow; accelerating death was sufficient to constitute the crime of homicide.

The traditional definition of death was adequate for centuries, but became outmoded and sometimes disastrous when technological advances allowed medical personnel to keep a person's heart and lungs functioning by artificial means. For example, assume that D shoots V in the head, causing severe and irreversible brain damage. Doctors order V to be attached to machines that keep V's heart and lungs functioning while waiting for the organ donation processes to authorize harvesting of V's organs for transplantation. A day later, upon doctors' orders, the machines are disconnected and V's heart is removed and transplanted. D is then prosecuted for murder but defends by asserting that D did not kill V; the doctors who removed V's heart are the real killers and should be prosecuted for intentional homicide. D alleges that V's heart and lungs were functioning until the machines were disconnected on doctors' orders. Under the traditional circulatory-respiratory test, the government may find it quite difficult or even impossible to prove that V was already dead when the doctors shut off the machines and removed V's heart.

2. Brain Death

To alleviate these concerns and to facilitate transplantation, American jurisdictions have added a new definition of death: *brain death.* The brain death criterion is *in addition to* the traditional heart-lung measure, so that both are applicable in most locales. A person is dead if he or she satisfies either test.

The Uniform Determination of Death Act, widely adopted by American states, defines death as either the "irreversible cessation of circulatory and respiratory functions" (the traditional view) or the "irreversible cessation of all functions of the entire brain, including the brain stem" (the brain death test). The Uniform Act provides that the determination of death under either approach is to be made "in accordance with accepted medical standards." The vague tests of death mean that the decision about a particular person's status is one involving professional medical judgment. Physicians ordinarily interpret the brain death standard as meaning that the person has no response to external stimuli (such as being stuck with a pin), no spontaneous muscular movements, no spontaneous respiration, and no reflexes. In addition, the person also has no brain waves (*i.e.*, a flat EEG) for a set period of time, although this measurement has some critics. Statutes often provide that one or two licensed physicians must certify brain death.

The brain death standard allows medical personnel to use external measures, such as pricking with a pin and using an EEG to measure brain activity, to assess whether the person is alive or dead without having to disconnect the machines that keep the heart and lungs functioning. Returning to the hypothetical above, if a brain death assessment indicates that V satisfies the criteria, V would be deemed dead and D could face homicide charges, even though V's heart was removed when V's heart and lungs still functioned, perhaps with the assistance of mechanical devices. The medical personnel could continue the use of the heart and lung machines and transplant V's organs without worrying about their personal liability for killing V, who was "legally dead" before the organs were removed.

Some statutes incorporate variations of the Uniform Act. *E.g., Alaska Stat.* *§11.41.140* ("A person is 'alive' if there is spontaneous respiratory or cardiac function or, when respiratory and cardiac function are maintained by artificial means, there is spontaneous brain function").

D. Special Causation Rule: Year and a Day

A person is guilty of homicide only if he or she is held to have *caused* the victim's death. Causation is discussed more specifically in Chapter 6, but bears special mention here because of a wrinkle in homicide cases. Perhaps because of the primitive state of knowledge about the human body and diseases, the common law embraced a special causation rule in homicide cases that held that a person was not responsible for another person's death if *death occurred more than a year and a day* from the fatal blow. The theory was that a person who lingered for this lengthy period may well have died from natural causes rather than the defendant's criminal actions.

Modern jurisdictions, including the Model Penal Code, have eliminated the year-and-a-day rule. Statutes or judicial decisions repeal the rule as no longer based on the considerable advances of modern medicine. The United States Supreme Court characterized the year-and-a-day rule as "archaic and outdated" and one "that has so clearly outlived its purpose." *Rogers v. Tennessee*, 532 U.S. 451 (2001). It is now accepted that victims of violence may linger far longer than a year before dying as the direct result of the defendant's conduct. Of course, in such cases the government must prove beyond a reasonable doubt that the homicide defendant caused the death of the long-lingering victim, a task that may be difficult or even impossible in some situations.

An interesting relative of the year-and-a-day rule is California's three-years-and-a-day rule. This statute creates a presumption, which the state can rebut, that a death occurring beyond three years from the fatal blow "was not criminal." *Cal. Penal Code § 194*. An even more serious statute is South Carolina's absolute bar to prosecute for homicide if death occurs more than three years between injury and death. *S.C. Code. § 16-3-5*.

E. Different Approaches to Homicide

In general terms, American homicide law is expressed in two broad patterns: (1) a structure first used in Pennsylvania (referred to as the traditional American approach/model), and (2) the more modern Model Penal Code. To simplify matters for the law student, only the traditional American and Model Penal Code approaches will be discussed in detail in this chapter.

The two approaches contain many similar elements, but differ in some significant respects. As one would expect, the MPC version is clearer than the traditional American model since the MPC includes definitions of key words, is far more complete (leaving less to case law) in describing the various homicide crimes, and omits outmoded and sometimes confusing terms such as "malice aforethought," "premeditated," "deliberation," and "lying in wait."

On the other hand, these two models share many features. For example, they provide a degree of leniency for a killing which is the product of a rash emotional response (called "heat of passion" in the traditional American model and "extreme emotional disturbance" in the MPC version), and both punish homicides that are the product of reckless (called "depraved heart" in the traditional American approach) or criminally negligent behavior.

F. Overview of Traditional American Model

Pennsylvania overhauled its homicide laws in 1794 in order to reduce the incidence of the death penalty. It provided a model of homicide that soon spread to other states and became the standard version of American homicide law. The 1794 Pennsylvania innovation divided murder into two degrees: first and second degree. The common law had recognized only one murder offense which was not divided into degrees. Pennsylvania rejected the common law one-type-of-murder approach and authorized the death penalty for first degree murder, but "only" life imprisonment for second degree.

Both of the categories in the Pennsylvania statute grew from the common law concept of "malice aforethought," although the Pennsylvania statute itself and many state statutes following this approach do not explicitly use the term "malice aforethought." The absence of specific reference to malice aforethought in these traditional American statutes modeled after Pennsylvania should not be read as dispensing with the concept, however, for case law in those jurisdictions routinely includes malice aforethought as an unexpressed, though viable, element in both first and second degree murder.

1. Text of 1794 Pennsylvania Murder Law

The Pennsylvania murder law of 1794, followed almost verbatim for many years in many other American jurisdictions, is as follows:

All murder, which shall be perpetrated by means of poison, or by lying in wait, or by another other kind of wilful, deliberate or premeditated killing, or which shall be committed in the perpetration or attempt to perpetrate any arson, rape, robbery or burglary shall be deemed murder in the first degree; and all other kinds of murder shall be deemed murder in the second degree.

2. Murder v. Manslaughter

The traditional American approach, based on the above Pennsylvania statute, divides homicides into two categories: murder and manslaughter. The fundamental distinction between them is the presence or absence of *malice afore-thought*, discussed in greater detail below. Murder, a common law crime, involves a killing with malice aforethought. Manslaughter lacks malice aforethought. The purpose of this common law distinction between murder and manslaughter was to separate people who kill into categories of those who are the most morally blameworthy and merit the death penalty (murder) and those of lesser moral depravity who should be spared the death penalty but nevertheless merit a serious punishment (manslaughter). Thus, a person who killed with malice aforethought was deemed more evil, more depraved than someone who did not. The traditional American model, reflecting the Pennsylvania statute, followed this common law approach of distinguishing murder from manslaughter based on the presence (murder) or absence (manslaughter) of malice aforethought. Further, as noted below, murder in the traditional American approach, is further subdivided into two categories: first degree murder and second degree murder. Manslaughter also has two divisions: voluntary and involuntary manslaughter.

G. Definition of Malice Aforethought

Under the traditional American model as well as the initial common law, the killer acts with *malice aforethought* for all murders and lacks malice aforethought for all manslaughters. This presents the obvious question of the meaning of "malice aforethought." As a starter, it must be recognized that the term is grossly misleading, for it requires neither "malice" nor "aforethought" as those words are used in ordinary parlance today. Thus, it does not require that the killer hate or even dislike the victim or have an intent or desire to kill the victim or anyone else. Moreover, many jurisdictions state that malice aforethought may be *express or implied*, further adding to the confusion.

The traditional general explications of malice aforethought indicate that the killer must exhibit a significant evil nature, but such generalizations are not very helpful in describing the actual meaning of the term. For example, a classic case states that malice aforethought exists when there is a "particular ill will" as well as when there is a "wickedness of disposition, hardness of heart, wanton conduct, cruelty, recklessness of consequences, and a mind regardless of social duty." *Commonwealth v. Carroll*, 194 A.2d 911 (Pa. 1963). Statutes following the traditional American model sometimes define malice aforethought in similar descriptive fashion. *See, e.g., Nev. Rev. Stat. § 200.020* (an abandoned and malignant heart). Sometimes this vague description, in whole or in part, actually was included verbatim in jury instructions used to define malice aforethought. This provided juries with little helpful guidance in deciding whether or not malice aforethought was present.

After studying centuries of case law discussing and defining this term, modern scholars usually conclude that malice aforethought is present if the killing occurs in one of the four following manners.

1. Intent to Kill

First, malice aforethought is present if the defendant *kills intentionally*. This means the defendant acted for the purpose of taking human life. Some jurisdictions soften the concept of intent by accepting *knowledge* as sufficient for malice aforethought. In these jurisdictions it is adequate if the defendant acted with the knowledge that death was substantially certain to result.

a. Natural and Probable Consequences

Many jurisdictions eased the prosecution's burden in proving a killing was intentional by recognizing a *presumption that a person intends the natural and probable consequences of his or her voluntary acts*. When the prosecution proved that the defendant pointed a gun at the victim and then pulled the trigger, the jury was authorized to find that the defendant intended to kill the victim since death was the natural and probable consequence of the defendant's acts. While this presumption was declared unconstitutional as shifting the burden of proof of a key element of the offense, the United States Supreme Court permitted the content of the presumption to be used as a *permissive inference* which the jury may, but is not required to, consider in deciding whether the defendant acted with the necessary intent to kill. *Sandstrom v. Montana*, 442 U.S. 510 (1979).

b. Deadly Weapon Rule

A related permissive inference is the so-called *deadly weapon rule*, which means the jury may, but is not required to, infer the intent to kill by the fact that the defendant intentionally used a deadly weapon on a vital part of the victim's body. Like the "natural and probable consequences" rule, the deadly weapon doctrine makes it easier for the prosecution to prove an intent to kill, which would constitute malice aforethought. It must be remembered, however, that the mere fact that the killer used a deadly weapon does not necessarily mean he or she had the intent to kill or is guilty of murder, for the homicide may have been accidental, the intent may have been to injure rather than kill, or the offense qualifies as voluntary manslaughter for a killing in the heat of passion.

The term "deadly weapon" is ordinarily defined as a weapon that, *in the manner it is used*, is likely to cause death or serious bodily injury. Thus, a loaded gun is a deadly weapon and an unloaded gun may be one if used as a club to strike the victim on the head.

2. Intent to Do Serious Bodily Injury

Second, malice aforethought is found when the killer acted with the *intent to do serious bodily injury*. This requires proof that the defendant's purpose in shooting the victim was to inflict a serious physical harm, though not to kill the victim. The intent to do serious bodily injury, as distinguished from mere "bodily injury," is assessed in the context of the surrounding circumstances, including what the defendant did and communicated. If the killer simply meant to frighten the victim by shooting and missing or just grazing the victim, this facet of malice aforethought is not established since there is no intent to do serious bodily injury.

3. Commission of a Felony (Felony Murder Rule)

The third version of malice aforethought is the *commission of a felony*. The traditional American version of homicide found malice aforethought when a homicide occurred during the commission or attempted commission of a felony (as opposed to a misdemeanor). An illustration would be a bank robbery where the robber accidentally dropped the pistol, which discharged and killed a bank customer. Though the defendant had no intent to kill or even harm the customer and the death was the product of a bizarre accident, the killing would be deemed to involve malice aforethought since it occurred during the commission of a felony, here the robbery. Felony murder is discussed in detail below.

4. Depraved Heart Carelessness

The fourth type of malice aforethought is often characterized as *depraved heart*, which means the defendant acted with extreme carelessness, frequently said to involve a wanton and wilful disregard of a risk to human life or, sometimes, "an abandoned and malignant heart." A good example would be a drunk driver who drives a car one hundred miles per hour the wrong way on a busy interstate highway and crashes into an oncoming car, killing the driver and three passengers in the other vehicle. The driver's extreme carelessness would likely be characterized as depraved heart and therefore constitute malice aforethought.

H. Categories of Traditional Homicide: Overview

1. First Degree Murder: In General

Under the traditional American model, reflecting the Pennsylvania statute, first degree murder is the most serious homicide, carrying the possibility of the death penalty in many jurisdictions. First degree murder, like second degree, requires the presence of malice aforethought, which is automatically present if the other elements of first degree murder are satisfied. In the traditional American model, first degree murder occurs in two ways. It includes a killing that is wilful, deliberate, and premeditated, or that occurs during the commission of one of a group of listed felonies. When the government proves first degree murder's elements of a "wilful" killing (intent to kill), or a killing during commission of a listed felony, it automatically also establishes malice aforethought.

2. Second Degree Murder: In General

Second degree murder in traditional American homicide law is a catch-all for murders (*i.e.*, killings with malice aforethought) that are not first degree murders because they do not contain the elements of first degree murder but do have malice aforethought. This includes homicides with the intent to kill (but the killing was not deliberate and premeditated), the intent to injure seriously, by means of depraved heart carelessness, or during the commission of a nonlisted felony.

To decide whether a homicide is second degree murder, a three-step process is helpful.

1. Step One: Was the killing committed with malice aforethought?
2. Step Two: If no, the crime is neither first nor second degree murder; it may be voluntary or involuntary manslaughter. If yes, because there is malice aforethought, is it first degree murder (willful, deliberate and premeditated or listed felony murder)? If yes, the issue is solved.
3. If no because there is malice aforethought but the crime is not first degree murder, then by default the crime is second degree murder.

3. Voluntary Manslaughter: In General

The traditional American version of voluntary manslaughter occurs when there is a killing in the heat of passion, without adequate cooling time, that was provoked such that a reasonable person would have acted rashly and the defendant was actually provoked into acting rashly.

4. Involuntary Manslaughter: In General

Involuntary manslaughter occurs in one of two ways: a killing through criminally negligent (sometimes characterized as reckless conduct) or during the commission of a misdemeanor (misdemeanor-manslaughter) rule.

I. Schematic Summary of Traditional Homicide

The traditional Pennsylvania-based homicide model can be summarized by the following table:

Crime	Means of Killing
First Degree Murder	Wilful,* deliberate, and premeditated Felony murder (listed felony)*
Second Degree Murder	Intent to kill* Intent to injure* Felony murder (nonlisted felony)* Depraved heart*
Voluntary Manslaughter	Heat of passion
Involuntary Manslaughter	Misdemeanor manslaughter Criminal negligence

* Constitutes Malice aforethought

J. Murder

Under the traditional American model of homicide, murder and manslaughter are distinguished by the presence of malice aforethought for murder and its absence for manslaughter. Murder is divided into two degrees: first and second.

1. First Degree Murder: Wilful, Deliberate, and Premeditated Killing

The traditional American approach divides murder into first and second degree. First degree is the more serious and carries a possible death sentence in many American jurisdictions. Under the traditional approach reflecting the Pennsylvania statute, first degree murder can occur in either of two ways: a killing that is wilful, deliberate, and premeditated (called the premeditation-deliberation prong); and one (called felony murder) that occurs during the commission of a felony that is on a short list of the most serious felonies.

a. Wilful, Deliberate, and Premeditated: In General

One avenue to a conviction for first degree murder under the traditional American approach is a killing that is *wilful, deliberate, and premeditated*. Often called the *premeditation-deliberation* formula, all three of these subjective mental states must be established by the government beyond a reasonable doubt. The stereotypical model for this variety of murder is the hired killer who stalks the victim and learns the victim's daily routine, carefully plans the killing, then calmly carries it out by shooting the victim with a sniper rifle while the victim is having lunch at the outdoor café where the victim dines each midday.

The need to prove each of the three *mens rea* subjective elements (willful, deliberate and premeditated) often provides a considerable challenge for the government. It is crucial to understand the definition of each element and appreciate how they differ from one another. Ordinarily proof of each of these elements is through circumstantial evidence and requires a careful analysis of the particular facts in the case, including how the homicide occurred. The defendant's motive (or lack of motive) as well as the defendant's conduct before, during, and after the event are of critical importance.

b. Wilful (sometimes spelled "Willful")

A *wilful* killing is one when the killer's purpose in engaging in the *actus reus* is to kill another person. In other words, it is an *intentional* killing, making this variety of first degree murder a specific intent crime. Since "wilful" refers to an intent to kill, a wilful killing, by definition, is murder rather than manslaughter because it is committed with malice aforethought. Recall that intent to kill is one way of proving malice aforethought.

For example, assume that D points a shotgun at V and pulls the trigger, killing V. The killing would be "wilful" if D's purpose was to kill V. It would not be "wilful" if D's goal was something else, such as to injure (but not kill) or frighten V or simply to show V how the shotgun worked and believing it was not loaded.

c. Deliberate

The second *mens rea* in the traditional American model's premeditation-deliberation prong of first degree murder is *deliberate*. In general, this means that the killer acted with a *cool state of mind*. Sometimes this subjective element is expressed as present if the killer carefully considered the acts that will occur or acted with a cool mind capable of reflection. The opposite of deliberation is characterized by acts in a heated state, mental impulsivity, rashness. One court characterized deliberation as an intent to kill carried out in a cool state of blood and not under the influence of violent passion. *State v. Beck,* 487 S.E.2d 751 (N.C. 1997). A Colorado statute defines deliberation along the same lines. *Colo. Stat. § 18-3-101* (deliberation means intentionally and that "the decision to commit the act has been made after the exercise of reflection and judgment concerning the act ... [and was not] committed in a hasty or impulsive manner").

Some jurisdictions that in general follow the traditional American model omit the deliberation requirement, finding a killing sufficient for first degree murder if it is intentional and premeditated. For example, the Minnesota provision punishes a premeditated killing but does not require deliberation. *Minn. Stat. Ann. § 609.185.*

d. Premeditated

The third prong of the premeditation-deliberation formula is that the killer *premeditate* the homicide. (There is some authority that premeditation was the "aforethought" in the early malice aforethought cases.) Case law suggests that premeditation under the traditional American model requires some advance planning occurring before the fatal blow is struck. Looking at the combined effect of the deliberation and premeditation requirements, it is sometimes said that these two subjective *mens rea* elements require the actor to have a cool mind capable of reflection (deliberation) and actually to reflect (premeditation) on the coming event. Thus, premeditation (and deliberation) would likely be found if the defendant purchased the gun three days before the killing and then carefully followed the victim to a remote area where the victim was shot multiple times. The same result if the defendant, before the homicide, had made elaborate escape plans.

While at first blush the premeditation rule would appear to exclude a spur-of-the-moment decision to kill immediately, it is common for case law to hold that premeditation may occur *in an instant.* Long range planning is not necessary. This view was stated eloquently in a famous Pennsylvania case: "no time is too short for a wicked man to frame in his mind the scheme of murder, and to contrive the means of accomplishing it." *Commonwealth v. Drum,* 58 Pa. 9 (1868).

An illustration of how short this time span may be is provided by the court that held that the time for premeditation "may be of the shortest possible duration and may be so short that it is instantaneous, and the purpose to kill may be formed at any moment before the homicide is committed." *State v. Harms,* 643 N.W.2d 359 (Neb. 2002). It should be obvious that this interpretation substantially weakens if not eliminates premeditation as a significant element distinguishing first degree murder from other homicides. Accordingly, many scholars argue that the premeditation-in-an-instant rule should be rejected as inconsistent with the concept behind requiring premeditation as an element of first degree murder. Perhaps this is why some locales require proof that the premeditation lasted for "more than a momentary duration." *State v. Nunes,* 788 A.2d 460 (R.I. 2002).

Because of concerns about the difficulties of proving and defining premeditation and the wisdom of even requiring it as an element, some American jurisdictions and the Model Penal Code do not include premeditation as an element. Ordinarily these locales punish an intentional killing, irrespective of whether it was done by premeditation (or deliberation). The existence or absence of premeditation may be a factor in sentencing.

e. Poison or Lying in Wait

i. Relationship to Wilful, Deliberate, and Premeditated

The traditional American first degree murder statute and many others based on it contain an odd and confusing provision to the effect that a first degree murder, through the premeditation-deliberation formula, may be perpetrated by means of *poison, or by lying in wait,* or by another kind of wilful, deliberate, and premeditated killing. Sometimes *torture* is added as a third method of killing. The poison lying-in-wait formulation, rejected in most modern criminal codes, raises the question of whether poison or lying in wait are simply illustrations of wilful, deliberate, and premeditated killings, or whether poison or lying in wait are alternate routes for liability for first degree murder and do not require additional proof of a wilful, deliberate, and premeditated killing. In other words, if D kills V by putting rat poison in her coffee, has D committed first degree murder by poison without any proof D acted deliberately and with premeditation?

Most (though not all) cases conclude that poison and lying in wait are given as illustrations of some ways that a killing may be accomplished in a manner that is wilful, deliberate, and premeditated. Even though poison or lying in wait is established, the prosecutor must still prove that the homicide was wilful, deliberate, and premeditated. Using the rat poison example above, in these jurisdictions the state could have to prove beyond a reasonable doubt that D's use of poison was part of a wilful, deliberate, and premeditated effort to kill V. If D accidentally put the rat poison in V's coffee, perhaps because D mistakenly thought the poison was coffee creamer, D would not be guilty of first degree murder since the killing was not wilful, deliberate, or premeditated. While this interpretation seems to ignore the strict language (any *other* kind of wilful, deliberate, or premeditated killing) of the traditional American first degree murder provision, it is still viable in many locales.

The matter is especially confusing when the proof is of lying in wait. Since in ordinary behavior one who kills with premeditation and deliberation may well lie in wait until the victim arrives, a number of decisions indicate that proof of lying in wait also is proof (sometimes characterized as the "functional equivalent") of intent, premeditation, and deliberation. *People v. Ruiz*, 44 Cal. 3d 589 (Cal. 1988). Some decisions also hold that the lying in wait need not occur immediately before the infliction of the fatal blow.

ii. Lying in Wait

The term "lying in wait" should not be taken literally, as requiring the defendant be prone and hidden. Rather the cases suggest there must be some period of "waiting, watching, and secrecy" with the intent to kill or do serious bodily injury. Judicial decisions occasionally describe lying in wait as involving concealment and waiting for the opportunity to act, plus a goal of surprising the victim. Case law sometimes gives "lying in wait" a rather expansive, nonliteral interpretation, including waiting in a parked car, taking a circuitous route to avoid being seen, concealing behind a building or other item, and waiting in the victim's house for the victim to return.

iii. Poison

The term "poison" is not difficult to define, but raises far more complex issues than it might appear. In general terms, it is a substance when introduced in the body is capable of causing death. It may be administered in virtually any way, such as by mouth, injection, inhalation, or application to the skin. Nowhere does guilt for first degree murder flow automatically when a person kills another through the use of poison. Thus, it is uniformly recognized that an accidental poisoning does not constitute first degree murder simply because of the method of talking life. Rather, in many jurisdictions there still must be proof that the poison was part of a wilful, deliberate, and premeditated killing. In other jurisdictions following the traditional American model, however, the term "poison" in the first degree murder statute is deemed not to require proof of a willful, deliberate, and premeditated killing. However, to prevent an accidental poisoning to be first degree murder, the statute is interpreted as requiring only proof of the intent to poison (to do the act resulting in death) with knowledge of the danger to life. The government need not prove the intent to kill. This distinction is usually irrelevant since people who knowingly administer poison to another person ordinarily intend to kill that person. But on rare occasions it is significant, as when the poisoner intended to make the homicide victim ill but not dead. *People v. Jennings*, 237 P.3d 474 (Cal. 2010).

f. Role of Motive

Motive, the reason behind an action, is not an element of murder, but may be circumstantial evidence of, or a lack of, intent, premeditation, and deliberation. For example, in one case the defendant had been angry at the victim for a long time, badly needed money, and had been scheming to resolve matters with the victim. These facts were deemed relevant on whether the defendant robbed, then killed the victim with intent, premeditation, and deliberation.

Sometimes even a laudable motive may prove intent, premeditation, and deliberation, as when the defendant kills in order to bring justice to someone who had done a terrible wrong or to prevent the victim from suffering any more from a horrible disease. (It is possible that the particular facts in one or both of these illustrations could involve adequate "heat of passion" to reduce the crime to voluntary manslaughter under the traditional American model of homicide.)

By way of contrast, motive may also help the defense argue against first degree murder. For example, assume D loves V but kills V with a shotgun and claims it was an accident. This affection may suggest that D did not kill V in a willful, deliberate, and premeditated manner, but rather did so accidentally when the gun discharged after D carelessly dropped it. On the other hand, if D shot V a few days after learning V had been unfaithful to D, D's anger at V may help the government establish a willful, deliberate, and premeditated first degree murder rather than an accidental killing.

2. First Degree Murder: Felony Murder (Listed Felony)

In addition to the premeditation-deliberation prong of first degree murder, the traditional American model using degrees of murder includes a felony murder alternative. A homicide occurring during the course of one of a small number of listed felonies constitutes first degree murder. The list of felonies qualifying for first degree murder often includes six to ten of the most serious crimes. Typically these include robbery, rape, kidnaping, arson, and murder. Modern additions often add child sexual abuse, aircraft piracy and certain terrorist acts. The inclusion of such serious felonies for first degree murder is designed to distinguish the worst of the worst (those committing a homicide while committing the most heinous crimes) from lesser morally blameworthy felons, deserving lower punishment for a killing during a less serious felony. As described more fully below, this application of the felony murder rule requires that the felony be the cause of the homicide.

In general terms, the prosecution in a jurisdiction following the traditional American approach may prefer to seek a conviction through the felony murder route than by establishing a wilful, deliberate and premeditated killing. The former requires only proof of the *mens rea* for the predicate felony, such as robbery; it does not mandate convincing the trier of fact that the defendant acted wilfully with deliberation and premeditation.

3. Second Degree Murder

As noted above, second degree murder was created in Pennsylvania and followed in many other jurisdictions when the common law crime of murder (which had no degrees) was subdivided into degrees, with only first degree carrying the death penalty. Second degree murder is a catch-all. Like first degree murder, second degree murder requires proof of malice aforethought. But defining second degree murder with particularity takes some effort because the traditional American definition is of little help. Adopting the vague Pennsylvania statute, the traditional American approach states a definition of first degree murder, then indicates that all other murders are of the second degree. This means that the exact parameters of second degree murder can only be ascertained by a three-step process, also described above.

First, there must be an assessment of whether the incident involved malice aforethought. If the answer is yes, then the crime is either first or second degree murder because malice aforethought is present for all murders but absent for all manslaughters. If the answer is no because malice aforethought is not present, then the crime is voluntary or involuntary manslaughter (or perhaps no crime at all).

For those killings that do involve malice aforethought, the next inquiry is whether the crime satisfies the definition of first degree murder (*i.e.,* premeditation-deliberation or felony murder with a listed felony). If so, the matter is resolved, but if not the crime, by default, is second degree murder. This analysis teaches that there are four varieties of second degree murder.

a. Intent to Kill (Without Premeditation and Deliberation)

Recall that first degree murder under the traditional American approach may be present if the killing is wilful, deliberate, and premeditated. But what if it is wilful, but either (or both) deliberation or premeditation cannot be proven? By a process of elimination, the crime is second degree murder. Here is the logic: the crime is a murder because the wilfulness (*i.e.*, intent to kill) constitutes malice aforethought, but it is not first degree murder since either deliberation or premeditation cannot be established. Since the crime involved malice aforethought and is therefore murder but not in the first degree, by default it is second degree murder.

b. Intent to Do Serious Bodily Injury

Second degree murder in the traditional American model may also occur if the killer's intent is to do serious bodily injury (or sometimes expressed as grievous bodily injury or great bodily harm). Again, the logic is that this intent constitutes malice aforethought, but the crime is not first degree because it lacks the wilfulness (*i.e.*, intent to kill) necessary for the greater offense. By default, the defendant may face charges of second degree murder. Thus, if D stabs V and intends only to wound V seriously, D may be guilty of second degree murder if V dies.

The harm that must be intended to constitute "serious bodily injury" includes that which is sufficiently egregious to risk loss of life or any other nontrivial physical injury.

c. Depraved Heart

The third way that second degree murder occurs in a traditional American jurisdiction is through a killing that is so careless that the behavior is characterized as *depraved heart*. At common law this was considered *implied malice* rather than express malice.

This type of malice aforethought involves extremely reckless conduct that has been described in various ways and lacks a generally accepted common law definition, though it clearly requires more carelessness than the ordinary negligence appropriate for tort relief and the "gross negligence" that would constitute involuntary manslaughter. One often-used description is conduct that evidences a wanton and wilful disregard of unreasonable human risk. Another version is an act that shows an extreme indifference to the value of human life. Still another, actually used in jury instructions, is conduct that manifests an "abandoned and malignant heart." Another iteration is the perpetration of "any act imminently dangerous to another and evincing a depraved mind regardless of human life." *Fla. Stat. Ann. § 782.04.* Note that death from this kind of extremely careless behavior is unintentional, perhaps even viewed as accidental.

There is a split of authority whether the concept of depraved heart carelessness has a subjective component that must be proven. Some jurisdictions assess depraved heart carelessness in purely objective terms, asking whether the degree of risk was excessive. In one case, for example, the defendant, playing "a game" with the victim, pointed a gun, which he erroneously thought was unloaded, at the victim and pulled the trigger twice. The New York court held that the defendant's personal belief about the gun's lethality was irrelevant. "Depraved indifference" second degree murder requires proof that the "objective circumstances bearing on the nature of a defendant's reckless conduct are such that the conduct creates a very substantial risk of death." *People v. St. Helen,* 742 N.Y.S.2d 640 (N.Y. Sup. Ct., App. Div. 2002).

Other iterations of the depraved heart approach include a subjective component. They require proof of an actual awareness of a serious risk, then an act in conscious disregard of this risk. This is the situation when the actor's mind, in theory, thinks something like, "Yes, I knew that there was a chance that I could kill or seriously injure someone but I went ahead anyway." The dullard who is too ignorant or has too poor judgment to perceive the risk would not be found to have acted with depraved heart carelessness in jurisdictions requiring subjective awareness of the risk.

On the other hand, if the defendant did not perceive the risk because he or she was simply too intoxicated to notice, in the vast number of jurisdictions the defendant would not be permitted to argue this version of an "intoxication defense." As a matter of law — often stated specifically in a statute — in these states, intoxication is not a permissible reason to fail to perceive the risk of death or serious bodily harm.

A classic illustration of depraved heart second degree murder occurred when the defendant played Russian roulette by placing one bullet in a revolver, spinning the cartridge cylinder, pointing the gun at another person's head, and pulling the trigger, risking that one bullet in the pistol would discharge when the trigger was pulled. When the gun discharged, killing the other person, the defendant's conduct was found to constitute malice aforethought since it was "an act of gross recklessness for which the defendant must reasonably anticipate that death to another is likely to result." *Commonwealth v. Malone,* 47 A.2d 445 (Pa. 1946).

Other typical illustrations of depraved heart conduct are the drunk driver who steers a car into a group of pedestrians, an angry employee who shoots a gun into a crowd of coworkers in the lunch room, engaging in a gunfight in a crowded street, stabbing someone with a knife, repeated beatings of an infant, and dropping a heavy rock from a bridge onto the busy highway below. Assuming that the killer neither intended to kill nor to injure seriously, his or her extreme carelessness would likely be sufficient to hold the killer responsible for second degree depraved heart murder in a jurisdiction requiring awareness of risk as well as in those that do not.

d. Felony-Murder

The fourth method of committing second degree murder in the traditional American homicide approach is a killing that occurs during a homicide not included in the list for first degree murder. However, as discussed more fully below, this expansive reading of the felony murder rule for second degree murder is rejected in many jurisdictions as too harsh and limited by the concepts of merger, causation, and the restriction that only felonies characterized as dangerous are sufficient to trigger the felony murder rule for second degree murder.

4. Felony Murder

a. Commission of Felony as Malice Aforethought

As noted above, the traditional American approach to homicide law held that malice aforethought is present when the defendant killed during the commission or attempted commission of a felony, often called the *predicate felony*. In the traditional American model that uses degrees of murder, the *felony murder* rule means that the crime is murder, either of the first or second degree. The defendant may be liable for murder under this approach even if the killing was unintended and the product of an accident. Thus, if D is robbing V and during that crime D's gun accidentally discharges killing V, D will be held for murder since the robbery constituted malice aforethought sufficient for murder of the first or second degree. The same result if a bank customer dies during the robbery from a heart attack brought on by the stress of the crime.

Felony murder may also be charged against multiple defendants involved in a crime that results in death, even if only one co-felon is directly responsible for the killing. This approach is a means to hold accountable those who participate in a felony even if they personally are not a direct cause of death. For example, if A and B rob V, and A then shoots V who refuses to hand over money, both A and B (both liable for robbery) may be responsible under the felony murder rule for V's death and both could be convicted of first or second degree murder in the traditional American model.

A small minority of American jurisdictions extend the concept of the felony murder and have created a crime called *attempted felony murder*. This very unusual crime reaches people who perpetrate or attempt to perpetrate a predicate felony covered by the felony murder rule and could, but do not, cause a death. *Fla. Stat. § 782.051.* An illustration would be a bank robber who shoots at, but misses, a bank guard during the escape from the crime.

b. Rationale for Felony Murder Rule

The felony murder rule is often justified as appropriate to deter people from committing felonies since the criminal may be held liable for murder irrespective of the lack of intent to kill or even injure anyone. A related argument is that it deters people from committing felonies carelessly or in a dangerous manner since they may be liable for the accidental events that arise during the crime. In theory at least, this means that a criminal who is familiar with the law of felony murder should be induced to commit a bank robbery with an unloaded gun in order to avoid at least the risk of being convicted of murder in case the gun accidentally discharges during the crime. Critics of the rule argue that it extends liability too far, punishing someone for murder even though the person never intended to do anything more serious than to commit the underlying felony.

c. Listed and Nonlisted Felonies

Felony murder laws differ markedly among the jurisdictions. Some simply do not include it in their homicide laws. Others specifically list the only felonies that may be the predicate felony, yet others specify the exact felonies acceptable for felony murder for some homicide offenses but have only general standards for which felonies may be used to establish other homicide crimes.

i. Traditional American (Pennsylvania) Approach

First degree murder laws that are based on the traditional American model and described in more detail above, often limit felony murder to a very small number of enumerated felonies and designate these specific crimes in the statute. These *listed felonies* might be the most serious and involve substantial potential harm. The typical list for first degree murder in the traditional American model ordinarily included such crimes as arson, robbery, rape, burglary, and murder (for example, killing B while in the process of killing A). Other jurisdictions that list the predicate felonies for first degree murder may extend the traditional American model list to crimes such as aggravated child abuse, aircraft piracy, and various acts of terrorism.

Technically, second degree murder under the traditional American model is available for a killing during any other felony (called *nonlisted felonies*). The commission of a nonlisted felony satisfies the rule that second degree murder required a killing with malice aforethought. Statutory modifications of the traditional American approach reject the idea that any nonlisted felony will satisfy second degree murder and, instead, may provide a list of crimes that will trigger the felony-murder rule for second degree murder; other jurisdictions allow the prosecutor the discretion to choose which felonies can be used as a basis for a felony murder charge for second degree murder.

For example, assume that D kidnaps V from a school yard and, by accident, V dies in an auto collision while D drives away from the school at a high rate of speed. In a jurisdiction following the traditional American approach, D may face charges of first or second degree murder under the felony murder rule since the kidnaping is a felony. The proper charge would be first degree murder if kidnaping is included as a listed felony in the first degree murder statute. If it is not on the first degree list, the proper crime would be second degree murder since the homicide occurred during the commission of a felony (not included in the first degree murder list) and therefore constituted felony murder.

ii. Other Approaches to Listing Felonies

While the traditional American approach provides a list of felonies qualifying for first degree murder but leaves unanswered which felonies suffice for second degree felony murder, many jurisdictions retain the concept of felony murder and have statutes with far more specific rules. For example, a statute may adopt a list of specific felonies that can establish felony murder for one or more types of homicide and refuse to recognize felony murder for any other homicide categories. The list in Florida includes almost twenty specific crimes.

d. Limits on Felony Murder: In General

Because felony murder is disfavored in the law, several limits to the rule have been adopted. While at one time in some locales second degree murder included a homicide occurring during any nonlisted felony, eventually it was recognized that there should be some limits on the felonies that would produce liability for second degree murder. Four such limits developed.

e. Merger (or Independent Felony Rule)

A rigid application of the felony murder rule could work significant injustice and cause some bizarre legal consequences. For example, involuntary manslaughter, discussed below, is a traditional low-level felony that involves a killing during the commission of a misdemeanor or through criminal negligence or recklessness. If a defendant is guilty of involuntary manslaughter, he or she has killed during the commission of a felony and, technically, could be held for second degree murder under the felony murder rule. Obviously, this result is absurd and would have the effect of eliminating involuntary manslaughter as a viable crime since every person guilty of involuntary manslaughter would automatically be guilty also of second degree murder (because involuntary manslaughter is surely a nonlisted felony).

Since the legislature never intended this result, the doctrine of *merger* (sometimes called the *independent felony rule*) evolved. Based on notions of statutory interpretation and the principle that a statute should be interpreted to further the legislature's intent in enacting it, the merger rule is a court-made concept providing that the legislature intended that certain felonies should not be the predicate offense for a felony murder prosecution. Often this approach is held to mean that the predicate felony must be independent of the act that kills the victim, involving by definition acts separate from those causing the death. Under this view, independent felonies include such crimes as robbery, rape, kidnaping, and arson. Nonindependent felonies include involuntary and voluntary manslaughter, plus felony assault and felony battery (often characterized as aggravated assault or aggravated battery). The exclusion of felony assault and battery as the predicate felony is the product of the observation that one of these occurs in just about every homicide—including those that would otherwise be voluntary or involuntary manslaughter. The argument is that the legislature did not mean to characterize virtually all homicides as murder by using a felony assault or battery as the predicate crime satisfying the felony murder rule.

A related approach used to exclude some felonies as predicate felonies for purposes of the felony murder rule is to ask whether the underlying felony had an *independent felonious purpose* other than killing or seriously injuring the victim. For example, if D kidnaps V, who dies from fright during the ordeal, in a jurisdiction using the independent felonious purpose rule felony murder would apply since the kidnaping had an independent felonious purpose unrelated to the death. The same would be true if the death had occurred when D robbed or raped V since there would be an independent felonious purpose in D's actions.

The independent felony rule may even arise in the context of an assault and prevent merger. In one case, for example, the court held that the crime of armed assault in a dwelling with intent to commit a felony was sufficiently independent of the homicide that the merger rule was inapplicable. *Commonwealth v. Gunter*, 692 N.E.2d 515 (Mass. 1998).

Not to be confused with the above discussion, there is another use of the word "merger" in felony murder cases. Say a defendant commits a robbery and someone is accidentally killed during the crime. Assume the felony murder rule will permit the robbery to be the predicate felony for second degree murder. May the defendant also be found guilty of robbery (*i.e.*, be found guilty or sentenced for both second degree murder and robbery)? Jurisdictions are split on this issue, though some hold that the robbery "merges" with the murder and the defendant may not be convicted (or in some states, sentenced) for both the murder and the robbery. *See State v. Dudley*, 566 S.E.2d 843 (N.C. App. 2002). Note how this view of merger differs from the one discussed above where the merged felony (such as assault) may not be used as the predicate felony, while here the felony may be so used but the defendant may not be sentenced for *both* the predicate felony (robbery) and murder (through felony murder).

f. Dangerous Felonies

At one point in English criminal law there was some suggestion that the commission of *any* felony constituted malice aforethought and therefore satisfied the felony murder rule. Over time, however, this view was rejected in virtually all jurisdictions with traditional American homicide laws and the scope of the felony murder rule was markedly limited by the rule that only *some* felonies qualify.

The underlying issue can be illustrated by the Case of the Unlucky Pranksters. Assume that a state has a rash of cemetery vandalism and passes a law making it a felony to tip over a grave marker. One Halloween night some inebriated pranksters go to a cemetery and push over a dozen tombstones. Unbeknownst to them, a homeless alcoholic woman is sleeping beneath one of the markers that is tipped over and she is crushed to death. Under a broad reading of the felony murder rule in a jurisdiction following the traditional American approach, the pranksters would be guilty of murder (second degree since it would likely be an unlisted felony) because they killed the victim during the commission of a felony, here cemetery vandalism.

To many students of criminal law theory, this result is wrong. While the defendants are guilty of vandalism and merit punishment for that, they are not the kind of dangerous persons who should be viewed as murderers. Indeed, their crime was very minor, a misdemeanor in most other jurisdictions, but they find themselves charged with murder because their jurisdiction classified the cemetery vandalism as a felony and they were unlucky enough to push over a grave marker beneath which someone happened to be sleeping.

To prevent this kind of overcriminalization, jurisdictions with traditional American homicide laws routinely limit the felony murder rule for second degree murder to *dangerous felonies*. (There is no such generic limit for first degree murder since that crime ordinarily lists felonies that lead to a conviction for that crime.)

i. Inherently Dangerous or Elements Approach

Dangerousness is assessed in one of two ways. Some jurisdictions, such as California, extend the felony murder rule to crimes that are *inherently dangerous*, which means the courts look at the elements of the crime in the abstract to determine whether it can be committed without creating a high probability that there would be a loss of life or at least serious bodily injury. *People v. Williams*, 11 Cal. Rptr.3d 114 (Cal. App. 2004). This approach (sometimes referred to as the *elements* approach) produces a line of judicial decisions indicating which felonies are classified as inherently dangerous and satisfy the felony murder rule. Sometimes this determination is difficult since some felonies, such as fraudulent breach of trust, extortion, or prison escape, may not be dangerous in the abstract but may be deadly in a particular situation.

ii. Dangerous Act Approach

Other jurisdictions adopt the *dangerous act* approach. They limit the felony murder rule for second degree murder to felonies that occurred while the defendant was doing an act dangerous to human life. They look at the facts of the particular crime, rather than just the elements of the felony, to determine whether the felony is sufficiently dangerous to merit felony murder treatment. One issue with this approach, called by some courts the "bootstrap problem," is that the presence of the dead body will sway a finding that the crime was inherently dangerous.

A classic case illustrates the differences in these two views. The defendant, a chiropractor, told the parents of a child with a deadly form of eye cancer that he could cure the cancer and that they should withdraw the child from traditional treatment, involving the surgical removal of the child's eye. The parents followed this advice, paid the defendant seven hundred dollars, and the child was treated for several months, eventually dying from the cancer. The California Supreme Court held that the defendant was guilty of grand theft for lying about his ability to cure the child, but refused to allow a jury instruction on felony murder. Following the "elements" approach to assessing whether grand theft was inherently dangerous and therefore a fit subject for felony murder, the Court held that grand theft was not in the inherently dangerous category and therefore could not be the predicate felony that triggers the felony murder rule. Had the California court followed the "dangerous act" approach, however, surely the defendant's conduct in promising to cure the child and accepting money for his services would be considered an act dangerous to human life and the grand theft would be sufficient to invoke the felony murder rule. *People v. Phillips*, 414 P.2d 353 (Cal. 1966).

g. Causation *(Res Gestae Rule)*

Another limit on the felony murder rule for both first and second degree murder is the principle that the death must be *caused* by the felony. This means that there must be a temporal and physical relationship between the felony and the death. In general terms this means that "but for" and, often, proximate cause rules must be satisfied. Causation is discussed in greater detail in Chapter 6.

i. Duration of Felony

For felony murder, causation means that the death occurred because of and during the *perpetration or attempted perpetration* (or *commission or attempted commission*) of the felony. A simple illustration of adequate causation is a defendant who burglarized the house of an eighty-six-year-old man, bound and gagged the victim who had emphysema and high blood pressure and suffered a mortal heart attack from the obstructed breathing and physical efforts to break free. The burglar would be held responsible for the felony murder of the victim. Another generally accepted illustration of causation in felony murder is a robbery by X and Y during which X accidentally kills codefendant Y. X would be held responsible for co-felon Y's death.

The concept of *perpetration* is sometimes quite broad, extending to escape from the crime itself. Sometimes the time frame is expressed as the *res gestae* of the crime, which means that there is a closeness in time and distance between the crime and the homicide. Some statutes state specifically that the felony murder rule extends to the *immediate flight* after the predicate felony. This means that the felony murder rule applies even to a killing during an escape, but often it is held that, for this purpose, the escape is over once the defendant reaches a place of at least temporary safety, sometimes referred to as a safe haven.

For example, assume that D commits arson of a building in order to collect insurance on it. During the fire, firefighter F is killed trying to rescue an inhabitant of the building. Also assume that police officer P is killed by D's car as D drives rapidly from the scene of the fire to avoid apprehension. Under the felony murder rule in a traditional American jurisdiction, D would be liable for the deaths of both firefighter F and police officer P since both occurred during the perpetration of the arson. If arson is a listed felony, D may be liable for first degree murder. But if officer P is killed a month later when trying to apprehend D who has been hiding in a remote cabin, the felony murder rule may be inapplicable since D had found a safe haven sufficient to stop the application of the felony murder rule. Essentially the felony had ended when the officer was killed.

ii. Death of Co-Felon

Several unusual situations have generated substantial discussion about the proper reach of the felony murder rule. One set of cases involves a felony by two accomplices, one of whom kills himself or herself accidentally during the commission of the felony. Is the other liable for the accomplice's death? The usual rule is that the felony murder rule applies in such cases, at least for co-felons who were present at the felony and participated in it. *People v. Billa*, 79 P.3d 542 (Cal. 2003) (two arsonists, one of whom accidentally set himself on fire and died).

iii. Killing by Non-Felon

Another unusual set of facts engendered special rules for causation in felony murder cases when the killing was done by someone other than a co-felon. Every possible combination seems to have occurred. For example, assume that X and Y rob a liquor store late at night. During the robbery, clerk C pulls out a pistol and kills felon X, or police officer P sees the robbery and shoots felon X during the escape. Can felon Y be charged with murder for the felony murder of co-felon X? Or what if clerk C or officer P shoots at X, misses, and kills innocent bystander I. Can felons X and Y be charged with murder for bystander I's death? Similarly, if police officer P accidentally shoots clerk C (the victim of the robbery!), can felons X and Y be held responsible under the felony murder rule? The matter is especially complicated if someone (the victim, police officer, bystander, or co-felon) is killed during the robbery but it is impossible to identify the killer. Perhaps it was X or Y, a police officer, or even a bystander who happened to see the incident and was armed.

Under a "but for" test of causation or even a general application of the principle that the felony murder rule applies to a killing during the perpetration of a felony, either felon could be responsible for the actions of clerk C and officer P in their response to the robbery. On the other hand, this extends liability quite far because the actions of clerk C and officer P are most likely not crimes since each has a defense to criminal charges (perhaps C and P acted in self defense, or could use the law enforcement or crime prevention defenses).

Agency Theory. Courts take two approaches to the issue. Under the *agency* theory, a felon is responsible only for those crimes committed by someone who is considered the felon's agent (normally a co-felon). Under this approach, since the killings above were committed by clerk C and officer P, felon Y is not responsible for them since neither is felon Y's agent. Sometimes this concept is expressed as holding each felon responsible only for the actions of other "participants" (*i.e.,* co-felons).

Proximate Cause Theory. The second approach, sometimes called the *proximate cause* view, holds a felon responsible for deaths that are reasonably foreseeable consequences of the felony. Under this test, it would likely be held that Y is responsible for the deaths caused by clerk C and officer P since it is foreseeable that both the liquor store clerk and the police officer would use deadly force in responding to the armed robbery and could easily kill one of the robbers or even an innocent bystander.

Some jurisdictions by statute reject the agency approach but still maintain proximate cause as a limit on the scope of their felony murder rule. *21 Okla. Stat. Ann § 701.7(B)*(liability for felony murder extends to death of anyone killed during commission of felony). *See Dickens v. State,* 106 P.3d 599 (Okla. Crim. App. 2005)(robbery victim killed co-felon; surviving felon is guilty of first degree murder since statute extends liability to any person killed during the felony and the death was foreseeable for an armed robbery).

h. Differentiating Among Felons

A small number of jurisdictions limit the felony murder rule by differentiating among participants based on the actions and relative moral blameworthiness of each. If X and Y commit a felony during which X shoots a police officer, in these jurisdictions Y may escape liability for felony murder (though not for the predicate felony) if Y did not commit or aid in the commission of the murder, was not armed with a dangerous weapon, and reasonably thought no other felon was so armed and no one intended to engage in conduct likely to cause serious bodily injury. *Conn. Gen. Stat. § 53a-54c; N.Y. Penal L. § 125.5(3).*

i. Reject Rule Entirely

Reasoning that the felony murder rule extends liability for murder too broadly, some jurisdictions, following the Model Penal Code, simply reject it as part of their homicide jurisprudence. England, which exported the felony murder rule to America, abolished it in 1957. In these jurisdictions a killer's liability is assessed by theories other than felony murder. For example, assume that a robber accidentally drops a gun during a bank robbery and kills a bank customer. The robber would be guilty of (a) robbery, and likely also of (b) second degree murder if the accident is characterized as depraved heart or of involuntary manslaughter if the defendant's conduct is defined simply as criminally negligent.

K. Manslaughter

Manslaughter, involving a killing committed without malice aforethought, is generally divided into two distinct categories: voluntary and involuntary in a jurisdiction following the traditional American model of homicide.

1. Voluntary Manslaughter

Voluntary manslaughter is a unique component of homicide law. It recognizes human frailties and includes an element of comparative fault (meaning the victim played a role in inducing the crime), which ordinarily is absent in the criminal law arena. In general terms, voluntary manslaughter under the American traditional model punishes someone who kills in the *sudden heat of passion* as the result of *legally sufficient provocation*. Note that voluntary manslaughter effectively reduces the gravity of an intentional killing but is not a defense that excuses or justifies the act. Thus, it differs markedly from self-defense, which would provide the killer with a complete defense to homicide. The defendant guilty of voluntary manslaughter commits a serious crime and may well face a prison sentence, though one shorter than he or she would have received had the crime been first or second degree murder.

Voluntary manslaughter ordinarily involves an intentional killing. While this may lead one to think that the crime should actually be first or second degree murder since the intent to kill would constitute malice aforethought, case law has long held that an intentional killing that satisfies the requirements of voluntary manslaughter does not show sufficient moral wickedness to amount to malice aforethought. Some statutes even address this issue directly, defining voluntary manslaughter, in addition to having the usual provocation and heat of passion elements, as an "intentional homicide that would otherwise be murder." Some decisions expand voluntary manslaughter to killings, otherwise satisfying the elements of the crime, that are of the intent-to-do-serious-bodily-injury variety (as by shooting the victim with the purpose of causing serious injury) or even depraved heart (as by pulling out a gun and pulling the trigger out of rage rather than a desire to hurt anyone).

a. Heat of Passion

By definition, voluntary manslaughter involves a killing *in the heat of passion*. This means that at the time of the homicide the defendant was in an extreme emotional state, perhaps characterized as anger, jealousy, fear, excitement, or even depression. In theory, the existence of the heat of passion negates the underlying values in malice aforethought and renders the defendant's acts not murder since there is no malice aforethought.

b. Insufficient Cooling Time

Voluntary manslaughter requires the killing to be spontaneous and rash. Often this is expressed in terms of *cooling time*. The defendant (some courts also require a reasonable person) must not have had sufficient time to cool off after the provocation. Some voluntary manslaughter cases take the concept literally, requiring that the homicide occur just after the provocation. The Nevada statute expresses this concept elegantly: "[I]f there should appear to have been an interval between the assault or provocation ... and the killing, sufficient for the voice of reason and humanity to be heard, the killing shall be attributed to deliberate revenge and punished as murder [rather than voluntary manslaughter.]" *Nev. Rev. Stat. § 200.060.*

Other cases are more forgiving, accepting the concept of *brooding* in which the defendant is provoked, then thinks about the matter over a course of time, getting angrier and angrier with each passing hour. Eventually, under this theory, the defendant explodes and kills the victim. In this situation some courts allow a voluntary manslaughter jury instruction despite the passage of time between the provocation and the killing. Often the matter is simply put in the hands of the jury to decide whether the defendant had cooled off or acted rashly because of the provocation.

c. Legally Sufficient Provocation

Voluntary manslaughter is a response to provocation. Many decisions under the traditional American approach hold that there can be no voluntary manslaughter if there were no provocation, no matter how inflamed or irrational the defendant had become. This is consistent with the underlying theory of voluntary manslaughter, which is that the defendant is less morally culpable because he or she was provoked into acting rashly because of the heat of passion directed at the person who provoked the defendant.

Case law has limited the provocation that will engender a voluntary manslaughter charge. Often the acceptable provocation is called *legally sufficient provocation*. This means that it must be of such gravity that it would cause even a reasonable person to act rashly from passion rather than calm reason and judgment. *See, e.g., Nev. Rev. Stat. §200.050* ("sufficient to excite an irresistible passion in a reasonable person"). Originally the common law accepted relatively few provocations. These included a serious battery, being subjected to an illegal arrest, serious injury to a close relative, and catching the defendant's spouse in adultery. Over time the restrictions were eased and more acts became recognized as triggering voluntary manslaughter.

Today the usual rule is that the jury is simply given a general standard and applies it to the facts. The standard is whether the provocation would be sufficient to make a reasonable person act rashly. But even under this generous approach, it is routinely held that a trespass on property or a slight battery is inadequate provocation. Similarly, "mere words" are insufficient provocation, no matter how cruel or personally offensive. However, words in combination with acts may suffice for legally sufficient provocation under the particular circumstances of the case. And even if words do not constitute provocation reducing the crime to voluntary manslaughter, in rare cases they may still mitigate the crime below first degree murder if they so inflame the defendant that he or she does not have the cool head required for deliberation under the law of first degree murder.

In one area, however, it may appear that words alone are adequate. So called *informational words* may qualify if they, for example, relate facts that would suffice for provocation. Thus, if an anonymous caller tells the defendant that the defendant's spouse is having an affair with another person, these words alone have been held sufficient to constitute legally sufficient provocation.

An obvious limit on provocation is the rule that the defendant may not have goaded the victim into the provocation. For example, if the defendant slaps the victim who, in response, shoves the defendant, the defendant may not rely on voluntary manslaughter if the defendant kills the victim and claims the victim's shove was adequate provocation for the homicide.

Some decisions extend voluntary manslaughter to what has been called *imperfect self defense*, which arises when the defendant is in a situation were self defense could be appropriate but some aspect of self defense is missing and the defendant nevertheless kills. For example, self defense extends to someone who reasonably believes that certain force is necessary, but is not applicable if the person's belief to that effect is unreasonable. In such cases where the belief as to the need for force or the amount of force that is appropriate to respond to the aggressor's use of force is unreasonable, there are decisions holding the defendant is guilty of voluntary manslaughter rather than murder. The provocation that was insufficient for self defense may still be adequate to satisfy the provocation element of voluntary manslaughter.

d. Reasonable Person Would Be Provoked

Voluntary manslaughter generally uses an objective standard by applying only when the provocation would have caused a *reasonable person to act rashly* and lose self control. This external test ordinarily does not take into consideration the fact that the defendant was thin-skinned, especially sensitive, or drunk. Model Penal Code § 210.3, discussed below, loosens the concept by stating that the "reasonable explanation or excuse" for the defendant's rash behavior is "determined from the viewpoint of a person in the actor's situation under the circumstances as [the actor] ... believes them to be." But the matter is not entirely objective. In assessing whether a reasonable person would have been provoked, most cases allow the jury to take into consideration the defendant's personal characteristics in assessing the gravity of the provocation.

e. Defendant Actually Provoked

Though often forgotten, it is clear that a defendant may have the "benefit" of voluntary manslaughter's reduced sanction for an intentional killing only if the defendant was *actually provoked* by the provocation. Thus, if the defendant were a particularly stoic person and were not provoked though a reasonable person would be, the defendant may not rely on voluntary manslaughter. Rather, the crime may well be first degree murder if wilful, deliberate, and premeditated, or second degree murder since there was likely an intent to kill or to injure seriously.

An interesting issue is when the defendant was actually provoked but was mistaken about the provocation. For example, what if the defendant became enraged when he heard a false rumor that his wife was having an affair and he immediately killed the wife's supposed lover? Though there are few cases on point, it is logical that a voluntary manslaughter charge would be appropriate since all the elements of voluntary manslaughter are satisfied.

2. Involuntary Manslaughter

The traditional American model includes the crime of involuntary manslaughter. Since the crime is manslaughter as opposed to murder, the offense does not involve malice aforethought and the killing is unintentional. There are two very different types of involuntary manslaughter: misdemeanor-manslaughter (also called unlawful act) and criminally negligent homicide. These two facets underlie the traditional rather obscure way of defining involuntary manslaughter: involuntary manslaughter involves an unlawful act (misdemeanor manslaughter) or a lawful act in an unlawful manner (criminally negligent homicide).

a. Criminal Negligence

A person who acts with criminal negligence that causes death may be guilty of involuntary manslaughter. Consistent with the view that criminal law does not criminalize the result of merely negligent conduct, which is the province of tort law, involuntary manslaughter traditionally applies to someone who kills as the result of *criminal* negligence, which involves an especially significant departure from the conduct of a reasonable person. Some jurisdictions call this variety of homicide *criminally negligent homicide* rather than involuntary manslaughter.

A few jurisdictions have softened this rule and extend involuntary manslaughter to a killing that is the product of ordinary negligence. Others take the opposite view and raise the bar considerably, providing that involuntary manslaughter requires proof of subjective awareness of the risk and then ignoring the known risk. This type of carelessness may be called "recklessness" in the particular locale. *Mo. Rev. Stat. § 565.024* (first degree involuntary manslaughter involves a reckless killing; second degree includes a criminally negligent killing).

It is common for involuntary manslaughter to be applied to someone whose negligence consists of an *omission* to act. As discussed more fully in Chapter 4 on *actus reus*, criminal liability may extend to an omission to act when the defendant had a duty to act. For example, a school teacher at a school crossing has a duty to ensure that children cross the street safely. If the teacher is drunk and passively watches a child cross the street in front of a truck that has not stopped, the teacher may be guilty of involuntary manslaughter if the truck strikes and kills the child. The teacher's criminal negligence consists of the failure to act while under a duty to do so. Crimes based on negligent omissions may conflict with other important values. For example, a few jurisdictions specifically respect a parent's right to make choices for children based on religious tenets and provide a defense to homicide when the child dies because the parents' religious beliefs led them to refuse medical treatment. *Ark. Code Ann. § 5-10-101.*

In a jurisdiction having a traditional American homicide law, if the defendant's careless acts cause a death, the trier of fact may be faced with a choice between involuntary manslaughter (for criminal negligence) and second degree murder (for depraved heart carelessness). The decision may depend on the specific facts of the accidental homicide and the definitions used for depraved heart and criminally negligent behavior. Often, depraved heart requires a subjective awareness of a serious risk and a decision to press on anyway ("I knew it was risky but what the heck"), while criminal negligence involves the failure to perceive the risk ("I should have seen the risk but failed to do so").

b. Misdemeanor Manslaughter (Unlawful Act Doctrine)

The second way of establishing involuntary manslaughter is the so-called misdemeanor manslaughter (or unlawful act) rule. A person is guilty of involuntary manslaughter if he or she commits a homicide during the commission of an unlawful act other than a felony triggering the felony murder rule. The unlawful act may be the commission of a misdemeanor or, in some locales, a felony otherwise excluded from the felony murder rule, or, rarely, even an act in violation of the law (perhaps including a municipal ordinance violation) though not amounting to a felony or misdemeanor.

The typical illustration of the unlawful act type of involuntary manslaughter is a homicide resulting from a traffic violation, such as speeding. Another is a death resulting from the illegal sale of liquor to an underage person or to someone known to be drunk.

As seen with the felony murder rule, many jurisdictions also limit coverage of the misdemeanor manslaughter rule by including only dangerous misdemeanors where there is a reasonable foreseeability of dangerousness (or including only *mala in se* misdemeanors—those considered evil in themselves as opposed to evil simply because the law makes them a misdemeanor).

Many modern jurisdictions, including the Model Penal Code, reject the unlawful act doctrine. They view it as imposing too great a liability for an accidental death resulting from the commission of a minor offense.

L. Model Penal Code and Other Modern Criminal Statutes

1. Overview of Traditional and Modern Homicide

While the Pennsylvania model of homicide was adopted by most American jurisdictions in the 1800s, over time many locales changed their homicide law. Often they adopted a modified version of the Model Penal Code. Sometimes their homicide laws were a hybrid that included elements of both the Pennsylvania approach (such as retaining felony murder) and the Model Penal Code (rejecting the premeditation-deliberation formula).

2. Overview of Model Penal Code Homicide Categories

The Model Penal Code rejects the traditional American approach in many ways, but does retain some of its categories. Model Penal Code §§ 210.1–210.4 has three criminal homicide crimes: murder, manslaughter, and negligent homicide. *Murder* is defined as a criminal homicide that occurs purposely, knowingly, or recklessly under circumstances manifesting extreme indifference to the value of human life. Reflecting a very distant relationship to felony murder, the MPC provides that the recklessness and indifference are presumed if the killer or an accomplice is engaged in the commission or attempt to commit or flight after committing a robbery, rape and other violent sexual intercourse, arson, burglary, kidnaping or felonious escape.

Manslaughter under the MPC is a homicide committed recklessly or, though technically murder, is committed under the influence of extreme mental or emotional disturbance for which there is a reasonable explanation or excuse. Taking its usual subjective approach, the MPC states that the reasonableness of the explanation or excuse is determined from the viewpoint of a person in the actor's situation under the circumstances as the actor believes them to be.

Negligent homicide in the MPC is a killing committed with criminal negligence, which is a gross deviation from the standard of a reasonable person.

3. Schematic Summary of Model Penal Code

Homicide Provisions

Crime	Means of Killing
Murder	Purposely or knowingly, or recklessly under circumstances manifesting extreme indifference to the value of human life
Manslaughter	Recklessly, or committed under influence of extreme emotional disturbance for which there is reasonable explanation or excuse
Negligent Homicide	By criminal negligence

4. Model Penal Code Compared with Traditional American Approach

The MPC and the traditional American approach share some similarities. Both have the crime of murder, though the MPC has only one "degree" of murder while the traditional American approach, using degrees of murder, adopts two categories: first and second degree. The MPC discards the malice aforethought and premeditation-deliberation formulas. While both the MPC and traditional American model consider a reckless homicide to be murder, the MPC requires that it be recklessness with an extreme indifference to the value of human life, obviously a most serious variety of carelessness that may require more callousness than the depraved heart facet of second degree murder under the traditional American approach. Reflecting vestiges of the traditional felony murder rule and first degree murder's list of felonies, the MPC establishes a presumption that the "extreme indifference to the value of human life" exists if the actor killed while involved in one of six enumerated serious felonies, including robbery and rape. Note, however, that liability for murder under the MPC is not automatic because the prosecution may still have to prove that the defendant acted recklessly during commission of the felony since the presumption, alone, may be insufficient to convince the trier of fact that the "extreme indifference" element is satisfied.

Both the MPC and traditional American models have the crime of manslaughter (called voluntary manslaughter in the traditional American model and simply manslaughter under the MPC) for killings as the result of extreme mental anguish. The MPC characterizes this state as "extreme emotional disturbance" while the traditional American model calls it "heat of passion." A related but important difference is that the traditional American model requires that the killing be the product of provocation, while the MPC merely indicates that the extreme emotional disturbance must have a "reasonable explanation or excuse," which may not satisfy the provocation requirement in traditional American jurisdictions.

The MPC adds a category of manslaughter occurring through a reckless killing, which is a less extreme variety of recklessness than will satisfy the MPC's definition of murder (which requires recklessness manifesting an extreme indifference to the value of human life). This MPC reckless manslaughter may be the equivalent of the depraved heart carelessness that the traditional American approach includes as second degree murder.

Both the MPC and the traditional American approach embrace criminal negligence as a culpability for criminal homicide. Under the MPC such negligence engenders liability for criminal negligent homicide and under the traditional model it is classified as involuntary manslaughter. Another distinction is the acceptance of the misdemeanor-manslaughter rule. While the traditional American model uses the misdemeanor-manslaughter approach, the MPC rejects it as it does the more serious felony murder rule.

M. Vehicular Homicide

Many American jurisdictions have added *vehicular homicide* (sometimes called *vehicular manslaughter*) to their homicide offenses. The crime may be less serious than second degree murder but more serious than involuntary manslaughter. It often requires that the defendant operate a *motor vehicle* (sometimes including *aircraft* and *watercraft* or, generally, a *vessel*) with gross negligence or recklessness, causing a death. A few states extend it to vehicular death caused by ordinary negligence and at least one makes it a strict liability crime if the death is the proximate cause of the driver's use of drugs or alcohol. *Colo. Rev. Stat. § 18-3-106.*

Typical examples of liability for vehicular homicide include drivers who kill because they were intoxicated by drugs or alcohol, fell asleep (not necessarily because of alcohol or drugs), knew they had bad brakes, had a seizure from known epilepsy, or drove too fast or on the wrong side of the road. Some locales limit vehicular homicide to defendants who are intoxicated, whose capacity to operate the vehicle is impaired by alcohol or drugs, or whose blood contains at least a specified concentration of alcohol.

N. Suicide and Assisting (or Aiding) or Attempting Suicide

The common law held that suicide by someone of sound mind and sufficient age was a felony. Even attempting, unsuccessfully, to kill yourself was a misdemeanor. And assisting someone in committing suicide was also a crime. Modern jurisdictions clearly reject the crime of suicide and attempted suicide. Model Penal Code § 210.5, for example, does not recognize the crime of suicide or attempted suicide. The reasoning is simple: punishment is both inappropriate and inefficacious since it is hardly likely to deter someone bent on self destruction.

1. Causing or Assisting Suicide

Most states today recognize a crime of causing or assisting someone else's suicide, sometimes called self-murder. A typical model makes it a crime knowingly to cause or assist another person to attempt a suicide. *Mo. Rev. Stat.* *§ 565.023(2)* (voluntary manslaughter includes knowingly assisting another in the commission of self-murder); *Alaska Stat. § 11.41.100* (first degree murder includes, with the intent to cause death, compelling or inducing any person to commit suicide through duress or deception); *Ark. Stat. Ann. § 5-10-106* (crime of physician-assisted suicide); *Fla. Stat. § 782.08* (is manslaughter deliberately to assist another person in commission of self-murder). Model Penal Code § 210.5, for example, includes a crime of causing suicide by force, duress or deception, and of assisting another person's suicide. The assisting suicide offense is a felony if the defendant "causes" the actual or attempted suicide.

A small minority of American jurisdictions do not criminalize assisting a suicide. The United States Supreme Court has upheld state laws that prohibit causing or assisting suicides, finding that the Due Process Clause does not include the right to assist someone in a suicide. *Washington v. Glucksberg*, 521 U.S. 702 (1997).

2. Killing Another While Attempting Suicide

An interesting fact situation arises when a person, while unsuccessfully attempting suicide, accidentally kills another person. The person who survives the attempted suicide may face homicide charges for the unintended death. For example, assume that S attempts suicide by jumping from a bridge. P, a police officer, sees S on the bridge and tries to intervene, but falls into the river below and is killed while attempting to rescue S. If S survives, he or she may be prosecuted for second degree murder (through depraved heart recklessness), or involuntary manslaughter (through criminal negligence or perhaps even the commission of a bridge-related misdemeanor).

Checkpoints

- The usual view is that the victim of homicide must be born alive, though some jurisdictions expand it to killing a fetus.

- The traditional definition of death is the irreversible cessation of circulatory and respiration functions. Most jurisdictions add an alternate brain death standard, present for the irreversible cessation of all functions of the entire brain, including the brain stem.

- The year and a day rule is a traditional limit on liability for homicide but is rejected in virtually all modern jurisdictions.

- Though American jurisdictions differ markedly in their homicide laws, the two major approaches are the traditional American view (based on the Pennsylvania statute) that revises the common law to include degrees of murder, and the Model Penal Code.

- Under the traditional American model, murder involves a killing with malice aforethought; manslaughter lacks malice aforethought.

- Malice aforethought is present when there is the intent to kill, intent to injure seriously, depraved heart carelessness, and the commission of a felony resulting in death.

- Modern jurisdictions severely limit the felony murder rule.

- Under the traditional American model, first degree murder includes a wilful, deliberate, and premeditated homicide or one occurring during the commission of a listed felony.

- Under the traditional American model, second degree murder is a homicide where there is the intent to kill (but not both deliberation and premeditation), the intent to injure seriously, the commission of certain felonies, and depraved heart recklessness.

- Under the traditional American model, voluntary manslaughter involves a killing in the heat of passion produced by legally sufficient provocation that would lead a reasonable person, and did lead the killer, to kill rashly and without adequate cooling time.

- Under the traditional American model, involuntary manslaughter is a killing by an unlawful act (the misdemeanor manslaughter rule) or by criminal negligence.

- The Model Penal Code has three homicide crimes: murder, manslaughter, and negligent homicide.

- A careless killing under the Model Penal Code may satisfy any of the three categories of homicide, depending on the gravity of the carelessness and the killer's subjective awareness of risk.

- Vehicular homicide is a new crime covering a killing through the careless operation of a vehicle; often the carelessness must be caused by intoxication.

- Suicide and attempting suicide are no longer crimes, but intentionally assisting or causing someone to commit suicide is a crime in most jurisdictions.

Chapter 9

Rape and Other Sexual Offenses

Roadmap

- The common law elements of rape
- Modern statutory development of rape and sexual assault crimes
- Resistance and the meaning of consent
- Types of fraud that will negate consent
- The elements of statutory rape
- Rape-shield statutes

A. Introduction

The offense of rape is among the most controversial in the criminal law. The common law approach to the crime has been heavily, and persuasively, criticized for its focus on the conduct of the victim, usually a woman, both during the commission of the offense and at other times unrelated to interaction with the perpetrator. The law of rape has undergone vast changes over the past thirty-five years, and the states take a number of different approaches to the crime. The variation between the laws means that generalizations are difficult, and the same statutory language may be interpreted in contrary ways.

B. Elements of Rape

Blackstone described common law *forcible rape* as "the carnal knowledge of a woman forcibly and against her will." The elements of the crime required the government to prove: (1) *sexual intercourse*, (2) *against a woman*, (3) *by force or threat*, and (4) *against her will and without consent*. Most often the common law required the victim to resist, and some courts described this requirement as undertaking the "utmost resistance" to the attack. The common law did not recognize a crime of rape if the victim were a male, although *sodomy* was an offense that did not require proof of force and could be prosecuted against both participants.

1. Modern Statutes

The modern reform in the states has changed the scope of the offense significantly. Some states renamed the crime *"criminal sexual conduct,"* and many added sexual assault as a separate offense. The statutes expand the offense to cover both penetration and sexual touchings, and usually add coverage beyond female victims by adopting gender-neutral language. The crime can include different degrees that permit greater or lesser punishment depending on whether the crime involved contact or actual intercourse, the type of victim involved, or if it resulted in specified harms to the victim. For example, Wisconsin makes it a first degree crime to have sexual contact or intercourse if it results in the victim becoming pregnant, while it is a second degree offense if, *inter alia*, the victim is injured or contracts a disease. *Wisc. Stat. Ann. 3940.225.* While common law rape was viewed as a type of assault crime, many of the modern sexual assault statutes incorporate notions of personal privacy and sexual autonomy within the scope of the prohibited conduct.

2. Sexual Intercourse

The sexual intercourse (or "carnal knowledge") element required that the perpetrator effect some penetration of the female victim, and even the *slightest penetration* was sufficient for conviction. Expert medical testimony that the female sex organ has been damaged or injured can provide evidence of sexual intercourse, although such harm is not required to prove the crime. The victim's testimony can be sufficient to establish this element.

Forcible rape does not require an emission, nor must there be a penetration for any specific period of time. For example, an impotent male can commit the crime of rape so long as the penis penetrates the victim's sex organ. Under the English common law, a boy under the age of fourteen was presumed to be unable to commit the crime, but contemporary statutes do not recognize such an exemption from liability.

3. Mens Rea

The common law did not include an explicit intent element for rape, and *general criminal intent* was often accepted as the applicable *mens rea* for the crime. There has been some dispute whether a *reasonable mistake of fact* about the victim's consent can be offered to a rape charge. If general intent requires that the defendant act voluntarily in pursuing a course of conduct that shows a morally blameworthy state of mind, then a defense that the man was mistaken about the woman's consent would appear to negate the moral blameworthiness aspect of general intent.

Some state courts, however, do not follow the moral blameworthiness approach and interpret the general criminal intent for rape as requiring only that the defendant intend to engage in sexual intercourse, so that even a reasonable mistake will not be a valid defense. Other states permit a mistake of fact defense regarding consent unless the defendant was *negligent* in believing the victim consented to the sexual intercourse. In these jurisdictions, to establish that the error was not negligent, the defendant must present some evidence on which a reasonable mistake could have been made regarding the victim's consent, otherwise an instruction on the issue will not be given. One court requires "substantial evidence that the defendant honestly and reasonably, but mistakenly, believed that the victim consented to sexual intercourse." *People v. Williams*, 841 P.2d 961 (Cal. 1992).

4. Force or Threat

The common law required that the sexual intercourse be the result of *force* ("forcible compulsion") or a *threat* of force upon the victim. Force involves some application of physical pressure to the victim, or the use of a weapon. The amount of force required has been subject to dispute, and it is difficult to separate the issue of force from consent, although courts generally require that each element be proven separately. The more common view of the amount of force needed to prove rape is that it must be greater than that required for the penetration of the victim's sex organ, but relatively little additional force has been found to be sufficient. In *State in the Interest of M.T.S.*, 609 A.2d 1266 (N.J. 1992), the New Jersey Supreme Court held that the force incident to penetration was sufficient to establish the element.

A threat adequate for rape must be to inflict *physical harm* on the victim or a third-party if the victim does not submit to the sexual intercourse. A threat of non-physical harm has been held to be insufficient to establish the force for rape. For example, a threat by a high school principal that he will not allow a student to graduate unless the students engages in sexual intercourse with him is coercive, but does not meet the "force" requirement for the crime of rape.

The victim's *fear of the assailant* alone is insufficient to prove force, although it can be evidence of the threat. In *State v. Rusk*, 424 A.2d 720 (Md. 1981), the Maryland Court of Appeals held that the reasonableness of the victim's "apprehension of fear was plainly a question of fact for the jury to determine." If a victim stated that she engaged in sexual intercourse because the defendant was significantly larger or stronger, and therefore she was afraid of him, that in itself would not be sufficient proof of force. However, an *implied threat* conveyed through the actions of the defendant, particularly if that person is a stranger to the victim, may be sufficient to establish the force element.

5. Consent

a. Requirement of Consent

An issue closely related to force under the common law is whether the sexual intercourse is *against the will* of the victim and *without her consent*. As proof that the intercourse was nonconsensual and therefore against the victim's will, the common law required that the victim respond to the threat of rape with the "*utmost resistance.*" As described by the Wisconsin Supreme Court, "[t]here must be the most vehement exercise of every possible physical means or faculty within the woman's power to resist the penetration of her person, and this must be shown to persist until the offense is consummated." *Brown v. State*, 106 N.W. 536 (Wis. 1906). Thus, verbal resistance, including screams and demands that the defendant cease the intercourse, could be insufficient proof of resistance. Modern reform of the rape laws has moved away from this view of proving a lack of consent as requiring the prosecution to show some measure of resistance. Courts also recognize that consent can be revoked even after sexual activity has begun. In *State v. Flynn*, 329 P.3d 429 (Kan. 2014), the Kansas Supreme Court held, "It is the continuation of nonconsensual intercourse by compulsion that makes the offender's act rape, not the offender's failure to immediately respond to the victim's withdrawal of consent."

b. Criticism of Consent Element

The resistance requirement for proof of rape has been heavily criticized, and most modern statutes and courts reject imposing on the prosecution the burden of proving any physical resistance by the victim. The view that victims must place their lives in danger, or increase the possibility that the perpetrator will inflict serious bodily harm, in order to demonstrate the lack of consent is inconsistent with other crimes in which the victim is not required to respond to force or a threat for the crime to occur. The absence of resistance can be a factor, however, in determining whether the victim consented to the sexual intercourse. To the extent that courts do not require proof of a significant application of force or recognize implied threats as sufficient to establish the non-consent element, then the victim's resistance may be relevant on the issue of consent and the absence of force.

c. Burden of Proof

The common law placed the *burden of proof* on the government to show that the victim did not consent to the intercourse. Some recent statutes do not make consent an element of the crime, but a defendant can raise it as a defense to a rape charge to negate whether there was force. In *State v. W.R., Jr.*, 336 P.3d 1134 (Wash. 2014), the Washington Supreme Court held that it violated due process to require a defendant to prove consent by a preponderance of the evidence, so that once there was some evidence of consent then the prosecution bears the burden of proving a lack of consent beyond a reasonable doubt. A different approach was adopted by New Jersey in *Interest of M.T.S.*, 609A. 2d 1266 (N.J. 1992), where the court held that absent explicit permission from the party, there is no consent to the sexual intercourse. Most jurisdictions have not moved to this point on the issue of consent, and even *Interest of M.T.S.* recognized that permission could be based on reasonable inferences from the conduct of the party.

Some states have removed a defendant's mistaken belief about the victim's consent as a defense to a charge. For example, Kansas provides that "it shall not be a defense that the offender did not know or have reason to know that the victim did not consent to the sexual intercourse,...." *Kan. Stat. Ann. §21-5503(e)*.

d. Verbal Resistance as Lack of Consent

Courts generally take the "*no means no*" response seriously and view a rejection of sexual intercourse as sufficient in itself to establish a lack of consent. For example, if a woman states that she does not wish to be with a person, continued requests for sexual intercourse need not be met by repeated denials to show that the woman has not consented. With the requirement of physical resistance eliminated or lowered in most states, so that a physical response is unnecessary to demonstrate the victim's lack of consent, *verbal resistance* has become more the focus. Therefore, today an explicit rejection of sexual intercourse will be accorded greater weight than at an earlier time in the development of American rape law.

e. Affirmative Consent

To combat the problems associated with unconsented sexual encounters on college campuses, California enacted a provision that requires colleges and universities in the state to adopt a student conduct policy requiring "affirmative consent" of both parties for sexual activity. *Cal. Ed. Code § 67386*. There must be an "affirmative, conscious, and voluntary agreement" for the conduct, and "[i]t is the responsibility of each person involved in the sexual activity to ensure that he or she has the affirmative consent of the other or others to engage in the sexual activity." The consent must be ongoing and can be revoked at any time, and a "[l]ack of protest or resistance does not mean consent, nor does silence mean consent." The policy covers complaints involving possible school disciplinary proceedings and does not directly affect the criminal law, although there may be an effort in the future to adopt heightened consent standards for a defendant seeking to avoid conviction for a sexual misconduct charge.

C. Special Situations

1. Acquaintance Rape

The most difficult rape cases to prove often involve situations when the parties are known to one another, and a significant number of cases involve intimate partners. This is what is sometimes referred to as "*acquaintance rape*" or "*date rape*" cases in which the participants have had some degree of interaction that colors their verbal and non-verbal communications. Particularly difficult cases involve rape charges when there is *no forensic evidence* to show a use of force, or the forensic proof is equivocal regarding whether the physical manifestation is consistent with non-consensual sexual relations. These are sometimes referred to as "he said, she said" cases in which the primary—and sometimes only—evidence is the *testimony of the participants* and their understanding of whether the victim did or did not consent to the encounter. Often, the perpetrator concedes that there were sexual relations, and asserts that he or she believed the victim consented. The outcome of the acquaintance rape case may depend on whether the prosecution bears the burden of proving nonconsent or the defendant must prove the victim consented, and whether a reasonable mistake as to consent is a defense.

2. Incapacity

If a woman suffered from an *incapacity*, which is a legal inability to consent to sexual intercourse, then the common law found that sexual intercourse with such a victim was rape regardless of the lack of force or absence of evidence of non-consent. Two common forms of incapacity are *unconsciousness* and *mental impairment*. Some modern statutes take a different approach by making the incapacity of the victim the equivalent of the use of force, rather than as evidence of a lack of consent. "Incapacity" is generally defined as a person incapable of *understanding* or *controlling* his or her conduct. For example, a person suffering from significant mental retardation would be unable to consent to sexual intercourse because this person would not be capable of understanding the nature of the sexual act. The defendant must be aware of the incapacity to be convicted of rape.

Certain so-called *"date rape" drugs*, such as GHB and Rohypnol, which are odorless and colorless, can render the person who ingests them physically unable to resist but otherwise conscious. Often the person has no memory of what occurred while under the drug's influence. If the defendant *secretly administers* such a drug to a person, or a third party does it with the *defendant's knowledge*, so that the victim is unable to resist sexual intercourse, then the defendant is guilty of rape regardless of any verbal expressions by the victim. Some modern statutes, in grading the offense of rape, make the use of intoxicants to permit sexual intercourse, even when the victim is not rendered unconscious, equivalent to the use of force.

If alcohol is given to a person without his or her knowledge and renders the person helpless or unable to understand the conduct, then sexual intercourse with the victim would constitute rape. Similarly, if alcohol is voluntarily consumed and the victim is rendered unconscious, then sexual intercourse would be a rape. Some modern statutes grade the crime in this circumstance as a lower offense. For example, Louisiana defines the lesser crime of "simple rape" as including "[w]hen the victim is incapable of resisting or of understanding the nature of the act by reason of a stupor or abnormal condition of mind produced by an intoxicating agent or any cause and the offender knew or should have known of the victim's incapacity." *La. Rev. Stat. 14:43.*

The more difficult case is when the victim *voluntarily ingests* the drug or alcohol and then seems to agree to sexual intercourse while appearing conscious but significantly inebriated. In that circumstance, the analysis will depend on the reasonableness of the defendant's belief that the victim consented, which will be affected by knowledge of the victim's condition and ability to meaningfully consent to the act. The majority of modern statutes do not make it a crime to engage in sexual intercourse with a person who is voluntarily intoxicated unless there is a lack of consent.

3. Fraud

In all areas of law, consent obtained by force or threat is not valid. A more difficult case is when one person misleads another so that the second person agrees to engage in sexual intercourse when the person otherwise would not have consented, *i.e.*, *fraud*. The common law divided fraud into two types: *fraud in the factum* and *fraud in the inducement*.

a. Fraud in the Factum

Fraud in the factum occurs when the defendant misleads the victim regarding the *nature* of the physical act, so that the person does not know it is sexual intercourse. Sexual intercourse that is the product of fraud in the factum is considered rape. For example, a doctor tells a female patient he will be conducting a pelvic exam involving a probe of her sex organs, and then inserts his penis into the victim's vagina. While the victim consented to a medical examination, there was no valid consent to the intercourse and the doctor is guilty of rape.

b. Fraud in the Inducement

Fraud in the inducement means that the person is misled by the defendant's *misstatements* or *omissions* about the factual circumstances surrounding the sexual intercourse, but the person understands that sexual intercourse is involved and consents to it. This type of fraud is not considered rape. For example, a defendant calls a woman and informs her that she has been infected with a serious disease, and the only way to obtain an innoculation against it is to engage in sexual intercourse with a man who has built up antibodies to the disease. The woman agrees to the sexual intercourse in order to ward off the disease. That is fraud in the inducement, and under the common law the defendant is not guilty of rape.

California adopted a provision that creates a lesser-degree of rape if a victim's "consent is procured by false or fraudulent representation or pretense that is made with the intent to create fear, and which does induce fear, and that would cause a reasonable person in like circumstances to act contrary to the person's free will, and does cause the victim to so act." *Cal. Penal Code § 261*. Note that fraud regarding a person's background, wealth, or romantic intentions would not come within this statutory prohibition, and so sexual intercourse as a result of such misstatements would not be rape.

c. Impersonation

Courts usually characterize as fraud in the factum the situation in which a defendant *impersonates the husband* of a woman and engages in sexual intercourse with her. For example, a man learns that his friend wears a mask at times when he has relations with his wife. Late one evening, while the husband is working, the man enters their apartment, dons the husband's mask, and then engages in sexual intercourse with the wife, who believes it is her husband. The defendant would be guilty of rape because the wife only consented to sexual intercourse with her husband and not the defendant, who induced the relations through fraud regarding the identity of the partner. Some courts have extended this analysis to couples in intimate, non-marital relationships, but others limit it to married couples. See *People v. Morales*, 150 Cal. Rptr. 3d 920 (Cal. App. 2d Dist. 2013).

4. Marital Immunity

The common law rule was that a man could not rape his wife, and therefore any sexual intercourse between them was not subject to prosecution for that crime. Sir Matthew Hale asserted that the marital bond meant that "the wife hath given up herself in this kind unto her husband, which she cannot retract." Under this outmoded view, the wife was, in effect, the property of the husband, and the law would not inquire into their sexual relations. The husband, however, still could be prosecuted for battery against his wife even if he could not be convicted of the more serious rape charge. The Model Penal Code continued this approach by limiting rape as a "male who has sexual intercourse with a female not his wife. . . ."

Modern rape and sexual assault statutes have eliminated the marital immunity, including a proposal to reform the Model Penal Code. Some limitations remain on prosecuting a spouse, such as South Carolina's requirement that a spouse must report the offense within 30 days unless they are not living together at the time of the offense. *S.C. Code § 16-3-615.* The majority of jurisdictions eliminated the marital immunity expressly, while others removed phrases such as "not his wife" or "to whom he is not married" from the definition of the offense. A few states remove the immunity if the husband and wife are separated but not divorced, while others permit it as a defense if there is no evidence of force or a threat.

D. Statutory Rape

Even though all sexual assault crimes are now incorporated into statutes, sexual intercourse involving a *young victim* traditionally has been called "*statutory rape*" because it was added to the common law forcible rape offense by statute. All states recognize as rape any sexual intercourse in which a participant is under a specified age, usually defined by statute as the age of consent. The rationale for the crime is that those under a specified age are incapable of making a reasoned decision to have sexual relations. In order to protect children from engaging in harmful conduct and to deter those who would prey on youth, the law will punish anyone who engages in such conduct with them based solely on the age of the victim.

Many modern statutes grade the offense depending on the age of the victim, without regard to any purported consent or lack of force. Sexual intercourse with a person under twelve usually will be punished the same as forcible rape, the most serious offense, while relations with victims under fourteen and sixteen can result in a conviction for a lesser charge or degree of sexual assault.

1. Age Element

a. Majority View: Strict Liability

Statutory rape is often described as a "*strict liability*" offense, but that is a misnomer. The crime requires the general intent to engage in sexual intercourse with the victim. In most jurisdictions, the *age* of the victim is a *strict liability element*, so that there is no *mistake of fact* defense regarding that attendant circumstance. For example, a defendant, who had impaired mental faculties, engaged in sexual intercourse with a neighbor who told him she was sixteen-years-old, when in fact she was just under fourteen. Although the defendant had no reason to believe otherwise, and his belief in her statement was reasonable, he would be guilty of statutory rape because the age element is one that does not require proof of any knowledge of age or intent other than general criminal intent; the mistake is irrelevant.

b. Minority View: Mistake Recognized

Some states reject the strict liability approach and permit defendants to raise a mistake of fact defense regarding the defendant's age. For example, Washington recognizes a defense "based upon declarations as to age by the alleged victim." *Wash. Rev. Code § 9A.44.030.*

2. Scope of Liability

Under the common law approach to statutory rape, both participants in the sexual relations could be prosecuted if each is under the age designated by the statute. Some states limit prosecutions to those cases in which there is a *minimum age difference* between the participants. If both are approximately the same age, then neither would be subject to prosecution, while typically if one is more than two or four years older than the other, the older one can be prosecuted. In addition, most statutes do not contain gender-specific language, so that a woman who engages in sexual intercourse with an underage boy can be convicted of statutory rape.

E. Proving Rape

1. Prosecuting Rape

Rape is one of the most difficult crimes to prosecute, particularly if the victim and defendant had a relationship before the conduct at issue and there is no evidence of force. The common law placed significant hurdles in the way of successful rape prosecutions, such as the *resistance* requirement that could result in a "not guilty" verdict, despite the woman's repeated verbal rejections of sexual intercourse, if the jury viewed her conduct as somehow falling short of the "utmost resistance." Another was the requirement enacted at one time in some states that prevented a conviction based on the *uncorroborated testimony* of the victim.

A third significant problem was that the victim's sexual history could be used as evidence to demonstrate that she was promiscuous and not someone evoking sympathy from jurors. Sometimes this background information was viewed as relevant on whether she consented to intercourse with the defendant. The approach was to "*put the victim on trial,*" which had the obvious effect of discouraging the reporting of the offense. The law operated under a concern that rape claims could be easily falsified, a suspicion not seen for other common law offenses like robbery or burglary. This attitude was reflected in Hale's assertion that "rape ... is an accusation easily to be made and hard to be proved, and harder to be defended by the party accused, tho never so innocent." For these reasons, rape is one of the most underreported offenses.

2. Rape Shield Statutes

In order to protect rape victims from the embarrassment of having to expose their sexual history to public scrutiny, all states and the federal government have enacted *rape-shield statutes* to limit the admissibility of evidence related to the victim's *past consensual sexual acts* and reputation for chastity. Federal Rule of Evidence 412 is typical in excluding both "[e]vidence offered to prove that any alleged victim engaged in other sexual behavior" and "[e]vidence offered to prove any alleged victim's sexual predisposition." Some critics of rape shield statutes argue that they sometimes exclude evidence that might be logically relevant on the issue of consent. On the other hand, the exclusion is justified to combat the penchant to use it to assail the character of the victim.

For example, a woman informs the police that a man with whom she is acquainted forced her to engage in sexual intercourse the prior evening while they were discussing a fight she had with her boyfriend. The man then drove her to the boyfriend's house, and a few hours later she went to the police station to report the crime. The man states that she consented, and the forensic evidence is unclear regarding whether there was forcible sexual intercourse. A hospital report indicates that the woman stated that she and her boyfriend engaged in sexual relations before she went to report the rape to the police. The man argues that the hospital report should be admitted to show that he did not rape her because a rape victim is unlikely to engage in consensual sexual relations after a traumatic experience.

Under the federal rape-shield statute, however, the evidence is not admissible because it is offered to prove the victim "engaged in other sexual behavior." Under Federal Evidence Rule 412 and similar state provisions, the only time evidence of a victim's sexual activity with *another person* is admissible is to show that another person is the source of semen, pregnancy, or a sexually-transmitted disease. The Rule also permits evidence of the victim's sexual background as proof of the defendant's own prior sexual encounters with the victim in order to show the victim consented to the sexual intercourse at issue in the case.

Despite the worthy purpose of rape shield statutes to protect the rape victim from public embarrassment, in unusual cases the rape shield exclusionary rules may violate the defendant's due process right to a *jury trial*, to *present a full defense*, and the Sixth Amendment right to *confront adverse witnesses*. This possibility is recognized by the federal evidence rule, which specifically provides for the admission of "evidence the exclusion of which would violate the constitutional rights of the defendant."

3. Prior Sexual Assaults

A more recent development in this area has been the enactment of statutes permitting evidence of a *defendant's prior sexual assaults* to show his or her character and to permit jurors to reason that the defendant may well be guilty of current sex abuse charges because he or she committed sexual assaults in the past. Federal Rule of Evidence 413(a) provides: "In a criminal case in which the defendant is accused of an offense of sexual assault, evidence of the defendant's commission of another offense or offenses of sexual assault is admissible, and may be considered for its bearing on any matter to which it is relevant." Note that the sexual assaults need not involve the same or similar victims, and the defendant does not have to have been convicted of a crime, just shown to have committed the offense. Although such *propensity* evidence normally is excluded from trial, in the case of sexual assaults a legislative determination has been made that the defendant's character for engaging in such conduct is important to the determination of guilt.

F. Model Penal Code

Model Penal Code § 213 sets forth a number of sexual assault offenses, including rape, gross sexual imposition, deviate sexual intercourse, and corruption of minors. While the Code expanded the types of conduct subject to prosecution beyond sexual intercourse, it adopted the approach of the common law before more recent statutory developments by limiting the crime to forcible sexual relations by men with women, and only when the victim is not the perpetrator's wife. It did move away from the common law by not requiring proof of the victim's lack of consent, nor does the woman have to physically resist. The Model Penal Code also retained the corroboration requirement for victim testimony, and required the judge to instruct the jury to view the victim's testimony "with special care in view of the emotional involvement of the witnesses and the difficulty of determining the truth with respect to alleged sexual activities carried out in private." These provisions, along with the gender-specific language limiting the crime, made this portion of the Code largely an anachronism.

An effort is now under way in the American Law Institute (ALI), which is responsible for drafting the Model Penal Code, to modernize the provisions for this offense. For example, a new proposed crime of "Sexual Intercourse Without Consent" would make it a misdemeanor to knowingly or recklessly have "sexual intercourse with a person who at the time of the act of sexual intercourse has not given consent to that act." This approach advances the position that affirmative consent, either by words or conduct, is always a prerequisite to sexual intercourse. The revision is still in the process of being drafted and has not yet been approved by the ALI, and a change in the Model Penal Code is likely to come in the near future.

Checkpoints

- Common law forcible rape was limited to sexual intercourse with a female victim.

- Modern statutes have expanded the crime to include sexual contact, and often provide for different degrees of the offense.

- Rape is a general intent crime, and a defense of mistake of fact may be available on the issue of consent.

- The common law placed the burden of proof on the prosecution to establish the victim did not consent, but some modern statutes remove that requirement, in which case consent is a defense to the crime that the defendant can offer.

- While the older common law cases required the victim to put up the "utmost resistance" to the attack, that is no longer required. Verbal resistance may be important to establishing that the crime was "against the will" or that the victim did not consent.

- Acquaintance or date rape cases are the most difficult to prosecute because of the prior relationship between the parties, the lack of forensic evidence of force in many cases, and the conflict between the recollections of the defendant and victim regarding consent.

- The common law found that consent was not valid when there was fraud in the factum, regarding the nature of the contact, but not if there was fraud in the inducement, regarding collateral issues but not the sexual act itself.

- Some modern statutes make it an offense for certain types of fraud that would not be prosecuted under the common law.

- Rape-shield statutes limit evidence about the victim that may be admitted at trial regarding prior sexual acts with third parties, although the defendant's right to confront witnesses may require the introduction of evidence that might otherwise be excluded by such statutes.

- The Model Penal Code provisions on sexual offenses are in the process of being revised.

Chapter 10

Assault, Battery, and Related Offenses

Roadmap

- The two varieties of assault
- The definition of battery and how it differs from assault
- The Model Penal Code's combined assault-battery crime
- Aggravated versions of assault and battery
- The defenses of consent and parental/teacher authority
- The definition of mayhem
- The definition of reckless endangerment
- The definition of stalking and how it differs from assault and battery

---

A. Assault, Battery, and Related Offenses: In General

A number of criminal laws punish behavior that harms a person but does not involve death. These range from offensive touching to causing serious bodily injury, from frightening to causing the risk of physical harm. Often punishment for these offenses is scaled according to the gravity of the harm the victim suffers. Assault and battery closely resemble their tort cousins and are the primary crimes in this category. Many modern criminal codes combine these two crimes into a single offense, often called assault. Other crimes punishing people for conduct involving physical or mental harm or the risk of such harm include mayhem, reckless endangerment, and stalking.

B. Assault

Assault is a pervasive crime that punishes two different types of behavior: attempted battery and frightening.

1. Attempted Battery

One variety of assault punishes an *attempted battery*, which means the defendant failed in an intentional effort to inflict bodily injury on the victim. An illustration would be B who tried to strike V with a fist but missed when V ducked. Note that this variety of assault requires an intent to do physical harm, not merely an intent to frighten someone. Thus, if B, above, swung at V but intentionally missed in an effort only to frighten V, B would not be guilty of the attempted battery-type of assault.

For the attempted-battery assault, the actor must come quite close to actually inflicting the harm. This differs from other inchoate "attempt" crimes, such as attempted murder, that may expand liability to preliminary acts occurring well before the intended harm was possible. Thus, a person may be guilty of attempted murder for buying a gun or driving with the gun toward the place where the shooting is to occur, but these acts would be too remote to satisfy the requirements for the attempted-battery version of assault.

Some jurisdictions further qualify the requirements for attempted-battery type of assault by mandating that at the time of the assault the defendant must have had the *present ability* to inflict the batter. An *apparent ability* is insufficient in these jurisdictions for an attempted-battery assault. Thus, in such a jurisdiction if D has a realistic toy gun and shoots it at V while yelling "Bang," D will not be guilty of assault of the attempted-battery type since D did not have the present ability to cause the harm, even if V thought the gun was real and believed he or she was being shot.

The attempted-battery version of assault focuses on the actions of the defendant rather than the reaction of the victim. A person may be guilty of this assault even if the victim were unaware that the defendant had carefully aimed a loaded rifle at the victim's head and pulled the trigger but the bullet missed its target when the victim sneezed.

Since assault includes an attempted battery, some cases have had to decide whether there is a crime of *attempted assault* of the attempted-battery type. In other words, can one attempt an attempted battery? Most authorities answer no, but strong arguments can be made there should be a crime of attempted assault of the apprehension-of-fear variety of assault. Thus, if D tries to frighten V by shooting a gun into the air but V is deaf and does hear the shot, one can argue D should be guilty of attempted assault for intentionally doing every-thing necessary to frighten V. The fact that V is deaf does not detract from the fact that D has exhibited a willingness to frighten D and has taken every step to do so. Looking at individual moral blameworthiness, D's culpability may be the same whether or not V actually was frightened.

2. Frightening

A second variety of assault reaches those who intentionally cause someone to be reasonably frightened of suffering immediate bodily harm. This crime, drawn from tort law, punishes those who intentionally cause fright rather than actual physical harm. Returning to the toy gun illustration above, while D, the actor who yelled "bang", would not be guilty of attempted-battery assault, he or she might be guilty of the apprehension-of-fear type of assault if the victim was aware of D's actions and frightened by them.

Note that no present ability to inflict the bodily harm is needed for this type of assault, but the victim must suffer actual fright from the experience. Thus, a person who points an unloaded gun at another and causes the victim to fear being shot is guilty of apprehension-of-fear assault even though there was no chance that the weapon could discharge.

Usually the victim is held to the standard of a *reasonable person* with nor-mal sensibilities. This means that the fright must be such that a reasonable person would suffer when presented with the defendant's conduct. If the par-ticular victim is especially sensitive and experiences fright when an ordinary person would not, the necessary harm for this type of assault is absent. For example, assume that D, with the intent to frighten V, points to the sidewalk near V's foot and says to V, "look at that ant." D would likely not be guilty of apprehension-of-fear assault if V, particularly fearful of ants because of a traumatic childhood experience, became terrified at the sight of the small creatures so near to V's body. V's fright response is simply unreasonable, though real.

Ordinarily for this type of assault the defendant must intend to frighten; merely being negligent or even reckless is insufficient. Thus, if D drives a car carelessly and frightens a passenger or person crossing the street, D is not guilty of apprehension-of-fear assault. On the other hand, if D drove too fast in order to frighten a passenger or person crossing the road, D would be liable for this type of assault.

C. Battery

1. Physical Harm

While by definition assault usually does not involve any physical contact, the common law crime of *battery* does. In the most general terms, a battery is physical contact without consent. The contact may involve various degrees of harm, ranging from serious bodily injury to any bodily injury to offensive contact.

2. *Mens Rea*

In every jurisdiction battery embraces intentional harm. The doctrine of transferred intent applies. This means that if D throws a rock at A intending to strike A but misses and hits B, D has committed a battery of B as if D had aimed the rock at B.

In addition, many locales also extend battery to reckless (sometimes requiring ignorance of a known risk) or even criminally negligent (serious deviation from the standard of care of a reasonable person) injuries. When a jurisdiction chooses to apply its criminal battery laws to physical harm caused by criminal negligence, it follows the long American tradition of punishing criminally negligent homicides. Criminal law usually does not penalize physical injury caused by ordinary negligence, which is remediable by tort law.

A few American jurisdictions even extend their battery crimes to harm caused by "unlawful" acts, which means the defendant committed the harm while engaged in a violation of another law, such as one defining a misdemeanor or municipal infraction.

D. Modern Combined Offense: Model Penal Code

Many modern criminal codes, recognizing that the lines between assault and battery are often blurred, combine them into one crime, often named "assault." These follow Model Penal Code § 2.11 which includes both the attempted battery and frightening facets of assault, as well as the causing injury ingredient in traditional battery.

More particularly, MPC § 2.11 contains two crimes: assault and aggravated assault. Assault, called "*simple assault*," is a misdemeanor that covers purposely, knowingly, or recklessly causing bodily injury (or even negligently by means of a deadly weapon) or attempting by "physical menace" to put another in fear of imminent serious bodily injury. The more serious crime, *aggravated assault*, reaches the person who attempts to cause serious bodily injury, or who causes serious bodily injury, purposely, knowingly, or recklessly under circumstances manifesting extreme indifference to the value of human life, or attempts to cause bodily injury with a deadly weapon.

Departing from the approach of many jurisdictions, the MPC's aggravated assault provisions do not include so-called assault-with-intent-to crimes, such as assault with intent to rape or murder. The MPC punishes these under attempt law (*i.e.,* attempted rape or attempted murder) rather than under assault law.

Note that the MPC strays from some traditional authority by not extending assault to unwanted physical contact; more significant harm is needed. The Code also does not cover harm caused by negligent behavior unless a deadly weapon is involved.

E. Conditional Assaults and Batteries

Sometimes a person will make a threat to do a physical harm unless the victim performs a specified activity. For example, D may threaten to kill V unless V gives D a kiss or money. In such cases, the common law has long held that this *conditional threat* is sufficient *mens rea* for frightening-assault since the victim suffered fear of the possibility of future harm.

F. Aggravated Versions of Assault and Battery

It is common for assault and battery laws to contain more than one offense or degree in order to recognize that certain factors make the crime more serious, meriting more severe sanctions. Routinely the least serious assaults and batteries are classified as misdemeanors. More serious versions are felonies and are frequently differentiated by the word "aggravated" or "with a deadly weapon" in their name. There are four types of aggravating elements.

1. Degree of Harm

Every jurisdiction treats batteries causing significant harm as aggravated offenses, often named aggravated assault or battery. Modern jurisdictions tend to describe the extra harm as "serious bodily injury" as distinguished from "bodily injury." Often these terms are defined in a way similar to MPC § 210.0. *Serious bodily injury* means bodily injury creating a substantial risk of death or which causes serious, permanent disfigurement, or protracted loss or impairment of the function of a bodily member or organ. *Bodily injury* refers to physical pain, illness, or any impairment of a physical condition; it does not embrace psychological trauma as the only injury.

2. Especially Grave Intent

It is common for jurisdictions to impose greater penalties for assaults committed with an especially grave purpose, usually the commission of a serious felony. Examples include crimes such as assault with intent to murder, rob, or rape. Proof of these offenses requires evidence of both the assault as well as the intent to commit the object crime (*e.g.*, murder).

3. Nature of Victim

Many jurisdictions give special protection to certain categories of victims. An assault or battery on someone in that group may be deemed an aggravated form of assault or battery and may carry additional punishment. Typical examples include victims who are elderly, pregnant, or otherwise especially vulnerable because of physical or mental disabilities, and public servants who are injured while performing their duties. This latter group may include assaults or batteries against police officers, firefighters, or school teachers who are injured while working. Sometimes the crime requires that the defendant know the victim's status at the time of the assault or battery.

4. Especially Dangerous Means of Inflicting Harm

Another aggravating factor is that the assault or battery was performed with a "deadly weapon," "dangerous instrument," or an item "likely to cause serious bodily injury or death." Thus, while assault with a fist may be deemed "simple assault," assault with a pistol may be aggravated assault carrying a much more severe sentence.

As one would expect, there has been much written about the meaning of *deadly weapon* in assault statutes. Many jurisdictions follow MPC § 210.0(4) and define it as a weapon, device, instrument, material or substance which in the manner it is used or intended to be used is known to be capable of producing death or serious bodily injury. Obviously, this includes all the usual suspects: knives, poisons, guns, and clubs. It also covers items not ordinarily characterized as deadly weapons but which may be used as such, including automobiles, a vicious dog or deadly snake, and even a jail cell's bars or cement floor (when the defendant slams the victim's head against the bars or floor).

Whether an unloaded gun is a deadly weapon for purposes of aggravated assault laws has been the subject of many cases. The rule that has emerged is that it is not ordinarily considered to be a deadly weapon since it cannot fire a bullet, but it could be so considered if the gun were used as a club and were of sufficient size and weight to inflict serious injury in the manner it was used or threatened.

For an aggravated assault or battery, note that the dangerous instrumentality must be used in the crime. If the defendant has a knife in his or her pocket but does not use it in any way in the assault, the crime would not be aggravated assault simply because of the presence of the knife on the defendant's person.

G. Special Defenses: Consent and Parental Authority

1. Consent

Assault and battery, like other crimes, are susceptible to the usual criminal defenses, such as insanity, self defense, defense of property, crime prevention, and the like, discussed later in this book. But, like sexual offenses, assault and battery ordinarily may be defended by establishing that the victim *consented* to the harm. In general terms, such consent is routinely recognized as a defense to minor injuries, but ordinarily not accepted for serious injuries. Thus, boxers consent to being hit by the opponent while in a boxing match (and thus the consent would be a defense to a battery charge), but they do not consent to being knifed during that same boxing match. Moreover, for public policy reasons, the criminal law does not allow consent as a defense to serious injury or death, unless the context makes consent appropriate. The latter exception is why a surgeon who performs an operation with the patient's valid consent does not commit a battery even though the patient may suffer serious injury or even death from the surgery.

Consent, of course, must be "legal" consent, recognized as valid under the law. Thus, a person who is mentally incompetent, intoxicated, or under age may lack the legal capacity to consent to a battery. The same is true if consent is obtained by force, duress, or deception. *MPC § 2.11.*

2. Special Responsibility for Care, Discipline, or Safety of Others

Many people in our society are tasked with the responsibility to care for others. Sometimes this responsibility comes from a job, relationship, or even an emergency situation. And sometimes the use of force is necessary to meet this responsibility. For example, a prison guard may need to use force to separate and restrain two prisoners in a fight, a parent may spank a child in order to punish the child for misbehavior, and a teacher may use force to restrain an out-of-control student. Jurisdictions routinely provide a defense to a criminal assault or battery charge when this force is used appropriately. Tort law is similar. Excessive force, however, may not protect against an assault or battery charge. *See, e.g., Ore. Rev. Stat. 161.205* (actor must "reasonably believe" force is necessary); *Model Penal Code § 3.08* (actor must believe — not "reasonably believe" — force is necessary). Often the force that may be used is limited to non-deadly force or that not known to create the risk of serious bodily injury. A standard approach is to ask whether the amount of force used was proportional to the harm threatened.

a. Parents and Guardians

The law has long recognized that parents (including step parents and guardians) have a legal privilege to use reasonable force in disciplining or otherwise helping their children. Some statutes characterize this as safeguarding or promoting the child's welfare. Occasionally this defense is extended to babysitters and other caregivers as well as to persons charged with the welfare of mentally or physically incompetent people. Thus, a parent who spanks a child using an appropriate amount of force does not commit a battery, even though the child feels pain and the parent intended to cause the discomfort. On the other hand, a parent who uses excessive force has no such privilege and may be guilty of battery or even aggravated battery if the harm is significant.

b. Teachers

Traditionally, teachers, like parents, are given a privilege to use reasonable force to discipline their pupils. The United States Supreme Court upheld a school teacher's right to paddle children without violating the Cruel and Unusual Punishment Clause of the Eighth Amendment. *Ingraham v. Wright*, 430 U.S. 651 (1977). In jurisdictions recognizing this privilege, teachers do not commit a battery when their actions are reasonable under the circumstances.

Some jurisdictions reject this common law privilege and have enacted statutes or administrative rules barring teachers from using such force other than in an emergency when necessary to protect a child from harm. Teachers who paddle children in violation of such rules may commit an assault or battery.

c. Correctional, Emergency and Transportation Workers

People, such as guards, and transportation and medical personnel, who work in hospitals, correctional institutions or provide emergency assistance or transportation services, may need to use force to do their jobs. For example, prison guards may have to use force to remove a prisoner from a cell or to prevent the prisoner from escaping, emergency room personnel may have to restrain an uncontrollable person who needs life-saving treatment, or bus or subway employees may have to deal with a drunk or mentally ill passenger. American law provides a defense if the force is reasonable under the circumstances.

d. Preventing Suicide

The privilege to use reasonable force is often extended to preventing a suicide or otherwise preventing serious physical injury.

H. Related Crimes: Reckless Endangerment, Mayhem, Stalking, and Harassment

Although assault and battery are the most frequently invoked crimes involving physical and mental harms, there are several other crimes, discussed in greater detail below, that also cover these harms to various degrees. *Mayhem*, an ancient crime, punishes physical disfigurement. *Reckless endangerment* covers conduct that puts someone in danger of physical harm. *Stalking*, a cousin of apprehension-of-fear assault, reaches repeated conduct that causes someone to fear harm.

1. Mayhem

Common law, and a minority of current criminal codes, recognize the narrowly-defined crime of *mayhem*, which makes it an offense for permanently rendering the victim incapable of self defense or fighting an enemy. The crime covers such actions as cutting off a hand or severely damaging a leg to the extent that the victim cannot walk. It also extends to permanent disfigurement, such as cutting off the victim's nose or ear. The crime of mayhem ordinarily requires the actor to have intentionally caused the harm, though sometimes "maliciously" will suffice. Recklessness or criminal negligence are insufficient mental states.

When a jurisdiction has modernized its criminal laws and has chosen to repeal its mayhem statutes, conduct formerly condemned as mayhem may be prosecuted as aggravated battery. The permanent harm sufficient for mayhem would likely satisfy the definition of serious bodily injury in aggravated battery statutes.

2. Reckless Endangerment

Many jurisdictions, following Model Penal Code § 211.2 , include *reckless endangerment* as a serious misdemeanor or low-level felony that punishes creating the risk of serious physical harm. It covers those who recklessly (or even negligently, in some jurisdictions) engage in conduct that places or could place another person in danger of death or serious bodily injury. This crime complements more specific offenses, such as reckless driving, discharging a weapon in public, or dropping items from bridges or tall buildings.

It should be noted that reckless endangerment reaches conduct that may not constitute an assault or battery since it deals with creating a *risk* of harm rather than causing actual harm. Reckless endangerment may occur even though the "victim" suffered neither physical harm nor fear of harm. For example, if D, while drunk, places his or her young children in the back of a pickup truck and takes them on a high-speed "fun ride" on a winding country road, D may be guilty of reckless endangerment for subjecting the children to the risk of serious physical injury, even though no one was injured and the children laughed with delight during the entire journey. Other reckless endangerment examples from case law include dropping a rock from a bridge onto a road below, shooting into an occupied house or car, blocking a road with a boulder, stabbing a person with a knife, and setting fire to a living room couch.

If the defendant's conduct creates no risk of physical injury, reckless endangerment is not established. For example, if the defendant points a toy gun at a victim and threatens to shoot, the lack of risk of harm takes the offense out of the realm of reckless endangerment, but the acts may still constitute an apprehension-of-fear assault.

If by the defendant's reckless acts the victim is injured, the crime may be reckless battery. If the victim is killed, the defendant may be guilty of a reckless homicide offense, which could constitute second degree murder or involuntary manslaughter under the traditional homicide categories.

3. Stalking and Harassment

Stalking is a relatively recent statutory crime that varies considerably among the states. In general terms, stalking laws are designed to stop people who make repeated efforts to harass someone and cause the victim to be in fear. Typical examples include individuals who repeatedly telephone or follow the victim, come to the victim's house or job, or threaten to harm the victim or victim's family.

More particularly, such laws punish people who repeatedly (often defined as more than once or constituting a pattern of activity or involving a course of conduct) are physically or visually close or make threats to someone or contact that person in a manner that induces fear in the person being harassed. Ordinarily the fear must be of physical harm, but some states also include causing fear of sexual intrusion or even property damage. Sometimes the test of fear is objective: conduct that would place a reasonable person in fear. Mental harm other than fear of physical injury may also be covered, such as acts causing the victim to suffer anxiety or emotional distress. Note that the government need not prove the defendant intended to carry out the threats; stalking occurs as long as the victim fears that the defendant will do so.

The *mens rea* of stalking is often twofold. First, the defendant must intend to do the prohibited acts, such as making repeated phone calls to the victim. Second, in many jurisdictions the defendant must do so for the purpose of causing the victim to be in fear or suffer mental anxiety and the like. Some states do not require the harm to be intentional; causing it knowingly or, in a few states, recklessly or, rarely, negligently, will suffice.

It is common for jurisdictions to add an *aggravated stalking* crime to their basic stalking offense. The more serious offense carries a greater punishment and, in many states, reaches people whose actions knowingly violated a court order prohibiting such contact. Another model is for aggravated stalking to cover defendants with a prior conviction for stalking or a similar crime, the use of a deadly weapon, or the victim's status as a minor.

Checkpoints

- Assault is a crime that covers both attempted battery and causing apprehension of battery.

- Battery requires physical contact.

- Modern statutes, such as the Model Penal Code, combine assault and battery into a single crime.

- Aggravated assault or battery is a more serious crime than ordinary assault or battery and is distinguished from those lesser crimes by requiring a greater degree of harm, an especially grave intent, a particular victim, or an especially dangerous means of committing the crime.

- Consent and the privilege that parents and teachers have to use reasonable force in performing their duties may be defenses to assault and battery if the amount of force is within the scope of the consent or reasonable under the circumstances for parents and teachers.

Checkpoints, *cont.*

- Mayhem is a crime involving the infliction of permanent disfigurement.
- Reckless endangerment is a crime punishing the reckless creation of the risk of physical harm.
- Stalking is a crime that punishes repeated efforts to harass the victim.

Chapter 11

Theft, Property Offenses, and Burglary

Roadmap
- Historical development of theft offenses
- Model Penal Code use of a consolidated theft offense
- Elements of common law larceny
- Differences between larceny and larceny by trick and larceny by bailee
- Elements of embezzlement
- Elements of false pretenses
- Differences between larceny, embezzlement, and false pretenses
- Elements of receiving stolen property
- Elements of robbery and larceny from the person
- Elements of extortion
- Elements of burglary

A. Overview

1. Historical Development of Theft and Related Crimes

Theft and related crimes have a long history and are often based on technical distinctions that no longer seem sensible. Accordingly, modern jurisdictions have dispensed with many of these distinctions and have created a far more simple approach to property-related crimes.

In general terms, *larceny* was the basic theft crime. It involved taking property from someone else's possession with the intent to deprive that person of it permanently. Because larceny did not reach certain thefts, such as those by bank tellers who take money from customers and pocket it, the English Parliament created the crime of *embezzlement* to cover those who obtain possession of property through a position of trust, then violate that trust by converting the property to their own use. While larceny and embezzlement covered many thefts, it did not reach those who told lies about past or present facts in order to obtain title (as opposed to possession) to property. Parliament then enacted the crime of *false pretenses* to cover this variety of thieves.

Larceny, embezzlement, and false pretenses are the three basic theft crimes that do not involve threats or violence. But if the thief obtained the property from the person or presence of the victim by using force or the threat of force, the crime was more serious—*robbery*. And if the property was obtained by threats of future harm, it was called *extortion*.

Another important offense, often involving a theft, is *burglary*, a common law felony that punishes an entry into a dwelling at night with the intent to commit a felony. Unlike the theft offenses, burglary is complete upon the breaking and entry into the home when the perpetrator intends to engage in any felony, including crimes of violence like murder and rape; it does not require that the victim suffer any loss or harm.

2. Modern Consolidated Theft Statutes

The common law theft offenses are built around technical distinctions rooted in the agrarian economy at the time. To a modern person trying to understand theft law, the distinctions drawn are often dubious, involving legal fictions that defy reality, yet were important historically to address new forms of misconduct that might have gone unpunished otherwise. In an effort to eliminate these outdated historical distinctions, most states have consolidated the various theft offenses into one provision. These new provisions create a generic theft offense that covers conduct that historically would be prosecuted as larceny, embezzlement, false pretenses, and the like.

The Model Penal Code provided a critically important impetus for the modernization of theft law when it adopted a unified approach to the theft offenses in § 223. One goal of the MPC revision was to eliminate many of the traditional distinctions in theft law to permit the prosecution to indict a thief without having to make decisions about technical issues such as whether the thief had possession or custody at the time the property was taken. Section 223.2(1) provides:

> Conduct denominated theft in this Article constitutes a single offense. An accusation of theft may be supported by evidence that it was committed in any manner that would be theft under this Article, notwithstanding the specification of a different manner in the indictment or information....

In addition to an ordinary taking, the combined theft offense includes obtaining property by deception, threat, and failing to make the required disposition of funds received.

California's consolidated theft statute, California Penal Code § 484, representing a modern approach to theft law, defines the consolidated theft offense as follows:

> Every person who shall feloniously steal, take, carry, lead, or drive away the personal property of another, or who shall fraudulently appropriate property which has been entrusted to him or her, or who shall knowingly and designedly, by any false or fraudulent representation or pretense, defraud any other person of money, labor or real or personal property, or who causes or procures others to report falsely of his or her wealth or mercantile character and by thus imposing upon any person, obtains credit and thereby fraudulently gets or obtains possession of money, or property or obtains the labor or service of another, is guilty of theft.

Another illustration of a consolidated theft statute is Colorado statute § 18-4-401:

> Theft. (1) A person commits theft when he knowingly obtains or exercises control over anything of value of another without authorization, or by threat or deception, and:
>
> (a) Intends to deprive the other person permanently of the use or benefit of the thing of value; or
>
> (b) Knowingly uses, conceals, or abandons the thing of value in such manner as to deprive the other person permanently of its use or benefit; or
>
> (c) Uses, conceals, or abandons the thing of value intending that such use, concealment, or abandonment will deprive the other person permanently of its use and benefit; or
>
> (d) Demands any consideration to which he is not legally entitled as a condition of restoring the thing of value to the other person.

The Colorado statute looks at the defendant's *mens rea* when the defendant either obtains or exercises control over the property. The "exercises control" element means that the statute covers someone who obtains the property with a clean mind but then, while exercising control over it, has a change of heart and decides to steal it. Note also that a consistent *mens rea* theme is that the thief intends to deprive the owner of the item permanently or at least knows that his or her treatment of the item will cause the permanent deprivation. Finally, the Colorado provision, like other consolidated statutes, reaches people who obtain or control property by various means: without permission, by threat, or by deception.

Despite the goal of eliminating many of the historical distinctions in theft law, some of the common law terminology remains important for applying such provisions. This is often because courts interpret the operative terms of the new consolidated theft statutes by referring to the historical meaning of the terms such as "fraud," "taking," and "steal."

B. Terminology

It is impossible to comprehend some of the arcane distinctions in American theft law without first understanding certain terminology derived mainly from property law. As important as these terms are, often it is difficult to state definitively the exact interest someone has in a particular item of property since the definitions are fuzzy, overlapping, and defy common sense. Modern statutes often eliminate them as relevant factors in theft law.

1. Custody

A person has *custody* of personal property when he or she has physical control over it, usually for a very short period of time and usually for a very limited purpose. For example, if you go to a craft fair and pick up a leather item in order to examine it, you have custody of that item while looking it over. You have physical control over it for a short time and for this limited purpose. For historical reasons, English courts held that a servant who received property from his or her master to deliver to a third party had custody, but not possession, of the property. As described below, the master retained constructive possession of the item.

2. Possession

Possession is similar to custody but involves a legally greater dominion over the property. Someone who is in possession of property has *actual* or *constructive* control of the property with the intent to possess it and the right to exclude others from possessing it at that time. Constructive possession is a legal fiction where the law deems a person to be in possession of an item that may not be in the person's immediate control but is within an area over which the defendant has some legal control or a sufficiently serious legal interest to be regarded as possessing the items.

For example, someone who rents a car has possession of that car. The renter has the right to exclusive use of it and to keep others from using it during the rental period. While driving the car, the renter has actual possession of it. The renter has constructive possession of it while the car is parked in the garage of the hotel where the renter is staying. Someone who steals the car from the garage has committed larceny from the renter because the taking was from the renter's constructive possession. Similarly, if a third-year law student loans a first year law student a casebook, the first-year student has possession of it for the duration of the loan. Someone who steals the dictionary from the borrower has committed larceny from that person.

Historically, English law held that if a third person gives property to a servant to deliver to the master, the servant had possession, not custody, of the property. But, as noted above in the discussion of custody, if the situation were reversed, the master gave property to the servant to deliver to the third person, the servant had mere custody of the property. This arcane distinction was important, as will be discussed below, because larceny was a theft from someone else's possession. If the thief (here, the servant) already had possession of property from the master and then decided to keep it, then he or she would not be guilty of larceny.

3. Ownership (Title)

A person who *owns* property has *title* to it. Although title is often defined in terms of a document or electronic record, it properly refers to the legal ownership of the property. The person who owns property may dispense with it as he or she wants (subject, of course, to environmental and other laws). Thus, the owner of a lawn mower may use it, sell it, give it away, blow it up, paint it, take it apart or even bury it. The expansive right that is inherent in ownership of property is in marked contrast to the limited rights of someone in possession of it and to the extremely limited rights of a person with custody. Ordinarily the person who has title to a piece of property also has possession of it. But sometimes ownership and title are separated, as when a car rental company owns a car but rents it to a customer. During the rental period the rental company still has title (*i.e.*, owns the car) and the customer has possession.

4. Abandoned

Property is abandoned if the person with title to it relinquishes all interest in the property. Abandoned property is not owned or possessed by anyone.

Someone who takes abandoned property does not commit a theft since it usually will belong to whomever picks it up first.

C. Larceny

As noted above, under the common law the basic theft offense was larceny, which required the prosecution to prove six elements: (1) a trespassory (2) taking and (3) carrying away of (4) personal property (5) of another person (6) with intent to steal. The prosecution had to prove each element beyond a reasonable doubt.

1. Trespass

In general terms, larceny requires that the property be obtained by *trespass*, which means without the consent of the victim or without some other legal justification for taking someone else's property. The concept of trespass in theft law does not refer to trespass on property (*i.e.*, entering property without permission). The trespass for larceny is similar to the tort of trespass to chattels, which involves interference in the goods of another. While initially the trespass for larceny referred to obtaining someone's property by stealth, such as by sneaking onto their property and taking a necklace from a jewelry box or by picking a pocket to obtain a wallet, it grew to include obtaining someone's property by fraud. The latter became known as the crime of larceny by trick, and is discussed below.

2. Taking

Larceny required not only a trespass but also mandated that the trespass involved some *taking*, which is sometimes described as the *caption* element of the offense. To constitute a taking sufficient for the crime of larceny, the thief must obtain actual control or dominion of the item, such that it dispossesses another of control over the property. Thus, a pickpocket who removes a wallet commits a larceny because he or she took property from the possession of the victim.

3. Carrying Away (Asportation)

The third element of a larceny is *carrying away* the property, or *asportation*, which involves the slightest movement of the property. The asportation requirement also provides circumstantial evidence of the defendant's intent to commit a larceny by demonstrating the desire to remove property from the control of the possessor. While some movement, even a "hair's breadth," will suffice in most jurisdictions, it must entail a change of position of the object, but the property need not be moved to a different location. The movement need not be a complete or successful removal of the property from the premises. For example, a shoplifter who places an item in his or her coat pocket with the intent to steal it commits a larceny even if stopped by an employee before leaving the store.

If the movement is insufficient to establish removal of the property, then a finding of the requisite intent to steal may also be lacking. Under the English common law, a defendant could still be convicted of attempted larceny even if there was no asportation, but that crime was a misdemeanor while a completed larceny was a felony subject to the death penalty. The asportation element is important to establishing whether the defendant completed the larceny, or whether it is only an attempt.

The Model Penal Code and modern theft statutes diminish the role of the asportation element, requiring only proof that the defendant gained possession of the property. The statutes do not focus as much on the actual movement of the property. Many states have combined the different common law crimes into a single statutory theft offense, but still may use common law terminology to some extent. When common law terminology is used in the modern theft provisions, the asportation element may be retained as a crucial element. For example, California's carjacking statute requires a "felonious taking of a motor vehicle" from the possession of another. The California Supreme Court held that the offense was based on larceny, so the "taking" element required proof of asportation of the car. *People v. Lopez*, 6 Cal. Rptr.3d 432 (Cal. 2003).

4. Personal Property

a. Personal v. Real Property

Under the common law, some items were not subject to prosecution as a larceny. To qualify for larceny, the property must be both tangible and capable of being possessed by an individual. Often this category was characterized as *personal property*. This excluded real property and any appurtenances, such as structures or physical improvements. Similarly, crops and trees that were in the ground were considered part of the real property and could not be the subject of a larceny action if a person entered the property and removed them, although that person could be prosecuted for a criminal trespass. If the crops or trees had been harvested, however, then they were considered the personal property of the landholder.

For example, if a farmer harvests hay and leaves it on the ground to be baled the next morning, and D takes the harvested hay to feed a horse, then D is guilty of larceny since the hay is the type of property covered by larceny. On the other hand, if D cut the farmer's hay while it was still in the ground and then fed it to the horse, D would not be guilty of larceny since the hay would be considered part of the land. Some jurisdictions stretched the traditional view and held that once the hay was separated from the ground, it could be the object of larceny, irrespective of whether it had just been cut or had been cut some time ago and was laying on the ground when taken for the horse.

b. Animals

Under traditional larceny law, animals that were wild on land or in the air or water were treated the same as crops and trees and could not be the object of larceny, while domesticated animals, such as horses or cattle, or animals that had been killed, were deemed personal property covered by larceny. Many jurisdictions plugged gaps in their larceny law by enacting specific statutes that brought the theft of certain animals, such as fish that had been caught, within the ambit of larceny. The Model Penal Code and modern theft laws dispense with these distinctions by extending their theft laws to cover taking both "movable" and "immovable" property or "anything of value" in which any person other than the actor has an interest.

c. Intangible Property; Services

Certain intangible property rights are represented by physical objects, such as a negotiable instrument, promissory note, or share certificate. Under the common law, these were not personal property so that their taking was not a larceny. Modern statutes have eliminated this technicality, so that title documents and securities are property for the purpose of theft prosecutions.

Services were also not covered by traditional larceny law as they were not considered personal property. Every jurisdiction has now expanded its theft law to cover theft of services. Sometimes this occurs by a statute punishing theft of particular services, such as electricity or cable television broadcasts. Modern consolidated theft laws, such as the Model Penal Code, routinely define services as among the items that the generic theft offense covers.

While of course the common law did not embrace the theft of technology that could not even have been contemplated, modern laws now reach computer files and electronic transmissions as the object of crimes akin to larceny, such as theft of access devices and authorization codes.

5. Of Another

a. Possession v. Ownership v. Custody

Larceny requires theft of the property *of another*. Although the trespassory taking and carrying away of property must be that of another person, ownership is not what determines whether the property is that of "another person." Larceny is a crime against possession and not ownership. The offense occurs when the victim is dispossessed of the property by the defendant, even if the defendant owns the property. For example, D gives a valuable bracelet to a pawn shop as security for a loan. Unable to repay the loan, D enters the pawn shop and takes it from a display case. D is guilty of larceny because the pawn shop had possession of the bracelet, even though D was still the lawful owner of the property.

Just as ownership must be distinguished from possession, custody must also be so distinguished for analyzing larceny. A key legal fiction created in the common law is the distinction between custody and possession. A person in actual physical control of an item may have either custody or possession. Recall that this matters because if the person had possession and then decided to convert the property to personal use, the crime was not larceny. But if the person had mere custody, with (constructive) possession residing in someone else, then the person committed larceny when he or she took the property.

For example, a person who goes to an automobile dealership may be allowed to test drive a car. If the person drives away, ostensibly for a test drive but then takes the car home and does not return it, there is a larceny if the person only has custody of the car and not legal possession of it. Custody means that the person has use of the property for a very limited purpose, while the person giving custody, who is usually the owner, retains constructive possession of it. The owner of the dealership would remain in constructive possession of the car used for the test drive, even though the driver obtained control of it through a voluntary act by the possessor, the dealership. Under this analysis, the driver could be charged with larceny because taking the car home is a trespassory taking of property from the owner's possession without valid consent. As discussed below, if the dealership allowed an employee to use the car and that person then converted it to personal use, that would be an embezzlement.

b. Lost and Mislaid Property

American personal property law has long distinguished between property that is *lost* (the owner does not know where it was placed, perhaps because it fell out of the owner's pocket) and *mislaid* (the owner intentionally put the property in a specific place then forgot where it was). For theft law, however, the two were treated the same. The owner was regarded as having constructive possession of the lost or mislaid property. This meant that someone who took the property may have committed larceny if he or she satisfied the other elements of that crime.

But the law imposed an additional requirement for lost and mislaid property. It was well-established that a finder of lost property must make every reasonable effort to find the owner when the person has the means to do so, or else the finder may be prosecuted for larceny. A person who found lost property and converted it to his or her own use was guilty of larceny if the person had knowledge of the true owner or a means of inquiry to locate the owner. For example, an unaddressed package is left on the front porch of a house. The homeowner opens that package and sees that it contains computer components that are similar to those seen at a neighbor's house. The homeowner must determine whether the items belong to the neighbor before taking permanent possession of the components, otherwise the person may be guilty of larceny.

On the other hand, if there is no basis on which to determine who might be the rightful possessor of the package, then the finder can use the property without committing a larceny. Model Penal Code § 223.5 largely reflects the common law approach by making it a crime if the defendant knows the property has "been lost, mislaid, or delivered under a mistake as to the nature [a real diamond ring was mislabeled as a fake diamond ring] or amount [$10,000 was delivered instead of $1,000] of the property or the identity of the recipient" and, "with purpose to deprive the owner thereof," he or she "fails to take reasonable measures to restore the property to a person entitled to have it."

c. Employees and Bailees

The distinction between possession and custody is particularly important in the context of employment relationships and bailments. In these cases, the issue is whether an employee who takes property is guilty of larceny. For ordinary employees provided with property of the business, the employee is deemed to have custody of it and the employer is considered to be in actual or constructive possession of it, at least for items that remain on the premises or are provided the employee for only temporary use to assist the enterprise. This means that if the employee steals the business property, he or she is guilty of larceny because the taking was from the possession of the owner of the business. For example, a laptop computer provided by the employer would remain in the constructive possession of the business even if the employee is allowed to take it home for a limited period of time to do work on it. The same computer provided to a traveling salesperson who uses it for extended trips and is authorized to use it for both business and personal transactions may well be considered to have been in the salesperson's possession, not just custody. Any taking in the latter situation would not be a larceny but rather an embezzlement.

The rule for bailees is more complex. A *bailment* is a relationship in which one person, the *bailor*, entrusts property to another person, the *bailee*, for a particular purpose. Often a bailment is created by contract. Examples of a bailment include a car left in a parking lot and jewelry left for repair. A bailment is important in civil law since the bailee has special responsibilities to care for the property left by the bailor. In theft law, the existence of a bailment is relevant because, for historical reasons, the bailee is deemed to have possession (not just custody) of the property. Thus, if the bailee takes the property for personal use, he or she is not guilty of larceny since the bailee had lawful possession and did not obtain it from the victim's possession.

The issue becomes even more complex in the context of shipping packages. For bailees, the analysis involves yet another legal fiction developed by the English common law courts to deal with a new form of theft. As the agrarian economy shifted to manufacturing, finished goods needed to be shipped long distances, a task undertaken by companies that could transport goods. The problem was that delivery personnel would sometimes steal the contents of a shipment, and the issue was whether they could be prosecuted for larceny when the property was voluntarily given to them. As a general rule, the person shipping the property was considered a bailor and the person transporting the item was the bailee. Thus, if a person transporting goods (considered a bailee) stole a package that was being transported, technically the theft was not larceny since the bailee had possession and the theft was not from the possession of the shipper, who had surrendered possession.

In an era when business interests were viewed as needing protection from thieves and safe delivery of goods was essential for commercial life, this result was unacceptable. The English courts "cured" the problem by engaging in a remarkable legal fiction. The bailor, usually the owner, was deemed to be in possession of the contents of the packages at the time of the misappropriation, while the bailee was ruled to have possession only of the outer package itself. In *The Carrier's Case*, 13 Edw. IV, f. 9, pl. 5 (Star Ch. and Exch. Ch. 1473), the English court adopted the "breaking bulk" doctrine, so that when a bailee of a package broke it open and misappropriated the contents, a larceny was committed since the thief took the contents from the constructive possession of the owner. The doctrine of breaking bulk was critical in a more modern context. In *United States v. Mafnas*, 701 F.2d 83 (9th Cir. 1983), an armored car driver was convicted of larceny under federal law for removing money from cash bags that he was transporting from a bank to its customers.

The court ruled that he had possession of the bags but committed larceny when he "broke bulk" and removed the contents of those bags since he had custody, but not possession, of the contents.

d. Illegal Possessor

As a crime against possession, the common law did not require that the victim of the larceny be a lawful possessor of the personal property. This creates the potentially anomalous situation in which a defendant can be charged with stealing from a thief who took the property in a prior larceny or other unlawful act. In short, a thief can steal from a thief. The same principle applies if the item taken from the victim is contraband which no one could possess legally. Similarly, even if the owner of the property loses possession through illegal means, this does not legitimize an unlawful retaking of this property. For example, D loses a watch in an unlawful dice game and afterwards takes it from W, who won the watch in the game. D is guilty of larceny because W had possession of it, even though the means of acquiring it was illegal. Modern theft statutes and the Model Penal Code retain the same rule that a larceny occurs even though the victim had obtained possession of the property unlawfully.

6. Intent to Steal

Larceny is a specific intent crime, requiring proof that the defendant intended to permanently deprive the possessor of the property. Note that the intent (*animus furandi*) is only to deprive, but not necessarily for the sake of obtaining a gain from the act (*lucri causa*). For example, it is a larceny to take a law school rival's notes and destroy them, even though the defendant does not realize any direct pecuniary gain from the trespassory taking of the property.

a. Claim of Right

As discussed above, even if one is an owner of property, it is a larceny to take it from another person who has lawful possession of it. As a specific intent crime, however, the owner's mistake regarding the propriety of another person's possession of the property can be a defense to the larceny charge in certain circumstances. For example, an owner of a store sees a person leaving with an item tucked inside a pocket. Believing the person is a shoplifter, the owner takes the item from the person, when in fact the person had paid for it and so did not steal it. Even though the owner took the item from someone in lawful possession of it, the owner would have a valid defense to a larceny charge so long as the store owner had a good faith belief that the person did not have a right to possess it and the owner simply wanted to regain his or her own property. The rationale is that the owner did not intend to deprive the person of lawful possession of the property since the owner thought that he or she had a rightful claim to possess it.

Similarly, if the customer with the item in a pocket thought that a friend who came into the store had already paid for the item, that customer's good faith belief that he or she was entitled to possession of the item would furnish a defense to a larceny (or shoplifting) charge. Model Penal Code § 223.1(3) provides an affirmative defense to a theft charge if the defendant "(a) was unaware that the property or service was that of another; or (b) acted under an honest claim of right to the property or service involved or that he had a right to acquire or dispose of it as he did...."

b. Permanent

Larceny requires that the defendant intend to *permanently*, rather than temporarily, deprive the owner/possessor of the property. The word "permanently," however, should not be taken literally, for case law holds that this element is satisfied if the thief intends to take the property for a substantial period of time or for sufficient time to deprive the item of its value. Thus, if D takes V's car and intends to keep it for six months, then return it, D has committed larceny since the taking was for a substantial period of time. Similarly, if D steals a block of ice and plans to put it in a large bucket and leave it in the bright sun for 8 hours, then returns it to V in the form of water, D has committed larceny of the ice block because the period of time essentially deprived the victim of the value of the property.

The fact that taking an auto for only a short period of time is a defense to larceny led many jurisdictions to pass statutes creating the separate crime of *joyriding*, which punishes a temporary taking of a vehicle. If the use of the property puts is at a substantial risk of a complete loss to the possessor, however, many courts will infer an intent to permanently deprive. Similarly, taking an item that is perishable would be a permanent deprivation because of the risk of loss.

c. Continuing Trespass

The common law element of a specific intent to steal meant that the defendant's intent at the moment of the trespassory taking determined whether the conduct was a larceny. There are occasions when a person takes property temporarily and then decides to keep it. For example, a person takes another's iPod to listen to it, expecting to return it before the owner notices it missing; later that day, after using it, the person decides to keep it. At the time of the taking, there was no intent to deprive permanently, so there would not be the requisite concurrence of the elements for a larceny. Many jurisdictions solved this problem by adopting the *continuing trespass* doctrine, under which each moment that the defendant retains possession of the item is a separate caption and asportation. The larceny occurs at the moment the defendant forms the intent to permanently retain the item.

d. Single Larceny Doctrine

In cases where the defendant steals more than one item, it is necessary to determine whether the defendant is guilty of one larceny offense or multiple violations. The answer is important for two reasons. First, the sentence may be much greater if the defendant is convicted of multiple theft crimes since the judge may order a prison term for each violation to be served consecutively. In addition, multiple convictions may affect the sentence in a subsequent case under recidivist statutes. Second, theft crimes are often graded by the value of the items taken in the crime. If several items are taken and it is viewed as a single crime, the value of those items may be aggregated for purposes of determining the sentence.

Several rules have evolved to address this issue. If a defendant takes different items from the same general location, the single larceny doctrine looks to the circumstances of the offense to determine whether a defendant intended to commit multiple offenses or only one larceny. When the evidence supports a finding that the thefts were part of a continuous act or plan, a single larceny has occurred. Circumstances to be considered in assessing the defendant's intent are the location of the items stolen, the lapse of time between the takings, the number of victims, and whether there are intervening events between the takings.

For example, a person who carries three televisions from a store to a van parked outside is likely guilty of a single larceny, while taking a television from three separate stores and loading them in the van at each location is more likely to be considered three separate violations.

7. Valuing Property

Many states have different degrees of larceny depending on the value of the property taken. Traditionally there were two categories of larceny: *grand* and *petit*. Theft of an item of less than a certain value, such as $1,000, was deemed petit larceny and punished as a misdemeanor. On the other hand, if the item stolen was worth more than $1,000, it may be a felony punishable by a longer term of imprisonment. These distinctions can be very important under recidivist sentencing statutes. Many modern theft statutes further refine sentencing in theft cases by using gradations based on the value of the stolen items. For example, some jurisdictions have up to six levels of theft: less than $1,000, $1,001 to $4,999, etc. Stealing an item worth $100 may be a misdemeanor, while taking a valuable car worth $50,000 may constitute a very serious felony.

The value of stolen property is the amount that the thief would have to pay if the items or services were purchased in the open market, even for property not for sale, such as free goods or gifts. Most stolen property is in used condition and its value is the fair market value at the time it was stolen, not when it was purchased. The defendant usually does not have to specifically intend to take an item of any particular value, and it is a larceny to take even worthless property. The value of stolen retail merchandise does not include any sales tax that would be charged, so that theft of a bracelet that sells for $999 would not become a more serious crime because a consumer would pay more than $1,000 with the addition of the sales tax.

D. Larceny by Trick

Recall that larceny requires the offender to take the property by means of a trespass, defined in terms of lacking the consent of the victim. But what if the offender tells lies in order to induce the victim to voluntarily give the offender possession of the item? One could argue that the crime is not larceny since the defendant did not obtain the property by trespass when the victim consented to the transfer.

The common law dealt with this situation by stretching the boundaries of larceny by recognizing the offense of *larceny by trick*. In *Pear's Case*, 168 Eng.Rep. 208 (Cr.Cas.Res.1779), the English court found that a thief committed this form of larceny when he obtained possession of a horse by telling the owner that he intended to use it for only half a day, but actually he planned to sell it at an auction. Although it appeared that the owner voluntarily gave possession to the thief, this apparent consent was obtained by fraud and so was not viewed as lawful consent. In other words, the English court was willing to stretch the crime of larceny to include the situation where possession is obtained by fraud. After *Pear's Case*, larceny included physically taking from someone else's actual or constructive possession, as by picking a pocket or removing from a purse, as well as obtaining possession by fraud.

E. Embezzlement

In the late eighteenth century, the English common law courts were less willing to expand the elements of larceny to include new species of theft. Recall that larceny required a trespassory taking of property from someone else's possession. A thief who acquired possession lawfully with the consent of the previous possessor, and then wrongfully converted the property to his or her own use, did not commit a larceny since there was no trespassory taking from another person's possession.

The pivotal case is *King v. Bazeley*, 168 Eng.Rep. 517 (Cr.Cas.Res.1799), where a bank clerk was given money by a customer to deposit in the bank. The clerk took the money from the customer with a "clean mind," then changed his mind and decided to retain the money rather than deposit it in the bank. He was found not guilty of larceny because he never wrongfully took the property from anyone's possession. The third party bank customer voluntarily gave the clerk possession of the money, and the bank never came into possession of it. Thus, the clerk, who acquired lawful possession of the property from the customer, did not commit larceny since he did not obtain possession with an evil mind. The English court refused to create a new fiction that the bank somehow had constructive possession or the customer retained constructive possession of the money at the time the clerk decided to pocket the money.

In response, Parliament passed the first *embezzlement* statute to cover the case of an employee who received property rightfully—with a "clean mind"— as part of his or her job or position of trust and then had a change of heart and wrongfully decided to convert the property to the employee's own use. The early embezzlement statutes reached only a few categories of people, such as employees and agents, but later embezzlement laws broadened coverage to almost anyone who received possession of property through a position of trust and then wrongfully converted it. Some of the newer statutes reject the name "embezzlement" and call the crime *fraudulent breach of trust* or *fraudulent conversion*. Consolidated theft statutes include the crime of embezzlement in their generic theft offense, thus rejecting the notion that embezzlement is a discrete crime separate from other basic theft offenses.

1. Entrustment

Embezzlement is different from larceny because the victim entrusts the property to the defendant, *i.e.,* gives possession voluntarily, and the defendant then converts it to personal use. Common types of entrustments are employees who take or receive money or property on behalf of an employer (*e.g.,* the bank teller or retail clerk), businesses that receive items for repair or service (*e.g.*, the watch repair or dry cleaning shop), and fiduciaries who administer or manage property on behalf of the beneficiary (*e.g.*, lawyers and investment managers). In each of these situations, the thief acquires lawful possession of the property, and then commits embezzlement when he or she misuses it for personal purposes.

2. Conversion

Embezzlement occurs when there is a fraudulent conversion of personal property by the person with otherwise lawful possession. The harm from the offense is the breach of trust by the perpetrator, while larceny is focused more on the potential breach of the peace by the initial trespassory taking of property from the victim. The *conversion* in embezzlement must be a serious interference in the owner's property rights by the defendant who takes the property for "his or her own use." There need not be any pecuniary gain from the conversion and the embezzler actually may not get anything personally from the conversion. The focus on serious interference distinguishes embezzlement from larceny, which requires only an asportation (*i.e.*, slight movement).

For example, an expensive watch left for repair would not be converted if the technician took it home overnight to work on it. There would be a conversion if the technician sold the watch, removed the parts to put into another watch, gave it to a friend, destroyed it, or said it would be returned only if the owner paid an extra $1,000 "repair fee."

3. Fraud

Like larceny, embezzlement is a *specific intent* offense, but the intent is to *fraudulently convert* the property to personal use, but not to permanently deprive. The crime is based on the violation of the entrustment and the abuse of an otherwise lawful possession of the item, so the length of the misuse can be irrelevant to embezzlement. For example, a worker at an auto repair shop takes a customer's car for a week-long trip to a distant city and then returns it before the customer comes to pick it up. The worker would be guilty of embezzlement by using a car for an unauthorized purpose if the owner did not give permission for the worker to take the car for personal use. The worker knows that the absence of permission means that the car is only to be used for the limited purpose of repairing it, and returning the car to the owner would not obviate the embezzlement. As with larceny, a mistake as to ownership (perhaps the person thought he or she had a right to the property) or the scope of the entrustment (actor thought the use of the property was consistent with the entrustment) would be a valid defense to an embezzlement charge since the actor would not have the necessary *mens rea* for the crime. Similarly, if the intent is to return the exact same property within a short period of time, the crime may not be embezzlement because the actions were not sufficient to constitute a conversion. But the intent to return equivalent property, such as a sum of money equal to that an accountant took from a client's bank account, would likely not be a defense to embezzlement in many jurisdictions.

4. Larceny-Embezzlement Distinctions

Distinguishing between larceny and embezzlement begins by ascertaining whether the defendant has lawful possession of the property or only custody of it. Embezzlement occurs when the person with lawful possession then converts it to his or her own use. Larceny is present when the person takes the property from someone else's possession but is not given possession. For larceny, often the person will have custody when he or she takes the property, which is still in the constructive possession of the victim. The crime of larceny by trick, a variety of larceny, occurs when the person obtains possession by misrepresentation. Thus, if the person obtains possession rightfully (*i.e.*, with the consent of the previous possessor who gives possession without use of trickery) then converts the property, the crime is embezzlement. But if the person obtains possession by deception, the crime is larceny by trick rather than embezzlement. And the crime is larceny if the person simply takes the property from the victim's possession without using tricks or getting the consent of the victim.

Another critical difference between larceny and embezzlement is the person's *mens rea* at the time he or she acquired the property. If the defendant used deception to obtain possession of the property, the crime is larceny by trick (a variety of larceny discussed above), not embezzlement. Embezzlement, technically at least, requires that the person have a pure mind when first getting the property, and then convert it after having a change of heart.

F. False Pretenses

1. False Pretenses v. Larceny by Trick

Similar to the gap-filling that occurred when Parliament enacted an embezzlement law to overcome the limitations in larceny, in the eighteenth century it created the crime of *false pretenses* to address thefts involving a transfer of ownership rather than possession, which took the crime outside the common law offense of larceny. False pretenses is a statutory offense in which the defendant, intending to defraud the victim, knowingly misrepresents a present or past fact which induces the victim to give the defendant *title* to property. Since both false pretenses and larceny by trick involve misrepresenting facts in order to induce another person to give the offender an interest in property, the two crimes are often confused. The distinction between them is based on what interest the defendant obtained by means of the misrepresentation. If a defendant acquired title to the property from the owner through a material misstatement or omission, the offense is false pretenses. If the defendant merely acquires possession through false statements, then the crime is larceny by trick.

2. Elements of False Pretenses

a. False Statement of Past or Present Fact

False pretenses, like larceny by trick, requires a factual misstatement by the defendant. The statement must relate to a *past or present fact* and not future conduct or conditions. It may be delivered in writing, orally, or by other conduct that conveys information. For example, a person borrows money and agrees to repay it over a certain period of time. If at the time the loan is made the borrower had insufficient assets to repay the loan, the person did not engage in false pretenses, even if the borrower knew at the time of the transaction that repayment would not be made. The agreement to repay is a promise about future conduct, and so would not constitute false pretenses even though it relates to a present factual situation, *i.e.,* the ability to repay. However, the result may be different if at the time the loan was made the defendant told the victim that the defendant had $10,000 in the bank and would withdraw it tomorrow to pay off the debt. If the defendant lied and did not have a bank account with that amount of money in it, he or she would have committed false pretenses. The defendant would have made a false statement about a present fact. Modern statutes address this by adopting other crimes that penalize making false statements about future conduct, such as the federal bank, mail, and wire fraud provisions.

i. Omission

An omission can be the basis for a false pretenses charge if the defendant has a duty to make disclosure to the victim. This duty may arise from a fiduciary obligation created by law, for example for lawyers and trustees, or through an agency relationship, such as an employee. A contract can also give rise to a duty to disclose information, such as that obligating real estate brokers to convey certain information to their clients. The failure to disclose must relate to a past or present fact, and it must be material to the transaction.

ii. Puffery

One of the most difficult areas in determining whether a statement is false involves *sales pitches* and other types of *puffery* about the value, nature, or status of an item. A statement of opinion ordinarily cannot be the basis for a false pretenses prosecution since it does not involve a statement of fact. Yet many statements of opinion contain, or reflect, factual assertions, which creates difficult questions of liability for false pretenses. For example, a car salesperson stating "I think this car is a good value" appears to be giving an opinion because it reflects just the speaker's personal conclusion. Yet the statement "this car is a good value because it was only driven by a grandmother to church on Sunday" connects the determination of value with a factual assertion regarding the prior use of the vehicle. If the previous owner was a more typical driver than represented by the car salesperson, then that statement could be the basis for a false pretenses charge even though it incorporates an opinion. Similarly, if the odometer were rolled back to reflect a lower mileage, that would be a false statement even though the seller never used any particular words to convey an assertion of value. The usual test for whether a statement is false, rather than mere puffery, is based on what a reasonable listener would conclude.

b. Falsity

False pretenses requires the defendant to make a statement that he or she believes is *false* and that actually is false. Thus, if the defendant mistakenly thinks he or she is telling a falsehood about a present or past fact but is wrong and the statement is actually true, the crime of false pretenses is not established. For example, if the defendant states that a fine Persian rug is worth $5,000, believing it is worth only $500, the defendant does not commit false pretenses if the rug really is worth $5,000 and the defendant had simply been ignorant of its true value. The theory is that although the defendant intentionally lied, no one was actually injured since the defendant's representations were, in fact, accurate.

c. Intent and Knowledge

False pretenses requires the government to prove two *mens rea* elements: *knowledge* that the fact is false and an *intent to defraud*. If the defendant has a good faith belief that the statements were not false, or that there was no duty to disclose, then that is a valid defense to a false pretenses charge. The intent to defraud is usually inferred from the knowing misstatement or omission, because if one uses a false statement to obtain title it is reasonable to infer that it was made for that purpose.

d. Reliance (Materiality)

The victim must *rely* on the false statement, which must be *material* to the transaction transferring title, *i.e.,* important to it. Some authorities described materiality as so significant that it causes the transaction to occur. Thus, a misrepresentation is not material if the victim knew the defendant was lying, did not care whether the fact was true or false, or regarded the misrepresented fact of little importance in the decision to transfer title.

In the situation in which a person makes a number of statements, some true and others false, reliance can be shown if the false statement substantially contributed to the transfer of title. For example, a salesperson who informs a potential purchaser that "this car is a good value because it was only driven by a grandmother to church on Sunday" could be guilty of false pretenses if that is not the case and the assertion is material to the transaction. It is not a defense to a charge of false pretenses that the purchaser was gullible, or could have discovered the truth by investigating further. Like other areas of the law, the contributory negligence of a victim does not absolve a defendant of responsibility for false statements of past or present fact.

G. Forgery

Forgery is a crime related to — and often confused with — false pretenses. Forgery involves someone who, with the intent to defraud, *alters or executes a document* that is not what it purports to be. In other words, the person has created or altered a document that is not genuine. The usual illustration is the thief who steals a check, signs the name of the person to whom the check is made out, and cashes it at a bank. In some jurisdictions this conduct satisfies the requirements for false pretenses and is prosecuted as such. In others the offender would be guilty of the separate crime of forgery.

In some jurisdictions, a major distinction between false pretenses and forgery is that a forgery occurs even if the defendant does not receive any property. This might occur if the defendant signs someone else's name to a stolen check and attempts to pass it at a bank. When the bank teller spots the forgery and refuses to pay, the defendant may still have committed a forgery under state law. Another possibility is attempted false pretenses.

H. Receiving Stolen Property

Theft crimes ordinarily punish those who directly obtain property from the victim. Receiving stolen property, however, is a crime that reaches the person who makes many thefts financially worthwhile by providing a market for the stolen items. Thus, a person who breaks into a house and takes a television can be found guilty of both burglary and larceny. If the thief then sells the stolen television to a professional buyer, referred to as a *fence*, the buyer may be guilty of *receiving stolen property*. In general terms, receiving stolen property reaches those who take property that has been stolen with knowledge that it was obtained unlawfully and with the intent to deprive the owner or possessor of the property. Modern jurisdictions that have adopted a consolidated theft crime include receiving stolen property within the reach of the generic theft offense. Ordinarily, receiving stolen property is punished the same as the theft of that property.

1. Receiving or Concealing

For receiving stolen property, the property is *received* when the defendant obtains *actual or constructive possession* of it. The latter would occur if the defendant ordered the thief to leave the stolen television in the defendant's garage while the defendant was at work. Some modern statutes have expanded the reach of the crime beyond receiving and also cover someone who *conceals* property with knowledge that it was stolen and with the intent to deprive the owner or possessor of it. The word "conceals" would cover the person who obtains property without knowing its origins, then keeps it after later discovering it had been acquired from someone who had stolen it.

2. Stolen Property

Since the crime may be defined as receiving *stolen property*, an extensive case law has developed defining this non-legal term. Ordinarily property is considered to be stolen if it was obtained by larceny or robbery, and in some jurisdictions by embezzlement and even false pretenses. It may be considered "theft" under consolidated statutes that combine many similar theft crimes into one generic one.

3. Knowledge Property Was Stolen

The *mens rea* for this offense requires proving the defendant had knowledge that the property was stolen. This is a subjective test, requiring the defendant personally to be aware of how the property was acquired. Often this knowledge is established by circumstantial evidence, such as the defendant paid a ridiculously low price for the item or the circumstances of the transaction were such that the defendant's knowledge is apparent. Some locales permit jurors to infer knowledge from possession of recently stolen property. In addition, the prosecution can rely on willful blindness to establish a defendant's knowledge.

4. Intent to Deprive Owner

A second mental element is that the defendant intended to deprive the owner of the property. This may be established by such circumstantial evidence as proof that the defendant acquired the property for his or her personal use or just to assist the initial thief in disposing of it. On the other hand, the necessary intent to deprive is absent if the defendant acquired the property in order to return it to the rightful owner.

I. Robbery

1. Definition

Robbery, often punished by a lengthy prison term, is an aggravated form of larceny. The offense entails a larceny coupled with the use of force or a threat of violence to dispossess the victim of the property. Robbery is deemed a very serious crime, a felony in every jurisdiction, because it presents the real danger of immediate serious physical harm to the victim.

Often robbery can be characterized as "larceny plus two." It includes the elements of larceny (trespassory taking and carrying away the personal property of another with intent to deprive the other of it permanently or for a substantial period of time) plus two additional elements: the theft must occur by force or the threat of immediate force, and the taking must be from the person or presence of the victim. Because the actual or potential bodily harm is the primary concern with robbery, it occurs irrespective of the value of the items taken.

2. Elements

a. Force or Threat of Immediate Force

The central element of robbery is that it is a taking accomplished by the use or threat of immediate force. Thus, a threat to reveal the victim's secret past unless the person gives the defendant a sum of money would not amount to robbery since the threat did not involve force or the threat of immediate force. (The crime may be extortion rather than robbery.)

The force or threat of immediate force used to take the property need not be significant, but it must entail more than the force required to obtain possession of the item. For example, pulling a necklace from the victim would not be a robbery so long as the force was only that necessary to gain control of it, although it would be a larceny. Putting a hand on the person's back to gain leverage in order to pull the necklace off could be a robbery because the force would be in addition to that required for control of the item. Similarly, if the robber attempted to pull off the necklace and the victim resisted, causing the robber to use additional force to obtain the jewelry, the force may be sufficient to constitute a robbery.

Although ordinarily the use or threat of immediate force is addressed to the victim ("Give me your money or I will shoot you"), robbery also embraces threats or actual force to a third party. For example, a robbery occurs when the robber threatens to do physical harm to the victim, the victim's family or friends, or even to other people in the immediate vicinity of the victim. Robbery usually requires that the threat be for immediate physical harm. A threat of future harm may be the crime of extortion rather than robbery.

b. Timing of Use of Force

Robbery traditionally requires the use or threat of force or violence before or at the time of the taking and must be the reason that the taking occurs. Thus, a key issue may be the exact moment when the theft occurred. For example, the manager of a jewelry store observed D place a watch in her jacket pocket and leave the store. The manager follows D into the parking lot and demands its return. At that point, D takes out a gun, orders the manager to step back, and then flees. Under the traditional common law approach, the defendant may not be guilty of robbery since the use of force did not occur at the time of the initial taking of the property. Many jurisdictions, however, now take a more inclusive approach by extending robbery to cover force used "in the course of "a taking or used "to retain possession" of the stolen items. In these jurisdictions, D's use of force in the parking lot made this a robbery since it was in the course of the taking of the property from the store or was used to retain possession of it. Other locales may reach the same result by using the fiction of constructive possession: D is guilty of armed robbery because the store (through the manager) still had constructive possession of the watch when the force was used in the parking lot.

c. Person or Presence of Victim

A distinguishing characteristic of robbery is that it requires a taking from the person or presence of the victim. This *proximity* requirement is a significant reason that robbery is deemed so serious since it greatly increases the likelihood of harm to the victim. A taking is from the *person* of the victim if it is on the victim's body, such as a watch or ring, or in the victim's clothing, such as in a pocket. Moreover, it is considered to be from the victim's person when the thief actually takes something within the immediate physical control of the victim, such as a purse on a table next to the victim or a briefcase at the person's feet.

A theft from the victim's *presence* is actually more inclusive than it might seem since it includes both the actual and constructive presence of the victim. The key is that the area is sufficiently close to the victim to be under the victim's control so that the victim could have prevented the theft had the robber not used force or the threat of force. For example, if the item is taken from an area near the victim, even though the victim could not physically see the robber take the item, it may be deemed to have been taken from the victim's presence. This might occur if the robber blindfolds and ties up the victim, then removes money from a safe a few feet from the victim. The concept of constructive possession has even been extended to cover the situation when the victim is tied up in one room and the thief takes property in another room of the same house.

3. Aggravated Robbery

It is common for a jurisdiction to provide for an increased penalty if a dangerous or deadly weapon is used in a robbery. In many states this is designated an *armed robbery*. The exact wording of the aggravated robbery statute may be crucial in assessing liability. If the statute requires a deadly weapon, it is satisfied only if the weapon was capable of causing death or serious bodily injury in the manner it was used. Thus, even an unloaded gun could be a deadly weapon if used to strike the victim in the head. Some locales interpret the term "deadly" even more broadly to include an unloaded pistol, regardless of how it was used.

On the other hand, if the aggravated robbery statute applies to a robbery involving a "dangerous weapon," the term may be satisfied by items that by their nature are capable of causing serious injury or death, and also things that can be used or displayed in a way such that they reasonably appear capable of causing serious harm. An object that on closer inspection could not inflict serious injury or death can still be a dangerous weapon in some jurisdictions if it would have been reasonable to believe that it was capable of inflicting such injury. For example, a defendant who displays a toy gun that appears to be a real firearm while demanding that a clerk open the cash register may be guilty of armed robbery, depending on the applicable robbery statute, even though the toy gun could not cause any substantial harm.

In one case, a court upheld an armed robbery conviction when the victim reasonably perceived that an object in the defendant's pocket was a gun even though it was only hairbrush. *Commonwealth v. Johnson*, 543 N.E.2d 22 (Mass. Ct. App. 1989). However, simply stating that one has a gun or knife is insufficient in itself to constitute an armed robbery, unless a statute provides that statements or conduct conveying that the person is armed with a dangerous weapon can be sufficient. *See, e.g., Or. Rev. Stat. § 164.405(1)(b)* (armed robbery if defendant "[r]epresents by word or conduct that the person is armed with what purports to be a dangerous or deadly weapon").

4. Larceny From the Person

Larceny involves a nonviolent taking of property and robbery consists of one with actual or threatened immediate violence. There is an intermediate class of cases where the offender takes property from the person of the victim but does not use enough force to amount to a robbery. Many jurisdictions reach this conduct by enacting crimes called *larceny from the person* or *purse snatching*. Since this crime poses a greater risk of physical harm than larceny but not as great as robbery, it is punished by a potential prison term between that authorized for those two offenses.

The elements of larceny from the person are the same as ordinary larceny, plus the requirement that the taking be from the victim. Sometimes the concept of "from the person" is viewed expansively, even extending to items within the victim's immediate presence. For example, in *Garland v. Commonwealth*, 446 S.E.2d 628 (Va. Ct. App. 1992), the defendant frightened a cashier when he reached across to steal money from the cash drawer. The cashier was not physically touching the cash drawer, but the thief's hands came within inches of the cashier in order to get the money. The court held that the money was within the cashier's immediate control so that the taking satisfied the elements of larceny from the person. The court found that there had been a "constructive trespass" of the person of the victim.

J. Extortion

The crime of *extortion*, which includes *blackmail*, is usually classified as more serious than larceny, embezzlement, and false pretenses but less serious than robbery. Originally, extortion involved a public official who took a fee, without authority to do so, as the price for performing public responsibilities. Today, extortion is a part of every jurisdiction's criminal law but differs markedly from one locale to another.

The heart of extortion is that it involves taking property by threat of present or future harm to a person or property. Thus, extortion and robbery may overlap, each covering a taking through the means of an immediate physical threat. In such overlap cases, often the prosecution will charge the defendant with the more serious crime—robbery. Some extortion statutes stray far from requiring physical harm and even include threats to harm property or reputation, to disclose a disgraceful secret, or to accuse the victim of having committed a crime.

Extortion statues may require that the defendant actually take the property, though some extortion laws are broad enough to embrace threats to obtain property irrespective of whether the property actually changes hands. Some extend beyond a taking of property to cover threats to cause someone to do something he or she is not obligated to do. For example, the latter version of extortion would occur if someone threatened to kill a politician unless the politician withdrew as a candidate from a future election.

Many modern extortion statutes include a defense that allows a person to demand the return of property or reasonable compensation for a loss. For example, if X steals Y's lawn mower and Y threatens to call the police unless X returns the mower, modern extortion statutes would provide Y with a defense to an extortion charge since Y is only threatening what Y has a right to threaten and the action sought is reasonable under the circumstances. The result would be different if Y said she would report X to the police unless X returned the mower plus gave Y $10,000 "for her time and stress."

Some modern jurisdictions include extortion in their consolidated theft offense, while others retain it as a separate, and often more serious, offense.

K. Burglary

1. Definition

Burglary was a common law crime designed to protect the sanctity of the home from nighttime invasion by someone intending to commit a felony inside of it. The offense represents an effort to provide special security for a person's sanctuary during the night when he or she is sleeping and most vulnerable to criminals. Under the common law, the elements of burglary are (1) breaking and (2) entering of (3) a dwelling (4) of another (5) in the nighttime with (6) the intent to commit a felony therein.

Traditional burglary requires the government to prove both that the perpetrator had the intent to break and enter along with the intent to commit a felony therein. The specific intent to commit a felony must be formed before the breaking and entering. While proof that the defendant actually committed a felony inside the building is unnecessary, at the moment of the unauthorized entry the actor must intend to commit a felony. In that regard, burglary can be viewed as a form of attempted crime, because the purpose to commit the felony upon entry is the key, not the actual commission of the intended offense.

While it is common to describe a person who enters a home or other structure to commit a theft as a "burglar," the crime is much broader than just a theft offense. The particular crime that will be committed after the entry can be any felony, so that an entry with the intent to commit a murder or rape can be charged as a burglary. Modern jurisdictions have markedly expanded the reach of burglary by eliminating or altering many of the traditional elements.

2. Elements

a. Breaking

Traditional burglary requires that the offender *break into a structure*. A breaking occurs when the defendant moves to a material degree something that barred entry to the structure in some way, such as a closed door or window or even a curtain covering an opening. The breaking can be of an interior door and need not be just an exterior entry. The structure does not have to be damaged, nor is significant force required to constitute the breaking. Entry through an open door or window, however, does not amount to a breaking. Similarly, no breaking occurs when the defendant is invited to enter the building, perhaps as a guest. But if entry is obtained by fraud, such as a misrepresentation that the defendant is an employee of the gas company investigating a reported leak, courts often hold there was a constructive breaking sufficient to satisfy burglary law.

Many modern criminal codes dispense with the requirement of a breaking, simply reaching those who enter or remain in a building without permission.

b. Entering

Traditional burglary also requires that the burglar commit an *entry* in addition to the breaking. The entry is accomplished by the intrusion into the building of any part of the body, such as an arm, foot, or even a finger. In some cases, the use of an instrument, such as a flashlight or cane, can be sufficient to effectuate the entry. The entry may be only for an instant, as when a burglar enters a house then leaves immediately upon hearing noises suggesting it is occupied.

A defendant's entry may be proven either through direct evidence, such as an eyewitness observing the defendant entering the structure or physical evidence showing the defendant was inside the structure, or by circumstantial evidence indicating the defendant's presence inside the structure. In many jurisdictions it is not a burglary if a person is invited into a structure and then decides to steal an item or commit another felony after entry because there was no breaking. On the other hand, in some jurisdictions it would be a burglary if the person were permitted on the first floor of a home and then sneaks upstairs, opens the door to the master bedroom, and steals money inside a dresser drawer. There would have been both a breaking and entry in these locales since the defendant was invited only to enter the first floor but committed a breaking and entering when, without permission, he or she went into the upstairs bedroom.

c. Dwelling

Traditional burglary was designed to protect the home from invasion by a felon. Accordingly, by definition it required that the offender break and enter a structure that was a *dwelling*. A structure satisfied this element when it was a place that people inhabited, irrespective of the presence or absence of any occupants at the time of the burglary. Thus, a building is a dwelling even when the inhabitants are away on vacation or are absent for an evening or a few hours, or conduct a business on the premises where they live. Buildings physically close to a house, such as an outhouse or barn or garage, may be considered part of the *curtilage* of the home and therefore included within the definition of dwelling. Similarly, a hotel room or rented apartment may be considered a dwelling.

Modern burglary statutes routinely reject the requirement that the structure be a dwelling, often covering any building or even "structure." However, it is common for today's burglary provisions to increase the penalty if the structure is occupied, thus retaining a vestige of the dwelling house rule at the heart of common law burglary. Some burglary statutes also greatly expand the offense by reaching entry into a vehicle or business with the intent to commit a crime.

d. Of Another

Burglary required that the dwelling that was burglarized be that *of another*. This means that the burglar could not be guilty if he or she had the right to inhabit the building. However, since the issue was the right to inhabit rather than ownership, it was possible for the owner of a house to burglarize it in unusual circumstances. For example, if the owner rented it to someone else and then broke and entered it during the rental period without the right to do so, the owner may be guilty of burglary since the property would be considered to be "of another."

Many modern statutes revise the "of another" requirement by stating that the entry must be unprivileged or without permission. In most situations this means that the same people who would be liable under the traditional "of another" rule would also be liable under the more modern language.

e. At Night

Traditional burglary required that the breaking and entry occur *at night*. This was defined as the period of time when the countenance of a person could not be ascertained by natural light. Modern burglary statutes often drop the requirement that the burglary occur at night, but may make a nighttime entry an aggravated form of the offense carrying a stiffer penalty. When a modern statute makes distinctions on whether the crime occurred during the day or night, the statute often defines those temporal terms. A frequent approach identifies the period between sunset and sunrise or thirty minutes before sunrise and after sunset at "night."

f. With Intent to Commit a Felony Therein

Burglary is a specific intent crime. The traditional approach required the offender to break and enter with the *intent to commit a felony inside the dwelling*. Since the requirement was that the offender intend to commit a felony, it was not a burglary if the intent was only to enter without committing an offense inside or to commit a misdemeanor upon entry. Thus, it was not a burglary if the offender intended only to look around the house, then killed someone found there. He or she lacked the intent to commit a felony at the time of the breaking and entry.

Modern burglary statutes retain the concept of burglary as a specific intent crime, but often expand intent to include a wider range of offenses. Offenders who broke into a house for the purpose of stealing items posed special problems since it may be difficult to prove the intent to commit a felony if the jurisdiction punished petty theft (such as theft of items worth less than $1,000) as a misdemeanor. How could the prosecutor prove that at the time of the entry the defendant intended to steal something with a value over the threshold amount? To eliminate this issue, many jurisdictions today extend their burglary statutes to people intending to commit a felony or any theft.

Checkpoints

- Larceny was the first nonviolent theft offense; embezzlement and false pretenses were added to fill in gaps in larceny.

- Elements of common law larceny: (1) a trespassory (2) taking and (3) carrying away ("asportation") of (4) personal property (5) of another person (6) with intent to steal.

- Larceny is a crime of depriving possession, not ownership, so the trespassory taking element involves proof that a possessor was deprived of the property.

- Possession does not require actual physical control of the property, so a taking from a person with constructive possession is also larceny.

- A thief or other wrongdoer can have sufficient possession of property to satisfy the requirements of larceny, so taking from that person can be a larceny even though their possession is unlawful.

- The common law developed a number of fictions to allow prosecutions for larceny even where the taking appeared to be voluntary or the defendant had control of the item.

- In some circumstances an employee or agent may only have custody of property, so the employee or agent's taking of the property may deprive the owner of constructive possession and be larceny.

- A bailee ordinarily has rightful possession of property but may be guilty of larceny by bailee if he or she takes the property. Under the break bulk doctrine, the bailee may only have possession of the container but not its contents.

- The asportation element in larceny requires only the slightest movement, so long as it establishes the requisite deprivation of possession. Some modern statutes dispense with this element.

- Common law larceny limited property to tangible items, while modern theft statutes expand the property subject to a theft to include intangibles and services.

- Larceny is a specific intent crime, and the intent is to permanently deprive the victim of possession of the property.

- Larceny by trick, a subcategory of larceny, is when a person makes a false statement to obtain possession of the property. The consent to transfer the property, therefore, is not voluntary.

Checkpoints, *cont.*

- A larceny defendant can offer a mistake defense, including the belief that one has a valid claim of right to possess the property.

- Embezzlement is the unlawful conversion of property by someone who, while serving in a position of trust, was given possession of the property and who had a "clean mind" at the time of acquiring possession.

- The intent for the crime of embezzlement is to fraudulently convert the property to personal use, but a defendant need not intend to permanently deprive another of possession, so a temporary use of the property can be sufficient for embezzlement.

- False pretenses involves the transfer of ownership, not possession, by means of a material misstatement or omission of past or present fact.

- False pretenses involves a specific intent to obtain ownership by means of false statements that are not mere puffery or promises of future performance.

- Many modern jurisdictions have adopted a consolidated theft statute that eliminates many of the elements of the traditional theft crimes and replaces crimes such as larceny, embezzlement, and false pretenses, and sometimes even extortion.

- Extortion is a crime involving the use of threats of present or future harm, often physical harm, to obtain property or, in some jurisdictions, other actions against the will of the victim. In some locales extortion and robbery overlap.

- Robbery is larceny from the person or presence of the victim coupled with the use of force or a threat of violence at the time of the taking.

- Traditional burglary is the breaking and entry into a home of another at night with the intent to commit a felony therein.

- Modern burglary statutes expand the coverage of burglary by dispensing with the requirements of breaking and entry, and by covering burglaries at times other than night and in structures other than a dwelling.

Chapter 12

Criminal Enterprises

Roadmap

- Statutes make the operation of a criminal enterprise a separate crime
- Membership in the organization can be a basis for a criminal prosecution
- The violation does not require a separate conviction for individual criminal conduct

---

A. Introduction

A particular concern of the criminal law in recent years is the rise of criminal organizations, from the Mafia to drug cartels to street gangs. A wide variety of traditional criminal laws reach the illegal activities of these groups. For example, the agreement to engage in criminal conduct may be punished under the conspiracy laws, and the acts themselves may engender separate criminal liability. Thus, if three gang members agree to kill a rival and one commits the murder, each may be guilty of conspiracy to commit murder as well as first degree murder for the homicide.

Concerned that these traditional avenues were not effective means to eradicate organized crime, legislatures adopted statutes making the operation of the criminal organization a separate offense from the particular crimes committed by its members. These new laws often require proof of an ongoing criminal entity and the participation of individuals in its activities. While conspiracy law can reach the agreement to join together in a criminal plan, the federal and state governments recognize an additional need to address long-term criminal organizations that can include multiple members engaging in a variety of criminal acts. Along the same line, laws have been adopted to constrain the finances of these organizations through money laundering statutes that make it a crime to transfer the proceeds of illegal activities. These laws reach not only the perpetrators of the crimes but also those who facilitate the transfer of funds.

B. RICO

The Racketeer Influenced and Corrupt Organization Act—better known as RICO—was enacted as part of the Organized Crime Control Act of 1970, the main statute targeting organized criminal activity. The statute, located at 18 U.S.C. § 1961 *et seq.*, targets criminal enterprises that operate both through legitimate businesses and as illegal organizations—called an "association in fact"—by creating a new offense based on the commission of a series of criminal acts. RICO requires the government to prove that the defendant engaged in two or more acts that constitute a "pattern of racketeering activity," which the statute defines to include state law crimes such as murder, robbery, and loan-sharking, along with a long list of federal offenses, such as mail and wire fraud. Importantly, a RICO violation does not require that the defendant be convicted of the underlying offenses, only that the government prove that the acts show beyond a reasonable doubt that the defendants engaged in a "pattern of racketeering activity." In addition, the collection of an unlawful debt can be the underlying activity for a RICO prosecution. The constitutional basis for the statute is the Commerce Clause, which requires proof that the activities were in or affected interstate commerce.

1. Types of Violations

One of Congress' aims in adopting RICO was to attack the perceived infiltration of legitimate businesses by organized crime, although the law can also be used against completely illegitimate organized crime groups. Two types of RICO violations specifically targeted the spread of organized crime to mainstream businesses. Section 1962(a) of RICO prohibits "any person who has received any income derived ... from a pattern of racketeering activity" from using those funds to acquire an interest in or control of another enterprise involving or affecting interstate commerce. Section 1962(b) prohibits any person from acquiring or maintaining an interest in such an interstate enterprise "through a pattern of racketeering activity." These provisions protect legitimate operations from being taken over by organized crime through classic strong-arm tactics that seek to expand the power of the criminal organization through control of ostensibly legitimate enterprises that can then be used as a cover for continuing criminal acts.

Section 1962(c), which is the most commonly charged subsection, is a catch-all provision that makes it a crime to conduct or participate in the operation of an interstate enterprise's affairs through a pattern of racketeering activity. Section 1962(d) makes it a crime to engage in a conspiracy to violate the RICO statute.

RICO prosecutions can, and often do, include more than one type of prohibited conduct.

Sections 1962(a) and (b), which target what Congress perceived as the more egregious tactics of criminal organizations, in fact have not proven to be of much use against such enterprises. Section 1962(a) imposes a high burden of proof on the government: it must show not only the intentional commission of the acts that constitute a pattern of racketeering activity, but further, that the defendant knew that the funds used to invest in the enterprise were the product of that pattern. Similarly, § 1962(b) requires proof of the pattern plus evidence that the defendant sought to gain or maintain control of an enterprise by the underlying criminal activity. When the prosecutor proves the predicate pattern, that likely demonstrates a violation of § 1962(c), which only requires proof that the defendant conducted or participated in the operation of an enterprise through the pattern of racketeering activity.

2. Application of RICO

In its early years, prosecutors seldom used RICO provisions because of the complexity of the statute and unfamiliarity with targeting organizations as a separate criminal offense. Although prosecutors initially focused on organized crime and other violent groups, they have since applied the statute to a wide variety of non-violent situations, including public corruption cases in which the RICO enterprise is identified as a public office, such as an executive or legislative office. While RICO's original target was organized crime groups, courts have held that the statutory language is not limited to such groups and covers any person who engages in a pattern of racketeering activity through an enterprise, such as a corporation, political or legislative office, or non-profit organization. In addition to a term of imprisonment, the statute also contains a broad asset forfeiture provision and authorizes private damages actions for violations, which is uncommon in the criminal law.

C. Street Gangs

A significant problem in inner cities are street gangs that control neighborhoods through violence and intimidation. Some gangs have developed into national organizations that rival other criminal enterprises, although most remain local groups with fluid membership and leadership. Areas infested with gangs, usually populated by low-income residents, often see a significant increase in violent crimes, such as drive-by shootings and drug dealing. While

RICO can and has been used to address these groups, a number of states also enacted statutes that specifically address this type of organization. Anti-gang measures include provisions adopted in both civil and criminal codes, and the application of laws to both juveniles and adults. Statutes include prohibiting the tattooing of minors, because gang symbols are popular tattoos, and authorizing public housing tenants who suffer a gang-related injury to seek the eviction of a gang member from the public housing units. Some states have enacted statutes making parents civilly liable for encouraging gang activity by their children. Moreover, in some jurisdictions crimes committed as part of gang activity can trigger an enhanced penalty.

1. STEP

California was the first state to adopt a separate criminal statute based on gang membership. Called the Street Terrorism Enforcement and Prevention Act (STEP), the law makes it a crime for a person to actively and knowingly participate in a criminal street gang, and prohibits the willful promotion, furtherance, or assistance to the gang in committing a felony. The law also makes it a crime to coerce another into participating in a street gang. Like RICO, STEP authorizes the issuance of an injunction to restrict gang members' public association with one another, the wearing of gang apparel, the use of gang hand signs, and limiting movement by gang members within an identified area. The legal basis for injunctive relief is that the gangs constitute a "public nuisance" and that governments traditionally have the authority to abate a nuisance that is injurious to the general public. The California Supreme Court upheld the constitutionality of the statute's injunctive provisions in *People ex rel. Gallo v. Acuna*, 929 P.2d 596 (Cal. 1997), holding that the prohibition on association with other gang members did not violate the First Amendment rights of the individual members.

2. Vagueness Challenge

An issue with these statutes is whether the broad definition of gang membership and the enhanced punishments based on being a member violate the Constitution. The Supreme Court addressed the constitutionality of a local anti-gang ordinance in *City of Chicago v. Morales*, 527 U.S. 41 (1999), involving a loitering ordinance targeting gangs. The statute required a police officer, on observing a person whom he or she reasonably believed to be a "criminal street gang member" loitering in any public place with one or more other persons, to order all such persons to disperse, and a failure to obey such an order was a criminal violation. The Court held the statute was unconstitutionally vague because it failed to provide fair notice of the prohibited conduct, and was also impermissibly vague in failing to establish minimal guidelines for enforcement of the provision. The statute's definition of "loiter" as meaning "to remain in any one place with no apparent purpose" did not provide sufficient notice of what conduct was prohibited. A plurality of the Court noted that it would be difficult to imagine how anyone standing in a public place with a group of people would know if he or she had an "apparent purpose" or not. The Court did not, however, find a violation of the First Amendment right to association in the definition of a "criminal street gang" as "any ongoing organization, association in fact or group of three or more persons, whether formal or informal."

D. Money Laundering

Unlike RICO's attempt to protect legitimate businesses from organized crime, the federal money laundering statute, located at 18 U.S.C. §§ 1956-1957, has been much more effective in attacking the supporting infrastructure of criminal activities. One of Congress's goals in adopting the statute was "to stem the flow of illicit profits back to the criminal enterprise, where profits provide the capital needed to expand criminal activity." The initial focus was on drug-related activity, but the statute has since been expanded to cover a wide range of criminal conduct, including white collar crime and terror financing. To achieve the goal of reaching the illicit profits, the money laundering statute expanded the scope of liability beyond those who participate directly in the criminal activity to include the ostensibly legitimate merchant or professional who receives the proceeds of criminal activity in exchange for goods and services while turning a blind eye to its source.

1. Elements of § 1956

Similar in structure to RICO, the money laundering statute builds upon other crimes as the basis for imposing liability for the separate offense of money laundering. Under the statute, the government must prove that the funds are the proceeds of "specified unlawful activity," which is defined by reference to a long list of federal crimes from which the criminal profits are derived. The money laundering statute also includes all of the acts that can constitute a "pattern of racketeering activity" for a RICO violation as meeting the requirement of "specified unlawful activity."

The second principal element the government must prove under § 1956 is that the defendant engaged in a "financial transaction," which is broadly defined to include any transaction that affects interstate or foreign commerce, or that involves the use of a "financial institution." The latter term includes not just banks but also stock brokers, casinos, check-cashing firms, mortgage companies, and a wide array of entities that engage in monetary transactions.

Section 1956 of the money laundering statute moves beyond the underlying criminal activity by imposing liability on those who act with the knowledge that the financial transaction is designed "to conceal or disguise the nature, the location, the source, the ownership, or the control of the proceeds of specified unlawful activity." Under this provision, the shopkeeper or moneychanger who converts the proceeds of criminal acts into common items of commerce can be held liable for the distinct offense of money laundering.

The government is required to prove two different elements of knowledge for a § 1956 violation: first, that the defendant knows the funds are the proceeds of "some form of unlawful activity," and, second, the defendant's knowledge that the financial transaction will conceal the source or ownership of the proceeds. Inferring knowledge from the circumstances of the transactions, courts have found that it is enough that the criminal who was exchanging ill-gotten gains sought to conceal or disguise the proceeds and that the businessperson knew of that design. Section 1956 also reaches those who deliberately structure transactions to avoid financial reporting requirements.

2. Elements of § 1957

A second means of reaching normal businesses that assist criminal organizations in laundering their profits is § 1957, which punishes any person who knowingly engages in a monetary transaction in criminally derived property with a value greater than $10,000. As with § 1956, under § 1957 the defendant must know that the funds are proceeds obtained from a criminal offense, although one need not know the particular violation, and that specified unlawful activity in fact generated the property. A § 1957 violation, however, only requires proof of the defendant's knowledge of the relation of the proceeds to the underlying criminal activity, without regard to whether the criminal using the proceeds sought to conceal or disguise the source of the funds.

There are two important differences between §§ 1956 and 1957. First, § 1957 prosecutions require that the particular transaction involve property with a value greater than $10,000, which is not an element under § 1956. Second, § 1957 applies to any "monetary transaction" while § 1956 uses the term "financial transaction." The definition of a "monetary transaction" requires the use of a financial institution, while a "financial transaction" can involve two private individuals, neither of whom may qualify as a "financial institution."

Checkpoints

- RICO requires either proof of a "pattern of racketeering activity" that involves the control or operation of an "enterprise" or collection of an unlawful debt.

- States have enacted street gang statutes that include civil injunctive provisions along with criminal prohibitions to limit gang activity in neighborhoods, but may be susceptible to challenges based on the First Amendment and Due Process.

- Money laundering statutes allow prosecutors to proceed against individuals, including merchants, who facilitate transactions in the proceeds of specified unlawful activity.

Chapter 13

Accomplice Liability

Roadmap

- Accomplice liability is derivative from the acts of the perpetrator
- The common law divisions: principals and accessories
- The modern statutory approach of accomplice liability
- The *actus reus* of accomplice liability
- The *mens rea* for accomplice liability
- An "innocent instrumentality" exempts participants
- The Model Penal Code approach to accomplice liability

A. Introduction

Many crimes involve multiple parties to the course of conduct, and assessing the liability of each is an important facet of the criminal law. For example, A enlists B and C to rob a bank. A plans the bank robbery, B drives the getaway car, and C enters the bank with a pistol and takes the money. What is the liability of A, B, and C for the bank robbery? Can all three be convicted of bank robbery even though only one actually entered the bank with a weapon?

The answer is provided by a set of rules for *accomplice liability*. These rules require distinguishing the basis for liability through an assessment of each participant's particular role in the offense. A basic principle of accomplice liability is that the liability of one person may be *derivative* of the criminal conduct of another person. Under this analysis, a person who provides some aid for a crime, such as driving the getaway vehicle from a robbery or shouting encouragement to an assailant, can be convicted of the *same offense* as the person who actually robs the store or beats the victim. Returning to the bank robbery hypothetical above, this means that A (who planned the robbery) and B (who drove the getaway car) may be convicted of bank robbery and punished to the same extent as C (who actually robbed the bank). In other words, accomplice liability principles result in convicting A, B, and C of bank robbery, as if each had been responsible for the conduct.

1. Scope of Liability

In the common law there were four levels of participation in a crime: (1) principal in the first degree, (2) principal in the second degree, (3) accessory before the fact, and (4) accessory after the fact. In some cases, the liability of one defendant was conditioned on the successful prosecution of another.

Modern laws largely moved toward a more simplified treatment of those who assist others in the commission of an offense by applying *accomplice* (sometimes called *accessory*) liability to permit punishment of all participants regardless of their role or whether one participant is not convicted of the offense. In short, all accomplices (who assist in the crime) as well as the principal actor (who actually did the crime) are treated the same way and deemed liable for the crime that was committed. Even in modern jurisdictions, however, assessing a person's role in an offense remains important for understanding what the prosecution must prove about that defendant's intent and what acts apart from the actual commission of the crime will suffice to impose liability.

2. Aiding and Abetting

The liability of an accomplice under modern law is frequently described as *aiding and abetting* a crime. Many terms are used to describe what it means to provide the assistance necessary to be an accomplice, such as *aid, abet, counsel, encourage, solicit, induce, procure,* or *advise*. These words are an attempt to describe what conduct is sufficient to meet the standard for assessing the liability of the person who does not engage in the particular act(s) that constitute the offense. Accomplice liability holds one person *responsible* for the acts of another, so the liability is *derivative* of the conduct of the other person. The accomplice must engage in particular conduct in providing the assistance that can advance the commission of the crime, although, as discussed below, that assistance need not be successful or even known to the perpetrator.

3. Nature of Assistance

When the prosecution uses an accomplice theory as the basis for proving an accused's criminal liability, it must show that the person provided some assistance in the commission of the offense by the primary violator and that the accomplice acted with the requisite *mens rea* for the commission of the target offense. The most important point to understand about accomplice liability is that it is *not* a separate crime, so one cannot be guilty of aiding and abetting an offense. Instead, it is a *theory of liability* in which the prosecution proves a person committed a crime by assisting another in the acts that make up the offense.

The accomplice is guilty of the crime to the same extent as the actual perpetrator. For example, if A purchases a gun for D to use in robbing a bank, then in some circumstances A can be held liable for the robbery even if the only person present in the bank is D and if A was not in the same state at the time of the robbery. A's pre-crime assistance is the means by which the prosecution will prove that more than one person can be convicted of the crime, even though A was not present for the offense. In this scenario, A and D may each be convicted of bank robbery and each could receive a lengthy prison term.

B. Common Law Divisions

The common law categorized participants in crime by a set of complex and rigid categories that affected the timing of a criminal trial and the potential liability of those who assisted in the commission of an offense. An important reason for this division of defendants was that those responsible for the actual commission of a felony would suffer the death penalty, so the categories permitted the courts to differentiate among participants and avoid having the maximum penalty imposed on all participants. Under the common law, participants in a crime were classified as either a *principal* or an *accessory*. Principals were subdivided into principals of the first and second degree; accessories were subdivided into accessories before and after the fact.

1. First Degree Principal

At common law, the *first degree principal* is the actual perpetrator of the crime who commits the acts or omissions with the requisite *mens rea* for the offense. More than one person can be designated a first degree principal. For example, if two people strike V, both can be guilty of battery as principals in the first degree. The first degree principal is ordinarily physically present at the crime scene. But in certain situations the first degree principal may be deemed constructively present, such as when the person leaves a bomb at the victim's home and is far away when it explodes.

This category also includes the person who uses an innocent instrumentality to commit the crime. If D asks A to bring an item from a store to D's car, falsely stating that D has already paid for it, D is the first degree principal even though A actually took and carried away the property for the larceny. D is deemed to have performed the acts of the *innocent instrumentality* (discussed below).

2. Second Degree Principal

The *second degree principal* is a person who was actually or constructively present at the commission of the crime, and provided (or was prepared to render) some assistance to the first degree principal in committing the crime. *Constructive presence* ordinarily means that the person is in close proximity to the location of the offense to provide assistance, but is not directly present when the crime occurs. For example, the driver of the getaway car outside the bank waiting to transport the co-felon after commission of the robbery is a principal in the second degree. Another example is the lookout, who may be blocks away from the house being burgled but strategically placed to warn the burglar if the police are driving in the neighborhood. The lookout is a principal in the second degree even though he or she does not see the police and therefore never alerts the burglars inside the house.

3. Accessory Before the Fact

An *accessory before the fact* is a person who was not actually or constructively present at the scene of the offense, but who counseled, advised, directed, or aided its commission. The accessory before the fact may have originated the criminal plan, or provided some assistance along the way. For example, the person who provides a schematic drawing of the bank and a way to avoid setting off the alarm is an accessory before the fact to the bank robbery so long as that person is in a different location at the time of the offense. The distinguishing characteristic between a principal in the second degree and an accessory before the fact is that the latter is not actually or constructively present at the scene of the crime.

4. Accessory After the Fact

An *accessory after the fact* is a person who purposely assists a felon in escaping capture and prosecution for the offense. The accessory must have knowledge of the felon's criminal conduct, and the aid must come after the completion of the offense. The accessory after the fact is markedly different from either degree of principal and from an accessory before the fact. While both degrees of principals and the accessory before the fact are liable for the crime committed, the *accessory after the fact* is not liable for the crime committed but rather is guilty of a separate offense that is akin to obstruction of justice or misprision of a felony. The punishment for an accessory after the fact is often relatively modest, irrespective of the gravity of the felony committed by the principle.

For example, X sees a friend run from a liquor store and the friend asks X to be hidden in the back of the X's car because the police are trying to apprehend the friend. X may be considered a second degree principal because he or she assists the perpetrator of the crime at the scene. On the other hand, if the friend encounters X the day after the robbery and asks to be hidden because the police are searching the neighborhood for the liquor store robber, then X is an accessory after the fact for rendering such aid.

5. Procedural Rules

Under the English common law, the punishment for a felony was death. Concerned that this penalty was too harsh for accessories, the law developed a number of procedural rules to shield accessories from that ultimate punishment. One significant limitation on the liability of those who assisted in a crime was the rule that in felony cases an accessory could not be convicted without the prior conviction of the principal in the first degree. The principal's *flight from the jurisdiction, death before trial, immunity from prosecution*, or *acquittal* on the charge barred prosecution of the accessory. Unlike an accessory, however, a principal in the second degree could be convicted notwithstanding the prior acquittal of the first degree principal.

The procedural bar applied only to the prosecution of accessories in felony cases. In a misdemeanor or treason prosecution, all participants in the offense were treated as principals, so the acquittal of the actual perpetrator did not prevent the conviction of an accessory.

These procedural rules meant that the accessory could not be tried *before* the principal(s) in the offense, although all the defendants could be tried jointly. If the principal was acquitted, then the accessory would also be acquitted, regardless of the reason. For example, if the first degree principal offered an insanity defense and the jury acquitted on that basis, then the accessory could not be convicted regardless of the accessory's mental state or intent in rendering assistance. Similarly, in post-trial proceedings, if the principal's conviction was reversed on appeal or a pardon granted, the accessory's conviction could not stand.

Another historical limit was that the accessory's conviction could not be for an offense greater than the principal's. There was an exception for a murder prosecution, where the accessory could be guilty of murder even though the principal was only guilty of voluntary manslaughter for acting under a heat of passion.

C. Modern Statutory Approach

The modern statutory approach eliminates the distinction between principals and accessories before the fact, treating them all as principals in the crime and imposing the same punishment. This approach is also used in the federal system. For example, a federal statute, 18 U.S.C. § 2(a), provides: "Whoever commits an offense against the United States or aids, abets, counsels, commands, induces or procures its commission, is punishable as a principal."

1. Historical Development

This modern simplification has a long history. To overcome the rigid categories created by the common law, statutes were adopted in both England and the United States that substantially changed the liability of accessories. In 1848, the English Parliament enacted a statute providing that an accessory before the fact would be treated in all respects the same as the principal, so that the accessory could be convicted even if the principal was acquitted. Several American legislatures followed Parliament's lead, and Congress adopted similar laws for the Alaskan territory and the District of Columbia that eliminated the distinction between an accessory before the fact and a principal. Today, almost every state dispenses with the distinction between principals and accessories before the fact, with each punished the same.

Most jurisdictions now have a separate criminal statute for an accessory after the fact, separating this category from principals and accessories before the fact, who are liable for the substantive offense. The punishment for this offense, considered a version of harboring a fugitive or obstruction of justice, is often much less than the sentence for the actual crime because the accessory after the fact has not played a role in the commission of an offense and lacks the *mens rea* for the actual crime.

2. Charging the Offense

While the fate of other defendants is now largely irrelevant to the conviction of an accessory, the distinction between principals and accessories remains important for proving liability based on an aiding and abetting theory. In some jurisdictions the charging document will allege how a defendant committed a

crime, so the distinction between the actual perpetrator and the person providing assistance can remain important as the theory of liability. Other jurisdictions
make no reference to accomplice liability in the charging document, and the
theory will be offered to the jury through instructions at the conclusion of the
trial. But in order for an accomplice to be found guilty of aiding in the commission of a crime, a *principal* must have committed the offense.

A defendant may not be convicted on an accomplice theory of liability if the
guilt of the principal has not been established, but the *identity of the principal*
is not necessary so long as the existence of a guilty principal is proven. For example, D is the driver of a getaway car from a bank robbery that is foiled when
police officers arrive at the scene after being notified by a silent alarm from the
bank. The robber inside the bank is alerted by the approaching police sirens and
quickly exits the building, never to be apprehended, while the driver is arrested
and charged with attempted bank robbery. Even if the government cannot identify the actual perpetrator, it can establish that *a* principal attempted to rob the
bank, and therefore the driver can be convicted as an accomplice to the offense.

3. Multiple Defendants

In order to convict a defendant, the prosecution must prove beyond a reasonable doubt its theory for holding the defendant liable, whether the person
was acting as a principal or as an accomplice to the perpetrator's conduct. In some
cases, the evidence will not be clear about which person among multiple defendants engaged in the actual criminal conduct. The prosecution can charge
defendants with the crime as both principals and accomplices. A jury may return a guilty verdict so long as the evidence supports the individual being either
a principal or accessory, because the distinction is not relevant to punishment.
For example, two people beat and rob a victim, who dies from the attack. Even
when it is not clear which person's blow was fatal, each can be charged as the
principal and with aiding the other in the commission of the crime. Unanim-
ity is not required as to whether the individual was the principal or an accomplice so long as the jurors agree to a finding of guilt beyond a reasonable doubt.

D. *Actus Reus*

1. Nature of Assistance

The accomplice provides assistance to the principal for the commission of the
crime. A wide variety of conduct, including just words, can suffice to establish

the requisite aid for liability. The assistance need not be great, nor must it be important to the commission of the crime. For example, helping load a weapon that the perpetrator could have loaded just as easily can still constitute aiding a crime. Similarly, supplying a weapon, even if it is not used in the actual commission of an offense, can be the basis for the accomplice's conviction.

The easier accomplice cases involve actual *physical assistance*, such as driving the getaway car, providing a weapon, or scouting the location for the offense. Similarly, verbal encouragement of a crime makes one an accomplice, regardless of whether the principal acted upon those words or even heard them. Encouragement means to countenance or approve the criminal conduct through words, gestures, looks, or signs. For example, while two people are beating the victim, a companion standing to the side shouts, "Go ahead and kill him." Even if the battery concludes without the victim dying, or with the perpetrators never increasing the force or frequency of their blows, the companion is liable as an accomplice to the battery, or even attempted murder, for encouraging the conduct.

2. Mere Presence

The more difficult cases involve a person who is present at the location of the crime but who does not provide any overt assistance or encouragement in the offense. Courts are fond of saying that *"mere presence"* at a crime scene, either alone or coupled with a refusal to interfere, is insufficient to support a conviction unless the person has a duty to prevent the harm or render assistance. For example, if the victim's companion standing to the side watches the victim being beaten by two perpetrators but says or does nothing to encourage or prevent the attack, that person is not guilty as an accomplice. The analysis would be different, however, if that person was a police officer, who has a duty to protect others from physical harm. The officer could be an accomplice because the failure to help the victim rendered aid to the principals.

Presence alone can be a form of assistance if it is part of a show of force in the commission of the crime or if the person is acting as a lookout for others. In these instances, the accomplice may not actually do anything that provides direct aid, but the possibility of providing such assistance advances the crime.

The perpetrator need not know that someone is providing assistance for the accomplice to be liable for the offense. For example, A sees D inside a bank committing a robbery, and notices a car down the street with its engine running but with no one in it. A sees a police officer approaching the deserted car. Desiring to help D escape from the robbery, A then calls out, "Officer, I think the owner went into that store across the street to pick something up. You can find the person in there." The officer goes to find the owner, and the robber leaves the bank and jumps into the car to escape. A is liable as an accomplice to the bank robbery for providing the assistance unbeknownst to D.

E. Mens Rea

Convicting a person as an accomplice requires the prosecution to prove *two mental states*: first, the intent to assist another in the commission of the offense, and second, the *mens rea* required for a violation of the object offense(s).

1. Two *Mens Rea* Elements

The first *mens rea* is often referred to as a specific intent, and it requires that the defendant intend to assist another person commit a criminal act with knowledge that it will promote or facilitate the offense. Second, the defendant must have the *mens rea* required for the offense committed by the principal. If that offense involves a specific intent, then the prosecution must prove the defendant intended both to assist in the crime and intended the particular violation or result prohibited by the criminal statute that was violated.

For example, A provides a schematic drawing of the security system of a jewelry store to D, who enters the store after hours by disabling the security system and steals a one million dollar diamond. A is an accomplice to larceny if A intended to assist D with knowledge that D would steal from the store, and if A has the *mens rea* required by the larceny statute: the intent to permanently deprive the store of its property. The proof of the two intents could be inferred from A providing the schematic drawing to D in exchange for a payment or receiving a cut of the proceeds from the crime. On the other hand, A would lack the necessary mental states and would not be an accomplice if D misled A into thinking that D is an employee of the store and needs to make a routine review of the security system for flaws.

Under this analysis, an accomplice can be liable for an offense that requires proof of recklessness or negligence, or even a strict liability crime with no intent element. While it may appear to be illogical that a person can intend conduct that is reckless (or negligent), the rationale is that the assistance is what makes the accomplice liable. The *mens rea* for the underlying offense can be inferred from the specific intent to assist, so the fact that it is a lower level of *mens rea* that does not require proof of a subjective state of mind does not mean the accomplice should avoid liability. For example, A and D are drinking beer at a bar and D becomes obviously inebriated. A encourages D to drive home, telling D that the alcohol will make him or her a better driver. While driving on a highway, D veers across the median and hits an oncoming car, killing the driver. A would be liable as an accomplice to D's drunk driving, which may be a strict liability offense, and for the reckless homicide charge arising from the driver's death.

2. Knowledge Alone

Knowledge of the criminal purpose of another is *not sufficient* by itself to establish the specific intent to assist in the crime. This issue arises most commonly in cases in which the principal obtained a good or service that was used in the offense and the supplier can be shown to have knowledge of the reason for the purchase. For example, D wants to release an internet virus that will disable many computers, in violation of state computer crime laws. To accomplish this, D needs a new computer with certain hardware that does not appear on any registries. D tells A of D's needs and A sells D the necessary computer. In demonstrating it before the sale is completed, A learns what D plans on doing with the new computer. If A sells D the computer, and D then releases the virus that causes millions of dollars of damages, A is not liable as an accomplice to D's computer crime even though A has knowledge of the criminal purpose. Absent proof of a criminal intent beyond knowledge of D's plan, there is no criminal culpability as an accomplice.

Inferring the accomplice's intent to commit the target offense from the conduct is particularly difficult in cases in which the person served as a lookout but did not otherwise participate in the commission of the offense. A defendant's mere presence at the scene of the crime or association with the perpetrators is not proof of an intentional participation in the crime, even if the defendant had knowledge of the criminal activity.

3. Greater Offense

The person who assists in the commission of a crime must have the *mens rea* for that offense, and can even be convicted of a *greater offense* than the perpetrator of the crime. When a person with the mental state necessary for an accomplice helps or induces another to engage in a crime, the accomplice's guilt is determined by the combined acts of all the participants as well as that person's own *mens rea*. If the accomplice's mental state is more culpable than the perpetrator's, then the accomplice may be found guilty of a greater offense. For example, D is agitated because he just saw his wife kissing V, a neighbor. A, a friend of D's who hates V and wants V to die, encourages D to attack V.

Because of D's personal anger and A's prodding, D is enraged and jumps on V from behind, beating him with a wrench that results in V's death. While D may have a good heat of passion defense to reduce a murder charge to voluntary manslaughter, A could be found guilty of murder because he has the intent to kill V through D's conduct. D would not be an innocent instrumentality because the intent in attacking V was to commit a crime.

4. Natural and Probable Consequences

An accomplice's liability for criminal conduct can include both the crime the person actually intended to assist, and also any offense that is a *natural and probable consequence* of the commission of the target offense. For example, if A encourages D to assault V, and due to a particular medical condition the attack causes V to die, then A is guilty of reckless homicide even though the killing was unintended. This is because the death would be a natural and probable consequence of the assault.

The doctrine permits the accomplice to be held liable for the reckless or negligent acts of the perpetrator even when the accomplice never intended a particular result or had any role in it occurring except to aid a different crime so long as that offense is a natural and probable consequence of the intended offense. Most jurisdictions treat accomplices identically to principals, so the majority view is that there is no distinction between them for liability for both the crime aided and additional offenses that are a foreseeable result of the intended crime. A few states reject liability for unintended offenses because the natural and probable consequences doctrine permits a defendant to be convicted of a specific intent crime where he or she did not possess the *mens rea* required for the offense.

The natural and probable consequences doctrine must be distinguished from the situation in which a defendant intends to aid one offense but the perpetrator commits a different, more serious crime. It is not necessarily the case that an accomplice who aids in a crime is "in for a dime, in for a dollar" and therefore responsible for any crime committed. For example, A asks D to drive him to a location where he will beat up a member of a rival gang. When D drives to the place where the assault will occur, A leaps out of the car and shoots and kills the rival gang member. D would not be liable for murder unless it can be shown that there was advance knowledge of the intended crime, although a conviction for assault would be permissible. If A showed D the gun while driving to the location, and told D to slow down so the victim could be shot in a drive-by shooting, then that could be sufficient to establish A's liability as an accomplice to murder even though the initial plan was to commit an assault. In *Waddington v. Sarausad*, 555 U.S. 179 (2009), the Supreme Court explained that "an accomplice who knows of one crime — the dime — is not guilty of a greater crime — the dollar — if he has no knowledge of that greater crime."

F. Abandonment

Similar to the rules for conspiracy and attempt, a person who abandons the criminal act for which assistance was provided may be able to avoid liability if the criminal act later takes place. This principle, designed to encourage criminals to abandon a planned crime, is adopted in many modern criminal codes which vary in the exact requirements for a legally recognized abandonment. Although the rules of abandonment — sometimes called withdrawal — vary among different jurisdictions, most require that it be voluntary and effectuate a complete cessation from the criminal course of conduct. Thus, it cannot be based on a decision to postpone the crime or out of fear of being caught. Some jurisdictions require that the individual communicate the withdrawal from the criminal activity to *both* law enforcement and the perpetrators of the offense.

In general, the person must attempt to "undo" the assistance that he or she had rendered. For example, if A provided D with a key to enter a house to steal a television, A may abandon the theft only if A retrieves the key or otherwise prevents the crime from occurring. A change of heart alone after providing assistance is insufficient to establish abandonment because the assistance has already occurred.

G. Innocent Instrumentality and Exempt Participants

1. Innocent Instrumentality

Although logic may suggest that accomplice liability would apply, it is widely held that this doctrine is inapplicable when one person uses another to commit a crime, and the person being used does not know that the conduct amounts to an offense. The person being used to commit the crime is viewed as an *innocent instrumentality*. The person who uses this hapless individual to commit the crime would be considered the actual perpetrator, even though he or she may not be physically present at the scene of the crime and may have committed no act directly involving its perpetration.

Under this approach, the acts of the innocent instrumentality are attributed to the person who instigated the crime. For example, D asks X to retrieve a purse from a nearby grocery cart, saying, "Could you please grab my purse over there while I load my car?" X assumes that it is D's purse, but it is not and D intends to steal it from a person who left it temporarily to return to the store. X would be an innocent instrumentality, and D would be liable for the theft even though D never physically removed the bag. Similarly, if an animal trainer uses an animal to commit the crime, then accomplice liability is not relevant to the determination of the trainer's criminal liability because the animal is, in effect, an extension of the trainer who uses it to commit the crime.

2. Exempt Participants

Another limit on accomplice liability is the product of legislative intent. A person is not an accomplice to a crime if that person is a member of the class of individuals protected by the statutory prohibition. Courts reason that the legislature did not intend to extend accomplice liability such that the victim is liable for the crime perpetrated on that victim. For example, many rape statutes prohibit sexual relations with a person under the age of sixteen. If a sixteen-year-old male engages in such conduct with a fifteen-year-old female, that female cannot be convicted of the offense as an accomplice, even though she was a willing participant in the male's offense. However, if the fifteen-year-old female encouraged the male to have sexual relations with another fifteen-year-old victim, then she could be an accomplice because the rape statute only protects the victim and not those who assist in the commission of the illegal act.

H. Model Penal Code

1. Scope of Liability

The Model Penal Code does not refer to principals or accessories, avoiding the common law categories and their limitations in favor of a more simplified approach that holds the accomplice liable for that person's own acts and intent. Its rejection of the common law is clear in § 2.06(7), which is similar to the modern statutory approach to accomplice liability. The section provides that the accomplice may be convicted even "though the person claimed to have committed the offense has not been prosecuted or convicted or has been convicted of a different offense or degree of offense or has an immunity to prosecution or conviction or has been acquitted."

Section 2.06(1) provides that "[a] person is guilty of an offense if it is committed by his own conduct or by the conduct of another person for which he is legally accountable, or both." Thus, X is guilty for the crimes X commits as well as for the conduct of someone else for whom X is legally accountable. X may be responsible for *both* X's own crimes as well as those of the person for whom X is accountable.

Under § 2.06(2), one person is "legally accountable" for the conduct of another if the person acts "with the kind of culpability that is sufficient for the commission of the offense" and (1) causes an "innocent or irresponsible" person to engage in the conduct; (2) if the MPC or other law provides that one person is accountable for another's conduct; or (3) if the person is an "accomplice" as that term is defined by the MPC.

2. Innocent and Irresponsible Party

The first MPC category corresponds in large part to the innocent instrumentality doctrine under the common law. What the MPC makes clear is that the person being held accountable must *cause* the "innocent person to engage in the criminal conduct," and the instrumentality can be a person who is only "irresponsible" but not necessarily innocent. For example, D provides I, who is clearly insane, with a weapon and encourages I to attack a person whom I believes is a threat. Under the MPC, D's actions would make D liable for I's acts, even though I would have a valid insanity defense to a charge.

3. Definition of Accomplice

The MPC makes a person "legally accountable" for another's conduct if the person is an *accomplice* in the commission of an offense. Section 2.06(3)(a) defines an accomplice as a person who, acting "with the purpose of promoting or facilitating the commission of the offense," (1) *solicits* a crime; (2) *aids, agrees to aid, or attempts to aid* another in planning or committing a crime; or (3) *fails to prevent a crime* while having a legal duty to prevent its commission.

Unlike many states that view solicitation to commit a crime as insufficient in itself to constitute being an accomplice to the crime, the MPC makes this conduct sufficient not only for a solicitation charge but also as an accomplice to that offense. Solicitation is defined in § 5.02(1), which makes it an offense for a person who "commands, encourages or requests another to engage in specific conduct that would constitute such crime or an attempt to commit such crime...." (see Chapter 14)

4. Agreement to Aid

Section 2.06(3)(a)(ii) defines an accomplice as a person who, among other acts, *agrees to aid* another person in the planning or commission of an offense. An agreement to aid a crime is similar to a conspiracy (see Chapter 16). However, liability as an accomplice can be established even if the formal elements of a conspiracy cannot be proven. For the crime of conspiracy, there must be proof of an agreement and knowledge of the criminal purpose of the agreement. For accomplice liability, on the other hand, a narrower agreement to provide some assistance without joining a broader conspiratorial agreement would be sufficient to make one an accomplice to the crime aided. For example, D asks A's assistance in stealing a truck to transport some items, but A is not told of the nature of the items to be hauled in the truck. A locates an unlocked truck and shows D how to hotwire the engine. D steals the truck and uses it to transport a large amount of illegal narcotics. A is liable as an accomplice in the theft of the truck, but is not necessarily liable for conspiracy or any drug crimes arising from the subsequent use of the stolen vehicle.

5. Attempting to Aid

The most significant change by the MPC from the common law of accomplice liability is in defining an accomplice as someone who, among other acts, *attempts to aid* in the planning or commission of a crime. Under the common law, attempted assistance might not be sufficient to establish accomplice liability if the principal did not commit the object offense or did not undertake sufficient acts to constitute an attempt to commit the crime. Under the MPC, however, a person can be guilty as an accomplice to an attempt offense even if the perpetrator would not be liable because the perpetrator's acts do not amount to an attempt since they do not constitute a substantial step toward the commission of the crime. Model Penal Code § 5.01(3), which defines attempt, provides that "[a] person who engages in conduct designed to aid another to commit a crime that would establish his complicity under Section 2.06 if the crime were committed by such other person, is guilty of an attempt to commit the crime, *although the crime is not committed or attempted by such other person.*" The common law would not permit such a result because no principal committed the attempt offense, so there is no crime to aid.

6. Purpose of Promoting or Facilitating Offense

Section 2.06(3) provides that a person is an accomplice if the conduct is with the "purpose of promoting or facilitating the commission of the offense." *Purpose* is the highest *mens rea* level in the MPC, requiring that "it is his conscious object to engage in conduct of that nature or to cause such a result."

a. Recklessness and Negligence

While in many cases the conduct of an accomplice must be done for the purpose of promoting or facilitating the crime, like the common law the MPC recognizes accomplice liability for a crime that only requires proof of recklessness or negligence. This embraces the situation where X is charged with being an accomplice to Y who acted recklessly causing death. Y will be charged with reckless homicide for Y's own reckless behavior. X's own acts or omissions in causing that result may lead to charges that X is an accomplice to the reckless homicide.

b. Result Crime

Section 2.06(4) states that for result crimes, such as homicide based on recklessness, a person is liable as an accomplice for providing assistance in the "conduct causing such result" so long as the person "acts with the kind of culpability, if any, with respect to that result that is sufficient for the commission of the offense." In other words, a person may be an accomplice to a crime that requires a reckless or negligent result so long as he or she acts recklessly or with criminal negligence with regard to that result. Note that this is a departure from the rule in § 2.06(3) that the accomplice must have the purpose of promoting or facilitating the crime.

c. No Natural and Probable Consequences Doctrine

The requirement that the accomplice act with the same kind of culpability for the result that would be required for commission of the actual offense means that the natural and probable consequences doctrine does not apply to the same extent as under the common law. In an example above, A helped D steal a truck that D then used to transport illegal narcotics. Under the common law's natural and probable consequences doctrine, A could be held liable for any crimes committed by the principal if they were a foreseeable result of the crime assisted. Under the MPC, however, A would not be liable for the narcotics transportation because A did not have the culpability required for that offense, which would likely require proof of knowledge of the narcotics and a purpose to transport them. Even if A were suspicious of D's reason for stealing the truck, that would not be sufficient to establish the intent for the offense through accomplice liability.

7. Abandonment

Similar to attempt and conspiracy (see Chapters 15 and 16), §2.06(6) authorizes defendants charged with accomplice liability to assert a defense of abandonment. The accomplice must stop any participation in the offense *prior to* its commission, and then must take one of two further steps: (1) "wholly deprives" his or her earlier assistance of any effectiveness in the commission of the offense, or (2) timely warns the proper authorities or otherwise makes a "proper effort" to prevent its commission. In practical terms, these may be difficult to demonstrate if the perpetrator goes through with the crime despite the accomplice's decision to end his or her participation in it.

Checkpoints

- Accomplice liability is derivative of the criminal conduct of the perpetrator. It is not a separate offense, but a theory to convict a person of a crime in which the person did not engage in the *actus reus* of the offense.

- The common law divided participants in a crime into two categories: principal and accessory.

- Principals were the perpetrators physically present at the crime, and were divided into first degree principal (the actual perpetrator) and second degree principal (present and assisting in the crime). Accessories were divided into those before the fact and after the fact.

- Under the common law, an accessory could not be convicted of a felony if the principal was not convicted for any reason.

- The modern statutory approach to accomplice liability treats all participants as principals to the crime, except that an accessory after the fact is now punished for a separate crime, such as harboring a fugitive or obstruction of justice.

- To convict a defendant as an accomplice, the government must show that a principal committed the conduct for the crime, but the actual perpetrator need not be convicted or even identified.

- The assistance provided to be an accomplice need not be significant, but mere presence at the scene of a crime is usually insufficient to establish a defendant's liability as an accomplice.

Checkpoints, *cont.*

- The government must prove two mental states: the intent to assist another in the commission of the offense, and second, the *mens rea* required for a conviction for that offense.

- The natural and probable consequences doctrine can establish an accomplice's liability for any crimes that arise out of the assisted offense.

- The Model Penal Code recognizes accomplice liability for an attempt to aid a crime, even if the perpetrator never engaged in conduct that would constitute an attempt to commit the crime.

Chapter 14

Solicitation

Roadmap

- Elements of solicitation
- The *mens rea* of solicitation
- Solicitation as an inchoate offense
- Whether a solicitation must be communicated to the other person
- Solicitation alone as insufficient *actus reus* for an attempt
- Merger of solicitation with both the target offense and conspiracy

---

A. Introduction

Solicitation is the crime of asking another person to join in a course of criminal conduct with the intent that the other person commit the target crime or participate in its commission. As an inchoate offense, the crime of solicitation virtually always will have occurred prior to the completion of the target criminal activity, and thus permits prosecution for conduct early in its planning stages.

Many solicitation prosecutions occur when an undercover police officer is the recipient of the communication, or the person solicited feigns agreement and informs the authorities. For example, D asks S to kill D's wife, offering to pay fifty thousand dollars. S is an undercover police officer who pretends to be a hired killer and obtains a payment from D for the murder. When D is arrested, a charge of attempted murder or conspiracy is usually impossible because S took no steps toward killing the victim and did not conspire to commit the crime, assuming it is a jurisdiction that follows the majority rule requiring at least two conspirators. The only offense D can be charged with is solicitation to murder because the crime did not advance any further toward completion.

B. Historical Development

The early common law limited the offense to solicitations of perjury in a judicial proceeding or conduct related to bribery of a public official. In the early nineteenth century, courts expanded the crime of solicitation to cover requests to commit felonies and serious misdemeanors involving a breach of the peace or other injuries to the public welfare. Modern statutes vary in the type of criminal activity that can be solicited, with some limiting the object crime to felonies, while other statutes apply solicitation only to certain specified crimes. Other jurisdictions and Model Penal Code § 5.02(1) extend solicitation laws to misdemeanors.

C. Modern Statutes

Almost every state has enacted a solicitation statute. The Illinois statute provides, "[a] person commits solicitation when, with intent that an offense be committed, other than first degree murder, he commands, encourages or requests another to commit that offense." *720 ILCS § 5/8-1*. New Hampshire, following the approach taken in Model Penal Code § 5.02(1), defines the offense as "[a] person is guilty of criminal solicitation if, with a purpose that another engage in conduct constituting a crime, he commands, solicits or requests such other person to engage in such conduct." *N.H. Rev. Stat. § 629:2*. Note that the description includes "solicits" as one means of committing the crime, which shows how legislatures struggle to define the offense in a coherent way. Wisconsin's solicitation statute focuses primarily on establishing intent: "whoever, with intent that a felony be committed, advises another to commit that crime under circumstances that indicate unequivocally that he or she has the intent…." *Wisc. Stat. Ann. § 939.30*.

D. Punishment

The crime of solicitation is usually, although not always, punished less severely than an attempt to commit the crime being solicited. For example, Tennessee provides that solicitation is "two classifications lower than the most serious offense solicited" unless the object offense is a less serious misdemeanor, in which case the solicitation is not a crime. *Tenn. Code Ann. § 39-12-107(b)*. The rationale for punishing solicitation less severely than attempt is that the attempt virtually always involves actions that are closer to the achievement of the object crime, thus making it more dangerous than a mere solicitation to commit the object crime. For solicitation to commit murder, however, some states have enacted statutes authorizing up to life imprisonment because of the dangerousness of the crime sought.

E. Elements

1. *Actus Reus*

The crime of solicitation involves communication, either oral or written, of a request that another person commit a crime. The language to describe this effort usually involves one or more of the following terms: command, encourage, request, advise, counsel, incite, order, invite, and hire. The communication must be sufficiently clear so that the recipient understands that the conduct will involve a crime by that person, or by the two together. The crime is complete upon the communication, so the solicitee need not perform the crime, nor even attempt it or undertake an overt act for a conspiracy. For example, D asks S to enter a house and remove the television from the living room, and S refuses. Despite S's refusal to join in the burglary, D is guilty of solicitation of burglary because the crime occurs when the request is communicated to S, whose response is irrelevant. This is consistent with the underlying policy of solicitation which aims at punishing and discouraging those who try to enlist others in criminal activity.

a. Indirect Assistance

A request for assistance in committing a crime is not a solicitation if the recipient is not being asked to participate directly in the criminal conduct. For example, D tells S, "I need to borrow your gun to rob a liquor store." D's statement is not a criminal solicitation because S is not being asked to commit the robbery, only to serve as D's accomplice. Modal Penal Code § 5.02(1) rejects this conclusion and includes within the definition of solicitation a request that another person engage in conduct that "would establish his complicity in its commission or attempted commission." This more expansive coverage would make D's request to S a solicitation because if S responded positively to the communication to supply the gun to use in a liquor store robbery, that would make S complicit in the robbery, *i.e.*, an accomplice.

b. Innocent Instrumentality

Solicitation differs from the situation when a primary party uses another person to commit a crime unbeknownst to the other person. For example, D asks S to go into the house across the street and remove the television from the living room because D claims to have lent it to the neighbor, but is unable to retrieve it due to a bad back. If S does as D requests, and D does not own the television but wants to steal it from the neighbor, then S will not be liable for larceny (or burglary) because S had no intent to steal (or commit a felony upon entry). D, however, is liable for larceny of the television despite not having physically engaged in the conduct. In other words, the law treats D as if D had personally committed the act performed by the innocent agent. D is the perpetrator — or principal in the first degree — of the crime and S is the "innocent instrumentality" (see Chapter 13). When D asks S to perform the act, there is no solicitation because D is not asking another person to engage in criminal conduct.

2. Mens Rea

Solicitation requires that the accused act with specific intent. This means that the solicitor's purpose is to have the recipient of the communication engage in the offense solicited. The *mens rea* of solicitation can be met irrespective of whether the act solicited can be accomplished, as long as the accused has the specific intent to commit the crime and knowledge that the crime can be accomplished. The use of an innocent instrumentality would not constitute a solicitation because the recipient is only asked to engage in the conduct, but that person would not be requested to commit a crime. For example, if D asks S to steal a necklace from a particular person knowing that the intended victim is not wearing the necklace at that time, then S cannot commit the larceny since there is no necklace to steal and D is not asking S to commit a larceny because of D's knowledge that the crime could not take place. The common understanding of solicitation was that it does not cover a request to commit only an attempted crime that could not be completed. On the other hand, if D mistakenly thought the victim was wearing the necklace, then a solicitation occurred because factual impossibility is not a defense to the solicitation and the defendant's intent that S engage in the theft would be sufficient proof of the *mens rea* element of solicitation.

If the object of the solicitation is a crime that entails a particular result, such as a homicide offense which requires someone to be killed, then the defendant must intend that the solicitee achieve that criminal result and not merely engage in conduct that causes the result. For example, D asks S, who is obviously drunk, to drive D and some friends home from a bar. While traveling on a highway, S crosses the center lane and hits an oncoming vehicle, killing its driver. D is not guilty of solicitation to commit manslaughter (or vehicular homicide) because D only asked S to engage in the conduct (driving the car) that led to the death but did not seek that particular outcome from the conduct. In other words, D did not intend for the crime (homicide) to occur, so D lacked the *mens rea* required for a solicitation to murder.

F. Uncommunicated Solicitation

Courts divide over the issue of whether the intended recipient of the communication, or an intermediary, must actually receive the communication in order for the offense to take place. For example, if D leaves a phone message for S asking S to assist D in stealing a car, is D liable for solicitation if S never retrieves or finds out about the phone message? If the rationale for solicitation is to punish those who intend to have a crime committed by another, then whether the communication reaches its intended recipient would seem to be irrelevant. On the other hand, if the harm is from the possibility that the communication will be acted upon, then the failure to communicate with the recipient means there is no threat of a crime taking place and therefore no harm caused by the defendant's conduct. Some states deal with the issue explicitly by prohibiting a defense to a solicitation charge that the request was not successfully delivered. Model Penal Code § 5.02(2) provides that it is "immaterial" to liability for solicitation "that the actor fails to communicate with the person he solicits to commit a crime if his conduct was designed to effect such communication."

In *State v. Cotton*, 790 P.2d 1050 (N.M. Ct. App. 1990), an incarcerated defendant wrote two letters to his wife asking her to dissuade their daughter from testifying against him in a molestation prosecution, but the letters were intercepted at the jail. The court overturned the solicitation conviction because the statute did not specifically permit a prosecution for an uncommunicated solicitation, and the court found an "implicit legislative intent" to require that the solicitation reach the intended recipient or an intermediary. Under this analysis, the crime does not take place until the receipt of the criminal request, even though the defendant's intent to have another engage in criminal activity is clear. Similarly, in *State v. Saephanh*, 94 Cal. Rptr. 2d 910 (Cal. Ct. App. 2000), the California Court of Appeals found that the statute's requirement of "solicits another" meant that the communication must reach the intended recipient; it is not enough that the defendant has done everything possible to make the communication.

The opposite approach is represented in Model Penal Code § 5.02(2) and a number of states that follow its approach. These jurisdictions permit a prosecution for unreceived solicitations so long as the defendant tries to communicate with the recipient. The MPC provision provides, "It is immaterial ... that the actor fails to communicate with the person he solicits to commit a crime if his conduct was designed to effect such communication."

When an intended solicitation does not reach the solicitee, the defendant could be found guilty of *attempted solicitation* if the state applies its attempt statute to solicitation. In *Saephanh*, the California court held that the general attempt statute applied to solicitations, so that a solicitation intercepted by prison authorities constituted an attempted solicitation.

G. Solicitation and Attempt

Solicitation is similar to a criminal attempt because it is a preliminary step toward the completion of a crime. Attempt law generally distinguishes between conduct that is so early in the sequence of events that it is deemed to be *preparatory* and not yet an attempt, and actions later in the progress of the crime that cross into *perpetration* of the offense and are sufficient to constitute an attempt. A majority of courts hold that the act of solicitation alone is insufficient to establish an attempt to commit the object offense. Solicitation by its nature involves inciting or encouraging another person to commit a crime in the future, so it is ordinarily preparatory to the commission of the object offense and does not involve actions that reach the perpetration stage of the crime.

Some courts, however, have upheld attempt charges when the solicitor undertakes additional acts to assist the solicitee in the commission of the crime and these additional acts, in addition to the solicitation, are of sufficient gravity that they satisfy one of the tests for an attempt crime (see Chapter 15). For example, a wife who hires two undercover officers posing as professional killers to murder her husband, pays a portion of the consideration in advance, identifies the husband's office location and car, and points out a possible site for disposing of the body has likely engaged in sufficient conduct to be guilty of attempted murder and not just solicitation to commit murder.

H. Merger

Solicitation is preparatory to the crimes of conspiracy and attempt to commit the object offense. In most jurisdictions this means that the crime of solicitation is held to merge into three other crimes if the evidence establishes the commission of that greater offense: (1) attempt, (2) conspiracy, and (3) the object crime. The result is that a person convicted of attempt, conspiracy, or the object crime may not *in addition* be convicted or sentenced for solicitation to commit the object crime. *See Model Penal Code § 5.05(3)* (barring convictions for more than one inchoate crime for conduct designed to commit the same crime); *§ 1.07(1)(b)* (barring conviction for both an inchoate crime and the object crime).

For example, A asks B to assist A in the commission of an arson of A's own warehouse so that A can collect insurance for the fire. B follows the plan and buys a flammable liquid and drives to the warehouse in the middle of the night intending to set the fire. If B is arrested as he or she arrives at the warehouse, both A and B may be guilty of attempted arson, but A may not also be convicted of solicitation for arson since the solicitation is deemed to merge with the attempt. Similarly, if A and B are charged with conspiracy to commit arson, A may not also be convicted of solicitation to commit arson because the solicitation merges with the conspiracy charge. Finally, if B is arrested after setting the fire, A and B may be guilty of arson (most likely A is an accessory before the fact and B is the principal), but A may not be convicted in addition of solicitation to commit arson as the solicitation crime merges with the object crime — arson.

I. Defenses

1. Renunciation and Entrapment

In many jurisdictions, solicitation is complete upon the communication of the request, and its receipt if that is also required. Any subsequent change of heart by the solicitor is irrelevant to the crime and so is not a defense. For example, if D solicits S to commit a theft, D is guilty of solicitation of theft when the communication is made, irrespective of S's response or whether D later has a change of mind and decides not to follow through with the heist.

Some modern jurisdictions, however, have enacted a *renunciation defense* designed to encourage people involved in criminal activity to change their mind and not commit the object offense. Model Penal Code § 5.02(3) provides "an affirmative defense that the actor, after soliciting another person to commit a crime, persuaded him not to do so or otherwise prevented the commission of the crime, under circumstances manifesting a complete and voluntary renunciation of his criminal purpose." This defense also applies to the crimes of attempt and conspiracy. Another defense may be *entrapment* because many solicitation charges involve undercover police operations (see Chapter 17).

2. Solicitor Cannot Be Convicted of Crime Solicited

Another rare defense arises when the solicitor cannot be convicted of the crime being solicited. For example, in many states an underage girl who asks her older boyfriend to engage in sexual relations with her could not be convicted of statutory rape because state law may bar a conviction of the victim. The theory is that the legislature did not intend for the underage victim to be convicted of violating a crime designed to protect her from others rather than from herself. If the victim could not be prosecuted for statutory rape, she could also not be convicted of solicitation of statutory rape for the same policy reasons.

The opposite result occurs if the person solicited, rather than the solicitor, could not be convicted of the crime. For example, assume that D solicits S to bribe a public official. D does not know that S is insane. D may be guilty of solicitation even though S, because of insanity, could not be guilty of bribery had the object crime been completed. The underlying theory is that D's guilt is based on D's actions and intent to commit the crime, and does not depend on whether anyone else could be responsible for the object crime. Thus, solicitation focuses on the danger created by the person who initiates criminal activity, irrespective of whether that activity ever occurs or whether the defendant ever successfully entices another person into joining the scheme.

Checkpoints

- Solicitation is a request that another person commit the crime or participate in the criminal activity.

- Asking another person to engage in conduct as an innocent instrumentality is not a solicitation.

- The solicitor must intend that the solicitee engage in the crime and not just the conduct that can lead to the offense.

- Some courts require that the solicitation be received by the solicited person before criminal liability attaches, precluding criminal charges for uncommunicated solicitations.

- Solicitation alone is not proof of an attempt to commit the crime.

- Solicitation merges into the object offense, an attempt to commit it, and conspiracy, so a defendant cannot be punished for both solicitation and the target offense, an attempt, or a conspiracy.

Chapter 15

Attempt and Related Preparatory Crimes

Roadmap

- The elements of attempt
- The meaning and importance of preparation and perpetration
- The tests used to determine whether the conduct goes beyond mere preparation
- Impossibility as a defense to attempt
- Abandonment as a defense to attempt
- The crime of communicating a threat
- The crime of possession of burglary tools
- The crime of assault

A. In General

The law of criminal attempts deals with defendants who do not, for one reason or another, succeed in completing their crime. For example, if a person takes out a gun, aims it, and then purposefully shoots and kills another person, a homicide charge is a likely result, probably first degree murder. If a second person aims a gun at another person but it misfires, or it hits but does not kill the victim, that may be a different crime: *attempted* murder. While the intent for each is identical, and the perpetrators caused a significant social harm (or, for attempt, at least the *risk* of serious harm), the criminal charges will not be the same because of the differing results. One may be guilty of murder while the other, because of luck or poor aim, cannot be convicted of murder because there has not been an unlawful killing. This individual may, however, be guilty of attempted murder.

1. Terminology

An analysis of attempt requires an understanding of two crimes: attempt and the target offense. *Attempt* is a crime in itself, carrying its own punishment. The offense may be charged as a discrete offense or as a *lesser-included* offense, and it is inextricably linked to the crime being attempted, called the *target* (or *object*) offense. Often a person convicted of an attempt is actually guilty of an offense called *attempted X*, where X is the target crime. For example, the person who shoots and only wounds a victim likely would be guilty of *attempted murder*, not simply of *attempt*. Similarly, someone arrested shortly before breaking into a house intending to steal something inside it would be guilty of *attempted burglary*.

2. Rationale for Attempt

Attempt punishes conduct that occurs in the steps leading toward commission of the target crime. If the target crime occurs, the defendant will be convicted of that crime rather than for the attempt to achieve that crime. Since attempt punishes acts that may, in themselves, be harmless to society, attempt crimes punish the *risk of harm* rather than actual harm. This distinguishes attempt from crimes such as murder or theft that require the offender to cause a harmful result.

While attempt does not punish someone solely for causing a result that is harmful to society, it is clear that it punishes those who have exhibited dangerousness and merit public intervention to prevent them from reaching their criminal objective; or, who sought to achieve a crime but failed for some extrinsic reason. It has been said that attempt protects society from people who intend to injure it.

For example, assume that D decides to rob a bank. D first scouts various banks, then selects one to rob, buys a gun, and is driving to the bank. If D is arrested in his or her car at this point, D may well be convicted of attempted bank robbery. Attempt law would in most jurisdictions hold D liable for a crime even though there is no actual harm, based on the policy decision that law enforcement authorities should be able to intervene to stop D's criminal scheme and that its punitive policies should be extended to someone like D who has manifested dangerousness.

3. Common Law and Modern Recognition

The common law did not begin to punish attempts as separate offenses until the late eighteenth century, and then only punished these activities as a misdemeanor. Today, every jurisdiction by statute punishes an attempt to commit a crime. Criminal codes often contain two varieties of attempt crimes. First, all jurisdictions have *general* attempt statutes that create a generic offense for an attempt to commit virtually any crime authorized by state law. For example, a jurisdiction with a first degree murder statute may have no crime specifically making attempted first degree murder an offense, but the general attempt law can be used to reach people who attempt to commit first degree murder. That same general provision may also reach those who attempt such crimes as rape, arson, or theft.

Second, many states have enacted *specific* attempt provisions or provide for enhanced punishment for those who attempt a particular identified crime. While a general attempt statute might provide for punishment up to half the authorized prison term for the object offense, a specific attempt statute could authorize punishment equal to that which would be imposed if the offense took place. These narrowly focused attempt laws enable the legislature to fine-tune the punishment for a limited number of offenses. For example, the California statute provides "if the crime attempted is willful, deliberate, and premeditated murder ... the person guilty of that attempt shall be punished by imprisonment in the state prison for life with the possibility of parole." *Cal. Penal Code § 664(a)*.

4. Punishment for Attempt

The grading of the crime of attempt is dependent on the target offense the defendant sought to accomplish. Thus, an attempt to commit a misdemeanor will be treated as a misdemeanor while an attempt to commit a felony is usually a felony. The underlying theory is that the gravity of the sanction for attempt should be consistent with, though not necessarily the same as, that for the crime attempted.

a. General Rule: Lesser Punishment Than for Target Crime

As a general rule, most jurisdictions authorize a lesser punishment for attempts to commit a crime than for completed offenses. The rationale is that the person who commits only an attempt has not caused the same harm as someone who completes the target crime and thus the "unsuccessful" criminal deserves a lesser punishment. Under this approach, some states allow punishment for attempt of up to one-half the authorized term for the target offense. A related sentencing model, present in many modern jurisdictions that classify their crimes into a small number of categories, is for an attempt to be classified one grade below that for the crime attempted. For example, if robbery is a Class B felony, an attempted robbery would be punished as a Class C felony.

b. Minority Rule: Same Punishment as Target Crime

A minority of jurisdictions, following Model Penal Code § 5.05(1), depart from the usual rule and make an attempt punishable in the same way as the most serious crime attempted. The Hawaii statute provides, "An attempt to commit a crime is an offense of the same class and grade as the most serious offense" attempted. *Haw. Rev. Stat. § 705-502.* The MPC explains this approach as based on the fact that the "antisocial disposition" of the defendant "and the demonstrated need for a corrective sanction" are the same irrespective of whether the target crime actually occurs. *See MPC § 5.05, comment.*

In jurisdictions adopting this approach, the person whose shot kills the intended victim is exactly the same in terms of mental culpability and danger to society as the one whose bullet misses the target or only injures the victim. These jurisdictions focus on the mental culpability of the offender and depart from the majority by not using their sentencing scheme to recognize a difference in terms of the actual harm the offender caused.

5. Attempt as Lesser Included Offense

For most offenses, attempt is a *lesser-included offense* of the target crime. The jury charge may include both the elements of the target crime and the attempt to commit that offense. This means that if the government fails to prove the completion of the target crime, the defendant can still be found guilty of an attempt even if it is not mentioned explicitly in the charging document. For example, if a defendant is charged with embezzlement but the jury hears the prosecution's proof and concludes that the defendant never actually converted the money to personal use, the defendant may be found guilty of attempted embezzlement for the unsuccessful efforts to obtain the money.

For many crimes, a defendant who commits the target crime also satisfies the elements needed for an attempt to commit that crime, thereby technically making the person criminally liable for both offenses. For example, in a jurisdiction that defined murder as the "intentional killing" of a human being, if D intentionally kills V, D would also be guilty of attempted murder since he or she would satisfy both the *mens rea* and *actus reus* necessary for an attempt conviction. Despite the fact that guilt for both crimes could be established, it is generally accepted in most states that a person cannot be convicted of both the target offense and an attempt to commit the target offense, absent unusual circumstances. If the same facts would establish the crime and an attempt, then the attempt is understood to *merge* into the completed offense and would not be a separate crime. The Double Jeopardy Clause bars multiple punishments for the same offense if the legislature did not intend that the crimes be prosecuted as separate offenses.

Many state statutes reflect the legislative intent to prohibit double convictions by specifically barring convictions for both the target crime and the attempt to commit that same target crime. For example, the Georgia statute provides, "A person may be convicted of the offense of criminal attempt if the crime attempted was actually committed in pursuance of the attempt but may not be convicted of both the criminal attempt and the completed crime." *Ga. Code Ann. § 16-4-2.*

6. Relationship to Solicitation and Conspiracy

Attempt, solicitation, and conspiracy are often classified as *inchoate* crimes. This means they are not the offender's ultimate criminal objective. They are committed as part of a scheme to commit the target crime. Concerned that aggressive prosecutors may try to convict offenders of two or more of these inchoate crimes, legislatures have enacted statutes limiting such prosecutions.

One such restriction, noted above, is that the defendant may not be convicted of both the target crime and the attempt to commit that crime. If D intentionally kills V, D may be guilty of intentional homicide but not also of attempted murder for that same killing.

Some states bar convictions of more than one of the three inchoate crimes for conduct directed toward the same target offense. For example, A solicits B to assist in stealing a valuable painting from a museum and both are arrested while trying to remove the painting from the wall. A may have committed three crimes: solicitation of B, conspiracy with B, and attempted theft of the painting. The Alaska statute provides, "A person may not be convicted of more than one crime ... for conduct designed to commit or culminate in commission of the same crime." *Alas. Stat. Ann. § 11.31.140.* Under the statute, A may only be convicted of one of the three inchoate crimes. A number of states allow a conviction for both attempt and conspiracy, but would preclude a solicitation conviction because that offense merges into the others.

7. Overview of Elements of Attempt

An important limitation on the scope of attempt crimes is the principle that a person is not liable solely based on evil intentions or bad thoughts. A criminal violation requires an act, the *actus reus*, coupled with the requisite intent. Merely proving a person's intention to commit a crime is usually insufficient for liability. At common law, two elements were required for conduct to be deemed a criminal attempt: (1) *intent* to commit the crime allegedly attempted;

and (2) sufficient *acts in furtherance* of that intent. Moderns attempt statutes often expand on these definitions, as discussed below.

8. Proof of Elements

The best way to think about an attempt crime is to view the defendant's conduct as occurring along a continuum, and asking whether the evidence is sufficient to establish (a) the *actus reus* of the offense and (b) the *mens rea*. Attempt is a specific intent crime, meaning that the prosecutor must prove that the defendant intended to commit the target offense. At what point along the continuum is the defendant's conduct sufficient to establish the act and intent for an attempt?

The government often uses the same evidence to meet its burden of proof on both the *actus reus* and *mens rea* elements of attempt. In most cases, intent is inferred from the acts taken toward completion of the crime, so a key issue is whether the accused has "done enough" to justify an inference of criminal intent.

Most attempt charges involve a result crime, such as murder, arson, or theft. Because a certain outcome must occur for the target offense, it is often easier to prove an attempt if the target crime involves an identifiable result because particular acts leading toward that result are a good indication that the defendant intends to commit the target crime.

For example, assume a person, dressed in black and armed with a high-powered rifle, is found hiding in shrubbery near the office of an enemy late one evening. The jury could easily conclude from these facts that the defendant had the intent to kill and was guilty of attempted murder. Similarly, a person entering a store with stolen merchandise and receipts most likely is attempting to defraud the cashier into giving a cash refund for stolen items, a type of larceny.

An interesting question is whether the government can prove attempt for a conduct or status crime, such as driving while intoxicated or being a felon in possession of a weapon. There is no theoretical reason why these types of offenses cannot be charged as attempts, but it is difficult to determine what conduct rises to the level of a criminal attempt short of completing the crime.

B. *Actus Reus* of Attempt

1. Preparation and Perpetration

The law of attempt has long provided that more than thoughts alone are necessary for an attempt. Some *conduct* is required, but what conduct is sufficient? This issue is complex because offenders, such as hired assassins, may take many steps in trying to commit a murder, while others may try to accomplish the offense in one movement, like the rash killer who is provoked and responds immediately.

The law of attempt has long recognized that the defendant's actions must be more than a minor act. Some authorities explain this by observing that preliminary acts do not indicate the offender's social dangerousness and should not be punished as attempt. Thus, the *actus reus* of attempt requires the act be of sufficient importance that it goes beyond what has historically been called mere *preparation* into the realm called *perpetration*. An attempt occurs only when the actor has crossed this barely discernible line.

The government must prove beyond a reasonable doubt that the defendant committed sufficient acts to satisfy the jurisdiction's definition of attempt. This presents a challenge to law enforcement who, of course, may want to intervene as early as possible to thwart a criminal scheme. Yet they may also feel conflicted because they may want to wait and monitor the situation until the offender takes enough steps to constitute the crime of attempt. In this way they can obtain a conviction for a more serious crime (attempt) than they could if they make an early intervention before the defendant's conduct amounted to an attempt.

Assume that on Monday, D forms the idea to kill a particular politician. On Tuesday, D searches the internet for the victim's schedule. On Wednesday, D goes to the hotel where the victim will speak the next day and plans how to kill the victim and escape safely. On Thursday, D puts a rifle in the trunk of a car and drives to the hotel where the crime will occur. As D enters the hotel with the rifle hidden in a long coat, security personnel apprehend him or her. If the government wants to try D for attempted murder, it must prove that the actions were of sufficient magnitude to cross the line from preparation to perpetration.

It should be obvious that there is no precise dividing line between preparation (not an attempt) and perpetration (possibly an attempt). The question of whether the conduct has advanced sufficiently for criminal liability to attach is submitted to the trier of fact unless the court decides as a matter of law that it could not constitute perpetration. In the above hypothetical, when D entered the hotel with the rifle on Thursday, sufficient acts likely occurred to satisfy the *actus reus* of attempt in any jurisdiction. But if the security authorities learned about D's plan and arrested him or her on an earlier day, at what point would D have attempted the killing: on Monday, after forming the idea; on Tuesday, when determining the victim's schedule; or on Wednesday, when scouting the hotel? What if D were arrested while driving to the hotel, would that be sufficient to constitute perpetration and not mere preparation?

2. Tests of Conduct Sufficient for Attempt

Courts have used different tests to determine if the conduct has gone beyond mere preparation. While a number of verbal descriptions of the appropriate test have been offered in cases, they can be difficult to distinguish and even more difficult to apply. It is clear that attempt cases are decided on their own peculiar facts, but the test used in a particular jurisdiction may favor one side or the other and will focus the lawyers on what conduct should be emphasized in advocating for their clients. Because of the vague descriptive words used to describe the various tests of the *actus reus* of attempt, there is significant flexibility in the application of the standard.

a. Dangerous Proximity

Pioneered by Justice Holmes, first in Massachusetts and then on the Supreme Court, this test looks primarily at the physical aspects of the conduct to determine how close a defendant was to the actual commission of the offense. The underlying theory is that the defendant should be deterred only when the conduct reaches the point of dangerousness. Language used by courts includes describing the conduct as "a direct movement toward the commission of the offense after the preparations are made," or where the defendant "is so near to the result that the danger of success is very great." The greater the gravity of the target crime, the more remote the conduct can be from completion of the target offense. The focus on physical proximity can lead to an acquittal of a defendant who seeks to commit a crime but is unable to get close enough to do so.

In *People v. Rizzo*, 158 N.E. 888 (N.Y. 1927), the New York Court of Appeals overturned the conviction for attempted robbery of four defendants who drove around the city searching in vain for a person who they believed would withdraw a large sum of cash to meet a payroll. After being observed by the police, the defendants were arrested when one entered a building where the victim was thought to be, but in fact was not. The court found that while the police work was exemplary, the defendants were not close enough to their intended victim and so an attempt had not occurred. The defendants were still in the preparatory stage when apprehended.

b. Last Act

The strictest approach is a requirement that the person engage in the *last proximate act*, that is, have done everything the person believes necessary to bring about the intended result. Under this approach, a court would not find an attempt until the defendant had virtually pointed the gun at the victim and pulled the trigger or entered the bank with drawn pistol and demanded money.

While courts have moved away from this test as the sole measure of attempt, many jurisdictions still use it as an alternate one. Reflecting the significant influence of the Model Penal Code, often it is an alternative to the substantial step approach discussed below. In these jurisdictions, D would commit an attempt by either doing everything needed to accomplish the target crime (last act test) or by taking a substantial step, corroborative of criminal purpose, toward that goal.

Indeed, the last act approach is not surprising since it would be shocking if conduct that satisfies this test is not sufficient to constitute an attempt. After all, the defendant has done everything in the plan to commit the target offense. Connecticut, adopting this approach as one way an attempt may be committed, provides that an attempt occurs when a person "intentionally engages in conduct that would constitute the crime if attendant circumstances were as he believes them to be." *Conn. Gen. Stat. § 53a-49(a)*.

c. Indispensable Element

Some courts follow a less rigid formula that looks to whether an act, over which the defendant has no control, remained to be done to commit the target crime. The emphasis under this analysis is less on what the accused has done than what remains to be done, so the time and place of an intended crime take on considerable importance. An illustration would be a scheme where X did the first part of a crime and Y committed the final part. An attempt would not occur as long as Y had not taken action.

d. Probable Desistance

Under this test, the accused's conduct must pass the point where most people would think better of their conduct and voluntarily desist. The focus is on whether the conduct is sufficient to infer a defendant's intent, and whether that intent reached the point at which the criminal object is sufficiently clear. The Wisconsin statute requires proof that "the actor does acts toward the commission of the crime which demonstrate unequivocally, under all the circumstances, that the actor formed that intent and would commit the crime except for the intervention of another person or some other extraneous factor." *Wis. Stat. Ann. § 639.42*.

The probable desistance analysis is an objective test in some locales. The factfinder determines whether a reasonable person reached the point of being firmly committed to the criminal plan, not whether the particular defendant might have desisted from the crime. The probable desistance test would permit a conviction for attempt at an earlier point than the dangerous proximity test because the focus is on confirming the firmness of the defendant's intent to engage in the crime, which could be shown well before the person reaches the point of nearly committing the crime. For example, under the facts of *People v. Rizzo*, the defendants would likely be convicted of attempted robbery because their conduct had reached the point that they were committed to the criminal scheme and failed only because of the police intervention.

*e. Unequivocality/*Res Ipsa Loquitur

Under this test, what transforms a person's conduct from preparation into perpetration is undertaking an act that can have no other purpose than the commission of the target offense. This approach invokes the tort doctrine of *res ipsa loquitur*, which means "the thing speaks for itself," under which an accident itself, if unexplained, affords reasonable evidence of a want of proper care to establish tort liability for the harm. In the criminal law context, the act is such that it demonstrates the defendant's intent to commit the crime without need for further evidence of how close the person came to completing the crime. The question is whether any particular act short of committing the crime can be said to demonstrate unequivocally a person's decision to engage in criminal conduct.

For example, a person who enters a liquor store and brandishes a weapon at a clerk behind the cash register can be convicted of attempted armed robbery, but the same person who is arrested on the sidewalk while approaching the store would not necessarily have engaged in an act that demonstrates unequivocally the intent to rob the store. The test is similar to the dangerous proximity approach that looks to clear conduct close to the commission of the crime as the prerequisite to liability for an attempt.

f. Substantial Step

Model Penal Code § 5.01(1)(c) and the majority of jurisdictions allow a conviction for an attempt if a person "purposely does or omits to do anything which, under the circumstances as he believes them to be, is an act or omission constituting a *substantial step* in a course of conduct planned to culminate in his commission of the crime." Perhaps out of concern that the trier of fact will reject evidence that the legislature deems sufficient to amount to a substantial step, some statutes specifically list conduct that as a matter of law may not be deemed insufficient if strongly corroborative of criminal purpose. The list includes lying in wait, enticing the victim to go to the place where the crime is to occur, "reconnoitering" or unlawfully entering the place contemplated for the crime, or possession of materials that serve no other lawful use and are to be used in the commission of the crime. *Conn. Gen. Stat. § 53a-49.*

In the substantial step jurisdictions, the government must also prove that the substantial step is "strongly corroborative" of the person's intent to engage in the crime. This has been characterized as focusing on the danger posed by an actor who has manifested a firm disposition to commit a crime. Unlike the unequivocality approach, however, the usual interpretation of "strongly corroborative of criminal purpose" is that the government need not demonstrate the person's clear intent to engage in the illegal act. "Some verification" of that intent is sufficient. Moreover, the actor does not have to reach a point at which the crime is likely to occur, or the person would be unlikely to desist.

In moving away from the focus of the common law on how close the defendant's conduct comes to committing the crime, the "strongly corroborative" element asks whether the defendant's conduct has advanced sufficiently to show that the person intends to commit a crime, at which point the person is guilty of an attempt. This subjectivist approach can result in greater liability for attempts. Conviction may be more difficult, however, in the minority of "strongly corroborative" jurisdictions that raise the bar and specify that the substantial step "must leave no reasonable doubt as to the defendant's intention to commit" the target crime. *Del. Code Ann. § 532.*

For example, in the *People v. Rizzo* case, when the four thieves began driving around the city looking for the payroll courier, a jury could find that they had taken a substantial step sufficient to permit a conviction for attempted robbery. Similarly, the person approaching the liquor store armed with a weapon could be convicted of attempted robbery even though under other tests the conduct may not have advanced sufficiently to meet the requirement for an attempt.

g. Accomplices

A significant change by the Model Penal Code from the common law of accomplice liability is in defining an accomplice as someone who, among other acts, *attempts to aid* in the planning or commission of a crime. Under the common law, attempted assistance might not be sufficient to establish accomplice liability if the principal did not commit the object offense or did not undertake sufficient acts to constitute an attempt to commit the crime. Under the MPC, however, a person can be guilty as an accomplice to an attempt offense even if the perpetrator would not be liable because the perpetrator's acts do not amount to an attempt since they do not constitute a substantial step toward the commission of the crime. Model Penal Code § 5.01(3), which defines attempt, provides that "[a] person who engages in conduct designed to aid another to commit a crime that would establish his complicity under Section 2.06 if the crime were committed by such other person, is guilty of an attempt to commit the crime, *although the crime is not committed or attempted by such other person."*

For example, A, to assist D in a robbery, provides D with a description of the operation of a check-cashing store, including when it receives its currency shipments and the time when the guards change shifts. The next day, D is arrested on an unrelated charge and A's information is discovered, so the robbery neither occurs nor was it attempted, unless the preliminary planned is sufficient to show a substantial step toward commission of the offense. If it is not a substantial step, then D cannot be charged with attempted robbery of the store under the attempt rules of § 5.01(1)(c). A, however, can be held liable as an accomplice for the attempt to aid D, even though D did not do enough to be personally guilty of attempted robbery.

The common law would not permit such a result because no principal committed the attempt offense, so there is no crime to aid. The MPC, however, focuses on the intent of the accomplice as the basis for criminal liability. The purpose to aid a robbery means the attempted assistance is sufficient for a conviction. Note further that the concept of "attempted aid" means that the assistance may be ineffectual to assist in any way in the ultimate crime. The key is that the aid was attempted, not that it mattered. Similarly, if the aid was attempted it may be sufficient for accomplice liability even if the principal actor was unaware that he or she had been aided.

C. *Mens Rea* of Attempt

1. *Mens Rea* Elements

Attempt statutes vary in their precise wording, but in general terms attempt laws contain three *mens rea* elements. The government must prove that the defendant acted with: (1) the *intent* to commit the target offense, (2) the intent to engage in the conduct constituting the attempt, and (3) the *mens rea* required for the target offense. Often facts proving one of these also establishes the others.

a. Intent to Commit Target Offense

The most obvious *mens rea* of attempt is the *intent to commit the target offense.* For example, state attempt statutes may require the person to "intend to commit" the target crime (*Kans. Stat. Ann. § 21-3301(a)*), or perform conduct "intended to culminate in his or her commission of" the target crime (*Neb. Rev. Stat. § 28-201(1)(b)*).

This specific intent element does not mean the actor must know the law or even the elements of the target crime. Rather, the defendant must have the intent to commit the target crime in a general sense. For example, for attempted arson there must be the intent to set fire to a building and for attempted robbery the intent to take property by force. For attempted murder, the defendant must have the intent to take human life; the intent to commit serious bodily injury is usually insufficient. In one unusual illustrative case, the defendant fired one bullet at two police officers and was convicted of two counts of attempted murder on the theory that he intended to kill them both. *People v. Chinchilla*, 60 Cal. Rptr.2d 761 (1997).

Since general intent will not suffice and a more specific intent is required for the crime of attempt, courts routinely hold that an attempt charge cannot stand when the defendant is only reckless or negligent. The necessary specific intent is lacking. For example, assume that D drinks too much and then is arrested as he walks to his car, which he is planning on driving through a crowded intersection. D is not guilty of reckless endangerment (reckless conduct exposing someone to the risk of serious injury) because D has not yet endangered anyone, but could D be guilty of *attempted* reckless endangerment? The answer is "no" because D lacks the intent to be reckless that would be required for the crime of attempted reckless endangerment. In other words, the defendant lacked the specific intent needed for an attempt.

b. Intent to Engage in the Conduct Constituting the Attempt

A second *mens rea* of attempt is the intent to do the conduct that satisfies the *actus reus* of attempt. For example, an attempt statute may reach someone who "intentionally engages in conduct" which would constitute the target offense if the circumstances were as the actor believed them to be. *Ariz. Rev. Stat. § 13-1001(A)(1)*. This would occur if the defendant mailed a letter bomb to an enemy, expecting it to explode when opened. Some courts refer to the second intent as requiring proof of *knowledge* that the acts will lead to the commission of the target offense.

c. Mens Rea *for Target Crime*

Attempt is not a completely separate crime, and so the defendant must also have the *mens rea* for the object offense. Sometimes this requirement is stated specifically in the attempt law. A common formulation is that a conviction for attempt requires the government to prove that the defendant acted "with the kind of culpability otherwise required for commission of" the target offense. *Colo. Rev. Stat. § 18-2-101(1)*. For example, if the target crime is arson, which requires the intent to set fire to a building, a defendant guilty of attempted arson must act with the intent to set fire to a building.

2. Illustration: Attempted Homicide

For a specific intent crime, the prosecution will have to show both the intent to commit the offense and intent to engage in the acts constituting the attempt, plus the *mens rea* for the target crime. Assume that D shot a rifle at V, but missed.

Can D be convicted of attempted first degree murder, defined as a killing that is wilful, deliberate, and premeditated? To be guilty, the government would have to prove that D's action were sufficient for the *actus reus* of attempt (they surely were under any test) and that D satisfied both the *mens rea* of attempt as well as that for first degree murder, the target offense. If the proof showed that D had a plan to kill V, it is likely D would be guilty of attempted first degree murder since the prosecution could establish the necessary *mens rea* elements: intent to kill (for attempt) and wilful, deliberate, and premeditated killing (for first degree murder).

Some states recognize the charge of attempted second degree murder because intent to kill, a *mens rea* for this crime in many jurisdictions, may be inferred from circumstantial evidence that does not establish premeditation but does show the killing was the result sought by the defendant. In the above hypothetical, this might be the case if D shot at V for the purpose of killing V but did not do so with both premeditation and deliberation.

A defendant can be charged with attempted *voluntary* manslaughter because that crime requires proof of a defendant's intent to kill mitigated by an adequate provocation, so a violent response to a provocation that does not result in death can be charged as an attempt. This could occur if D, outraged and adequately provoked to satisfy the elements of voluntary manslaughter, shot and missed V. The crime would have been voluntary manslaughter had D's shot been true.

An attempt to commit criminally negligent homicide would not be possible, however, because attempt crimes require specific intent, and a negligent act is not performed intentionally. Thus, D is not guilty of attempted criminally negligent homicide even though shooting at V is surely a criminally negligent act. Similarly, a charge of attempted felony-murder would be impermissible because the killing is an unintended consequence of the underlying felony and not a desired result. For attempted felony murder, the defendant would have to have the intent to kill.

3. Evidence of *Mens Rea* Elements

As with all issues of proof of a defendant's mental state, proof of intent often is based on *circumstantial evidence*, including the defendant's words and conduct, the overall plan, and the actions of everyone involved in the scheme. It can be difficult to determine what the defendant intended if the crime did not reach the point at which it was nearly a completed offense.

Some courts ease the government's proof of intent by instructing the jury that it may, but is not required to, infer that a person intends the *natural and probable consequences* of the conduct. This inference would allow the jury to find that a person, who fired a weapon into the passenger compartment of a vehicle that cut in front of the perpetrator's car, intended to kill the driver because the death would be a natural and probable consequence of the shooting.

Another similar inference is that intent to kill may be inferred from the use of a deadly weapon directed at a vital part of the victim's body. Other illustrations from case law are that the intent to kill was found to be present when the defendant did such actions as threaten to kill the victim and repeatedly stab the victim in the torso.

One case involved a man who, knowing he was infected with the Human Immunodeficiency Virus (HIV), raped three women without taking precautions to avoid spreading the virus. He was charged with three counts of attempted murder. The appellate court reversed because of insufficient evidence of the intent to kill. The court held that the "natural and probable consequences" inference would not establish intent to kill since death was not the "probable" result of the victims' exposure to the virus. To establish the necessary intent to kill, the government would have had to introduce such evidence as the defendant's oral statements indicating the intent to kill, as occurred when a prisoner with HIV spat on a guard and believed this would kill the guard. *Smallwood v. State*, 680 A.2d 512 (Md. 1996).

D. Impossibility

In some cases, the defendant's act could never result in the completion of the target crime because an attendant circumstance does not exist or a result could not be accomplished. For example, a defendant may try to kill someone by blowing up the person's house, but, unbeknownst to the defendant, no one has lived in the house for months. In such cases defendants often argue that they should not be convicted of attempted murder because it was *impossible* to commit the crime. Another example is someone who pays money to bribe a person thought to be a juror but who, in fact, is an undercover police officer. The defense to a charge of attempted bribery of a juror may be that the crime was impossible since no juror was bribed.

1. Overlapping and Vague Categories

The common law divided impossibility claims into two types: *factual impossibility* and *legal impossibility*. Legal impossibility is now further divided into *hybrid legal impossibility* and *pure* or *true legal impossibility*. While factual impossibility was not a defense to an attempt charge, legal impossibility was a valid defense. The problem with this simple division is that cases cannot be so easily distinguished, and the law in this area can be contradictory. For example, shooting at an empty bed where the victim usually slept was determined to be factual impossibility in one case, while shooting at a tree stump believed to be a person was found to be legal impossibility in another. Similarly, engaging in sexual intercourse with a woman who had died a short time earlier was attempted rape, but shooting a corpse thinking the person was alive was legal impossibility for attempted murder.

2. Traditional Categories: Factual and Legal Impossibility

a. Factual Impossibility

Factual impossibility is when the defendant is mistaken about the facts surrounding the crime such that it cannot be accomplished. The law of attempt does not recognize factual impossibility as a defense and the defendant can still be held liable for an attempt crime.

The classic example used to demonstrate factual impossibility is the case of the unlucky pickpocket who attempts to steal from an empty pocket. The frustrated thief could not be convicted of theft since nothing was taken, but could be held criminally liable for attempted theft despite the fact that the pocket was empty. The reasoning is that if the pocket had contained money, the theft crime could have taken place. Similarly, the defendant who shoots bullets into the head of a dummy, thinking it is a human being, could be guilty of attempted murder as if the dummy were in fact a human. The defendant is held accountable for the attempted crime because this "factual" impossibility does not negate the defendant's intent to commit the crime.

A common modern scenario raising impossibility questions involves undercover police operations targeting people seeking to have sexual relations with minors by contacting them through the internet. Posing as a boy or girl under the age of consent, adult police officers arrange a meeting with the correspondent and then charge the person with attempted criminal sexual conduct with an underage victim. The defendant's presence at the meeting place is usually sufficient to show conduct beyond mere preparation. The absence of an actual underage victim can be viewed as either factual impossibility or legal impossibility. Most courts put this conduct in the factual impossibility category because the defendant's intent to engage in the conduct is clear from the communications and the defendant was merely mistaken about a fact—the age of the victim. *E.g., In re Doe*, 855 A.2d 1100 (D.C. 2004) (for crime of attempted enticement of a child, the fact that victim was not a minor, unbeknownst to the defendant, is factual impossibility and no defense).

b. Legal Impossibility

Legal impossibility occurs when the defendant has made efforts to do something that is not a crime. Case law today recognizes two types of legal impossibility: hybrid and true. Hybrid involves a factual situation that can be characterized as either factual or legal, and involves a defendant who is mistaken about a legal status, while pure legal impossibility clearly involves a case where no crime would have occurred.

i. Hybrid Legal Impossibility

Hybrid legal impossibility is present when the defendant has an illegal goal, but could not accomplish the crime because of a mistake about the legal status of a relevant factor. One case cited the following examples of hybrid impossibility: receiving unstolen property believing it to have been stolen (charged with attempted receiving stolen property), picking the pocket of a stone image of a human (attempted theft), offering a bribe to a "juror" who was not actually a juror (attempted bribery of a juror), shooting a stuffed animal thinking it was a deer that was being shot out of season (attempted hunting out of season), and shooting a corpse or tree stump believing it to be alive (attempted murder). *People v. Thousand*, 631 N.W.2d 694 (Mich. 2001).

In a case like the attempted murder involving a dummy, the defense may argue that the impossibility is not factual, but rather it is legal impossibility because an element of the crime is missing since there was no human victim. Legal impossibility has historically been a defense to an attempt charge. The classic example of legal impossibility is *People v. Jaffe*, 78 N.E. 169 (N.Y. 1906), in which the court held that a person accepting goods which he believed to have been stolen, but which were not then stolen goods because the authorities had already recovered them, was not guilty of an attempt to receive stolen goods because it was legally impossible for the crime to occur without stolen goods involved in the transaction.

It is important to distinguish an impossibility defense from a *mistake defense* based on the defendant's misapprehension of a legal requirement for conduct. As discussed in Chapter 5, for a specific intent crime, a defendant's subjective belief can negate the intent for the crime. For example, assume that a defendant takes property, erroneously believing it is abandoned, and is charged with theft, which includes a *mens rea* element that the defendant had the intent to deprive the owner of the property. The defendant may offer a defense of mistake, arguing that he or she lacked the necessary *mens rea* because of the erroneous belief about the legal status of the object as abandoned. This is not a legal impossibility defense, but a mistake defense that, by proving that the defendant had no intent to deprive the owner of the "abandoned" property, seeks to disprove the *mens rea* of the theft crime.

ii. "True" Legal Impossibility

While, as discussed below, today most jurisdictions do not recognize either factual or legal impossibility, in the case of "true" or "pure" legal impossibility there may be no crime for which the accused could be prosecuted, making this variety of legal impossibility a viable defense. A "true" legal impossibility is when there would be no crime even if the object of the crime had been fully accomplished. The legislature has not criminalized the defendant's conduct or the results that he or she sought to bring about. Although the defendant may be quite surprised that he or she was not involved in criminal behavior, the defendant's belief is not sufficient to make conduct criminal.

For example, a defendant forges a prescription to obtain a drug that was recently approved for over-the-counter sales without a prescription. The defendant was unaware of the change in the law and thought that a prescription was needed for the drug. If the defendant were charged with attempting to purchase a narcotic without a valid prescription, "true" legal impossibility would be a good defense because no crime could take place if the defendant obtained the drug. The legislature had not criminalized the purchase of that particular drug, though the defendant may have been mistaken about the legal status of purchasing the medication. Since it was not a crime to purchase that drug, it also was not a crime to attempt to purchase it.

Note that while the defendant could not be convicted of attempted purchase of a narcotic drug, he or she could be charged with actual or attempted forgery of the prescription. That offense is not dependent on the drug requiring a prescription; it only requires a forged signature on a medical prescription.

3. Elimination of Factual and Legal Impossibility

Many jurisdictions today have eliminated both factual and hybrid legal impossibility as a defense to attempt. True legal impossibility remains a defense in every jurisdiction.

A typical provision removing the defenses states that factual or legal impossibility is not a defense "if such crime could have been committed had the attendant circumstances been as the accused believed them to be." *Ga. Code Ann. § 16-4-4*. Thus, for purposes of the law of attempt, the facts are treated as the defendant thought they were, including the legal status of something crucial to the crime.

Under this approach, the pickpocket who reaches into an empty pocket to steal a wallet would be guilty of attempted theft. The court would view this factual impossibility situation as if the pocket had contained the wallet the defendant believed was there. Similarly, the person who purchased "stolen" goods believing them to have been stolen, though the items had not in fact been stolen, would be guilty of attempted receiving stolen property, despite the status of the goods possibly making the issue one of legal impossibility. For purposes of liability for attempt, this modern view would treat the goods as stolen, because the defendant believed them to be.

4. Inherent Impossibility

Though perhaps the product of overly active academic minds, there is another category of impossibility, called *inherent impossibility*. In some bizarre circumstances a person, perhaps of unsound mind or at least with little common sense, may take steps to commit a serious crime but uses means that make the crime inherently impossible to accomplish. The common illustration is someone who sticks pins in the head of a doll fashioned to look like a particular person, believing that the person will die because of the pins. Assuming that the defendant cannot successfully assert an insanity defense, may he or she be guilty of attempted murder?

A few jurisdictions specifically recognize that in such cases the criminal law should acknowledge the lack of public harm and refrain from imposing full criminal liability for attempt. Model Penal Code § 5.05(2) provides that in such cases when neither the conduct nor the actor presents a public danger, the trial court has the authority to lower the level of the crime or even to dismiss the prosecution. A few states are more specific, giving a statutory defense when the "conduct charged to constitute the offense [of attempt] is inherently unlikely to result or to culminate in the commission of a crime; and neither the conduct nor the defendant presents a public danger warranting imposition of criminal liability." *Ark. Code Ann. §5-3-101.*

E. Abandonment (or Renunciation)

States divide over whether a person's decision to abandon a course of conduct should relieve liability for an attempt crime. For example, D decides to rob a bank, puts a gun in the car and drives toward the bank, then changes his or her mind in the bank's parking lot. Of course D is not guilty of bank robbery since D quit the scheme before any robbery occurred. The issue is whether D engaged in sufficient conduct to commit the crime of *attempted* bank robbery, and if so, does the fact that D abandoned the plan serve as a defense to the attempt offense.

1. Common Law

a. Did Not Recognize Abandonment Defense

The common law did not recognize an abandonment (or renunciation) defense because, once the defendant's conduct crossed the line from preparation to perpetration, the crime of attempt was complete and liability should attach. The defendant's decision to forego committing the target crime did not "erase" the attempt crime that was already completed.

b. Absence of Formal Abandonment Defense

Even if a jurisdiction does not recognize an abandonment defense, a defendant's decision to desist from the course of conduct leading to the crime can be the basis to argue that there is insufficient evidence of perpetration to prove an attempt. The abandonment can also be used to infer that the accused did not have the requisite intent to attempt the target offense. Another advantage of abandonment is that it may relieve the defendant of responsibility for the target crime if any accomplices persist in carrying out the plan.

2. Modern Statutes: Recognition of Abandonment (or Renunciation) Defense

The modern trend is toward recognition of the defense. The Model Penal Code and many modern state statutes include a provision that abandonment of a criminal attempt is an affirmative defense to a charge. Often these statutes call the defense "renunciation." Several reasons support this policy decision. First, some argue that providing an abandonment defense encourages offenders to quit before committing the target crime. The abandonment defense is considered an incentive. Another argument is that a true voluntary cessation of the criminal conduct tends to negate the dangerousness of the actor.

In those jurisdictions that recognize the defense, the defendant must abandon the effort to commit the crime *before* its consummation. The abandonment must involve a complete and voluntary renunciation of the criminal goal. To qualify for this defense, several steps must occur.

a. Voluntary

The abandonment defense is usually available only to offenders who *voluntarily* give up the scheme. To be considered voluntary, the decision to abandon must originate with the defendant, not as a result of extrinsic factors that increase the probability of detection or the difficulty of committing the target crime. For example, assume that D, while opening a window of a house D is going to burglarize, sees the homeowner coming down the stairs to investigate the noise created by the window. If D hides in the bushes in the back yard and is arrested there, D would not be eligible for an abandonment defense because the crime ceased due to extrinsic factors, such as the fear of discovery, rather than D's personal motive to give up a criminal course of conduct.

b. Complete

The abandonment defense is generally only available if the defendant's decision was not only voluntary but also *complete*. This means that the offender not only desisted from this particular episode but also gave up the idea of committing the crime. If the defendant remained committed to completing the offense at another time or location or against another victim, the desistance would not qualify for the defense since it would not be deemed a complete abandonment.

c. Prevent Commission of Target Crime

A common feature of virtually all abandonment provisions is that the defendant has a defense to attempt only if he or she somehow prevents commission of the target crime. If the defendant voluntarily and completely abandons the plan but accomplices proceed and commit it, the defendant may not use the abandonment defense to avoid liability for attempt. The rationale is that the defense is an incentive for the defendant, who has significant knowledge about the target crime, to use that information to prevent that crime from occurring.

The statutes are vague about what the defendant must do to prevent the target crime from occurring. Some use language such as "taking further and affirmative steps" to prevent the crime. *See Ala. Code § 13A-4-2(c)*. Another approach requires the defendant to notify law enforcement authorities if necessary to stop the target offense from occurring.

For example, if D mails a bomb to his or her enemy, D may have an abandonment defense for attempted murder only if D somehow prevents the bomb from killing the victim. D could accomplish this by retrieving the bomb, warning the recipient, or informing law enforcement in time for it to be found and defused. The issue can be more complex if D is one of many participants involved in committing the target crime. D may have to do whatever is necessary to stop the others from accomplishing their criminal goal. Perhaps D could dissuade them from proceeding, or could warn the victim or police.

A minority of jurisdictions recognize that sometimes the defendant's best efforts cannot prevent commission of the target crime. These jurisdictions do not require the impossible. Their goal is to encourage participants to take whatever steps are most likely to result in the ultimate crime from occurring. The defendant need only give "timely warning" to law enforcement authorities or take other reasonable steps to prevent the target crime. *Ariz. Rev. Stat. § 13-1005*. The warning must be given in sufficient time to permit the law enforcement personnel to prevent the target crime.

F. Criminalizing Preparatory Conduct

An attempt charge reaches acts that are committed as part of a course of conduct leading to commission of the target crime. In general terms, the law of attempt requires the government to prove criminality based on what can be inferred from the evidence regarding how a course of events would have developed and what the defendant's state of mind was in pursuing the conduct.

Attempt is only one way that this preliminary conduct is made criminal. Often legislatures create other crimes that punish actions early in a sequence of events. Sometimes these separate crimes reach actions that would be deemed in the "preparation" rather than "perpetration" stage and therefore, would not satisfy the *actus reus* of attempt.

1. Communicating a Threat

Some legislatures have enacted statutes that make it a crime to *communicate a threat*, even if the threat is never received or the recipient is not harmed by the conduct. The transmission of the threat may not rise to the level of an assault or an attempted battery, but the preparatory conduct itself is made a criminal act so that the person can be convicted before there is a substantial step toward a more serious offense. It is not necessary to show that the threat induced fear in the named victim, and a conviction under such a statute can be upheld even though the communication was not delivered to the person threatened.

2. Possession of Burglary Tools

Most states have a statutory crime that punishes the *possession of burglar's tools*. It reaches people who possess certain implements with the intent to use them in committing a burglary. The statutes often include a list of implements covered by the crime. A typical list is: an explosive, tool, instrument or other article adapted, designed, or commonly used in a burglary. If a person is stopped short of completing the requisite breaking and entry for a burglary while using a tool to accomplish the crime, he or she may be charged with both attempted burglary and possession of burglar's tools.

The separate crime of possession of burglary tools may occur, however, at such an early stage that the offender has not engaged in a sufficient *actus reus* to constitute an attempted burglary. The burglary tool statute criminalizes conduct — possession — that is not necessarily sufficiently close to the target offense to satisfy the *actus reus* of attempt.

What constitutes a burglary tool often cannot be determined from a particular item's innate characteristics, but only from the context in which it is to be used. An item of common household usage might not be sufficient to establish the defendant's intent to possess a burglary tool. There are tools, however, so peculiarly adapted to the commission of a burglary or trespass that they are sufficient to establish the defendant's intent to use them to commit a crime.

3. Assault as Attempted Battery

Under the common law, the crime of *assault* can cover several types of conduct. One is an *attempt to commit a battery* where the defendant engages in conduct designed to injure the victim. For example, if D swings at V intending to knock V down, but misses V entirely, D may be guilty of assault of the attempted-battery type. Many jurisdictions that prosecute the attempted-battery type of assault add an additional element: the government must also prove that the defendant has the *present ability* to commit the assault. Present ability is similar to the perpetration requirement for an attempt crime, in that a person who does not have the present ability to cause a battery will not have reached a point where liability can be assessed for an assault. This type of assault should be distinguished from conduct intentionally causing the victim to be in reasonable fear of immediate bodily harm which is discussed in Chapter 10.

Assault of the attempted-battery variety requires an intent to injure, but what if D's goal were to kill V? Many jurisdictions did not have the crimes of assault with intent to murder. Instead, an assault with this specific intent is simply treated as "attempted murder." In addition to attempted murder, this crime would also qualify for the far less serious crime of "assault" because it was an attempted battery. To increase the penalty for serious assaults, some jurisdictions recognized the offense of assault with intent to commit murder as a crime separate from attempted murder. Many modern jurisdictions have the offense of "aggravated assault" to impose a more severe punishment when the defendant intends to cause serious bodily injury or uses a deadly weapon in an assault.

Since this variety of assault is actually an attempted battery, many courts hold that there is no such crime as *attempted assault*. They adopt the rule that one cannot attempt to commit an attempt. Using this same rationale, some courts have even held that the offense of *attempted battery* does not exist because assault law already punishes an attempt to commit a battery.

G. Model Penal Code

The Model Penal Code takes a subjective approach to attempt, with the focus on "the actor's disposition." This is clearest in the *mens rea* requirements for an attempt. In general terms, the government must prove that the defendant acted with the purpose to commit a crime, and the belief that the conduct would lead to the commission of the target offense. The acts must be a "substantial step" toward the commission of the crime that is "strongly corroborative" of the defendant's purpose.

1. *Actus Reus* and *Mens Rea*

Section 5.01(1) states that an attempt requires the defendant to have the purpose to commit the offense and have the *mens rea* of the target crime. If the target crime requires the "intent to kill," a person charged with attempt must act with that intent in addition to the purpose of accomplishing the result. A charge of attempt under the MPC also requires the actor to engage in conduct designed to accomplish the target offense. Three situations satisfy the requirement of purposeful action.

a. Done Everything Toward Completion

The Model Penal Code provides that an attempt occurs in two situations when the actor has done all that he or she thinks is necessary to accomplish the target offense: (1) the actor "purposely engages in conduct that would constitute the crime if the *attendant circumstances* were as he believes them to be" (§ 5.01(1)(a)); or (2) "when causing a particular *result* is an element of the crime, does or omits to do anything with the purpose of causing or with the belief that it will cause such result without further conduct on his part ..." (§ 5.01(1)(b)).

Note that under § 5.01(1)(a) there are two *mens rea* components. First, the prosecution must show that the defendant acted for the *purpose* of committing the target crime. Second, the defendant *believed* that the crime would occur without the need for any further action. For example, a defendant shoots at a tree stump, believing it is a person and desiring to kill that person. Under the MPC the defendant would be guilty of attempted murder because if the attendant circumstance (a human victim) had been present as the defendant believed, then the crime of murder could have occurred.

Similarly, under § 501(1)(b), if a defendant acts with the purpose of causing the expected outcome or *believes* the result will occur without further action, the defendant may have committed an attempt. For example, a defendant picks up an unloaded weapon, aims it at V, and pulls the trigger. If the defendant believed the gun was loaded, the crime would be attempted murder, even though the crime could not have occurred. Since the defendant did something (point the weapon and pull the trigger) with the belief that he or she had done everything necessary for the homicide, the crime of attempted murder would have occurred.

b. Substantial Step

While the above two elements involve a defendant who does all he or she plans to do to commit the target crime, the MPC also provides attempt liability for those who take a *substantial step* toward the target crime. Section 5.01(1)(c) authorizes prosecution for a person who purposely acts in a way that he or she believes is "a substantial step in a course of conduct planned to culminate in" the commission of the target crime. As with the other forms of attempt liability, the government must prove two mental elements: the defendant's purpose in engaging in conduct that would be a substantial step, and the belief that the attendant circumstances are such that the crime can occur.

Section 5.01(2) further provides that the substantial step be *strongly corroborative of the actor's criminal purpose.*" This is required because this form of attempt liability arises when the defendant does not take all the steps necessary to commit the crime. The focus is on how the conduct demonstrates the person's intent rather than on just how close the actor came to completing the crime. The MPC provides examples of certain types of conduct that "shall not be held insufficient as a matter of law" to show the requisite intent: lying in wait; enticing a victim to go to the place for the crime; reconnoitering the place for the crime; unlawful entry; possession of specially designed materials for the crime or items that serve no lawful purpose at or near the place for the crime; and soliciting innocent intermediaries.

2. Aiding an Attempt

The MPC also expands attempt liability in § 5.01(3) by making it a crime to aid another in the commission of an offense even if "the crime is not committed or attempted by such other person." For example, D provides P with a weapon to use in robbing a store in exchange for twenty-five percent of the proceeds. A week before the crime is to take place, P decides not to rob the store and throws the gun away. Even if P is not liable for attempted robbery, D would be guilty of an attempted robbery because the *purpose* of the conduct was to aid in the commission of a crime and the assistance would have made D an *accomplice* if P committed the robbery. The common law does not permit liability for the accomplice in this circumstance, but the MPC's subjective approach allows a conviction because D's intent to assist in the commission of a crime is clear, and the assistance occurred, so criminal liability can attach.

3. Renunciation

Model Penal Code § 5.01(4) recognizes an affirmative defense of *renunciation* if the person "prevented the successful commission of the offense attempted, solicited or conspired, under circumstances manifesting a complete and voluntary renunciation of the person's criminal purpose." Simply terminating involvement in a criminal plan may be insufficient if others will complete the offense. The MPC makes the defense unavailable if the motivation for desisting from the crime is an increased possibility of detection or circumstances that make the crime more difficult to accomplish. Similarly, any renunciation of the actor's criminal purpose is insufficient "if it is motivated by a decision to postpone the criminal conduct until a more advantageous time or to transfer the criminal effort to another but similar objective or victim."

4. Impossibility Defense

Sections 5.01(1)(a) and (b) make a defendant liable if the person engages in conduct purposely believing it will result in a crime, so the failure to complete the offense is irrelevant. While § 5.01(1)(c) requires that the substantial step toward commission of the crime be "strongly corroborative" of the actor's intent, that same requirement is not present for attempts under § 5.01(1)(a) or (b). Because the subjective approach of the MPC focuses on the intent of the accused, impossibility is only a defense if it negates the *mens rea* of the target crime.

Checkpoints

- Attempt is a specific intent crime.

- An attempt occurs when conduct passes from preparation to perpetration.

- Courts use different tests for determining when the defendant has moved beyond preparation to an attempted act, with the Model Penal Code requiring that the accused commit a substantial step toward the commission of the crime.

- Under the Model Penal Code, a person can be guilty as an accomplice to an attempt offense even if the perpetrator would not be liable because the conduct does not amount to an attempt, while the common law would not recognize attempt liability in this situation.

- The *mens rea* of intent to commit the target crime may be proven by direct and circumstantial evidence of the actor's intent and inferences, such as a person intends the natural and probable consequences of his or her acts.

- Factual and legal impossibility are not defenses to attempt, although a "pure" legal impossibility will preclude a conviction.

- Abandonment can be a defense to a crime of attempt, but only when the abandonment is voluntary and complete.

- Conduct that would not rise to the level of attempt can be made a crime by the legislature, such as possession of burglary tools.

- The Model Penal Code's substantial step test makes it easier to convict a person of attempt so long as the conduct is "strongly corroborative" of the defendant's intent.

- Aiding an attempt is sufficient for liability under the Model Penal Code even if the perpetrator does not engage in an attempt to commit the crime.

- Some jurisdictions make it a crime to communicate a threat.

- The crime of assault ordinarily includes an attempted battery as well as an intentional frightening.

Chapter 16

Conspiracy

Roadmap

- The rationale for conspiracy being a separate crime
- The definition of an agreement in conspiracy law
- The intent for a conspiracy
- The overt act requirement
- The parties to a conspiracy
- Proving a conspiracy
- The limitations of the conspiracy offense
- The scope of conspiratorial liability
- Conspiracy under the Model Penal Code

A. Introduction

Conspiracy is an *inchoate* offense committed as part of an agreement to do what is often called the *object or target crime*. For example, A and B may enter a conspiracy to commit a murder. Their goal is the murder, not necessarily to conspire, which is simply a means for them to achieve the homicide. Even though the conspiracy itself is a way to achieve the goal, it is punished, in most jurisdictions, as a separate offense apart from any crime growing out of the agreement. Thus, if the conspirators actually follow through with the plan and commit the murder (or attempt to do so), often they may be punished for *both* conspiracy and the offense.

1. Danger of Group Criminality

The key to understanding conspiracy is the fact that it is a crime that punishes *group criminality*. The unique actual and potential harm posed by group—as opposed to individual—criminal activity explains why conspiracy has long been accepted as an offense distinct from any other crime the conspirators commit. According to the Supreme Court:

> [C]ollective criminal agreement — partnership in crime — presents a greater potential threat to the public than individual delicts. Concerted action both increases the likelihood that the criminal object will be successfully attained and decreases the probability that the individuals involved will depart from their path of criminality. Group association for criminal purposes often, if not normally, makes possible the attainment of ends more complex than those which one criminal could accomplish. Nor is the danger of a conspiratorial group limited to the particular end toward which it has embarked. Combination in crime makes more likely the commission of crimes unrelated to the original purpose for which the group was formed. In sum, the danger which a conspiracy generates is not confined to the substantive offense which is the immediate aim of the enterprise.

Callanan v. United States, 364 U.S. 587 (1961).

2. Historical Development

The conspiracy offense is traceable to early English statutes that made it a crime for a combination of people to procure a false indictment, bring a false appeal, or maintain vexatious law suits. The English courts expanded the crime by focusing on the agreement as the *actus reus* of the offense, and later extended conspiracy to include agreements to commit any crime. Although there are now statutes in the United States that make it a crime to conspire to engage in specific illegal conduct, such as a conspiracy to import illegal narcotics, every state and the federal government also have broad conspiracy statutes that track the common law scope of the offense.

3. Advantages to Prosecution

Conspiracy has been described by Judge Learned Hand as "that darling of the modern prosecutor's nursery" because it provides significant advantages in prosecuting groups for criminal activity. One advantage is that conspiracy may reach conduct that occurs at the earliest stages of criminal activity. Since the crime of conspiracy is complete when the defendants enter into the criminal agreement and commit an overt act (if required), prosecutors can charge a conspiracy even when the conduct never proceed as far as necessary to constitute an attempt to commit the object crime. For example, if A and B agree to commit a murder and A performs a relatively unimportant overt act in furtherance of the plan, then both may be guilty of conspiracy to commit murder but neither may be guilty of attempted murder since no one engaged in an act sufficient to establish an attempt.

Conspiracy presents prosecutors with other advantages. For example, the prosecution can bring together all conspirators for a joint trial, which can enhance the possibility of "guilt by association." In addition, prosecutors have great flexibility in choosing the venue in a conspiracy case because jurisdiction can be found where any overt act occurred or where the parties formed the agreement. This may enable prosecutors to choose a forum that is more convenient for the government and less advantageous for the defendants. Finally, as discussed below, a conspiracy charge may increase the evidence the prosecutor can introduce at trial by allowing the admission of statements made by one conspirator during the course of the conspiracy that would otherwise be subject to exclusion as hearsay.

B. The Conspiratorial Agreement

1. What Constitutes an Agreement

Conspiracy requires an *agreement* between two or more people, although it is not a contract in the legal sense. Perhaps it is better to think of the agreement as an understanding more than a formal contract. The agreement does not need to be in writing, nor does it require specific statements by the parties. In *Iannelli v. United States*, 420 U.S. 770 (1975), the Supreme Court stated that "[t]he agreement need not be shown to have been explicit. It can instead be inferred from the facts and circumstances of the case." The conspiracy can be established by evidence as slight as a nod of the head or conduct demonstrating concerted group activity.

2. Proof of Agreement

Most conspiracies are proven by *circumstantial evidence*, and the agreement usually is implied from the surrounding circumstances or by inference from the actions of the parties. The key is that the prosecution must prove the parties had an understanding as to the common criminal purpose among the members of the conspiracy. For example, X and Y enter a bank together, and X walks to a teller while Y stands by the door with a hand in the front coat pocket. X gives a note to the teller indicating X is armed and demanding money. The teller complies, and the two robbers leave the bank together and are arrested a short time later, each with half the money. Based on their actions in concert and sharing of the proceeds, there would be sufficient evidence for a jury to find that there was an agreement that the two would rob the bank.

As courts are fond of noting, a conspiracy by its nature is a *clandestine act*, so there will be few cases in which evidence of an actual agreement exists. The prosecution, however, must prove that the defendants entered into the *same agreement* to commit a crime, or a series of crimes, and not just that they engaged in the same type of conduct at approximately the same time. Although circumstantial evidence can establish the agreement, courts frequently state that they will examine such evidence with great care. A jury may infer an agreement from other facts, but each link in the chain of inferences must be sufficiently strong to avoid mere *speculation* as to the conspiratorial agreement.

For example, D provides information about a company about to be bought by another company to his girlfriend, X, so that she can trade on it and make a large amount of money. Unbeknownst to D, the girlfriend is also secretly dating G, and the girlfriend gives the information to G so that G, the secret lover, can trade on it. While D conspired with his girlfriend X to commit insider trading, there is no agreement between D and G, the secret lover, even though they are both involved in the same misconduct. The government would not have sufficient circumstantial evidence that D and G had an agreement. The crime is based on the agreement, not the particular crimes even if the offenses are similar.

3. Object of Conspiracy

Under the common law, the agreement necessary for a conspiracy was to commit either an unlawful act or to achieve a lawful goal by criminal or unlawful means. Modern conspiracy statutes now provide that the agreement is to commit a *felony* or, in some jurisdictions, *any crime*. The object of the conspiracy need not be a single criminal act, and can encompass a *continuing course of illegal conduct*, such as drug distribution, prostitution, and loan sharking. In addition, the conspiracy can change to incorporate additional criminal objects so long as the members agree to the new crimes. For example, if A and B conspire to distribute drugs, over time they may also agree to commit a bank robbery to finance the purchase of more drugs. Model Penal Code § 5.03(3) provides that "[i]f a person conspires to commit a number of crimes, he is guilty of only one conspiracy so long as such multiple crimes are the object of the same agreement or continuous conspiratorial relationship."

4. Accomplice Liability and Conspiracy

Frequently, a person who is an *accomplice* to a crime is also a conspirator. In many cases, the accomplice will know the criminal object of the perpetrator and likely agrees to the commission of the offense, so the assistance the accomplice renders to the perpetrator can be proof of the conspiratorial agreement between the accomplice and the perpetrator.

It is not necessarily the case, however, that aiding or abetting a crime in itself makes one a party to a broader criminal agreement. It could be that the accomplice does not know of the ultimate criminal purpose, and so cannot be said to have joined the agreement with other conspirators. For example, D is in a conspiracy with five other people to smuggle drugs across the border. A may be asked to steal a car to help D engage in conduct that A believes may well be criminal, but is not sure what the crime will be. Thus, A knows that the car will be used for a criminal purpose but does not know that it will be used for the illegal drug activity. If A steals the car and gives it to D, A may be an accomplice to D's crime but not a member of a broader drug conspiracy between D and others. Even though A is not liable for the main conspiracy with people other than D, it is likely that there is a separate conspiracy between A and D that can be charged as a separate offense. Because of the limits of A's knowledge, perhaps this conspiracy between A and D is simply to commit auto theft.

5. No Merger of Conspiracy and Object Crime

The majority rule is that conspiracy is a separate offense from any substantive crimes committed in the course of the conspiracy. Unlike solicitation (see Chapter 14) and attempt (see Chapter 15), which merge with the target offense, in most jurisdictions conspiracy can be charged and punished in addition to any punishment for the object(s) of the conspiracy. Therefore, it is possible for a defendant to be found not guilty of the object crime but guilty of a conspiracy to commit that offense because it is the agreement that constitutes the *actus reus* of conspiracy and not the actual (or attempted) commission of the substantive offense.

C. *Mens Rea* of Conspiracy

1. Intent to Agree

Conspiracy requires proof of two *mens rea* elements. The first is the specific *intent to agree* to combine for a common criminal objective; the second is *knowledge* of the unlawful act that is the object of the agreement. The first intent is closely related to the proof of the conspiratorial agreement. Note that the agreement may cover more than one object offense and is still considered to be a single conspiracy. The nature of an agreement is that the parties give their assent to a particular criminal goal, which can have multiple objects, so the evidence of the existence of the agreement will usually suffice to prove the intent to agree. Similarly, a failure to prove the agreement or its particular scope may mean that the defendants did not have the intent to enter into an agreement.

One issue that can arise regarding the intent to agree is if one party to an agreement cannot form the requisite intent. For example, D and X decide they will burn down the house of a common enemy. At the time the plan is formed, D is legally insane by not being able to appreciate the wrongfulness of the conduct. In that circumstance, D would assert a successful insanity defense and therefore not be liable for a conspiracy. In the majority of jurisdictions that require an agreement among two or more persons (but not in those that follow the Model Penal Code's unilateral approach, discussed below), X would also not be liable for a conspiracy because there was no agreement between two persons to commit a crime. D was simply incapable of agreeing because of his or her mental disability.

An agreement to kill a person would be a conspiracy to commit first degree murder because the agreement is sufficient proof of deliberation and premeditation. Some states also recognize the crime of conspiracy to commit second degree murder. There cannot be a conspiracy to commit involuntary manslaughter or any other offense with a *mens rea* of recklessness or negligence because of the specific intent requirement needed for the agreement.

2. Knowledge of Criminal Objective

The government does not have to prove that a conspirator had knowledge of all the circumstances of the agreement or knew all the participants in the conspiracy. The key is whether there is knowledge of the common criminal objective arising from the agreement. In some cases, knowledge can be the basis to infer the requisite specific intent to agree, but knowledge alone is insufficient to establish liability for a conspiracy. A defendant must know that he or she is entering into a conspiratorial agreement, so the prosecution must establish the defendant's knowledge that the agreement incorporated a criminal object.

a. Scope of Knowledge

Knowledge of the criminal object does not necessarily mean that the conspirators must be aware of all the details of the crime to be committed. The agreement is to commit an illegal act, or a lawful act by unlawful means, but that agreement does not mean that the conspirators must comprehend all the *attendant circumstances* required for a conviction. For example, two defendants agree to mug an acceptable victim on a Sunday evening. They drive around and see an older woman walking alone on a deserted downtown street. One defendant alights from the car, knocks the woman to the ground, and steals her purse. They are apprehended a short time later with her credit cards, and charged with conspiracy to assault a federal official engaged in the course of her duties; the victim was a federal district court judge walking to her chambers to finish writing an opinion. Although the defendants can plausibly assert they did not agree to mug a federal official, they can still be held liable for conspiring to violate the statute because the status of the victim is relevant only for jurisdiction.

For example, in *United States v. Feola*, 420 U.S. 671 (1975), the Supreme Court did not require the defendants to know that the victim was a federal officer when they attempted to rob undercover drug agents of the money they brought to purchase drugs from the defendants. According to the Court, an agreement to engage in wrongful conduct—an assault—is sufficient without regard to the status of the victim, which is the basis for permitting federal jurisdiction but need not come within the scope of the illegal agreement.

b. Deliberate Indifference

Proof of knowledge can be shown if the prosecution establishes that the defendant *consciously avoided* learning of the criminal object of an agreement. For example, D receives inside information about a corporate takeover from a relative who is an employee of an investment bank working on the deal. D buys shares in the target company, reaping a substantial profit. At trial, D testifies that he or she did not know that the relative was prohibited from disclosing the information or that it was impermissible to trade on it, but never asked the relative why the information was being provided or its source. An "ostrich" or *deliberate ignorance* instruction (see Chapter 5) would be appropriate to permit a jury to infer knowledge of the criminal object of the agreement when there is sufficient evidence that the defendant was aware of a high probability that the agreement involved a crime but consciously avoided confirming that fact. A defendant's conscious avoidance of knowledge of the unlawful aims of the conspiracy is the equivalent of knowledge of those unlawful aims, so long as there is proof of an intent to agree to achieving the unlawful end.

3. Corrupt Motive

Some states require proof of a *corrupt motive* when the object of a conspiracy is a *malum prohibitum* crime that the conspirators may not recognize as unlawful, at least when they agreed to the act. A "corrupt motive" means that the actor intended to break the law, had an evil purpose, or had a reason to do something that is wrong. This is like an ignorance defense, that the conduct was such that a defendant may not reasonably know it was illegal, and so absent a corrupt motive the parties should not be held liable for the agreement. Even in those jurisdictions that require such proof, the issue is narrow because of the general presumption that ignorance of the law is not an excuse.

4. Merchants and Suppliers

The issue of intent for conspiracy becomes especially difficult in cases involving the seller of goods or services when the individual knows the purchaser will use them to commit a crime. When is knowledge of the illegal use of the goods sufficient to permit the jury to conclude that the provider had the intent needed for conspiracy? A key question is whether it was a single or isolated transaction, or a continuing course of conduct. This is particularly applicable to merchants and suppliers, who may well know, or can easily infer, the criminal object of the customer.

a. United States v. Falcone

The leading case in this area, *United States v. Falcone*, 109 F.2d 579 (2d Cir. 1940), involved a conspiracy to operate illegal stills. Falcone sold large quantities of sugar to grocers who, in turn, sold it to distillers to make illegal liquor. The Court of Appeals found that Falcone knew that the grocers were supplying the distillers, then turned to the question whether Falcone was in a conspiracy with the distillers. The court first expressed a concern that suppliers of goods could be too easily considered conspirators in an era when "so many prosecutors seek to sweep within the drag-net of conspiracy all those who have been associated in any degree whatever with the main offenders." Using terms that have been repeated by countless courts, the *Falcone* court stated that for a conspiracy it "is not enough that he does not forego a normally lawful activity [selling sugar], of the fruits of which he knows that others will make an unlawful use; he must in some sense promote their venture himself, make it his own, have a stake in the outcome." Falcone was found to lack the needed personal involvement in the venture to make him a conspirator with the people to whom he supplied sugar. This approach has led many courts to state that knowledge, and even tacit approval, of a criminal plan in not sufficient *by itself* to prove an intent to enter into an agreement.

b. Factors

Cases discussing the issue of when a merchant's or seller's knowledge morphs into the intent required for a conspiracy often rely on a number of factors:

1. the *quantity* of the sales;
2. whether the *price for the goods* was the usual one or was *inflated*;
3. any *ongoing relationship* between the seller and purchaser;
4. any evidence of a *stake in the criminal venture*;
5. the *impetus* for the transactions; and
6. the *nature of the goods or services* sold, *i.e.,* whether they are common or involve dangerous products or any special attributes for use in criminal conduct.

In some instances, courts refer to the status of the item that was supplied as lawful or unlawful as a basis for distinguishing between liability for a conspiracy, although it is difficult to find the agreement simply based on supplying something used to commit a crime, even if that item is illegal.

c. Nature of Goods or Services

The intent for conspiracy is especially likely to be found if the only use of the goods or services was illegal, such as providing a wire service reporting only the results of horse races, distributing a newsletter listing only the names, addresses, and sexual proclivities of prostitutes, or selling loaded dice to casinos. In *People v. Lauria*, 59 Cal. Rptr.2d 628 (Cal. App. 1967), an oft-cited case, the court dismissed a charge of conspiracy to commit prostitution against the operator of a telephone answering service used by prostitutes to receive messages from their clientele. Although the defendant clearly knew the reason why the prostitutes were using the telephone service, the absence of a "stake in the enterprise" or other indicia of participation in the criminal object meant that there was insufficient proof of an intent "to further the enterprise" needed for a conspiracy conviction. The *Lauria* court noted that the result would be different had there been more proof of intent, such as had the defendant given the prostitutes advice on how best to use the answering service to maximize their income.

In contrast to *Lauria*, there are some cases which seem to suggest that knowledge will satisfy intent more easily if the item supplied is especially dangerous. The leading case involving a dangerous product, *Direct Sales Co. v. United States*, 319 U.S. 703 (1943), concerned a drug manufacturer and mail order wholesaler that sold a large quantity of illegal drugs to a physician who then dispensed them illegally. The Supreme Court held that the defendant drug wholesaler could be found to be in a conspiracy with the physician because the evidence could be interpreted as showing the defendant knew of the illegal distribution of its drugs. Moreover, the dangerous nature of the commodity (plus the large quantity of the drugs sold the physician along with the duration of the business dealings between the two) could justify a conclusion that there is "informed and interested cooperation, stimulation, [and] instigation." This could prove the existence of a conspiratorial agreement since it may establish that the defendant "joins both mind and hand" with the physician to make the physician's unlawful deeds possible.

D. Overt Acts

The majority of conspiracy statutes require the government to prove an *overt act* in furtherance of the agreement, something the common law did not mandate. When proof of an overt act is an element of the offense, it does not have to be criminal in itself, only a step in the process of committing the object of the conspiracy. The overt act need not be sufficiently substantial to satisfy the *actus reus* necessary to constitute an attempt to commit the crime, so that otherwise *innocent conduct*—such as renting a car, purchasing a weapon, or placing a telephone call—may be an overt act sufficient to establish the conspiracy if it relates to the criminal object of the agreement. Moreover, a single overt act by any conspirator is sufficient, and the government need not prove separate overt acts by each member to establish the existence of the conspiracy.

An overt act may involve virtually any type of activity. For example, if two people agree to steal goods from an abandoned building, an overt act could be a telephone call to rent a van to transport the loot, obtaining plans for the building, enlisting another person to act as lookout, or even walking past the building to ascertain whether it has external security cameras. While it is a minimal evidentiary requirement, the overt act element is viewed as a means of separating mere talk about a possible crime from actual conspiracies that may actually reach fruition.

Federal drug conspiracy statutes do not require proof of an overt act. Thus, prosecutors can seek a conviction merely upon proof of the agreement and *mens rea* without any outward manifestation of the criminal purpose.

E. Parties to a Conspiracy

1. Plurality

The common law rule, followed in most jurisdictions, is that a conspiracy requires at least *two parties* to the agreement. If one of the two parties *feigns* agreement, then there is no conspiracy. If there are three parties involved, however, and one of them feigns agreement but the other two actually do agree, there is a conspiracy between the two who are committed to the crime. For example, D wants his wife murdered and calls an old friend from the military for help. While pretending to agree to assist him, the friend contacts the police, who arrange to put the defendant in touch with an undercover officer representing himself as a killer for hire. After agreeing to pay the undercover officer for the killing and providing details of his wife's whereabouts, D is arrested after giving the officer the money. While D can be held liable for solicitation (see Chapter 14), in most jurisdictions he is not guilty of conspiracy nor an attempt to kill his wife. Neither the undercover officer nor the friend actually agreed to commit the killing, so there is no conspiracy even though in D's mind he certainly agreed to the commission of the crime. But if the friend agrees and contacts someone who turns out to be an undercover officer, then there is a conspiracy involving D and the friend.

Many jurisdictions, including those adopting the Model Penal Code's conspiracy provision, recognize a *unitary* approach to conspiracy, allowing prosecutors to proceed when the accused believes there is an agreement even if there is no second party to it. In the example above, D would be liable for conspiracy to kill his wife under the unitary model because D believed there were others conspiring with him and in his mind there was an agreement. The theory is that D is as morally blameworthy whether or not his belief is correct about the involvement of the other conspirator.

2. Verdict

Although more than one person is usually required for a conspiracy, it is not necessary that the prosecution *charge* or *convict* all parties to the agreement. For example, it is common for the charging document to allege that others, perhaps currently unknown, also participated in the conspiracy and so are *unindicted co-conspirators*. Thus, an indictment or criminal information can allege that "A and others unknown at this time conspired to distribute cocaine." The prosecutor must prove that there were at least two parties to the agreement if the jurisdiction requires a plurality, and that the defendant is one of them, but the *identity* of the other conspirators is unnecessary to secure the conviction of A for the drug conspiracy.

3. Inconsistent Verdicts

Issues arise whether a conspiracy exists when one person is convicted and an alleged co-conspirator is acquitted. Historically, *inconsistent verdicts* were impermissible, so that if the prosecutor alleged a two-person conspiracy and one of the alleged conspirators was found not guilty, the other alleged conspirator could not be convicted. This rule did not apply when only one person was tried for conspiracy and another person, perhaps of unknown identity, was listed as an "unindicted conspirator." The single known conspirator could still be convicted but the trier of fact would have to conclude that this person was indeed in a conspiracy with another person whose identity was unknown.

In recent years, courts largely have moved away from prohibiting inconsistent verdicts where one defendant is found not guilty and another guilty of entering into a conspiratorial agreement. Courts rely on the fact that a jury may feel particular sympathy for one defendant, which could explain the inconsistent verdict. In modern jurisdictions, even in a joint trial, an acquittal of one conspirator usually does not affect the conviction of any co-conspirator.

4. Variance

The government often proves a conspiracy charge by asking the jury to infer that apparently coordinated conduct demonstrates the existence of an agreement. The problem is that proof of the commission of the object offense is not sufficient in itself to prove an agreement. Moreover, the fact that different actors committed the same crime does not prove that they entered an agreement. Because the government's proof is usually circumstantial, the courts struggle with determining the scope of an agreement, and whether all the defendants entered into a *common agreement*. The government is required to prove the offense it charges in its indictment or information.

If it charges one conspiracy when in fact there were two separate agreements, then there may be a *fatal variance* between the charge and the proof adduced at trial, requiring reversal of a conspiracy conviction. In addition, if the government fails to prove that the defendants were members of the same conspiracy, then the evidence against one defendant would not be admissible against another defendant (under the co-conspirator evidence rule) who was not a member of that conspiracy. If the evidence against one conspirator was erroneously admitted against the other, the mistake may cause sufficient prejudice and lead to a reversal of a conviction for the substantive offense.

5. Types of Conspiracies

Courts frequently assert that the conspirators need not know one another personally or ever have met in order to be convicted as members of the same conspiracy. In some conspiracies, ignorance of the exact identity of other members—especially the ringleaders—is desired to limit the damage if one or more members are arrested and cooperate with the government.

To be members of the same conspiracy, courts require proof that each person knew that others were involved in the criminal enterprise, and that those participants were a functional part of the conspiracy. But the prosecution need not show the defendants were aware of the exact identity of other conspirators or even the precise number of participants involved in the conspiracy. For example, in a large scale drug distribution conspiracy, the importer will know generally that other people, perhaps even tens or hundreds of others, are responsible for cutting and packaging the drugs for sale in a variety of locations. Despite the fact that the many people involved in the scheme do not know one another and have never been in the same location, the importer can be a member of the same conspiracy as lower-level figures.

a. Scope of Agreement

Determining the scope of the agreement becomes problematic as the size of the conspiracy and complexity of its criminal objects grow. For example, if one person buys stolen property from five different thieves in order to resell it (*i.e.*, a fence), is there a single conspiracy to traffic in stolen property, with six people joining an agreement, or are there five separate conspiracies that share a common buyer and criminal object? As described by one court, "conspiracies are as complex as the versatility of human nature and federal protection against them is not to be measured by spokes, hubs, wheels, rims, chains or any one or all of today's galaxy of mechanical molecular or atomic forces." *United States v. Perez*, 489 F.2d 51 (5th Cir. 1973). The key is whether the evidence supports an agreement among a range of individuals involved in a continuing course of conduct, or whether the connection is insufficient for a jury to infer that the defendants are part of a unified criminal enterprise. For example, in *United States v. Bruno*, 105 F.2d 921 (2d Cir. 1939), the court upheld a conviction involving a single conspiracy of eighty-seven defendants whose criminal object was to smuggle narcotics into New York and then distribute them in New York City along with locations in Texas and Louisiana. The agreement required the cooperation of smugglers, middlemen and two groups of retailers, one in New York and one in Texas/Louisiana, so all were members of the same conspiracy despite its far-flung nature.

b. Hub-and-Spoke and Chain Conspiracies

In looking at whether there is a single agreement or multiple conspiracies, the courts have described how the agreement can be viewed in different ways, using the metaphors of a "*wheel*" conspiracy—with a hub and spokes—and a "*chain*" conspiracy. The exact category—whether spoke or chain—does not, in itself, answer whether there is one or multiple conspiracies, but the structure may help in resolving the issue. Two major cases illustrate how courts approach the issue of the number of conspiracies involved in a complex criminal scheme. In *Kotteakos v. United States*, 328 U.S. 750 (1946), defendant Brown assisted eight different groups, totaling thirty-one defendants, fraudulently obtain government loans. Seven were convicted of a single conspiracy. The Supreme Court reversed the conspiracy conviction for a wheel conspiracy involving a central "hub" figure, whose associates were the "spokes," finding that there was no unifying agreement among the different groups that operated separately. Thus, there were at least eight conspiracies rather than one large one, and participants (who were "spokes") in a particular conspiracy with Brown were not necessarily in a conspiracy with people who were in other conspiracies with him. In other words, certain single conspirators were in a conspiracy with Brown, the hub, but not with other spokes in the wheel, who were in their own conspiracies with Brown. To establish that all the participants were in one large conspiracy rather than a number of small ones, the government would have had to establish some unifying agreement among the conspirators, sometimes called the "rim" to play out the metaphor. The fact that each was in a conspiracy with Brown was not, in itself, sufficient to make them in a conspiracy with one another.

In contrast, in *Blumenthal v. United States*, 332 U.S. 539 (1947), the unidentified owner of a liquor wholesaler distributed alcohol to two distributors, who in turn provided it to salesmen who sold it in violation of wartime price controls. The Court upheld a conspiracy conviction against the distributors and salesmen for a chain conspiracy, with several "links" leading linearly from a source. Even though the salesmen did not know the identity of the wholesaler, each link knew that the others existed, knew of the scheme to sell at excessive prices, and aided in carrying out the plan.

F. Co-Conspirator Statements

1. Not Excluded as Hearsay

The paucity of direct evidence of an agreement and its scope can make it a difficult crime for the prosecution to prove beyond a reasonable doubt. An important aid to prosecutors is an exception to the general ban on hearsay evidence. The co-conspirator's statement rule allows the government to introduce certain co-conspirator statements as substantive evidence to prove the existence of the conspiracy and other issues. Many of the co-conspirator's statements would be inadmissible hearsay if made by someone outside of the conspiracy. For co-conspirator statements, however, the rules of evidence allow the admission of statements made by one conspirator *during the course* of and *in furtherance* of a conspiracy. Importantly, this evidence can be used *against every member of the conspiracy*, regardless of whether that conspirator participated in the statement.

This approach expands the range of relevant evidence available to prove the existence of the conspiracy and the participation of its members. For example, a statement by one conspirator, C, that another person, P, has joined the criminal enterprise can be used to prove that a conspiracy exists and that P and C are part of it. This may enable the government to prove its case against P even though P never said anything about the conspiracy and there may be no other evidence of P's participation.

2. Standard of Proof

For a co-conspirator's statement to be admissible, the government must establish by a preponderance of the evidence that (1) a conspiracy existed at the time the statement was made *by the declarant*; (2) the declarant was a *member of that conspiracy* at the time of the statement; and, (3) the statements contributed to (*"in furtherance of"*) the ultimate goal of the conspiracy.

An important issue is what evidence must be introduced to establish the existence of the conspiracy before the co-conspirator's statement can be used at trial. The burden is on the party offering the statement to show by a preponderance of the evidence that the statement was made during the course of and in furtherance of the conspiracy. While a charge of conspiracy must be proven beyond a reasonable doubt for a valid criminal conviction, the *evidentiary* issue of whether a conspiracy existed at the time of the statement is determined under the preponderance standard, that it is more likely than not there was a conspiracy and the statement otherwise meets the requirements of the evidence rules for admission.

3. Considering the Statement

The court can consider the co-conspirator's statement itself in deciding whether a conspiracy exists that would allow admission of the statement—a process often called *bootstrapping*—but the statements alone cannot be the only evidence of the conspiracy. Federal Rule of Evidence 801(d)(2) provides that "[t]he statement must be considered but does not by itself establish ... the existence of the conspiracy or participation in it...." For example, a statement by D to a friend that "X and I need you to provide us with an alibi for tonight" could be considered by a court as evidence of a conspiracy so long as there was other evidence, such as concerted criminal activity by D and X, to show that a conspiracy existed. If the court finds there was a conspiracy, then the statement would be admissible against D *and* X even though X had nothing to do with the conversation and may not even know it took place.

4. Timing of the Statement

A temporal limitation on co-conspirator statements requires the government to prove that the conspiracy was still in operation at the time of the statement, so that it was made "during the course of" the conspiracy. This foundational element may require the court to assess when the conspiracy started and when it ended.

A common issue is the admissibility of a statement, made after the crime was completed, by a co-conspirator who is trying to conceal the crime or avoid detection. In *Krulewitch v. United States*, 336 U.S. 440 (1949), the government sought to introduce the statement of an alleged conspirator urging a cover-up of the criminal conduct of another conspirator. The statement was made after the crime ended and while both participants in the conversation were under arrest, but before charges were filed. The government argued that any statement by a conspirator designed to conceal the existence of a conspiracy was part of the conspiracy, which continues so long as it has not been detected. According to the government, the statement was covered by the co-conspirator exception to the hearsay rule and was admissible to establish the existence of the conspiracy. The Supreme Court rejected the argument as overbroad because "under this rule plausible arguments could generally be made in conspiracy cases that most out-of-court statements offered in evidence tended to shield co-conspirators."

In order to use statements made after the primary criminal object of the conspiracy has occurred, the government must show that a cover-up of the crime was an important aspect of the agreement so that the conspiracy continues forward and includes the cover-up. For example, D and X agree to burn down a building owned by D and submit an insurance claim fraudulently stating it was an accident. After the fire, the insurance company conducts an investigation and denies the claim, which D appeals to a higher authority in the insurance company. While awaiting the results of the appeal, X speaks with a friend about how to get the insurance company to pay the claim, explaining how they set the fire so that it would not look like arson. X's statement would be admissible in the ensuing insurance fraud case because an important part of the conspiracy to burn the building and collect the insurance proceeds is to keep the true nature of the fire from being discovered, so the agreement continues while the efforts to collect the insurance claim are ongoing.

5. Pre-Existing Conspiracy

An important expansion of the admissibility of a co-conspirator's statement occurs when a defendant joins an already-existent conspiracy by entering into the agreement with other members. In this circumstance, most courts hold that statements made by other co-conspirators are admissible against the later-joining member, even if they were made before the person joined the criminal agreement.

G. Limitations on Conspiracy

1. Wharton's Rule

In those relatively few instances when a crime by its very nature requires the agreement of two people to engage in the conduct constituting the offense, courts have precluded use of conspiracy as a separate charge based on the same agreement under what is called "Wharton's Rule," named for the author of a nineteenth century criminal law treatise. In other words, if by definition a crime must be committed by at least two people, then if only those two people commit that crime they may not also be convicted of conspiracy to commit that crime. In *Iannelli v. United States*, 420 U.S. 770 (1975), the Supreme

Court explained, "The classic Wharton's Rule offenses—adultery, incest, bigamy, duelling—are crimes that are characterized by the general congruence of the agreement and the completed substantive offense. The parties to the agreement are the only persons who participate in commission of the substantive offense, and the immediate consequences of the crime rest on the parties themselves rather than on society at large."

The statute defining the crime must provide that both participants are culpable for the conduct, so that the crime cannot be committed by a single person. For example, two lovers who were married to others could not be prosecuted for a conspiracy to commit adultery because the crime itself requires two participants. If there are more participants in the agreement than the minimum number required for the offense, however, then a conspiracy charge can be brought against all participants. For example, if a friend of the married man provides him with the keys to his house for the trysts, then there can be a conspiracy to commit adultery between the three.

Modern cases applying Wharton's Rule include bribery, gambling, extortion, sale of stolen property, and simple drug sales. At one time, Wharton's Rule was characterized as based on double jeopardy principles. In recent years, however, Wharton's Rule has been significantly limited by using it as a means for interpreting legislation and not always as a bar to prosecution for conspiracy. In *Iannelli*, the defendants were charged with conspiracy and gambling, arguing that Wharton's Rule precluded conviction for conspiracy because the statute required at least five participants in the gambling enterprise. The Supreme Court held that Wharton's Rule only acts "as a judicial presumption, to be applied in the absence of legislative intent to the contrary." If the legislature wishes to make the parties to the substantive offense liable for conspiracy in addition to the object offense, then that can be done and Wharton's Rule does not make a conspiracy conviction impermissible as a violation of the double jeopardy protection. This occurred in *Iannelli*, where the Supreme Court found that Congress intended to permit punishment for both gambling and conspiracy.

2. Protected Class of Victims

A related doctrine limiting conspiracy liability is that a person who is within the class of individuals protected by the criminal statute usually cannot be prosecuted for conspiring to commit the crime in which that person is the victim. For example, an older federal statute, the Mann Act, made it a crime to transport a woman across state lines for immoral purposes. In *Gebardi v. United States*, 287 U.S. 112 (1932), the Supreme Court overturned the conviction of a man and woman for conspiracy to violate the law for traveling together to engage in immoral conduct. The Court held that "we perceive in the failure of the Mann Act to condemn the woman's participation in those transportations which are effected with her mere consent, evidence of an affirmative legislative policy to leave her acquiescence unpunished." If a woman and man, however, agreed to transport *another* woman across state lines for the immoral purpose, they could be charged with conspiracy because the statute does not make all women immune from prosecution. A similar situation arises under the statutory rape law, which would prevent the underage participant in the sexual relations from being charged with conspiracy. *The Queen v. Tyrrell*, 1 QB 710 (1893). The same analysis would also apply to an aiding and abetting charge.

3. Withdrawal, Abandonment, and Renunciation

Sometimes people cease involvement in a conspiracy. This may have a significant impact on criminal liability for the conspiracy as well as for other related crimes.

a. Withdrawal: Formation, Termination, and Liability for Future Acts

Withdrawal from a conspiracy (sometimes called "abandoning," as in Model Penal Code § 5.03(7)) can provide significant benefits to the person who elects to cease involvement in the scheme. If a person withdraws from an agreement before any overt act is undertaken, if that is a requirement to prove a conspiracy, then the person would not be guilty of conspiracy; the person was never in a conspiracy. If no one commits an overt act, then the conspiracy itself never existed in this jurisdiction.

Once a person is in a conspiracy, "a defendant's membership in the ongoing unlawful scheme continues until he withdraws." *Smith v. United States*, 133 S. Ct. 714 (2013). However, a conspiracy ends when all conspirators withdraw from it or the agreement ceases to operate. In addition, collateral effects of the conspiracy end with regard to the person who withdrew. Thus, the withdrawal starts the running of the statute of limitations for the withdrawing conspirator. In *Smith v. United States*, the Supreme Court stated, "[w]ithdrawal also starts the clock running on the time within which the defendant may be prosecuted, and provides a complete defense when the withdrawal occurs beyond the applicable statute-of-limitations period." Statements made by a conspirator in furtherance of the conspiracy would not be admissible against the withdrawing conspirator if they were made after the withdrawal.

Another significant benefit of withdrawal, as *Smith* explained, is that "[w]ith-drawal terminates the defendant's liability for post-withdrawal acts of his co-conspirators, but he remains guilty of conspiracy." For example, assume a conspiracy to rob a bank. If the conspirator successfully withdrew from the conspiracy before the bank robbery, that person would not be liable for the robbery or under *Pinkerton* (see infra) for any crimes that occurred during the commission of that offense, such as an assault on a teller or the killing of a guard during the escape. The conspirator who withdrew would still be guilty of the conspiracy to commit bank robbery.

The exact requirements for a withdrawal are frequently the product of case law rather than statute. Many jurisdictions require significant positive action rather than passive conduct. Thus, hiding from other conspirators and avoiding contact with them may be insufficient. A prevailing view is that withdrawal must be unequivocal and requires an affirmative act of disassociation inconsistent with the goals of the conspiracy that was communicated to other conspirators in a manner reasonably calculated to reach them. Some courts even state that the withdrawal must be made in time for the remaining conspirators to decide to abandon the scheme.

Some jurisdictions also require that the criminal objective not be achieved by the remaining conspirators. In *Smith v. United States*, the defendant was in jail for six years during which the five-year statute of limitations for conspiracy ran out. The Supreme Court held he was nevertheless still in the conspiracy during that time because he had not taken affirmative measures to withdraw from it.

Model Penal Code § 5.03(7) provides that a conspirator terminates his or her involvement only by advising other conspirators of the abandonment or informing law enforcement of the scheme and his or her participation in it. The Code does not require that the conspirator thwart the success of the conspiracy if the remaining members choose to go ahead with the crime.

b. Renunciation: Liability for Existing Conspiracy

Since the agreement forms the basis of conspiracy, if there is an agreement and an overt act in furtherance of the conspiracy—assuming one is needed—then a conspirator's subsequent withdrawal from the scheme is irrelevant in many, though not all, jurisdictions on the issue whether the person is criminally liable for the conspiracy. Under this traditional view, the conspiracy is complete once the actors enter the agreement and one of them commits an overt act. Thus, if A and B agree to commit a crime and A takes a step (an overt act) to effectuate the plan, then A and B are guilty of conspiracy even if B has a change of mind and leaves the conspiracy well before the object offense occurs. The withdrawal from the conspiracy is not recognized by the common law as a defense to the conspiracy itself unless the conspiracy statute permits such a defense.

Some modern jurisdictions disagree with the traditional view that liability for a conspiracy cannot be "erased" by a subsequent abandonment. These jurisdictions have enacted a statute that allows a *renunciation* (sometimes, confusingly, called an abandonment) to be a defense to the conspiracy itself. This differs from the withdrawal/abandonment discussed above which is not a defense to an existing conspiracy but rather defines the duration of a conspiracy and the effect of a conspiracy on those who withdraw from it. These renunciation statutes, following Model Penal Code § 5.03(6), are based on the proposition that permitting abandonment as a defense to the conspiracy encourages criminals to leave the agreement and not follow through with the object offense. Thus, the law provides a significant incentive for conspirators to abandon their plans, perhaps serving the goal of preventing crime.

In order to reap the benefits of a renunciation defense, the usual requirement is that the conspirator manifests a complete withdrawal that is not caused by either fear of discovery or the inability to complete the criminal object of the agreement. It requires an *affirmative act* showing the person is leaving the conspiracy, and not simply drifting away from the criminal enterprise. This can require both communication with the co-conspirators of the withdrawal and, if the plan is close to reaching fruition, some effort to defeat the object offense. Some courts further require people who renounce the agreement to notify the authorities to prevent the crime or to somehow get other parties to the conspiracy to stop their involvement in it.

Model Penal Code § 5.03(6) authorizes a defense of *renunciation of criminal purpose*, defined as thwarting the success of the conspiracy under circumstances "manifesting a complete and voluntary renunciation of" criminal purpose. For example, three people decide to rob a bank after it receives large cash deposits on a Friday afternoon. One of the three notifies the others on Friday morning that he or she will no longer participate in the crime. Under MPC § 5.03(6), the person will also have to make sure the conspiracy does not succeed and will have to establish a voluntary and complete renunciation of criminal purpose, meaning that he or she has voluntarily abandoned the criminal object.

c. Example

A person leaving a conspiracy may accomplish both a withdrawal and a renunciation by satisfying the requirements for each. For example, A, B, and C are in a conspiracy to steal copper pipes from construction sites, and if necessary have committed an overt act in furtherance of the agreement. C notifies A and B that C is no longer involved with the criminal plan. One week later, A and B also decide not to steal copper pipes. C successfully withdrew from the conspiracy by communicating the abandonment to the co-conspirators and the statute of limitations will begin to run at that point. Statements made by co-conspirators will not be admissible against C if made after C's abandonment. However, if A and B committed any pipe thefts during the week after C's renunciation, C's renunciation may be ineffective to shield him from liability for the conspiracy because C did not thwart the success of the conspiracy. However, if A and B stopped stealing pipes in response to C's abandonment, C's renunciation will be effective as a defense to the conspiracy charge.

4. Impossibility

While impossibility presents many difficult issues in determining whether an attempt to commit a crime has taken place (see Chapter 15), the analysis is much simpler for a conspiracy. So long as the agreement seeks the attainment of a criminal object, then the defendants can be found guilty even if they could not have committed the specific crime contemplated because it could not be accomplished. For example, two defendants agree to kill a common enemy. They acquire a gun and plan the date and time for the killing. Unbeknownst to them, the intended victim died the day before they agreed to the killing. The defendants would be liable for conspiracy to commit murder because impossibility is not a defense to a conspiracy charge, which punishes group conduct before an attempt occurs. Similarly, if the intended victim were alive and the police arrest one of the conspirators prior to the killing, leading the other to give up on the plan, they could still be charged with conspiracy. In *United States v. Jimenez Recio*, 537 U.S. 270 (2003), the Supreme Court stated, "A conspiracy does not automatically terminate simply because the Government, unbeknownst to some of the conspirators, has defeated the conspiracy's object."

An opposite result occurs if the objective of the conspiracy is not a crime. Often characterized as legal impossibility, this principle holds that there is no conspiracy if the misdeed to be committed has not been determined to be a crime in the jurisdiction. For example, if A and B agree to import into the United States a certain over-the-counter drug from Canada, thinking the importation violates federal drug law, A and B are not guilty of a conspiracy to import illegal drugs if it turns out that federal drug law allows the particular drug to be brought into the United States in the manner A and B planned. Another way to analyze this "defense" is that, irrespective of the actor's intent, there is no conspiracy because the agreement was not to commit a crime (or unlawful act or felony), which is an element of a conspiracy.

H. Liability for Substantive Offenses

1. Scope of Liability

A member of a conspiracy is liable for that offense, and also personally liable for any crime that person commits in connection with the agreement. Thus, if A and B conspire to kill V, and then B follows the agreed plan and shoots V while A stands guard outside, B is clearly guilty of both conspiracy to murder and first degree murder. In addition, in some jurisdictions that have adopted the *Pinkerton* rule, discussed below, each member of the conspiracy can be held liable for any substantive offense committed by *another conspirator* during the course of and in furtherance of the agreement. Importantly, this can include an offense that was not originally within the contemplation of the agreement, but was a foreseeable consequence of it. This is a type of vicarious liability for members of a conspiracy. For example, if a group of defendants agree to rob a jewelry store and dispose of the stolen jewelry, and one member's only role is to help sell the stolen goods, that person is liable for any reasonably foreseeable offenses committed during the commission of, and in furtherance of, the robbery. If a guard who tries to prevent the robbery is shot and killed by a co-conspirator, then every member of the conspiracy, including a conspirator not present, could be convicted of murder in addition to the conspiracy. This basis for liability is distinct from a possible charge as an accomplice to the robbery.

2. *Pinkerton* Rule

The Supreme Court held in *Pinkerton v. United States*, 328 U.S. 640 (1946), that a member of a conspiracy can be convicted for all foreseeable substantive offenses carried out in furtherance of the agreement. The Court upheld the conviction of a defendant for a crime committed by another conspirator even though the defendant was in jail and did not participate directly in its commission. The *Pinkerton* rule has broad implications for all conspirators because it *extends liability* for substantive crimes committed by any conspirator, with or without the participation or even knowledge of the other conspirators, if the offense is reasonably foreseeable and committed during and in furtherance of the conspiracy.

Under *Pinkerton*, the co-conspirator's offense must be a reasonably foreseeable consequence of the criminal agreement. In the example above, the killing of the jewelry store guard likely permitted completion of the robbery or flight, so it would be a foreseeable consequence of the fulfillment of the conspiracy's criminal object. On the other hand, if one of the conspirators robs a patron while stealing the jewelry from the store, the robbery of the customer is unlikely to be either in furtherance of the jewelry store robbery or a foreseeable outcome of the criminal agreement. While *Pinkerton* applies in federal conspiracy prosecutions, a number of states do not accept it.

3. Limit on Liability

Pinkerton liability will not extend to every possible offense committed in connection with a conspiracy. For example, two people agree to assist a local drug dealer by hiding narcotics in a house they share. The police search the house and discover the drugs, arresting the two conspirators who hid the drugs. One of the two has a gun hidden in a drawer at the time of the arrest, and is a convicted felon. While that person can be charged with the offense of being a felon in possession of a weapon, a court rejected the application of *Pinkerton* to hold the second conspirator liable for that offense because it was based only on the status of the conspirator as a felon and not any criminal act related to the object of the agreement. *United States v. Walls*, 225 F.3d 858 (7th Cir. 2000).

4. Nature of Intent

The *Pinkerton* doctrine applies in cases in which the defendant did not have the level of intent required by the substantive offense for which he or she was charged. For example, a group of gang members decide to beat a member of another gang who is found in their territory. As they beat the opposing gang member, one of the conspirators takes out a gun and shoots and kills the victim. The others participating in the beating will be liable for murder, most likely first degree murder, even though they did not personally have the *mens rea* for that crime when undertaking the criminal conduct. This extension of criminal liability is viewed as a means to deter *collective criminal agreements* to protect the public from the danger inherent in group criminality. Courts explain that a combination to commit a crime makes it more likely that there will also be the commission of crimes unrelated to the original purpose for which the group was formed.

5. No Need to Charge Conspiracy

While *Pinkerton* creates liability for every member of the conspiracy, the government is not required to charge a conspiracy to invoke the doctrine. *Pinkerton* is a rule imposing vicarious liability for the criminal act of other conspirators, and it applies regardless of whether the government actually charges the conspiracy offense. Like proof of any criminal offense, the government must establish the elements of the conspiracy beyond a reasonable doubt, so prosecutors usually charge that offense in addition to any substantive crimes. For example, if X and Y agree to rob V and while they are fleeing the robbery X kills a police officer trying to apprehend him, X and Y may be charged with the robbery of V and the murder of the police officer, even if the prosecutor decides not to charge them with a conspiracy. The *Pinkerton* rule would apply, making Y liable for the officer's death irrespective of the fact that no conspiracy was formally charged and they never agreed to the killing. The prosecutor still must prove the existence of a conspiracy and that the killing was during the course of and in furtherance of the agreement in order to have the *Pinkerton* rule apply. Note the similarity between the *Pinkerton* rule and the felony-murder doctrine as both allow for vicarious liability for a crime not directly perpetrated by a defendant but related to a course of conduct resulting in an offense.

I. Model Penal Code

1. Elements

The Model Penal Code follows the same approach as the common law in making the agreement the focal point of the crime. Section 5.03(1) defines conspiracy as when a person "agrees with such other person or persons that they or one or more of them will engage in conduct that constitutes such crime or an attempt or solicitation to commit such crime," or agrees to aid in the planning or commission of the criminal object. The MPC requires proof of an overt act for a conspiracy to commit a misdemeanor or third-degree felony, but not for a first or second degree felony. For example, burglary is a second degree felony if it is perpetrated in a dwelling at night or there is an attempt to harm an occupant, otherwise it is a third degree felony.

2. Mens Rea

The MPC's highest *mens rea* level is required, that the person agree with "the purpose of promoting or facilitating" the object offense. Based on this intent requirement, the MPC rejects the *Pinkerton* doctrine that holds a conspirator liable for all crimes committed by other conspirators during the conspiracy that were foreseeable and in furtherance of the agreement.

3. Members of a Conspiracy

A defendant can be guilty of joining a larger conspiracy if it can be proven that he or she "knows that a person with whom he conspires to commit a crime has conspired with another person or persons to commit the same crime," regardless of whether the defendant is aware of the identity of the additional members. Thus, if A and B agree to distribute illegal drugs, A is also in the same drug conspiracy with C and D if A knows that B has conspired with others to carry out the same drug distribution offense, even if they are unknown to A.

4. Unilateral

In an important departure from the common law, the MPC adopts a *unilateral* approach to the criminal agreement that only requires the defendant agree with another person to commit a crime, but not that another person reach the same agreement. A primary purpose of this approach is to facilitate undercover police activity by permitting officers to run a "sting operation" and pretend to be involved in a crime. By defining conspiracy as the individual defendant's purpose to agree with another person, the MPC eliminates the requirement in the common law that another person reciprocate by actually joining the agreement.

For example, D asks A to help steal an expensive sports car later that evening, and A feigns agreement and informs the police. As D and A approach the vehicle, the police arrest D, who is charged with attempted auto theft and conspiracy. Under the MPC, D can be convicted of conspiracy because he or she had a purpose to agree to the criminal act with A and did, in D's mind, agree with A, even though A did not actually enter into the agreement. Under the common law, however, there would be no conspiracy liability because at least two people must enter into the same agreement, and A did not agree to steal the car. The unilateral approach eliminates any vestige of the older common law rules that the acquittal of all other members of a conspiracy means the remaining defendant must be acquitted, or that inconsistent verdicts are impermissible.

5. Renunciation and *Pinkerton*

Section 5.03(6) recognizes an affirmative defense of *renunciation*. A defendant who entered into a conspiracy can be acquitted of that crime if the person "thwarted the success of the conspiracy, under circumstances manifesting a complete and voluntary renunciation of his criminal purpose." The rationale for the defense is the focus on the defendant's intent, that a person who repudiates a criminal plan by defeating it should not be punished for that earlier illegal purpose. It is also designed to encourage people to quit criminal activity before completing the crime that was planned. The MPC rejects the *Pinkerton* doctrine of vicarious liability for the crimes of co-conspirators in the commentary to § 2.06, which provides for liability for the conduct of another person. One conspirator is not "legally accountable" for the conduct of other conspirators, and therefore cannot be convicted except when the person acts as an accomplice to the conduct of a coconspirator. The rationale is that a person should only be responsible for his or her own acts undertaken with the requisite criminal intent and not those of another person when there is no proof of a purpose to assist in the commission of the offense.

Checkpoints

- A conspiracy is an agreement to commit an unlawful act, or a lawful act by illegal means.

- The majority of jurisdictions require proof that two or more persons enter into the agreement, while the Model Penal Code and a minority of jurisdictions only require proof of the defendant's intent to agree.

- Two mental states are required for conspiracy: intent to agree and knowledge of the criminal objective of the agreement.

- Knowledge alone is insufficient to prove a conspiracy, but a defendant's knowledge of the illegal object can be proven based on willful blindness.

- A conspirator need not know all the other members of the conspiracy or each of its details so long as each member joins the same agreement.

- Statutes in some jurisdictions require proof of an overt act in connection with the conspiracy, and that act need only be a step in completing the object of the conspiracy and not a crime or an attempt to commit a crime.

- Conspiracies come in many forms, sometimes called "wheels" and "chains," and the focal point is proving whether there is a single agreement among all the members.

- The statement of one conspirator made during the course of and in furtherance of the conspiracy can be introduced as substantive evidence against all members of the conspiracy.

Checkpoints, *cont.*

- "Wharton's Rule" precludes a conspiracy charge for an offense that necessarily involve two persons for the crime, unless there is a third party joining the agreement.

- Abandonment is recognized in some jurisdictions as a defense to any crimes committed by another conspirator after the withdrawal, and may be a defense to a conspiracy charge when permitted by statute.

- Abandonment as a statutory defense must be voluntary and complete, and in some jurisdictions the defense requires notification be given to the authorities.

- Under the *Pinkerton* doctrine, which is not accepted in all jurisdictions, a conspirator is liable for all offenses carried out by any co-conspirator that are foreseeable and in furtherance of the conspiracy.

Chapter 17

Defenses in General, Alibi, and Entrapment

A. Overview

In a criminal case, the prosecution bears the burden of proof on all elements of the crimes with which the accused is charged. The defendant is under no obligation to present a defense and frequently does not do so. The defendant does have the option to present defenses subject to the legislative or judicial acceptance of the particular defense being presented by the accused. What makes something an available defense varies among the jurisdictions. There may also be different approaches on who has the burden of proof with respect to the defense.

1. Policy Basis of Defenses

Each defense represents a policy decision that the criminal law should not hold a person liable for one or more crimes in certain circumstances. For example, the insanity defense is based on the view that people should be held criminally responsible for their acts only when they meet minimal mental standards. In most locales, this means that people are excused from all criminal liability if at the time of the crime they were unable to control their actions or to appreciate the wrongfulness of what they did. Similarly, self-defense rests on the concept that in some extraordinary circumstances people have a natural right to defend themselves against immediate physical harm.

Just as each defense has a general policy basis, the contours of each defense are formed to further one or more policies. For example, as noted above, self-defense is based on the natural right of self-preservation. Some jurisdictions, however, have tempered self-defense by providing that the defendant must retreat before using deadly force in a public place if retreat could be done safely. The policy behind this limit on self-defense is to preserve life whenever possible. If, in a jurisdiction that requires retreat, V attacks D in a public place with deadly force, such as a knife, D must retreat rather than stand and fight if D could retreat safely. If D responds with deadly force rather than retreats, he or she may lose the right to use self-defense if charged with V's homicide.

2. Definition of "Defense"

There is some disagreement about what should be considered a formal "defense" in a criminal case. Some scholars maintain that the term "defense" includes all arguments that negate the prosecution's case. For example, a claim of insufficient evidence of the crime charged can be called a defense. Thus, a defendant's evidence showing that the prosecution failed to prove the accused had the *mens rea* element of the crime might be characterized as a "defense" to the crime.

Other scholars, however, take a narrower view of what is a "defense," limiting this characterization to issues that are separate from negating elements the prosecution must prove in its case-in-chief. Thus, in the narrower view, a defendant's argument that he or she lacked the necessary *mens rea* would be considered an effort to counter the prosecution's proof of one of the elements it must prove beyond a reasonable doubt, but would not be considered a "defense" in the same way as insanity or self-defense.

3. Multiple Defenses

The defense is not limited to presenting a single defense. Rather, the accused can offer inconsistent defenses and is entitled to a jury instruction on every legitimate defense presented. For example, the accused might argue that he or she acted in self-defense while also arguing involuntary intoxication. From a practical perspective, arguing inconsistent defenses might cause defense counsel to lose credibility and result in the trier of fact's rejection of both arguments.

4. Burden and Standard of Proof

While due process mandates that the prosecution has the burden of proving each element of a crime beyond a reasonable doubt, (see Chapter 7) states are free to allocate the various burdens for defenses. In general, defenses are not an issue until raised by the defendant. Ordinarily, the defense has the responsibility for the *burden of production*, which means putting on some proof (often called a *prima facie case*) of a defense. This makes the particular defense an issue in the case.

The *burden of persuasion*, which refers to which side must convince the trier of fact of the existence or nonexistence of the defense, varies markedly among jurisdictions depending on the particular defense. After the defendant satisfies the modest burden of production and thereby formally makes a defense an issue in the case, states adopt one of two approaches. Under the *burden shifting* model, the burden (called the burden of persuasion) shifts to the prosecution to prove that the defendant did *not* meet the requirements for the alleged defense. Under the *burden staying* model, the defendant retains the burden of persuasion and must prove the existence of the defense.

The *standard of proof* for defenses, which describes the degree of certainty needed to satisfy the burden of persuasion, varies considerably, ranging from a preponderance of evidence, to clear and convincing evidence, to beyond a reasonable doubt. Indeed, a single jurisdiction may have several categories of defenses and allocate a different standard of proof for each.

For example, insanity is a defense recognized by many jurisdictions. The defendant has the burden of production of introducing some proof that he or she was insane at the time of the crime. Who has the burden beyond that point can vary by jurisdiction. In some jurisdictions the prosecution will need to prove the defendant was sane at the time of the crime. Other jurisdictions will place the burden on the defendant to prove insanity at the time of the crime.

Many modern jurisdictions categorize defenses into "defenses" and "affirmative defenses." The defense counsel is typically required to prove an "affirmative defense." On the other hand, the prosecution must disprove a "defense." Some statutes will indicate clearly whether a given defense is a "defense" or an "affirmative defense." A typical example is New York: "(1) When a 'defense,' other than an 'affirmative defense,' defined by statute is raised at trial, the people have the burden of disproving such defense beyond a reasonable doubt. (2) When a defense declared by statute to be an 'affirmative defense' is raised at trial, the defendant has the burden of establishing such defense by a preponderance of the evidence." *N.Y. Penal Law § 25.00.*

5. Impact of Defenses

Defenses may affect a criminal case in different ways.

a. Complete Defense

A few defenses are a *complete defense* to all criminal liability arising from a course of conduct. Thus, a defendant who satisfies the jurisdiction's test of insanity or infancy is not responsible for any crime, irrespective of the defendant's conduct or the gravity of the harm.

b. Partial Defense

Some defenses may lead to an acquittal on one or more crimes but have no impact on others. An example of a *partial defense* is imperfect self-defense, which reduces the gravity of a homicide from murder to voluntary manslaughter. Another illustration is diminished capacity which allows a defendant to present expert testimony that he or she was mentally disabled and unable to deliberate or premeditate, as required for a conviction for first degree murder in many traditional jurisdictions. The same expert may also conclude that the defendant's particular mental condition was not a defense to a charge of reckless or negligent homicide since the mental disability that affected the capacity to premeditate or deliberate would not affect the defendant's capacity to satisfy the requirements for acting recklessly or with criminal negligence.

c. Negate Element of Crime

Another set of defenses enables the defendant to *disprove an element of the crime* at issue. Virtually always the element negated is the *mens rea*, such as intent, knowledge, purpose, and the like. A classic illustration is *intoxication*. The defendant may argue that he or she was so drunk as to be unable to have the intent required for liability. A related defense is *mistake* where the accused maintains that a mistake about a fact negates a mental element of the crime. The prototypical illustration is the person who leaves a black umbrella in a restaurant cloak room, then after the meal mistakenly takes another umbrella and leaves the building. The defendant is not guilty of larceny of the umbrella because that crime requires an intent to deprive the owner of it permanently.

Since the defendant believed that it was her umbrella, she lacked the *mens rea* for larceny.

B. Justifications and Excuses

The common law divided defenses into two categories: *justifications* and *excuses*. Both justifications and excuses involve conduct normally subject to the criminal laws, but permit an exoneration of the accused because of policy reasons reflecting the theoretical underpinning of the criminal law. For defenses characterized as *justifications*, often involving an actor who used force against another person, the accused's actions are deemed non-criminal because a greater good to society was served when the defendant engaged in the act. In other words, the defendant's behavior was consistent with what society thinks is appropriate for a person to do under the circumstances. Accordingly, the defendant is not considered to be morally blameworthy for conduct that furthered goals which society deems meritorious. Thus, the actor who kills in self-defense or who defends a third party against a physical assault is justified in committing the act because it may save that person from the harm caused by another party who had no right to attack the defendant or the person he or she protected. Other types of justification defenses are protection of property, the various law enforcement defenses that permit police and even citizens to use force to prevent crime and arrest criminals, and the right of a parent (or sometimes, school official) to use reasonable force to discipline or protect a child.

In contrast, an *excuse* defense would exculpate the accused because he or she should not be held accountable for the conduct, despite it being harmful and technically satisfying the elements of a crime. It focuses on the actor rather than the conduct. Thus, one who suffers from insanity, infancy, or is involuntarily intoxicated at the time of the offense, or who acted under duress, might be excused from being held criminally liable. The personal extenuating circumstances warrant that the individual should not be held accountable for the criminal act that had been committed. Another view is that under traditional views of moral blameworthiness, the person is not held criminally responsible for his or her conduct because of the mental illness or other extenuating circumstance.

The distinction between justifications and excuses was important historically because justified conduct was considered a benefit to society, while the excused conduct carried a greater stigma in society. Justified conduct could also be conduct used by accessories in claiming that they, too, should not be held criminally liable. In contrast, the insanity of the perpetrator does not excuse the sane act of an accomplice.

C. Right to Present a Defense

1. Generally

In general terms, an accused has a constitutional right to present a defense. The Supreme Court has continually held, as it did in *Holmes v. South Carolina*, 547 U.S. 319 (2006), that it is unconstitutional when excluded evidence significantly undermines the defendant's "meaningful opportunity to present a complete defense." *Holmes* involved a South Carolina trial court ruling excluding evidence that a third party committed the murder with which the defendant was charged. The constitutional violation is premised on either a deprivation of Due Process under the Fourteenth Amendment or the Sixth Amendment's Compulsory Process or Confrontation Clauses.

2. Exceptions to Right to Present a Defense

Like other rights, however, the right to present a defense is not absolute and is subject to some limitations. For example, a defense premised on clearly inadmissible evidence will not be permitted. Thus, the right to present a defense does not include the right to present polygraph evidence or to call a witness who will commit perjury. The evidence needs to serve a "legitimate interest[ ] in the criminal trial process." *United States v. Scheffer*, 523 U.S. 303 (1998).

Another limit on the defendant's ability to offer a defense is whether the particular jurisdiction recognizes the defense. Many states, by statute or judicial decision, limit the defenses to those clearly defined by the legislature in a statute. As such, common law defenses are not recognized unless codified in a statute. An illustration is a state that fails to include a "battered spouse" defense in its list of accepted defenses. This may preclude the presentation of witnesses about the battered spouse's situation because the jurisdiction does not recognize a battered spouse defense and the defense witnesses do not clearly fit within the confines of the legislature's definition of self-defense. In contrast, other jurisdictions might allow the accused more room to present a defense that does not meet the traditional elements of self-defense. This may be a defense that provides an explanation for the accused's conduct and one that the jury should consider in determining whether to exonerate the individual. For example, prior to the California legislature precluding a diminished capacity defense, the accused was able to present evidence related to the excessive consumption of "Twinkees."

Often the defense lawyer seeks to present sociological or psychological evidence about the defendant's mental condition that does not rise to the level of insanity. For example, a defendant may attempt to present a defense premised on television violence, arguing that the various influences on the accused should be admitted as proof so that the jury can fully evaluate why the accused engaged in this conduct. A court that precludes this form of testimony at trial may still decide to consider it as mitigating evidence to reduce a sentence.

Some jurisdictions reject certain traditional defenses because they are inconsistent with the legislature's determination of the appropriate public policy. For example, Idaho does not recognize insanity or any "mental condition" as a defense "to any charge of criminal conduct." *Idaho Code § 18-207*. Missouri bars proof of voluntary intoxication to negate *mens rea*. *Mo. Ann. Stat. § 562.076*. The Supreme Court generally upholds these policy choices as within the authority of state legislatures. Thus, in *Montana v. Egelhoff*, 518 U.S. 37 (1996), the Court rejected a due process challenge to the Montana rule barring evidence of voluntary intoxication to establish that the accused lacked the *mens rea* of killing purposely or knowingly. Some states have allowed a defendant to assert a "gay panic" defense when the accused claims that he or she was provoked to commit the crime because of the victim's sexual orientation or gender identity. Other states now follow the lead of an American Bar Association Resolution in curtailing the availability of this defense.

D. Cultural Defenses

Should the defense be allowed to present evidence on the "role of honor, paternalism, and street fighters" in a certain culture? Should the fact that Native American children were removed from their tribal families be considered by the jury in deciding whether the accused acted criminally in not taking a child to a physician? Should a sociological, national, or religious difference be considered by a jury in determining whether the accused acted with criminal liability? Courts differ in deciding whether a jury should be entitled to hear evidence related to a cultural defense. Courts that permit this testimony can allow it three different ways: (1) to negate an element of the offense (*e.g.*, intent); (2) to reinforce an accepted defense (*e.g.*, self-defense); (3) and as a separate defense as a facet of the defendant's right to present his or her case.

E. Alibi

Often the accused will assert that he or she did not commit the offense because he or she was someplace else at the time of the crime. This defense is referred to as an *alibi defense.* Unlike justification or excuse defenses, which admit the accused's involvement in the activity but seek exoneration based upon the circumstances, the alibi defense involves a claim that the defendant was not present at the time of the crime and is therefore *innocent of* the charges. If the defendant offers sufficient evidence of an alibi, in many locales the court will give an alibi instruction that tells the jury the prosecution has the burden of disproving the alibi beyond a reasonable doubt.

Courts distinguish alibi cases from cases questioning the perpetrator's identity. Thus, the defendant who says "I am not the five-foot nine-inch, blond-haired individual who committed this crime," would not be entitled to a jury instruction on alibi based upon this argument. In contrast, the individual who says that he or she was at home with Mom at the time of the crime might have an alibi instruction read to the jury.

1. What Is an Alibi?

For procedural reasons, it matters whether the defendant is offering a formal "alibi" defense or is simply arguing that he or she was not at the scene of the crime and is therefore innocent. In the latter situation, the accused is not providing evidence of being elsewhere, but is merely contesting the prosecution's proof that he or she was at the scene of the crime. For example, if the defense offers witnesses to say that the accused, charged with assault, was not at the scene of a fight where the assault allegedly occurred, the court needs to determine whether this constitutes an "alibi" and entitles the defendant to a jury instruction on alibi as well as triggering the procedural notice requirements, described below, mandated for an alibi defense. If the defendant is not claiming to have been at a particular location at the time of the offense, but rather contends only that he or she was not at the scene of the crime, courts may not consider this to be an alibi and permit this testimony, despite there being no alibi notice filed. Courts tend to find that the defense proof is merely rebuttal to the State's case and not an alibi that puts the accused in another location.

2. Notice of Intent to Use Alibi Defense

Cases where the defense offers an alibi present unique challenges for the prosecution, which could be unaware of the alibi defense until defense counsel's opening statement. Imagine the situation where the crime occurred in Detroit and defense counsel's opening statement indicates that the defense will present witnesses that the defendant was in San Francisco at the time of the crime that occurred in Detroit. If the prosecution did not know of this alibi, it may have no witnesses from San Francisco to rebut the defendant's surprise alibi witnesses. If the government witnesses who place the defendant in Detroit at the critical time are not strong witnesses, the defense witnesses who testify about the defendant's presence in San Francisco at the relevant time may persuade the jury that there is a reasonable doubt whether the defendant committed the offense.

To protect the prosecution from being surprised by an alibi defense, many jurisdictions have strict procedural rules requiring the defendant to provide the prosecution with advance notice of an intent to rely on alibi witnesses. For example, Oregon requires that "not less than five days before the trial of the cause, [the accused must] file and serve upon the district attorney a written notice of the purpose to offer such evidence, which notice shall state specifically the place or places where the defendant claims to have been at the time or times of the alleged offense together with the name and residence or business address of each witness upon whom the defendant intends to rely for alibi evidence." *Ore. Stat. § 135.455.* Unless good cause can be shown, the defense's alibi witnesses may be excluded when the defense fails to comply with an alibi notice requirement. A defendant who provides notice of an intent to offer an alibi defense usually is entitled to receive information from the prosecution about its witnesses who will rebut the defendant's alibi witnesses.

The rule barring defense alibi witnesses from testifying if the required notice is not given does not apply if the witness is the defendant as the defendant has a constitutional right to testify at his or her trial. If the defendant and other defense witnesses will testify about the alibi, the lack of notice may bar the witnesses other than the defendant. For example, the Kansas statute explicitly states that "no such notice shall be required to allow testimony as to alibi, by the defendant himself, in his own defense."

F. Entrapment

The *entrapment* defense is premised on the notion that the government should not use its virtually unlimited resources to turn its citizens from law abiding people into criminals. On the rare occasions when this occurs, the criminal law has long provided the accused with a defense to criminal charges. The real purpose is to deter police conduct that many regard as morally repugnant to notions of what law enforcement officials should be doing to combat crime.

The definition of entrapment is in part dependent upon which of two views is taken by a jurisdiction: the *objective* or *subjective* approach. The subjective approach looks at the defendant's *predisposition* to commit the crime. In contrast, an objective approach examines the extent of government conduct in enticing citizens to violate the criminal law. Under either approach, it is widely held that entrapment does not occur if law enforcement officials merely afford a person an opportunity to commit a crime. Some jurisdictions see the entrapment defense composed of two distinct, but related, elements: government inducement and lack of predisposition. *United States v. Mayfield*, 771 F.3d 417 (7th Cir. 2013).

1. Subjective Test

The *subjective* approach is used by the majority of states and the federal courts. The standard is that it is improper for law enforcement to "implant in the mind of an innocent person the disposition to commit the alleged offense and induce its commission in order that they may prosecute." *Sorrells v. United States*, 287 U.S. 435 (1932). Thus, when the prosecution is unable to show that the accused would have purchased the drugs but for the police continually calling the accused and trying to get him or her to buy these drugs, an entrapment defense may prevail. Many jurisdictions follow the Supreme Court's lead in *Jacobson v. United States*, 503 U.S. 540 (1992), and find that this initially is an issue of law for courts to decide.

If the defendant wants to assert entrapment but cannot convince the court that there was entrapment as a matter of law, he or she must present evidence to the trier of fact of being induced by the government to commit the crime. Many courts then treat entrapment as an affirmative defense requiring the defendant to shoulder the burden of persuasion to establish the government misconduct and the defendant's lack of predisposition to commit the offense. Other jurisdictions require the defense to bear the burden of production of entrapment by showing government inducement, as noted above, but then shift the burden of persuasion to the prosecution to show that the accused had the predisposition to commit the crime.

Courts use many different factors in assessing predisposition. The factors are: "(1) whether the defendant readily responded to the inducement offered; (2) the circumstances surrounding the illegal conduct; (3) the state of mind of a defendant before the government agents make any suggestion that the defendant shall commit a crime; (4) whether the defendant was engaged in an existing course of conduct similar to the crime for which the defendant is charged; (5) whether the defendant had already formed the design to commit the crime for which the defendant is charged; (6) the defendant's reputation; (7) the conduct of the defendant during negotiations with the undercover agent; (8) whether the defendant has refused to commit similar acts on other occasions; (9) the nature of the crime charged; (10) the degree of coercion which the law officers contributed to instigating the transaction relative to the defendant's criminal background." *United States v. Dion*, 762 F.2d 674 (8th Cir. 1985).

A good illustration is *Albaugh v. State*, 721 N.E.2d 1233 (Ind. 1999), where the court found the defendant was entrapped into driving while drunk. The defendant's truck broke down on a snowy night. Police went to his house and told him to move it immediately because it was a safety hazard. The defendant, who had been drinking for hours, tried to convince the police to postpone the move until morning, but relented when the police would not permit the delay. When the defendant finally got the truck started and drove away, he was arrested for drunk driving. The appellate court found that the defendant was entrapped because the police induced the crime and the defendant was not predisposed to commit it.

Because of concerns of prejudicing the defendant's case, often the rules of evidence bar proof of the defendant's criminal history. When the defendant raises entrapment and his or her predisposition becomes an issue, however, the rules of evidence change to allow the prosecution to introduce evidence about the defendant's criminal history. Fearing the negative reaction jurors may have to this proof of the defendant's "bad" character, many defendants refuse to offer an entrapment defense. Moreover, the reluctance to present an entrapment defense is augmented by the fact that the defendant presenting this defense essentially must admit that he or she did the acts prohibited by the criminal law. For example, an accused would be unwise to argue, "I did not sell the drugs to Undercover Agent X but if I did I was entrapped."

2. Objective Test

Model Penal Code § 2.13, followed by a minority of jurisdictions, adopts an *objective* approach to entrapment. As opposed to focusing on the accused's subjective predisposition to commit the crime, the objective approach examines the officer's conduct irrespective of the defendant's predisposition. An entrapment occurs when, in order to obtain evidence of the commission of a crime, a law enforcement official knowingly makes false representations to induce a belief that the conduct is not criminal, or employs methods that create a substantial risk that the offense will be committed by persons other than those who are ready to commit it. The defendant is entitled to an acquittal if he or she establishes by a preponderance of evidence that his or her conduct occurred in response to an entrapment, as defined above.

3. Entrapment by Estoppel

In addition to the traditional estoppel defense, a defendant can raise *entrapment by estoppel* when the person relies on an official statement of the law to engage in conduct, and that statement turns out to be erroneous and leads the person to commit a crime. The defendant bears the burden of proving, usually by a preponderance of the evidence, that a government official told the defendant that certain conduct was legal, and the defendant actually relied on the government official's statements. The defendant's reliance on the statement must be in good faith and reasonable in light of the identity of the government official, the point of law represented, and the substance of the statement. In determining reasonableness, a defendant's reliance is reasonable if the person sought the information to obey the law and was not put on notice to make further inquiries.

For example, a defendant convicted in state court for illegal possession of a machine gun, a felony, has the charge reduced to a misdemeanor because of good conduct while on probation. The defendant then speaks with a federal firearms licensee who erroneously advises the defendant that there is no problem owning a gun because the felony conviction had been reduced to a misdemeanor. If the defendant is charged with being a felon in possession of a weapon after purchasing a gun from a firearms dealer, an entrapment by estoppel defense might be offered to argue that the defendant has the right to rely on the representations of a federal firearms licensee who has been made aware of all the relevant facts by the defendant.

G. Outrageous Government Conduct

In addition to entrapment, defendants on occasion will argue, usually unsuccessfully, that the government engaged in outrageous behavior that should be prohibited under the Due Process Clause of the U.S. Constitution. In *United States v. Russell*, 411 U.S. 423 (1973), the Supreme Court reasoned that at some point the government's gross misbehavior in obtaining evidence of a crime bars the government from invoking the judicial process. Like entrapment's objective approach, the focus is on the government conduct as opposed to the actions of the accused. Outrageous government conduct, however, is not limited to situations of when the defendant might be predisposed to commit the crime. Rather, this defense includes all instances when the prosecution may have exceeded constitutional authority and violated the accused's due process rights.

Checkpoints

- The defense has no obligation to present a defense, but a right to present one when desired.

- At common law, defenses were divided into justifications and excuses.

- What constitutes a defense may differ depending upon state statute or court interpretation.

- Some states permit defendants the ability to present cultural defenses.

- An alibi defense claims innocence on the basis of the accused being elsewhere when the crime was committed.

- To avoid surprise at trial, many states require the accused to provide advance notice of presenting an alibi defense.

- Entrapment is a defense that can be approached either subjectively or objectively, with the majority of jurisdictions using a subjective approach.

- A subjective approach of entrapment focuses on the accused conduct and whether he or she had the predisposition to commit the offense absent police activity.

- Outrageous government conduct focuses exclusively on the police conduct to see if there has been a due process violation.

Chapter 18

Defending Self, Others, and Property

A. Introduction

As a general rule, if D strikes V with a fist, D has committed a crime. In most situations society condemns physical violence and punishes those who commit these acts. In some narrowly defined circumstances, however, the criminal law authorizes the use of reasonable force because that violence serves a permissible policy. The common law recognized defenses to crimes such as murder, manslaughter, and assault and battery based on the justification that the person was protecting him- or herself, another individual, property, or capturing a criminal. Most jurisdictions today have enacted statutes that define these defenses.

There are four basic circumstances when the criminal law recognizes that an individual is justified in the use of some measure of force against another person that would otherwise trigger liability for a crime. These are: (1) self-defense; (2) defense of others; (3) defense of property and habitation; and (4) crime prevention and arrest. Each is discussed below.

B. Self-Defense

1. Introduction

The law of *self-defense*, developed by the common law and now recognized in every jurisdiction, often by statute, provides that in certain circumstances a person may be justified in using force to defend him- or herself. Thus, an individual who is assaulted, or about to be assaulted, may stop the attacker through the use of reasonable force without incurring any criminal liability for that defensive action. Self-defense provides a *complete defense* to the charge. Therefore, the person who is prosecuted for assault, but acted in accordance with the requirements of self-defense, could be acquitted of this charge.

American courts traditionally recognized self-defense on the theory that each individual has a right to self-preservation and personal autonomy that allows force to be used in limited circumstances. One court expressed the traditional rationale eloquently: "Our law has recognized that self-preservation under such circumstances springs from a primal impulse and is an inherent right of natural law." *State v. Holland*, 138 S.E. 8 (N.C. 1927). Despite the universal acceptance of self-defense, courts are especially careful in applying it in the context of the use of deadly force because it effectively sanctions killings by private citizens without prior judicial authorization.

2. Elements of Self-Defense

It is generally held that there are seven elements necessary for an actor to assert a claim of self-defense. These are: (1) the use, or threat of the imminent use, of (2) unlawful (3) force (4) that does or could cause physical injury and (5) which a reasonable person would believe could not be avoided without the use of physical force, and the actor (6) defends by using only a reasonable amount of force and (7) was not responsible for the situation that prompted the need to use such force. These elements, however, may be modified by a particular jurisdiction and may also have exceptions depending on the facts. Additionally, in some cases the same evidence may be used to satisfy more than one element.

The Arizona self-defense statute, typical of those in many American jurisdictions, provides that "a person is justified in threatening or using physical force against another when and to the extent a reasonable person would believe that physical force is immediately necessary to protect himself against the other's use or attempted use of unlawful physical force." *Ariz. Rev. Stat. § 13-404(A)*. But the statute also provides that one cannot use self-defense in certain circumstances.

While it is easy to justify the use of force in self-defense when a stranger threatens a significant harm to a person, such as an attempted rape or armed robbery, it is much more difficult to determine the availability of the defense when there has been some measure of mutual threats, or an escalation of a confrontation from one involving only verbal sparring to the use of dangerous weapons. In these scenarios, the reasonableness of the use of force will depend on who, at the time the force was used or threatened, is deemed an *aggressor* and whether either participant sought to exit the confrontation before using force. For example, the Arizona self-defense statute does not allow a self-defense claim when "verbal provocation alone" triggered the violent response or "[i]f the person provoked the other's use or attempted use of unlawful physical force." *Ariz. Rev. Stat. § 13-404(B)*. Thus, the key issues in many cases involving self-defense are: (1) did the actor have a reasonable belief in the necessity to respond with force in the situation; (2) was the amount of force used reasonable under the circumstances; and (3) who started the altercation and was the actor responding to force or was he or she the aggressor?

a. Use or Threat of Imminent Physical Harm

Self-defense is generally limited to those situations in which a person faces *imminent* force. The force must be immediately present or threatened, not just a fearful perception of possible harm. For example, if A states, "I'll be back later to beat you up," the listener could not then use force to resist the potential attack. The harm threatened was not sufficiently imminent to satisfy self-defense. A conditional threat, however, can be sufficient to permit the use of force in self-defense. For example, if A states, "Get out of here now or I'll hit you over the head with this baseball bat," that may create a reasonable fear of imminent harm that would allow a use of force, especially if A was holding the bat while making the statement.

The imminence of force changes with the circumstances. If the attacker punches the victim in the face then withdraws, perhaps by running away, the defendant may not use self-defense to justify pursuing and subduing the attacker since the attacker's threat of immediate harm ended when he or she withdrew. Similarly, once the attacker is rendered harmless, perhaps by being knocked unconscious or gravely injured, the initial victim may not continue the attack and then claim self-defense. The danger had subsided and self-defense was no longer necessary.

Immediacy can be an issue in cases involving domestic violence. For example, a spouse who is battered in the daytime by his or her spouse may respond several hours later, killing the battering spouse when the individual is asleep. Some courts hold that self-defense fails under the immediacy requirement because there was no current danger posed by the battering spouse. Other courts, however, allow battered spouse evidence to demonstrate the continual abuse suffered by the spouse as a basis to establish the reasonable fear of harm in the near future.

b. Unlawful Force Used or Threatened

The threatened force must be *unlawful*, so that a police officer pointing a gun at a murder suspect in order to prevent the suspect's flight would be a lawful use of force and therefore would not allow the suspect to use self-defense as a justification to shoot the officer. The Indiana self-defense statute, for example, allows the use of force in response to what "the person reasonably believes to be the imminent use of unlawful force." *Ind. Code § 35-41-3-2(c)*. Following the theory that the force being resisted must be unlawful, the Indiana statute does not allow a self-defense claim if "the person is committing or is escaping after the commission of a crime." *Ind. Code § 35-41-3-2(g)*. Therefore, a thief who is confronted by a use of force from the owner of property to prevent the crime could not use self-defense to justify using force to resist the owner.

Most states prohibit the use of any force to *resist an arrest,* even if the person reasonably and accurately believes the arrest is unlawful. The Delaware statute provides, "The use of force is not justifiable under this section to resist an arrest which the defendant knows or should know is being made by a peace officer, whether or not the arrest is lawful." *11 Del. Code § 464(d)*. The underlying theory is that the person should use the legal system, not violence, to contest the arrest. One reason is that when a person resists arrest, the officers as well as the arrestee may suffer considerable physical harm.

c. Honest and Reasonable Belief Force Was Necessary

Self-defense is available in almost all jurisdictions only if the actor used force when both the actor and a reasonable person would believe that the force was necessary under the circumstances. The test is both subjective and objective. Some jurisdictions, however, use a solely subjective test.

i. Honest Belief Force Necessary

Obviously, force should not be allowed in self-defense unless the actor personally, subjectively believed the force was necessary at that time. If a reasonable person would believe that force was necessary in the situation but the actor, perhaps gifted with fearlessness, had no such belief, he or she could not use self-defense. The widespread rule is that self-defense requires that the actor's belief that force is necessary must be *both honest and reasonable.*

A few jurisdictions depart from the general rule and focus almost entirely on the honest belief requirement. A purely subjective test would consider only whether the individual believed that he or she was in danger and needed to respond to the perceived threat. Sometimes this is called the *honest belief* element. This subjective approach requires the trier of fact to place itself in the defendant's shoes and view the defendant's acts in light of all the facts and circumstances known to the defendant. The issue is whether the defendant had an honest belief in the need to use force to resist a threatened harm based from the person's viewpoint.

The Model Penal Code, adopting a minority rule that embraces only the honest belief approach and rejects the objective-reasonableness view, states that "the use of force upon or toward another person is justifiable when the actor believes that such force is immediately necessary for the purpose of protecting himself against the use of unlawful force by such other person on the present occasion." *MPC § 3.04. See also Ky. Rev. Stat. § 503.050* (use of physical force by a defendant upon another person is justified when the defendant believes that such force is necessary to protect himself against the use or imminent use of unlawful physical force by the other person). Even under the MPC, however, if the person's belief about the threat was mistaken due to recklessness or negligence, then the person would be liable for an offense based on these *mens rea* terms and could not use self-defense to escape criminal liability.

For example, V believes that all young men from a particular ethnic group intend to beat and rob V. This belief, however, obviously would not be accurate. One evening, as a young man from the ethnic group approaches, V uses a cane to beat him about the head and kills the young man. If V is charged with a homicide crime in a MPC jurisdiction that requires proof that V killed knowingly or purposely, V could offer the mistaken belief about the threat to support a self-defense argument. V would maintain that he or she actually believed that the force was needed at that time. On the other hand, if V is charged with reckless or criminally negligent homicide, under the MPC V could not use self-defense because V's mistaken belief about the need to use force was the product of V's negligent or reckless perceptions.

A key criticism of a purely subjective approach, such as that of the MPC, is that it allows a jury to consider the prejudices and idiosyncratic views of a defendant claiming to have acted in self-defense. Those advocating for the MPC approach may argue in response that it allows for individualized consideration of what the accused believes, as opposed to using a reasonable person standard.

ii. Reasonable Belief Force Necessary

In addition to requiring that the person asserting self-defense have an honest belief that force was needed at the time, most jurisdictions reject the MPC's purely subjective approach and also include an objective component for determining the validity of a self-defense claim, either by statute or judicial interpretation. In general terms, the force must be *both honestly and reasonably believed to be necessary* under the circumstances.

Modern statutes express the objective component by requiring that the use of force be based on a *reasonable belief* that the person was in danger of an attack. For example, the Georgia statute requires that the person claiming self-defense "reasonably believes that such force is necessary to defend himself or herself or a third person against such other's imminent use of unlawful force...." *Ga. Code Ann., § 16-3-21(a)*. This is consistent with the common law approach to self-defense, which required that a person who claimed self-defense must have entertained a reasonable belief in the necessity of using force.

Even if a defendant is mistaken about the need to use force, including deadly force, a self-defense claim can be proven as long as the mistake was reasonable. For example, late one evening in a parking lot V is confronted by X, who points a dark object at V and demands the keys to the car. V draws a concealed weapon and shoots, seriously wounding X. In deciding whether to charge V with assault with intent to kill, the prosecutor would have to consider whether V would have a good self-defense claim even if it turns out the person trying to steal the car was holding an unloaded weapon or a plastic object shaped to look like a gun. The reasonableness of V's belief that there was a threat of death or serious bodily harm must be evaluated from that person's point of view at the moment of the confrontation. In this case, it is likely the prosecutor would forego charges against V absent clear evidence that V's belief about the threat was not honestly held or was unreasonable.

A number of considerations go into determining the reasonableness of a person's belief in the necessity to use force. The Utah statute provides a list of factors to consider in determining the imminence of a threat or the reasonableness of the perception:

(a) the nature of the danger;
(b) the immediacy of the danger;
(c) the probability that the unlawful force would result in death or serious bodily injury;
(d) the other's prior violent acts or violent propensities; and
(e) any patterns of abuse or violence in the parties' relationship.

Utah Code Ann. § 76-2-402(5). As this list shows, the determination of what constitutes a reasonable belief that a person was in danger involves balancing both objective and subjective factors.

Some cases specifically hold that a belief of the need for force cannot be reasonable unless the aggressor has done some act that manifests an intent to cause the defender immediate physical harm. For example, pointing a pistol at the defender would suffice, but perhaps a "threatening attitude" may be insufficient in some situations.

iii. Balancing Objective and Subjective

In general, the objective aspect requires a determination of what a reasonable person in the defendant's situation would have believed or done. Many decisions note that the perspective is not that of either a coward or an unusually timid person, or an especially brave person, but rather of a person of ordinary firmness and reason.

This general statement, though accurate, does not shed light on the critical issue of what personal circumstances of the actor should be incorporated into the analysis. For example, courts struggle with the extent that prior experiences of the person are relevant. Should the trier of fact consider that the defendant had previously been robbed? A related issue is whether the physical characteristics of the participants should be a factor in the decision whether self-defense is appropriate in the situation. For example, should it be a "reasonable person" standard that does not take into account the gender of the person claiming self-defense, or should the trier of fact consider how a "reasonable man" or "reasonable woman" would respond?

Courts are divided in considering how many specific factors should be included in the reasonableness analysis. There is a growing trend to incorporate gender into the analysis, and also to take into consideration any disparities in age and physical size in the reasonableness calculation. This may be particularly important in cases involving domestic violence and battering relationships, as discussed below.

d. Proportionality

In addition to the requirement that the threat be imminent and that the actor have had a reasonable perception that force was necessary to repel the threatened or actual attack, it is also required that the force used by the person in response to the threat be *proportional*. This means that the *amount of force used must be reasonable under the circumstances.*

i. Reasonable Amount of Force

The usual rule is that the test is objective; would a reasonable person in that situation have believed that this amount of force was needed to resist the force that appeared to be offered by the aggressor. The reasonableness of the use of force will vary depending on the degree of force being resisted. If a person reasonably perceives that *deadly* force is threatened, then a commensurate degree of force may be used to resist. For example, A may kill B with a knife if B pulls a gun — even if unloaded or if a toy gun that appears to be authentic — on A and threatens to shoot A immediately. A's use of deadly force under the circumstances is both honest and reasonable. On the other hand, A cannot kill B with a gun when B is about to throw a tennis ball from across the room at A. The force that may be used is limited to that which is reasonably necessary to stop the individual who is attacking the accused.

If a reasonable person would perceive that only *non-deadly* force is involved, then the responsive force cannot exceed that amount of force so long as it is sufficient to protect the threatened person. For example, the Georgia statute states that "a person is justified in using force which is intended or likely to cause death or great bodily harm only if he or she reasonably believes that such force is necessary to prevent death or great bodily injury to himself or herself...." *Ga. Code Ann., § 16-3-21(a)*. Therefore, if it would be unreasonable in the context of the event for the actor to meet non-deadly force with deadly force that kills the aggressor, the person, whose quantity of force was unreasonable, may not use self-defense to avoid a homicide conviction. The actor, who killed while using unreasonable force, may still claim that the death was the product of heat of passion sufficient to mitigate a charge from murder to voluntary manslaughter (or attempted murder to attempted voluntary manslaughter) under the theory of imperfect self-defense, discussed below.

ii. Deadly and Non-Deadly Force

What constitutes deadly and non-deadly force may depend on both the type of weapon and its perceived use. Deadly weapons clearly include pistols, rifles, and shotguns as well as knives and swords. Fists, sticks, clubs, and even feet may also be deadly weapons in some situations.

The context of the use is also important. Thus, brandishing a heavy club combined with words indicating an intent to cause immediate harm makes the club a deadly weapon under the circumstances and may entitle the potential victim to use deadly force in self-defense. Similarly, factors such as the relative size, age, and health of the actors may be relevant in assessing whether the force was deadly force.

3. Imperfect Self-Defense

Imperfect self-defense is a doctrine used in many jurisdictions to reduce a charge from murder to voluntary manslaughter when the defendant meets some, but not all, the requirements for self-defense. There are two interrelated theoretical bases for this rule. First, in common law jurisdictions a murder requires the presence of malice aforethought, but manslaughter does not. Case law holds that a killing that occurs with some, but not all, the elements of self-defense may lack malice aforethought and therefore be manslaughter. For example, a person who is attacked but responds with unreasonable force may not qualify for self-defense but could be found guilty of voluntary manslaughter through imperfect self-defense. Moreover, imperfect self-defense is consistent with the elements of voluntary manslaughter. Recall that voluntary manslaughter often requires the killer to act in the heat of passion (or extreme emotional disturbance) caused by provocation. A physical attack is routinely considered sufficient provocation for this purpose. Thus, imperfect self-defense arises primarily in two situations: (1) the unreasonable belief of imminent threat, and; (2) unreasonable amount of force used.

a. Unreasonable Belief of Imminent Threat

Imperfect self-defense may be present when the accused has a subjective belief of being in imminent danger of death or serious bodily harm but the danger is not objectively reasonable. In this situation many courts recognize a claim of imperfect self-defense that may permit a conviction for voluntary manslaughter rather than murder. One court stated that imperfect self-defense is present when there was "an honest subjective belief on the part of the killer that his or her actions were necessary for his or her safety, even though an objective appraisal by reasonable people would have revealed not only that the actions were unnecessary, but also that the belief was unreasonable." *State v. Tierney*, 813 A.2d 560 (N.J. Supr. App. 2003).

For example, D sees an approaching youth who is reaching into a coat pocket. Believing the youth is taking out a weapon for a robbery, D takes out a pistol and fires, killing the youth. In fact, the youth was only reaching for a pack of cigarettes in the pocket, and had no intention of robbing D. Assuming D honestly believed the youth was going to use force, but the mistake was unreasonable, some states allow an instruction permitting the jury to find the defendant guilty of voluntary manslaughter rather than murder on a theory of imperfect self-defense. The unreasonable use of deadly force against the assailant does not justify the killing, but the crime and resultant punishment may be reduced. Imperfect self-defense generally is not a defense to an assault charge if the use of force did not cause a death. In the scenario above, if D only wounded the youth, then a charge of assault with intent to cause serious bodily injury or death would not be mitigated to a lesser offense.

b. Unreasonable Amount of Force Used

The second situation in which imperfect self-defense arises is when the defendant uses *excessive force* in responding to an imminent attack. This could occur when the assailant is the initial aggressor and uses obvious non-deadly force, and the defendant responds by escalating the confrontation through deadly force. Initially the defendant had a right of self-defense to use non-deadly force to resist the assailant's unlawful attack, but lost a self-defense claim by resorting to deadly force, which was excessive and unreasonable, even though the other person was the initial aggressor. Though unable to use self-defense, the defendant may be guilty only of voluntary manslaughter rather than some degree of murder.

4. Aggressor

A person who initiates a course of events that results in the use of force against another cannot claim self-defense if the initiator is determined to be the *aggressor*. The Missouri statute embraces this concept, permitting the use of force in self-defense "unless ... the actor was the initial aggressor." *Mo. Rev. Stat.* *§ 563.031(1)*. For example, assume that AG gets drunk and punches V in the face and then continues the attack. V responds by striking AG with a beer bottle. Since AG was the aggressor, AG may not use self-defense to justify a violent response (such as hitting V with a chair) to V's defensive use of the beer bottle. V, on the other hand, may rely on self-defense if charged with assault for using the beer bottle to repel AG, the initial aggressor. Obviously, other factors may enter into the viability of this defense, such as issues of proportionality.

a. Denying Self-Defense

There are several reasons for the principle that an aggressor may not use self-defense. First, the aggressor's force is virtually always *unlawful* which makes him or her ineligible for self-defense and the victim's response is lawful. Recall that self-defense is a reaction to the use of unlawful force *by the opponent*. A second rationale is that the use of self-defense by the person who initiated the violence is unreasonable under the circumstances. A reasonable person would not use force against someone who was simply offering reasonable force to resist the attack.

There is no single definition of who is the aggressor. It is generally viewed as the person who initiates a physical confrontation, as opposed to mere verbal sparring. Aggressive conduct includes brandishing a weapon, coupling verbal threats with some movement toward an assault, or using some measure of actual physical force against another person.

Sometimes the first person who uses or threatens to use immediate force is the aggressor. For example, assume that D makes a disparaging remark about V's clothes and V responds by threatening to beat up D and then advances in such a way as to make it clear that he or she intends to act on the threat. D can use reasonable force to repel V, and is not the considered to be aggressor for purposes of self-defense, even though D provoked the physical contact by making the remark.

The rule that one may not be an aggressor to use self-defense does not mean that the opportunity to use protective force is completely forfeited if one is the initial aggressor. The two situations when the initial aggressor may still rely on self-defense involve *withdrawal* and *escalation*.

b. Withdrawal

An aggressor who quits the affray and withdraws, and is then attacked by the initial victim, may have the right to claim self-defense. For example, the Missouri statute provides that the use of force is justifiable if "[h]e or she has withdrawn from the encounter and effectively communicated such withdrawal to such other person but the latter persists in continuing the incident by the use or threatened use of unlawful force." *Mo. Rev. Stat. § 563.031(1)(a)*. Thus, if D attacks V on day one and then goes home to sleep and calls V and apologizes, when V attacks D the next day, D may have a right to defend him or herself because although initially the aggressor, there was a withdrawal.

Arizona does not require the initial aggressor to actually retreat from the affray if it is not reasonably possible. The statute states that "[t]he person withdraws from the encounter or clearly communicates to the other his intent to

do so reasonably believing he cannot safely withdraw from the encounter...."
Ariz. Rev. Stat. § 13-404(B)(3)(a).

c. Escalation

An unreasonable response by the victim that escalates the situation may provide the initial aggressor with the right to claim self-defense. For example, assume that AG attacks R with fists. R responds by pulling out a knife and charging AG, making efforts to stab AG in the chest. In this case R's response, involving deadly force, may be deemed unreasonable and would therefore deprive R of the use of self-defense but would restore it to AG. Though AG was the initial aggressor, AG became the "victim" when R used excessive force to respond to AG's non-deadly attack.

5. Retreat

Since by definition self-defense is available when one person uses or threatens to use force against another person, the question arises whether the person asserting self-defense must use force only as a last resort. The issue is framed in terms of *retreat*. Does the person asserting self-defense have to retreat — leave the conflict when possible — rather than resorting to the use of force? The answer varies among the jurisdictions. Those that require retreat allow for situations when a person could not retreat safely or when the person is within his or her own home. It can also depend on whether deadly or non-deadly force is used in self-defense.

a. Safety

Whenever the law imposes a duty to retreat before using force in self-defense, it is clear that retreat is only necessary if it could be accomplished safely. Whether a safe retreat is possible is a product of the particular facts. For example, if AG Aggressor points a gun at D, D may respond with deadly force without retreating since one cannot retreat safely in the situation. On the other hand, if AG pulls a knife, D may be able to run away and avoid further confrontation. But if AG chases D and D runs into a dead end with no possible exit, D need not retreat any longer since no safe avenue is available. Similarly, if D has a physical disability that precludes flight, D need not retreat.

b. Castle Doctrine

States that do require retreat, may also provide an exception for when one is in his or her own home. Under the *castle doctrine*, a person is not required to retreat in his or her own home from a person using or threatening force. This approach is a reflection of the English common law view that "a person's home is his or her castle."

The castle doctrine is included in a number of self-defense statutes. For example, some statutes specify those persons in a home who have no duty to retreat, including the owner of the house and also a person who is a "guest or express or implied agent of the owner, lessor, or resident." *Alaska Stat. § 11-81-335(b)(1)(C).*

This issue becomes complicated when the attacker also lives in the same dwelling, such as when the aggressor is a spouse, roommate, child, or guest. Though most cases hold that there is no duty to retreat in this situation, a minority view is that the obligation to retreat is present if the attacker is a lawful dweller in the house.

The concept of castle, in which no retreat is required, is usually extended to the *curtilage* around a house, which is generally viewed as the area within close proximity to the home. Most cases also recognize that the "castle" includes the basement, attic, and an attached structure such as a porch, deck, or garage, and some decisions even extend the concept to outbuildings such as a barn. On the other hand, some cases are more restrictive, requiring retreat when a person is attacked in the driveway, lawn outside the home, or common area outside an apartment.

The castle may not be limited to the house and its surroundings. Some jurisdictions extend the concept of castle to a person's business or job. Others note that it does not apply to a vehicle, such as a car or truck.

c. Deadly Force

When deadly force is used in self-defense, jurisdictions differ as to whether the actor must retreat rather than take human life. The decision may also rest in part on whether the individual can retreat to complete safety or whether the individual is within his or her own home. Retreat is not required before the use of non-deadly force in self-defense.

A minority view maintains that life is more important than honor and requires a person to flee rather than use deadly force if flight could be accomplished safely. In many contexts this means that deadly force is only authorized as a *last resort*. The Connecticut statute provides that "a person is not justified in using deadly physical force upon another person if he or she knows that he or she can avoid the necessity of using such force with complete safety (1) by retreating." *Conn. Gen. Stat. § 53a-19(b).* Exceptions may exist here, such as when the person is in his or her dwelling.

For example, if a person being attacked could easily go into his or her house and avoid the need to use deadly force to respond to the attack, then the person must leave the scene and attempt to reach a place of safety before being able to respond with deadly force that will later require a claim of self-defense. As with the use of force in self-defense, the means of retreat must be *reasonably* available to the person, so that a reasonable mistake regarding the availability of an avenue of escape from the affray will not prevent the assertion of self-defense.

d. Stand Your Ground Laws

Some states have endorsed so-called *stand your ground* laws that make it clear there is no duty to retreat when a person is not engaged in any unlawful activity and confronted with force or a threat of force. For example, Florida law provides that "[a] person who uses or threatens to use deadly force in accordance with this subsection does not have a duty to retreat and has the right to stand his or her ground if the person using or threatening to use the deadly force is not engaged in a criminal activity and is in a place where he or she has a right to be." *Fla. Stat. §776.012(2)*. Although these statutes extend beyond the home, typically the use of force is limited to places the person is entitled to be.

Some argue that these statutes do not have any substantial effect on the operation of the law of self-defense as the majority of the states do not require retreat. For example, the Florida statute still limits the use of force to situations in which the person "reasonably believes" in the necessity of physical resistance, which is similar to the common law and modern statutory requirements for self-defense. Others respond that the emphasis on permitting a person to stand his or her ground goes beyond merely rejecting the retreat doctrine to emphasizing the ability to fight back.

6. Burden of Proof

States vary on the standard of proof and who bears that burden when self-defense is raised as an issue in the case. The standard rule is that the accused must produce evidence of self-defense (burden of production). The defense's burden of production might be met by cross-examining a witness as to whether the victim had threatened the defendant with a gun.

In states that have self-defense as an *affirmative defense*, it is common to require the defense to carry the burden of persuasion. Other states may require the defense to raise the issue, but then shift the burden to the prosecution to convince the trier of fact that the defendant did *not* act in self-defense. In these states, once the defense raises the issue by satisfying the burden of production, the prosecution would then need to show that the accused's conduct failed to meet the elements of self-defense.

States vary in the standard of proof used for self-defense. Some require proof by a preponderance of the evidence, while others use a higher standard, such as proof beyond a reasonable doubt. For example, in a burden shifting jurisdiction the prosecution may have to prove by a preponderance of the evidence that the accused did not act in self-defense.

7. Model Penal Code

a. Belief

Model Penal Code § 3.04(1) provides that "the use of force upon or toward another person is justifiable when the actor believes that such force is immediately necessary for the purpose of protecting himself against the use of unlawful force by such other person on the present occasion." The focus is on the person's subjective belief in the necessity of using force, including deadly force, although a reasonableness requirement will apply in certain circumstances. As the commentary points out, under MPC § 3.09 "if his belief is mistaken and is recklessly or negligently formed, he may then be prosecuted for an offense of recklessness or negligence...."

For example, if D honestly but mistakenly believes that A is about to pull out a knife to launch an attack, and so D shoots and kills A before the assault can begin, D may be able to assert a successful self-defense claim if charged with a crime that requires proof that D acted purposely or knowingly. Even if D's belief is unsupported by any objective facts or circumstances, the honest mistake would enable D to rely on self-defense. On the other hand, if D were charged with a lesser offense, such as manslaughter or negligent homicide, that included the *mens rea* elements of recklessness or criminal negligence, under the MPC the defendant could not rely on self-defense if the trier of fact finds that D's belief in the need for deadly force was based on a mistake that was recklessly or negligently formed. This is similar to the claim of "imperfect self-defense" to reduce a first or second degree murder charge to manslaughter because the belief in the necessity of using force was unreasonable.

b. Immediately Necessary

The use of force in self-defense under MPC § 3.04(1) is based on whether the actor believes that it is "immediately necessary" for protection against the application of unlawful force "on the present occasion." While this test may suggest that the threat must be of the imminent use of force, the commentary to the MPC indicates that a broader meaning is intended. The phrase "on the present occasion" means that the attack will be soon. The MPC's illustration is that self-defense is justified to prevent an attacker from leaving to find reinforcements and return to continue the attack with increased assistance "on the present occasion." *MPC § 3.04 comment.*

c. Unlawful Force

Under MPC § 3.04(1) self-defense is available to protect against what the defendant believes is the use of "unlawful force." Note that the use of force being resisted does not actually have to be unlawful; the MPC only requires that the actor *believes* it to be so.

MPC § 3.11(1) defines "unlawful force" as that which is "employed without the consent of the person against whom it is directed and the employment of which constitutes an offense or actionable tort or would constitute such offense or tort except for a defense (such as the absence of intent, negligence, or mental capacity; duress; youth; or diplomatic status) not amounting to a privilege to use the force." For example, if an insane person were to initiate an attack, force could be used in response even though the attacker would not be held criminally liable because of insanity.

An exception to the "unlawful force" rule is present when the use of force is by a peace officer effecting an arrest. MPC § 3.04(2)(a)(i) specifically denies the use of force to resist an arrest by a known police officer, even if it is unlawful. The person who believes that he or she is being unlawfully arrested should fight the arrest in the civil and criminal courts rather than on the street.

d. Deadly Force

The MPC substantially restricts the use of deadly force in self-defense. It prohibits the use of deadly force unless "the actor believes that such force is necessary to protect himself against death, serious bodily injury, kidnapping or sexual intercourse compelled by force or threat." *MPC § 3.04(2)(b).*

Similar to the common law, the MPC does not allow deadly force if the person "provoked the use of force against himself in the same encounter" with the purpose of using force to cause death or serious bodily harm. For example, if D begins to shove A and make insulting remarks, knowing A's short temper and proclivity for carrying a knife, D could not use deadly force if the confrontation were instigated to cause A to draw the knife.

The MPC limits the provocation analysis to the "same encounter." This may allow a person, who provoked an incident in order to be justified in killing the person who was provoked, to withdraw from the confrontation and thereby regain the right to use deadly force in self-defense. Like the common law, if D initiates a confrontation with A through the use of deadly force and then removes himself or herself from the situation, the MPC allows for a self-defense claim if A renews the attack after D's withdrawal.

The MPC incorporates a retreat rule before deadly force may be used. MPC § 3.04(2)(b)(ii) does not allow the use of deadly force if "the actor knows that he can avoid the necessity of using such force with complete safety by retreating or by surrendering possession of a thing to a person asserting a claim of right thereto or by complying with a demand that he abstain from any action that he has no duty to take...."

Similar to the common law, retreat is not required in the home. The MPC provision, however, makes it clear that if one is the initial aggressor in the home, then retreat is required before deadly force can be used, consistent with the "same encounter" limitation. The MPC also extends the retreat rule to the workplace, but requires retreat if the attack is by someone the defendant knows also works there.

C. Battered Spouse Syndrome

Although states do not recognize a battered spouse syndrome as a separate defense, a growing number of jurisdictions allow battered spouse syndrome evidence to support a claim of self-defense.

In some cases the use of force by a spouse in response to battering by his or her spouse may easily fit within the general requirements of self-defense. For example, if D spouse gets drunk and attacks V spouse with fists, V has a right to resist, consistent with the usual rules of self-defense.

A more difficult self-defense issue is presented when the victim uses force, including deadly force, when there is no present battering but the person actually believes that another attack is imminent. Often, the victim's fear of future harm is based on past attacks. For example, the spouse who argues that he or she was subjected to horrific battering for years, and finally responded by shooting the battering spouse while he or she was asleep, may be faced with the issue of not meeting the immediacy requirement for self-defense. *See State v. Norman*, 378 S.E.2d 8 (N.C. 1989).

Courts are divided on whether self-defense's immediacy requirement is met when a battered spouse does not act at the time of the abuse, but waits until a safer time to respond to the attack. Some courts allow testimony of battering to be admitted and provide an accompanying jury instruction to allow for consideration of this evidence as a component of the reasonableness analysis for self-defense. Other courts require a showing of necessity before allowing an instruction on self-defense. Thus, the accused, who kills a sleeping spouse in the middle of the night who had abused him or her hours before, may be able to present the evidence of abuse in some jurisdictions while being precluded from even receiving an instruction on self-defense in other states.

In response to the limitations imposed by the traditional self-defense analysis, a few states have adopted statutes to address the admissibility of battering evidence. For example the Missouri statute provides that "[e]vidence that the actor was suffering from the battered spouse syndrome shall be admissible upon the issue of whether the actor lawfully acted in self-defense or defense of another." *Mo. Rev. Stat. § 563.0331.* The Georgia statute provides that a defendant arguing a reasonable belief that the use of force, including deadly force, was "immediately necessary" can offer evidence "that the defendant had been the victim of acts of family violence or child abuse committed by the deceased." *Ga. Code Ann. § 16-3-21(d)(1).* Note that the Georgia statute is not limited to spousal abuse and also includes family violence, such as the abuse of a child that leads to killing the abusive parent.

The battering or family violence evidence provides the jury with information about the history of the accused having suffered prior abuse. It could include such evidence as testimony by witnesses to the victim's previous violent acts and medical reports resulting from trips to the emergency room after the accused was beaten by the victim. The defense evidence may also include an expert witness on the battered spouse syndrome. This expert testimony can be important to explain why the defendant remained in the battering relationship and why the person finally resorted to violence. The Georgia statute allows the admission of "[r]elevant expert testimony regarding the condition of the mind of the defendant at the time of the offense, including those relevant facts and circumstances relating to the family violence or child abuse that are the bases of the expert's opinion." *Ga. Code Ann. § 16-3-21(d)(2).*

While some states permit the jury to hear evidence of battering as a means to establish a claim of self-defense, courts have been unanimous in rejecting the use of such evidence when the victim of the abuse hires a third-party to kill the abuser. Courts find that the battering does not justify the conspiracy to kill and the planning involved for a murder.

D. Defense of Others

Just as American law permits a person to use force in self-defense, in some situations it allows a person to use force to protect someone else. For example, if D sees V being attacked by a robber, D may use force to protect V. If D, the rescuer, is charged with assault or even homicide for this use of force, he or she may assert the defense of others justification for the assaultive conduct. As with self-defense, there are different rules applicable as to whether this commendable use of force qualifies for a defense in a criminal case. If a rescuer uses unreasonable deadly force or unreasonably perceives the need to aid the victim and kills the alleged attacker, the rescuer may be entitled to a jury instruction on imperfect self-defense and qualify for voluntary manslaughter, as discussed more fully above in the context of self-defense.

As with self-defense, in virtually all jurisdictions a defense of others claim requires that there be a necessity and that the amount of force used be reasonable and proportional to the threat. For example, the Missouri statute provides that deadly force may be used only if "[h]e or she reasonably believes that such deadly force is necessary to protect himself or herself or her unborn child, *or another* against death, serious physical injury, or any forcible felony." *Mo. Rev. Stat. § 563.031.2(1)*.

Thus, the accused cannot wait until the next day to act against the person attacking the third party. Similarly, the force may not be applied after the initial attack for purposes of revenge or out of anger. The response must be immediate, and the amount of force allowed is that reasonably believed necessary to stop the person attacking the third party. The use of unreasonably excessive force defeats the ability to claim defense of another.

1. Common Law

a. Relationship Requirement

At early common law, defense of another required a personal relationship between the individual being defended and the accused. Thus, a parent could lawfully intercede when his or her child (or even fetus) was being threatened. Defending a stranger, however, was not justified. Some states still retain an aspect of this common law doctrine by requiring that there be a familial or legal relationship with the defended person. For example, in the State of Washington, a justifiable homicide for defending another is limited to "his or her husband, wife, parent, child, brother, or sister, or of any other person in his presence or company." *Wash. Code § 9A.16.050. See also S.D. Codified Laws § 20-9-8* ("[a]ny necessary force may be used to protect from wrongful injury of one's self, or a wife, husband, child, parent, or other relative, or member of one's family, or of a ward, servant, master, or guest."). Most statutes today have rejected this restriction and allow for a defense of others even when there is no relationship between the accused and the person being defended, who may be a total stranger.

In jurisdictions requiring some relationship between the person who was rescued and the person who performed the rescue, the latter was not necessarily denied a defense if he or she rescued a stranger. Though the defense of others rationale was not available because of the absence of the relationship, the rescuer could still use such defenses as crime prevention to justify the use of force to assist a stranger.

A related rule not only permits a defense of persons in a particular relationship, it may also *require efforts to defend another person*. American law has long created a number of situations where one person has a legal duty to provide reasonable protection to a person who is in a certain relationship with the rescuer. Obvious ones are the common law duty of a parent to protect a child. Countless other cases have discussed a myriad of situations, such as whether there is any duty for owners of premises to protect guests, renters, or intruders, or whether hospitals have a duty to protect their patients from violent acts.

b. Act-At-Peril Rule

The common law approach to defending others was based on the law of self-defense. This defense permitted a person to rescue another person from imminent physical harm by using the same amount of force that the person rescued could have used in self-defense. A problem with this approach is that the person acting to defend another *acted at peril* if he or she incorrectly assessed the situation and aided another person who could not use the same force for his or her own self-defense. The rule here became known as the *act-at-peril* or *alter ego* rule.

For example, D sees V on the ground with A standing over him or her pointing a gun. V cries out, "Please help me," at which point D comes to V's aid by approaching the two from behind and striking A on the back of the head. In fact, unbeknownst to D, A is an undercover police officer lawfully arresting V for selling drugs. Under this *act-at-peril* or *alter ego* rule, the person using the force stepped into the shoes of the person threatened. If V, the person rescued, could not use the force that D used, then D also could not justifiably use that force against A. Despite D's sincere desire (and even commendable efforts) to help a person who appeared to be in dire need of assistance, D would be liable for the assault or even murder if A were to die from the blow.

2. Reasonable Belief Rule

Since the *act-at-peril* or *alter ego* rule could deny a defense to individuals who risk personal safety to assist others facing imminent attack, legislatures and courts in most states have rejected this rule in order to encourage people to aid victims. The theory is that the law should protect a public-minded person who acts as a reasonable person in assessing a situation and decides to assist someone else at peril. These laws expand the ability of individuals to assert a defense of third parties by requiring only that the rescuer *reasonably believe* that the use of force is necessary, similar to the requirement for self-defense. For example, the Colorado statute provides that "a person is justified in using physical force upon another person in order to defend himself *or a third person* from what he reasonably believes to be the use or imminent use of unlawful physical force by that other person, and he may use a degree of force which he reasonably believes to be necessary for that purpose." *Colo. Rev. Stat. § 18-1-704(1).* The standard for the use of force is the same regardless of whether the threat is to oneself or another.

One impetus for the broadening of the defense of others were reports about the failure of bystanders to assist those in need. An often-cited illustration is the well-known case of Catherine "Kitty" Genovese when many bystanders watched passively as she was being openly murdered and screamed for assistance. The common law approach provided no incentive to assist and indeed deterred those who might want to render aid by opening these individuals to potential criminal liability.

3. Honest Belief Rule: Model Penal Code

Under the Model Penal Code, the requirements for using force, including deadly force, to protect another person are the same as those for self-defense. *See Commentary to § 3.05.* Thus, the use of force is based on the person's subjective belief in the necessity of such action, and will be a defense to any charge requiring proof that the defendant acted purposely or knowingly, while an unreasonable mistake could entail liability for a crime involving recklessness or negligence. The MPC's most significant change from the common law was dropping the requirement of any relationship between the person using force and the person being defended by allowing the use of force to defend "a third person."

Model Penal Code § 3.05 also rejects both the *act-at-peril* or *alter ego* rule and reasonable belief approaches in its adoption of an *honest belief* test. The rescuer may use force to protect a third party when the actor believes that such force is immediately necessary to protect the third party against the use of unlawful force. If the rescuer is wrong, even unreasonably so, he or she may still use a defense of others defense as long as the belief was honestly held.

Model Penal Code § 3.09 adds a wrinkle in cases where the rescuer is reckless or negligent in forming the belief that the use of force is necessary to aid a third person. Permitting the defendant to use defense of others if charged with intentional or knowing homicide, the MPC would still allow the defendant to be liable for a crime, such as negligent homicide, which has a mental culpability element of recklessness or criminal negligence. This could occur if D, while drunk, "rescues" V from the grasp of A by shooting and killing A but does not notice that A is a uniformed police officer who is yelling "You're under arrest!" while attempting to handcuff V. D could still be prosecuted for reckless or negligent homicide since D was reckless or negligent in forming the belief that such force was necessary in the situation.

The MPC also applies the retreat rules to the use of deadly force for protection of third parties, although retreat is not required unless the actor knows that he or she can retreat in complete safety while securing the complete safety of the person in peril. *MPC § 3.05(2)(a)*. Sometimes *both* the rescuer and person rescued must retreat if they could do so in complete safety and such retreat would be required under the law of self-defense.

E. Defense of Property and Habitation

Just as the criminal law allows force to be used to protect people from physical attack, it may also provide a defense for those who use force to protect property. The underlying theory is the basic principle that a person who owns or possesses property has an inherent right to protect it from deprivation by someone less entitled to it. While the law routinely allows a person to use force to protect property in some situations, it has long adopted the principle that life is more important than property and, accordingly, bans the use of deadly force merely to protect property. One consequence is that in some situations a person's property will be taken by a thief or other wrongdoer and the victim whose property was wrongly dispossessed simply is unable to recapture it. This expression of relative values represents the law's efforts to induce people to rely on judicial and other remedies rather than to take human life.

When the need to protect property is accompanied by a need also to protect oneself, then the rules of self-defense (as well as crime prevention, discussed below) are likely to also apply. For example, when a thief is about to steal an occupied automobile, the individual in the vehicle may reasonably perceive a threat of force to his or her person, in addition to fearing the theft of the property. Using force to resist the thief may be in self-defense, as well as in defense of property and crime prevention. But when a person is not in direct jeopardy, but still uses force against the person taking his or her property, the rules related to defense of property and crime prevention govern.

1. Elements

Under the common law, a defendant may claim defense of property if (1) reasonable non-deadly force is used to protect the property from trespass or theft, or to reclaim it immediately; (2) there is an immediate danger of the property being taken or destroyed; and, (3) there is a necessity to act to prevent the dispossession. Some jurisdictions do not allow a person to defend property with force if there was an opportunity to call the police. The defense applies to real or personal property, and anyone in lawful possession of property may use force to resist being dispossessed of it. Note that one need not be the owner of the property to use force, so the defense is available to one entrusted with possession. For example, if A gives B permission to borrow a car, B can use force to resist a thief seeking to steal it even though B is not the owner of the vehicle.

2. Limitations

The law places several limits on the use of force to protect property. These limits often relate to instances when the use of force is not authorized for the protection of property, to the amount of force that may be used, and to the use of deadly force.

a. Police Seizure of Property

Courts will not allow a defendant to argue defense of property when the accused uses force in response to a police seizure of property. Thus, even if the police are incorrect in impounding a vehicle, this does not give the owner of the automobile the right to forcibly resist the officer's efforts. The court system provides an avenue for judicial relief in these instances.

b. Time Frame for Use of Force

Similarly, in most states one may not use force to *regain* property at a later time after losing possession, even if one has a lawful claim of right to it. Once the thief succeeds in depriving another of possession of the property, force is no longer justified to effect a recapture of it. For example, D learns that V stole D's tools from a shed, and goes to V's house to reclaim them. If D sees V using the tools, D cannot attack V or use force to reclaim them. The law requires the use of the legal process, such as calling the police, to effect the return of property taken unlawfully. This limitation is similar to the immediacy requirement for self-defense and defense of others. It is designed to minimize the occasions when force is used to protect property.

The Texas statute is illustrative in that it provides that "[a] person unlawfully dispossessed of land or tangible, movable property by another is justified in using force against the other when and to the degree the actor reasonably believes the force is immediately necessary to reenter the land or recover the property if the actor uses the force immediately or in fresh pursuit after the dispossession." It is also required that "(1) the actor reasonably believes the other had no claim of right when he dispossessed the actor; or (2) the other accomplished the dispossession by using force, threat, or fraud against the actor." *Tex. Crim. Code Ann. § 9.41(b)*.

Note that this typical statute limits the time when force can be used to the period near the point of the dispossession. Additionally, the person using force to retake property must reasonably believe the other person has no claim of right to the property.

c. Reasonable Non-Deadly Force

Another limit on the use of force to protect property is the rule that the amount of force used must be reasonably proportional to the threat. A person could not severely beat someone trying to steal a bicycle if simply blocking access to it or pushing away an arm would suffice. This use of force would be excessive and unreasonable under the circumstances.

d. Deadly Force
i. Deadly Force Generally Barred

In recognition that life is more important than property, the common law and most states preclude the use of deadly force to protect property so long as there is no threat of death or serious bodily harm to anyone present. For example, the Colorado statute provides, "[a] person is justified in using reasonable and appropriate physical force upon another person when and to the extent that he reasonably believes it necessary to prevent what he reasonably believes to be an attempt by the other person to commit theft, criminal mischief, or criminal tampering involving property, but he may use deadly physical force under these circumstances only in defense of himself or another...." *Colo. Rev. Stat. § 18-1-706*.

Even if a threat of force is used to dispossess the theft victim of property, he or she may not use deadly force to resist the taking in some jurisdictions if the person making the threat asserts a claim of right to the property and the theft victim can dissipate the threat by giving up the property. This is similar to the retreat rule for self-defense. If one can defuse the threat by complying with the request by someone who claims to be entitled to the property, then deadly force may not be used. For example, the New Hampshire statute provides that if a person can, with complete safety, "[s]urrender property to a person asserting a claim of right thereto," then the use of deadly force to resist would not be justified. *N.H. Rev. Stat. Ann. § 627:4(III)*.

It is unclear whether a person can *threaten* deadly force against another to prevent being dispossessed of property even though the threat is not followed by the application of such force. For example, homeowner D sees a thief taking a snowblower from the garage. D shouts out, "I've got a gun and I'll kill you if you don't stop." The threat constitutes an assault if it places the thief in reasonable fear of an imminent battery, which is the purpose of the statement. While D could argue there was no intent to follow through on the threat, the prohibition against using deadly force would likely prevent D from offering a defense to an assault charge because there is no right to use the force threatened.

ii. Expanded Use of Deadly Force

A number of states have expanded the right to use deadly force through the enactment of laws that authorize the use of such force to thwart a range of crimes that may occur anywhere. These statutes authorize the use of force for *crime prevention* (a separate defense discussed below) rather than protection of property, but some of the crimes may directly or indirectly permit force to be used to prevent the wrongful taking or destruction of property. For example, the Arizona statute provides that "[a] person is justified in threatening or using both physical force and deadly physical force against another if and to the extent the person reasonably believes that physical force or deadly physical force is immediately necessary to prevent the other's commission of arson of an occupied structure..., burglary in the second or first degree..., kidnapping..., manslaughter..., second or first degree murder..., sexual conduct with a minor..., sexual assault..., child molestation..., armed robbery..., or aggravated assault ..." *Ariz. Rev. Stat. § 13-411[A]*. While the context in which a number of the identified offenses occur would also trigger the separate defenses of self-defense or defense of others, some of the listed crimes may not necessarily involve any threat of death or serious bodily harm, such as arson of an occupied structure or burglary.

This broad crime prevention defense to wrongdoing involving harm to property applies anywhere. The statute states that it "is not limited to the use or threatened use of physical or deadly physical force in a person's home, residence, place of business, land the person owns or leases, conveyance of any kind, or any other place in this state where a person has a right to be." *Ariz. Rev. Stat. § 13-411[D]*.

3. Defense of Habitation

a. Special Protection of Habitation

American and English law has traditionally recognized that a person's home is his or her "castle," a personal sanctuary that receives extensive protection in many parts of the law, especially criminal law. For example, the Fourth Amendment prohibits unreasonable searches in the home, and absent exigent circumstances a warrant is required to arrest a person who is in a home, even if the person is in the home of another at the time of the arrest.

b. Common Law

In recognition of the special role that a home, as distinguished from other property, is accorded in criminal law, the common law provided an especially broad defense for situations involving invasion of a home. The law allowed the use of deadly force if the occupant reasonably believed such force was necessary to prevent or repel an unlawful entry. For example, if reasonable under the circumstances, O, the owner and occupier of a house, can use force, including deadly force, to prevent D from coming through a sliding door in the back of the house, even if D was drunk at the time and mistook the house for that of a friend and had no intention of committing a crime upon entry.

The defense of habitation does not require that the person own the property, so that a renter or even an invited guest at the dwelling could use force to resist an invasion. Some states extend the concept far beyond a habitation, allowing the use of force to resist an entry into an occupied vehicle in addition to a person's residence. For example, the Florida statute provides a presumption that the use of deadly force is reasonable if another person tries to forcibly enter "a dwelling, residence, or occupied vehicle, or if that person had removed or was attempting to remove another against that person's will from the dwelling, residence, or occupied vehicle...." *Fla. Stat. Ann. 776.013(1)(a)*. Similarly, some statutes expand the defense to cover occupied buildings and related property, not just residences, so that one could rely on the defense to repel an invasion of a garage, storage shed, or business property.

Even if the householder has a reasonable belief that the home invader will commit only a property offense, such as theft or burglary, the common law defense of habitation in certain circumstances authorizes the use of deadly force when it might not be available under self-defense or defense of others. Defense of habitation is broader than the defense of property by allowing the accused greater leeway to use force, and a greater degree of force, when defending the home than in defending other types of property from criminal conduct.

c. Reasonable Belief of Harmful Conduct After Entry

Some jurisdictions limit the use of deadly force in defense of habitation to situations in which there is a reasonable threat in addition to the unauthorized entry. These states require that the occupant reasonably believe the invader intends to commit a felony or injure the occupant upon entry into the home. This limitation requires some basis for the use of force, including deadly force, beyond just the fact of any uninvited entry.

Some jurisdictions recognize a presumption that the person using force acted reasonably. The Utah statute contains a *presumption* that the occupant "acted reasonably and had a reasonable fear of imminent peril of death or serious bodily injury if the entry or attempted entry is unlawful and is made or attempted by use of force, or in a violent and tumultuous manner, or surreptitiously or by stealth, or for the purpose of committing a felony." *Utah Code Ann. § 76-2-405(2).* The focus here is on the method of entry as establishing what would be a reasonable perception of a threat to the occupant(s) authorizing the use of deadly force.

As with the defense of others, the use of force to defend one's habitation overlaps significantly with self-defense. For example, the law of self-defense may permit a person to use deadly force to resist an attempted rape or robbery, depending on the circumstances. The fact that the attack occurs in the home does not change the self-defense analysis to any significant degree.

On the other hand, the location of the attack or threat may lend greater credence to the claim that the occupant reasonably believed that the home intruder would commit a violent act if permitted to enter the dwelling. Thus, if a drunken neighbor tries to force open the front door of the house across the street late at night, thinking it was his or her own home, the occupant's perception that the invader posed a threat of serious harm may be reasonable when the occupant does not recognize the intruder. On the other hand, if the occupant recognized the invader as a harmless inebriated neighbor, then the narrower view of defense of habitation, requiring a reasonable belief in post-entry harm, would restrict the use of force in defense of the home. This result is similar to self-defense and defense of others that also impose a reasonableness limit on the use of force.

d. Demand

As a condition for using deadly force in defense of habitation, some states require that the occupant first seek a non-violent resolution by requesting the invader desist from the entry or commission of a crime while on the premises. This view reflects the policy behind the defense of property justification of avoiding the risk of death or serious physical harm whenever possible. The Maine statute provides that deadly force may be used "only if the person first demands the person against whom such deadly force is to be used to terminate the criminal trespass and the trespasser fails to immediately comply with the demand, unless the person reasonably believes that it would be dangerous to the person or a 3rd person to make the demand." *Me. Rev. Stat. Ann. § 104(4)*. Model Penal Code § 3.06(3) expands the rule to require a request to desist before using *any force* to protect property, unless the request would be useless, dangerous, or result in substantial harm to the property being protected.

4. Spring Guns and Other Devices

Courts have struggled with the propriety of using mechanical devices or traps as a means of defending property. These cases arise when an intruder is injured or killed by a weapon like a spring gun, which is triggered automatically, regardless of the occupant's presence, whenever a particular door is opened. Some property owners install these devices or rig traps to protect their property when the property is vacant or the owner is sleeping inside. If a burglar is injured by a spring gun, may the homeowner escape a criminal conviction by asserting that the force was permissible as a defense of habitation or property?

Most jurisdictions disapprove of spring guns and other mechanical devices that can kill or maim a person entering property because they do not discriminate between a lawful entrant, such as a police officer or fire fighter, and one who is trespassing on property. A claim of defense of habitation is often disallowed when someone is killed or injured by such devices, even when there is a posted warning about the item.

There is a split of authority whether a person setting the spring gun would have had a valid defense of habitation claim *if present* at the moment the device was triggered. In *People v. Ceballos*, 526 P.2d 241 (Cal. 1974), a leading case rejecting the use of spring guns when no one was present, two teenagers entered the defendant's garage intending to steal when a spring gun set by the defendant fired, hitting one teen in the face. In response to a charge of assault with a deadly weapon, the California Supreme Court held in dictum that the defendant, *had he been present* when the break-in occurred, could possibly have used a defense of habitation—assuming the garage met the requirements of a dwelling—because it was a forcible entry and the teens intended to commit a felony therein. California law would have required a finding that the felony threatened, or was reasonably believed to threaten, death or serious bodily harm.

In a similar case, the Georgia Supreme Court rejected a defendant's claim under the defense of habitation statute that authorizes the use of deadly force if the occupant reasonably believes deadly force is needed because the intruder intends to commit a felony. Defendant's absence from the dwelling when the spring gun fired meant that he could not form the requisite "reasonable belief" needed to use deadly force. *Bishop v. State,* 356 S.E.2d 503 (Ga. 1987). Had the defendant been present and able to control the firing of the spring gun, in some circumstances the *Bishop* court would have permitted the use of a habitation defense.

Model Penal Code § 3.06(5) reflects the general view that these devices should not be encouraged and allows a defense of property for the use of these devices only under three restrictive conditions: when the device is not designed to cause death or serious bodily injury, the use of the device is reasonable, and the device is typically used or the owner of the property makes reasonable efforts to let intruders know of its use.

5. Model Penal Code

a. Non-Deadly Force

The MPC reflects the common law that allows the use of *non-deadly* force in defense of property. Section 3.06(1) provides greater detail than the common law on when the right to use non-deadly force is triggered. First, it may be used "to prevent or terminate an unlawful entry or other trespass upon land or a trespass against or the unlawful carrying away of tangible, movable property" so long as the person believes he or she has possession of the property. Second, force may be used to reclaim property reasonably believed to have been unlawfully taken, so long as "the force is used immediately or on fresh pursuit after such dispossession."

b. Request to Desist

The MPC does impose some limits on the use of force even if the circumstances might otherwise allow for its use. Section 3.06(3)(a) requires that any use of force be preceded by a request to desist to the person seeking to take possession of the property, unless the request would be useless, dangerous, or cause substantial harm to the property being protected. In addition, in the case of a trespass, a person cannot use force if the "actor knows that the exclusion of the trespasser will expose [the trespasser] to substantial danger of serious bodily injury." For example, if D sees A removing hay from a barn on his or her property, D must first ask A to stop and leave the property. If D observes that

A is armed, or that there are a number of individuals involved in the theft, then the request need not be made because the request would be futile or doing so would entail a risk of serious bodily harm.

c. Deadly Force

i. Habitation

The MPC does not permit the use of deadly force in defense of property except in two circumstances. First, deadly force can be used if "the person against whom the force is used is attempting to dispossess him of his dwelling otherwise than under a claim of right to its possession." *MPC § 3.06(3)(d)(i)*. This is similar to the common law defense of habitation, although it is narrower than the more expansive common law view that would allow the use of deadly force to prevent an entry if the person sought to commit a crime after entering the home. For example, D could not use deadly force under this provision against A, who is caught attempting to remove stereo speakers from D's house through a front window. The MPC limits the use of deadly force to responding to an attempt to *dispossess* the occupant of the dwelling, which would not be supported by A's conduct involving only a theft of property.

ii. Serious Felony

The second basis for using deadly force in defense of property is MPC § 3.06(3)(d)(ii), which allows its use against a person who is "attempting to commit or consummate arson, burglary, robbery or other felonious theft or property destruction" and has employed or threatened the use of deadly force, or the use of non-deadly force (rather than deadly force) would expose the actor or someone in the actor's presence to death or serious bodily harm. Unlike the common law, the MPC allows the use of deadly force to protect property in any locale and not just the home if the offense is one of the above listed crimes.

d. Spring Guns and Similar Devices

The use of spring guns and other protective devices is only permissible under the MPC if "the device is not designed to cause or known to create a substantial risk of causing death or serious bodily injury." *MPC § 3.06(5)(a)*. Moreover, the device must be reasonable under the circumstances and be one typically used to prevent trespassers from entering. The limitations imposed by the MPC on the use of mechanical measures to protect property effectively prohibit the use of spring guns and other incendiary devices because of the risk of substantial harm they pose.

F. Crime Prevention and Arrest

The common law and modern statutes allow the use of force by the police and private citizens to prevent the commission of a crime and to arrest the person who commits the offense. The issue in this situation is the degree of force that can be used. Courts find that non-deadly force is available in virtually all situations, while deadly force can only be used in limited circumstances. As with the other defenses discussed in this chapter, the virtually unanimous view is that the need to use force and the amount of force used must be reasonable in the circumstances.

1. Crime Prevention

a. Non-Deadly Force to Prevent Crime

The common law rule is that a person can use *non-deadly force* to prevent a felony or misdemeanor so long as the force is reasonably necessary to prevent the crime. The felony is not limited to dangerous or other particular felonies.

b. Deadly Force

Jurisdictions differ in their approach to the use of *deadly force* to prevent crime. The distinctions often reflect the type of felony involved.

i. Any Felony

A minority view is that deadly force may be used to prevent the commission of *any felony*. One problem with this approach is that it allows deadly force for felonies that are not typically protected in self-defense law. For example, typically deadly force cannot be used to protect property, so allowing it to be used when there is a felony theft of property may result in a contradiction of traditional limitations. Assume that O sees D leaving O's home with a valuable vase and, to keep D from completing the larceny, shoots and kills D. O could not claim defense of property for a murder (or manslaughter) charge because there is no right to use deadly force to defend property. If the defense of crime prevention allows the use of deadly force for any felony, however, then there would be a legitimate defense if larceny is considered a felony in this jurisdiction.

ii. Forcible Felonies

The majority rule today authorizes deadly force to prevent some *serious felonies*, often characterized as forcible felonies or what some jurisdictions call an "atrocious" felony. For example, the Montana statute provides that a person "is justified in the use of force likely to cause death or serious bodily harm only if the person reasonably believes that such force is necessary to prevent the commission of a forcible felony." *Mont. Stat. Ann. 45-3-104.* The Florida statute is more specific and defines a forcible felony as "treason; murder; manslaughter; sexual battery; carjacking; home-invasion robbery; robbery; burglary; arson; kidnapping; aggravated assault; aggravated battery; aggravated stalking; aircraft piracy; unlawful throwing, placing, or discharging of a destructive device or bomb; and any other felony which involves the use or threat of physical force or violence against any individual." *Fla. Stat. Ann. § 776.08.*

Applying the forcible felony limitation means the homeowner O still may be able to use deadly force against the thief D caught removing the valuable vase if D's crime was a burglary — breaking and entering of a dwelling with the intent to commit a felony therein — even under the more restrictive approach to crime prevention. Burglary is routinely considered a forcible felony. On the other hand, a gas station owner could not use deadly force against a person who attempts to leave the station without paying for gas pumped into a car because theft of the gasoline would only be a larceny and not considered a forcible felony.

As with other defenses, the amount of force used to prevent the crime must be reasonable under the circumstances. Even if the crime to be prevented is a forcible felony, the actor may not use deadly force if a reasonable person would believe that nondeadly force would accomplish the same purpose.

c. Model Penal Code

Under the MPC non-deadly force may be used "to prevent such other person from committing suicide, inflicting serious bodily injury upon himself, committing or consummating the commission of a crime involving or threatening bodily injury, damage to or loss of property or a breach of the peace...." *MPC § 3.07(5)(a).* The limitations imposed by other Code provisions on the use of force in other contexts, such as self-defense or defense of property, apply equally to preventing a crime.

Deadly force is permissible for crime prevention under MPC § 3.07(5)(a)(ii) only if the actor believes (not reasonably believes) that commission of the crime poses a substantial risk of death or serious bodily harm to any person and the application of such force does not pose a threat to bystanders. Unlike the older common law rule of crime prevention that allowed the use of deadly force to prevent any homicide, the Code limits it to offenses that pose a significant threat to others, *i.e.,* forcible felonies.

2. Arrest

American law has traditionally authorized both law enforcement officers and private citizens to arrest people for breaking the criminal law. Concomitant with the authority to arrest is the authority to use reasonable force to effectuate that arrest. Though the law treats law enforcement officers and private citizens similarly in many respects, there are significant differences.

a. Police

i. Authority to Arrest

Of course the police have the authority to arrest people for violation of the criminal law. An arrest warrant provides specific authorization for the arrest. Even without a warrant, the police may arrest a suspected lawbreaker in some circumstances. For suspected *felonies*, the general rule is that the police may arrest whenever they have probable cause to believe the defendant committed the felony. The usual rules for *misdemeanors* are more restrictive. Traditionally police could arrest for a misdemeanor only if the misdemeanor was committed in the officer's presence.

The rule limiting the authority to arrest for a misdemeanor has caused problems in two areas: drunk driving and domestic violence. In both situations the police may have probable cause to believe the suspect committed the act. Typically, he or she might have driven while intoxicated, or committed a misdemeanor assault on a family member, but the officer cannot arrest the perpetrator because the officer did not personally see the crime. Many states statutes have reacted to this dilemma by enacting statutes authorizing the police to arrest in either case whenever they have probable cause, despite the fact that the offense is a misdemeanor.

ii. Use of Force to Effectuate Arrest

The criminal law allows law enforcement officers to use reasonable force to arrest someone engaged in criminal activity. Non-deadly force is routinely allowed for both felonies and misdemeanors. While the common law also authorized law enforcement officers to use deadly force to prevent any *felon* from absconding, today there are severe restrictions on the use of deadly force by law enforcement. In general terms, deadly force is permissible to make an arrest only if necessary in self-defense or to prevent the commission of a forcible or atrocious felony by the arrestee.

Much of the change in the approach to the use of deadly force to prevent crime or effect an arrest is traceable to the Supreme Court's decision in *Ten-*

nessee v. Garner, 471 U.S. 1 (1985). The Court held that the killing of an unarmed burglary suspect who was fleeing was improper even though the state rule in effect authorized the use of "all the necessary means to effect the arrest" of a suspect who was fleeing or forcibly resisting. The *Garner* Court found that the use of deadly force was a "seizure" governed by the Fourth Amendment's rule that such seizures must be "reasonable." While the use of deadly force is unreasonable under the Fourth Amendment to stop a non-dangerous misdemeanant or felon, it is permissible if the officer has probable cause to believe that the suspect poses a threat of serious physical harm to the officer or to others. Thus, the Court has recognized that law enforcement can use deadly force to shoot a fleeing suspect who may pose a risk to persons in the area. *Brousseau v. Haugen*, 543 U.S. 194 (2004). Two key factors in assessing whether the suspect is dangerous are the crime for which the suspect is being arrested and the conduct of the arrestee before and during the attempted arrest.

Tennessee v. Garner was a civil damages action, not a criminal prosecution, leaving states free to recognize a defense to a criminal charge when deadly force is used. State statutes generally implement *Tennessee v. Garner*. For example, the Illinois statute outlines the requirements for an officer to use deadly force in effecting an arrest. It provides that a law enforcement officer "is justified in using force likely to cause death or great bodily harm only when he reasonably believes that the force is necessary to prevent death or great bodily harm to himself or such other person, or when he reasonably believes both that: (1) such force is necessary to prevent the arrest from being defeated by resistance or escape; and (2) the person to be arrested has committed or attempted a forcible felony which involves the infliction or threatened infliction of great bodily harm or is attempting to escape by use of a deadly weapon, or otherwise indicates that he will endanger human life or inflict great bodily harm unless arrested without delay." *720 Ill. Comp. Stat. § 5/7-5.*

For example, officers approach to arrest D for a recent jewelry story shoplifting. Seeing the officers approach, D tries to escape by forcing open the door of a car waiting at a stoplight. The officers could use force, including deadly force, to prevent the commission of the carjacking, which is a forcible felony, because of the threat posed to others. On the other hand, under the defense allowing the use of force to effectuate an arrest, if the officers see D getting into an unoccupied vehicle in order to flee, they would not be authorized to shoot and kill D in order to prevent the escape from capture.

The Model Penal Code, though predating *Tennessee v. Garner*, generally follows its prescriptions. Section 3.07(2)(b) allows the use of force in arresting someone when "the actor believes that such force is immediately necessary to effect a lawful arrest." Notice needs to be given to the person being arrested, and if the arrest is pursuant to a warrant, then it needs to be a valid warrant or one that the individual believed was valid.

Deadly force may only be used if the following requirements are met: (1) the crime is a felony; (2) the person using force is authorized "to act as a peace officer or is assisting a person" believed to be a peace officer; (3) there is "no substantial risk of injury to innocent persons"; and, (4) the crime of the person being arrested involved "the use or threatened use of deadly force" or "there is a substantial risk" of serious injury if there is a delay in apprehending the individual. This approach is consistent with the Supreme Court's analysis of deadly force in *Tennessee v. Garner*. Under the MPC, deadly force may not be used by a private citizen in effecting an arrest except where the person is assisting a police officer.

iii. Availability of Self-defense

Although there are limitations on the amount of force that may be used to effectuate an arrest, actually the issue is more complex. An officer making an arrest may use reasonable force to do so and need not retreat. He or she is entitled to "stand ground" and even to "press on." If the arrestee resists by the use of force, the officer may use reasonable force under the circumstances, which have now changed by the arrestee's resistance to the arrest. Under some circumstances, noted in *Garner*, the officer may use even deadly force to make the arrest.

Moreover, the officer always has the right of self-defense in addition to the right to use force to effectuate an arrest. If the officer is in personal danger in the encounter, he or she may invoke the usual self-defense rules, including the use of deadly force when honestly and reasonably deemed necessary to protect the officer. For example, if an officer tries to arrest a suspect for a drug charge, the officer may use reasonable non-deadly force in doing so. Since the crime is not a forcible felony or the suspect at this time does not appear to pose a threat of harm, the officer may not use deadly force. If the suspect escalates the situation by pulling a knife on the officer, the officer may use even deadly force in self-defense since he or she is presented with the risk of immediate death or serious injury.

b. Private Citizens

i. Authority to Arrest

Private citizens were and are authorized to make a *citizen's arrest* in some circumstances. Like law enforcement officers, private citizens may arrest for any felony or misdemeanor committed in their presence. They may also arrest for a felony outside of their presence if, in fact, the felony was actually committed by the arrestee. Even if the private citizen makes an arrest with probable cause, the arrest is invalid unless the person arrested had actually committed the crime. In other words, the private citizen must be right. By way of contrast, the police officer need only have probable cause to make a lawful arrest for a felony. The arrest is lawful even if the officer, in fact, was wrong and the person arrested had committed no felony.

ii. Use of Force

A private citizen may use force to effectuate an arrest in some circumstances. When "deputized" by a law enforcement officer, in general the citizen may rely on the same authority as the officer in the use of force.

Absent serving as an agent of law enforcement, the private citizen may use reasonable non-deadly or even deadly force to make a citizen's arrest. *Tennessee v. Garner* does not apply to private citizens since their conduct is not a "seizure" governed by the Fourth Amendment. Accordingly, in a minority of jurisdictions a private citizen may use reasonable non-deadly or even deadly force to prevent the escape of a fleeing felon. *People v. Hampton*, 487 N.W.2d 843 (Mich. App. 1992).

Out of concern that untrained citizens may be prone to use inappropriate force that unnecessarily endangers both suspects and bystanders, today most jurisdictions have established a number of limits on a private citizen's use of deadly force to effectuate a citizen's arrest. The usual approach is to limit the use of deadly force to the arrest of people suspected of committing serious or even violent felonies or of posing a serious risk. *See, e.g., State v. Weddell*, 43 P.3d 987 (Nev. 2002)(private citizen may use deadly force in making an arrest only if the suspect poses a threat of serious bodily injury to the private citizen arrestor or to others).

The Missouri statute, for example, allows the use of such force only if the suspect committed a serious felony or murder in the person's presence or is "attempting to escape by use of a deadly weapon." *Mo. Stat. Ann. § 563.051(3).* Note that in these circumstances the citizen likely would have a valid self-defense or defense of others claim, so the defense allowing force to effectuate an arrest would be in addition to the other defenses.

Model Penal Code § 3.07(2)(b) goes even further and bans the use of deadly force by private citizens other than those assisting law enforcement officers.

Checkpoints

- Self-defense requires a necessity of an immediate threat.

- For self-defense, the response to the aggressor must be proportional.

- In assessing a self-defense claim, courts use a subjective, objective and a mixed test in examining the defendant's belief that he or she was in danger.

- States may place restrictive rules on when deadly force can be used in self-defense.

- Before using deadly force in self-defense, some states require the accused to retreat if he or she can retreat safely.

- There may be no duty to retreat before using deadly force if one is in one's home or business.

- Some states permit battered spouse testimony to support a claim of self-defense.

- The defense has the burden of production on self-defense and usually also has the burden of persuasion that he or she acted in self-defense. Jurisdictions differ on what standard of proof applies.

- At common law, defending others required that there be a relationship between the person defended and the accused, and a defendant acted-at-peril in defending a person being attacked, with mistaken beliefs not being excused.

- The more modern view for defense of others is that it is excused when the actor reasonably believes it is necessary to defend a person.

- The Model Penal Code only requires that the belief in the need to defend someone be honest, not necessarily reasonable.

- Defense of property may be allowed if necessary and if the force used is proportional.

- Usually deadly force will not be permitted to defend property.

- In some circumstances, deadly force may be used in defense of habitation.

- Law enforcement, and citizens assisting law enforcement, may be allowed to use force in making an arrest but there are limits to when deadly force can be used.

- Law enforcement and private citizens may use non-deadly and sometimes deadly force to prevent the commission of a crime. Often deadly force is only permissible to stop a dangerous felony.

Chapter 19

Necessity and Duress

Roadmap

- The rationale for necessity and duress defenses
- The elements of necessity and duress defenses
- Factors distinguishing these defenses
- When civil disobedience can be a defense

A. Generally

The criminal law recognizes two defenses—necessity and duress—that can offer relief to an actor who is charged with a criminal act that society deems should not be punished. *Necessity* is a defense that justifies conduct of the accused when he or she committed a criminal act to avoid a greater harm. In its most traditional form, it involved a nonhuman force, such as an act of nature that compelled the accused to commit the criminal act to avoid the greater harm. The law recognizes a defense for the conduct because the accused made a rational choice in selecting the *lesser of two evils*. Closely related is the defense of *duress*, which excuses a different type of conduct, oftentimes conduct induced by human coercion. Many states, as well as the Model Penal Code, have adopted statutes that provide the boundaries of these two defenses. Other states use the common law.

Initially the distinction between necessity and duress rested upon the source of the threat that caused the defendant to act. Natural forces were considered to be a basis for a necessity defense, while human threats excused conduct under the duress defense. Thus, stealing a car to escape a hurricane would be considered a *necessity*, while transporting narcotics to avoid having a drug lord kill a family member would be considered *duress*.

Modern statutes and case law often blur this distinction, and in some cases defendants argue both of these defenses for the same conduct, with courts

367

varying on which defense is appropriate. For example, a defendant may argue both necessity and duress when facing an escape from prison charge premised on intolerable conditions within the prison facility. Some courts will allow necessity as a defense, while others only permit duress for prison escape cases. In some jurisdictions, courts find that prison escapes for intolerable conditions do not warrant either defense. Although courts may differ as to the applicability of these defenses to a prison escape charge, and may perhaps only allow it when the conditions rise to the level of the prisoner being physically assaulted within the facility, a failure to surrender to prison or law enforcement officials at the earliest possible opportunity will negate the use of either of these defenses in such cases.

B. Necessity

1. Common Law

A defendant using a common law necessity defense, sometimes called a "choice of evils" defense, needs to demonstrate that: (1) the action was necessary as an emergency measure to avoid imminent injury; (2) the action taken was proportional to the injury being avoided; (3) there was no reasonable alternative to avoid the harm; and (4) there was a causal link between the defendant's criminal conduct and the harm he or she was seeking to abate. The defense does not apply if the accused caused the threatened harm or if the legislature explicitly precluded the defense by statute. For example, a Texas statute that allows for a necessity defense states that the "conduct is justified if … the legislative purpose to exclude the justification claimed for the conduct does not otherwise plainly appear." *Tex. Penal Code § 9.22.* States may designate necessity as an affirmative defense, thus requiring the accused to bear the burden of proving the elements of this defense.

In deciding if conduct is necessary as an emergency measure to avoid imminent injury, courts have held that a real emergency must exist for the harm to be considered imminent. Thus, a subjective belief that there is a threat of imminent harm is insufficient for this defense because courts will require proof of objective facts demonstrating that the harm was actually immediately threatened. For example, a defendant who steals an automobile to take someone to the hospital believing the person might need medical attention may be precluded from offering a necessity defense to a theft charge because the harm might not be certain, and because there is a reasonable alternative available, such as calling an ambulance.

2. Economic Harm

Some courts will not allow a necessity defense when it is premised on economic necessity. Thus, a parent who steals food to feed his or her child may be unsuccessful in using a necessity defense because courts may find that reasonable alternatives exist making it unnecessary under the circumstances for the defendant to choose to commit the crime. Other courts, however, permit economic harm to be the basis of a necessity defense.

3. Balancing Harm

Courts often balance both the harm caused by the crime and the harm avoided by commission of the crime. Thus, a court would weigh the harms from the two courses of conduct and only permit necessity as a defense when the harm from failure to act would exceed the harm as a result of the commission of the crime. Courts differ on whether necessity can be a defense to a murder charge.

4. Model Penal Code

Model Penal Code § 3.02 permits a more streamlined approach that omits the immediacy requirement. One can use this defense if, at the time the accused commits the criminal conduct, he or she believes — not reasonably believes — that the conduct will avoid the harm. The harm can be directed to the accused or to a third person. The harm avoided must be greater than that sought to be prevented by the criminal law violated. For example, if a mountain hiker is stranded by a sudden snowstorm and must break into a vacant cabin to survive the storm, the MPC would allow the defense of necessity if the hiker were charged with trespass for entering the cabin without permission. Clearly the harm avoided (death by exposure to the snowstorm) would exceed the harm addressed by the law creating the crime of trespass. Additionally, in contrast to the common law approach, the Model Penal Code does not preclude its use in homicide cases.

5. Civil Disobedience

In some cases, a defendant deliberately violates the law as an act of civil disobedience. A violation of a law that is the object of the protest is *direct* civil disobedience, while violating a law that is not the object of the protest is *indirect* civil disobedience. For example, it is indirect civil disobedience when a defendant illegally trespasses on government property to protest the government's violation of human rights law. This is because the accused is not protesting the trespass statute that is being violated, but rather protesting a failure to comply with human rights law. If the entry onto the land was committed to protest the trespass statute, then direct civil disobedience would apply.

Since people involved in direct civil disobedience want the statute violated to be invalidated, they ordinarily do not use necessity as a defense to prosecution. Although those accused with crimes may raise indirect civil disobedience as a valid necessity defense, courts seldom find it as a valid necessity defense. Some hold that the accused should not be allowed a necessity defense because there is no causal connection between the act of civil disobedience and the activity sought to be abated. Further, courts may preclude the necessity defense for an act of civil disobedience when there are legal alternatives available and the harm is not imminent, both of which are present in many cases where people attempt to use a necessity defense in the civil disobedience context.

C. Duress

Like necessity, duress is often an affirmative defense with the accused having the burden to prove its elements. At common law, courts recognized a duress defense because one could not rehabilitate or deter an individual from committing criminal conduct that was the product of improper coercion. Also, it was considered improper to punish someone whose free will to choose law-abiding behavior was overcome by another person's threats or physical abuse. The common law rule is that duress is not a defense to a homicide charge.

1. Elements

A defendant's crime may be excused by the duress defense when he or she was coerced to act by a threat of imminent death or serious bodily injury. Courts strictly apply the imminence requirement of this defense, precluding its use when the harm is to occur in the future. A reasonable belief of immediate harm, however, may be sufficient, even if that belief is incorrect. For example, a gun placed to the head of a bank employee may justify that person's unlawfully removing money from a bank safe to avoid being killed. A threat of harm to an individual's family can also be a basis for a duress defense. Economic damage, however, is usually insufficient for this defense. When the harm can be abated, the defense may not be used. Further, in many jurisdictions, duress is not allowed for the crime of murder, although the duress defense may be used to mitigate the crime to a lesser offense, such as manslaughter.

2. Model Penal Code

Model Penal Code § 2.09, like its necessity counterpart, does not require an element of imminence in the application of force. Rather, it simply requires that the use or threatened use of the force is of such gravity that "a person of reasonable firmness" in the situation "would have been unable to resist." Unlike the common law, however, the Model Penal Code does not preclude its use in homicide cases.

The Model Penal Code bars the duress defense to a crime when the defendant recklessly placed him- or herself in a situation where it was probable that the defendant would be subjected to duress. Similarly, under the MPC, duress is unavailable for a crime of criminal negligence such as when the defendant was negligent in placing him- or herself in the situation.

Checkpoints

- For necessity to be a defense, the harm threatened must be greater than the harm caused by the criminal conduct of the accused.

- At common law, a necessity defense required that the conduct of the accused be done as an emergency measure to avoid imminent injury, that it be proportional to the injury being avoided, that the accused had no reasonable alternative, and that the criminal conduct would abate the existing harm.

- Some courts will not allow a necessity defense for criminal activity designed to avoid economic harms or as a defense to murder.

- Direct civil disobedience and indirect civil disobedience are distinguished by whether the actor's crime is the object of the protest.

- Indirect civil disobedience is not recognized as a valid necessity defense.

- Duress is allowed as a defense because one cannot rehabilitate or deter improperly coerced conduct and because the actor's free will was overcome by coercion.

- At common law, duress can be a defense to criminal conduct when the accused has a reasonable belief of imminent harm. Duress is not a defense to a murder charge, but it may be used to mitigate a murder to a lesser charge.

- Necessity and duress are usually affirmative defenses with the defense bearing the burden of proof.

- The Model Penal Code does not require that the harm be immediate for necessity or duress.

Chapter 20

Competency, Insanity, and Diminished Capacity

Roadmap
- The theoretical basis for providing that incompetent defendants may not be tried, sentenced, or executed
- The tests for mental competence in criminal cases
- The theoretical basis for the rule that a criminally insane person is not responsible for his or her criminal acts
- The standard tests for criminal insanity and their strengths and weaknesses
- The unique procedures used in insanity defense cases
- How a diminished capacity defense operates as a partial defense

---

A. Overview

American criminal law recognizes that a defendant's mental status may have a significant impact on how the judicial process assesses criminal responsibility. Competency, insanity, and diminished capacity are three concepts that can factor into the resolution of a criminal case against an accused individual.

Competency is a pervasive concept that sets minimum mental standards to participate in various legal proceedings. The underlying theory is that a fair trial may be impossible if the defendant's mental condition is such that he or she cannot understand the proceedings or participate in the defense. A defendant who is *mentally incompetent* is deemed to be incapable of participating in various proceedings, such as a trial, sentencing hearing, or even execution. Competency refers to the person's mental condition at the time of the proceeding at issue.

Insanity refers to a limit on responsibility for criminal acts and raises profound questions about accountability for one's behavior. It assesses the defendant's mental status at the time of the crime rather than at the time of any court proceeding. In virtually every American jurisdiction a defendant who satisfies the applicable test of insanity has a complete defense to criminal liability and will be found not guilty of committing a crime, even though he or she did the act condemned by the criminal law. Some jurisdictions, however, have abolished an insanity defense although still allowing mental illness to be used to negate an element of the crime or as mitigation in homicide cases.

Diminished responsibility is a theory adopted in many American jurisdictions that provides a partial defense to criminal charges. It involves a careful assessment of a defendant's mental capacity to form a *mens rea* and may produce a ruling that, though the defendant is not criminally insane, he or she lacks the mental capacity to form a particular *mens rea* and cannot be convicted of a crime where that *mens rea* is an element. The defendant may be convicted, however, of other crimes that include *mens rea* elements other than those which this defendant lacks the mental capacity to have.

B. Competency

A fundamental facet of American criminal procedure, enforced by the Due Process Clause, is that the defendant who is *mentally incompetent* cannot be tried, sentenced, or executed as long as he or she is incompetent. The Supreme Court has explained this principle as a part of rights essential to a fair trial: the right to effective assistance of counsel; the right to summon, confront, and cross-examine witnesses; and the right to testify or to remain silent.

1. Tests of Competence

According to the Supreme Court, the general test of a defendant's mental competence for a trial or other judicial proceeding is whether the accused has sufficient mental ability to consult with his or her lawyer with a reasonable degree of rational understanding and a rational as well as factual understanding of the proceedings. *Dusky v. United States*, 362 U.S. 402 (1960). Model Penal Code §4.04 expresses this test more tersely in the language most courts use: a person is incompetent to participate in a judicial proceeding who "lacks the capacity to understand the proceedings against him or to assist in his own defense."

A person also cannot be executed while insane. *Ford v. Wainwright*, 477 U.S. 399 (1986). Although jurisdictions differ on the exact test used to assess whether the condemned prisoner is insane, a common feature is that the accused must be able to understand that the pending penalty is death and why that penalty was assessed. Some jurisdictions add the test used for judicial proceedings: can the accused assist in any legal defense efforts to thwart the execution. While to many it seems odd to bar the execution of incompetent death row inmates, the Supreme Court justified the ban, present in every state, as being naturally abhorrent, useless retribution, and offensive to humanity.

2. Determining Competency

The general rule is that every criminal defendant is presumed competent to engage in each proceeding. Accordingly, competency is usually not an issue unless raised by one of the parties. In this regard, the defense, the prosecutor, or judge may seek a competency examination if questions arise about the defendant's mental status. The judge must hold a hearing if there is a *bona fide* doubt as to the defendant's competence. The burden of proving incompetence is routinely placed on the defendant, who must establish incompetency by a preponderance of the evidence. *Medina v. California*, 505 U.S. 437 (1992).

Competency is determined by the trial judge, not jury, in one or more competency hearings. Once the issue of competency is raised, the trial court routinely conducts a hearing and orders the defendant to be evaluated by mental health professionals, often at a state mental hospital. After a formal evaluation is rendered, the court may have another competency hearing where the results are assessed. One or more mental health professionals may testify for one or both sides. Not infrequently, the accused is so obviously seriously mentally impaired that the two sides agree that he or she is not competent at that time. If the court finds that the defendant is not competent, the accused may be sent to a mental institution for further evaluation and treatment.

3. Effect of Incompetence

As a general rule, a defendant found incompetent to stand trial or participate in other proceedings is released (if a minor crime) or sent to a mental institution for observation and treatment. This can take several months, which according to the Supreme Court is considered a "reasonable period of time." Once he or she regains competence, the criminal prosecution may proceed.

If, after the mental evaluation, it is determined that in the foreseeable future there is no substantial probability that the accused will attain the necessary competence for the proceeding, the state must institute civil commitment procedures if it is to continue confinement. This means that the state may not hold someone indefinitely just because the person is incompetent to stand trial. There must be judicial proceedings assessing the defendant's mental health. If, in these civil commitment hearings, it is determined by at least clear and convincing evidence (some states raise the standard to proof beyond a reasonable doubt) that the person is dangerous to himself or to others, a court may order the defendant to be involuntarily confined in a mental institution or other such facility. Absent this proof, the accused, who has not been convicted of a crime, must be released from confinement.

The Supreme Court has allowed the government to use antipsychotic drugs—even involuntarily—on a criminal accused, when medically necessary and appropriate, in order to restore the accused to sufficient mental competence to participate in criminal proceedings. Less intrusive measures must be used if possible.

C. Insanity

In jurisdictions that permit an insanity defense, an individual accused of a crime who is found insane has a complete defense to a criminal charge and will be acquitted. Following an acquittal, a myriad of procedures are routinely followed that could lead to the person being sent to a mental hospital for evaluation and possibly treatment.

1. Theoretical Basis for Insanity Defense

The core of the insanity defense is that it embodies the principle that in the Anglo-American system of criminal justice, the criminal law reaches the conduct of those persons who are *morally blameworthy*. People whose mental processes lack certain qualities are deemed not morally blameworthy and therefore are excused from criminal liability. One rationale advanced for this is that people who are criminally insane lack the free will or volition to be held responsible for their behavior. Some commentators also argue that punishment is ineffective on the insane, who cannot appreciate why they are being punished, and it is also not useful as a deterrent. Retributivists maintain that the criminally insane are not accountable because they do not deserve, in a moral sense, to be punished. The Model Penal Code summarizes the issue as follows:

> Those who are irresponsible under the [insanity] test are plainly beyond the reach of the restraining influence of the law, and their condemnation would be both futile and unjust ... Moreover, the category defined by the [insanity defense] ... is so extreme that to the ordinary person the exculpation of those it encompasses bespeaks no weakness in the law.

Model Penal Code § 4.01, Explanatory Note.

2. Mental Disease or Defect

The insanity defense is ordinarily based on a finding that the defendant suffered from a *mental disease or defect*. While the meaning of these terms is rarely at issue since in many cases the accused obviously suffers from serious mental problems, on occasion there are definitional issues. It is generally recognized that, by definition, a *disease* may be subject to change, while a *defect*, such as serious retardation or brain injury, may not change over time. Beyond this unhelpful general description, only a few jurisdictions actually define either term by statute. Some states limit what can be considered for an insanity defense. For example, a California statute states that the insanity defense may not be based solely on "a personality or adjustment disorder, a seizure disorder, or an addiction to, or abuse of, intoxicating substances." *Cal. Penal Code § 29.8.*

Model Penal Code § 4.01(b) does not define either disease or defect but does eliminate from inclusion "an abnormality manifested only by repeated criminal or otherwise antisocial conduct." This exclusion means that sociopaths or psychopaths, whose mental condition is manifested by repeated criminal or antisocial conduct, cannot offer this diagnosis as a mental disease or defect qualifying for the insanity defense.

While ordinary intoxication, even that of an alcoholic, is routinely rejected as a disease sufficient for an insanity defense, *involuntary intoxication* may so qualify and be used to satisfy the elements of the insanity defense. For example, the Model Penal Code allows a defendant to argue that his or her involuntary intoxication caused a loss of substantial capacity to appreciate the criminality of the conduct or to conform the conduct to the requirements of the law. For this purpose, involuntary intoxication refers to intoxication induced by extraordinary means resulting in an intoxication that cannot be attributed to the offender's free will. One type of involuntary intoxication is an abnormal reaction to a legitimate substance, such as prescribed medication. Another is an intoxicant administered by trickery or force so that it cannot be said to have been ingested as the voluntary act of the offender.

3. Tests of Insanity

American jurisdictions have adopted specific tests used to ascertain whether a defendant was criminally insane at the time of the crime. It must be stressed that these tests of *criminal insanity* are not the same as those for competence to participate in a proceeding, discussed above, or for capacity to perform various legal tasks, such as write a will or enter a contract, or for mental disability sufficient to trigger a jurisdiction's civil commitment process, also discussed below.

a. M'Naghten *Test*

The basic test of insanity in American criminal courts has been the so-called *M'Naghten test*, stemming from an 1843 English case, *M'Naghten's Case*, 8 Eng. Rep. 718 (H.L. 1843). The House of Lords held that a person was criminally insane if at the time of the committing of the act, the party accused was laboring under such a *defect of reason*, from disease of the mind, as not to know the nature and quality of the act he was doing, or if he did know it, that he did *not know he was doing what was wrong.*

Note that the *M'Naghten* test, often misnamed the "right-wrong test," is a cognitive one, focusing on what the defendant *knew* at the time of the crime. The word *know* has been subjected to a variety of interpretations. One view looks simply at the defendant's awareness: Was the accused aware that he or she was taking money by force from a grocery store and that it was morally (or legally) wrong to do so? The second approach looks deeper into the defendant's emotional awareness of the conduct and the wrongfulness of it.

The *M'Naghten* test incorporates two types of knowledge. First, the defendant is insane if he or she did not know the *nature and quality* of the act. This *cognitive incapacity test,* as it is sometimes called, might occur if the defendant thought he or she were squeezing juice from a grapefruit when in actuality he or she was strangling his or her mother. Second, the alternate cognitive approach, often called the *right-wrong* test, asks whether the defendant knew the conduct was wrong. Courts differ in their interpretation of the word "wrong" in this test. Some ask whether the accused was aware that the conduct *violated the law.* The more pervasive view is that the test focuses on the defendant's knowledge that the conduct is both *morally* and *legally* wrong. Moral wrong does not refer to the accused's personal moral code but rather to the broader moral standards of society.

The two prongs of *M'Naghten* are still the test of criminal insanity in a number of American jurisdictions, though some states have modified it. Some locales adopt only the moral incapacity prong while others use only the cognitive incapacity approach.

Despite *M'Naghten's* impressive longevity, it has been subjected to criticism on several fronts. The most frequent argument is that its focus on the defendant's cognitive abilities overlooks other important mental health issues that should also be considered in assessing responsibility for crime. The primary one is whether the defendant, even with the ability to know the nature and quality of conduct as well as the moral dimensions of the behavior, could control his or her actions.

b. Irresistible Impulse Test

A number of jurisdictions accepted the criticism of *M'Naghten* and added an additional test of insanity, sometimes called the *volitional* or *irresistible impulse* test. Under this alternative approach, even if the accused is unable to satisfy either prong of *M'Naghten*, he or she may be found criminally insane if a mental disease deprived the accused of *will power to resist the insane impulse.* The approach is sometimes expressed by asking whether the defendant would have committed the crime if aware that a police officer were nearby observing the event. As expected, this test, too, is heavily criticized as focusing too much on sudden, momentary urges or impulses and ignoring those people whose criminal actions are the product of long-term thought processes, such as brooding or reflection. Another objection is that this test may be interpreted as requiring a total inability to resist forces impelling the criminal acts, yet psychiatrists maintain that less than total lack of control should be available, in some cases, to excuse criminal responsibility.

c. Durham *(Product) Test*

Because of concerns that the *M'Naghten*-Irresistible Impulse combined approach was still inadequate in that it did not embrace the full measure of mental activities that led a person to commit a crime, the United States Court of Appeals for the District of Columbia Circuit rejected both tests and adopted what became known as the *Durham* or *Product Test*. The *Durham* (Product) Test was first adopted in 1871 in New Hampshire. In *Durham v. United States*, 214 F.2d 862 (D.C. Cir. 1954), the court held that a person was criminally insane and not responsible for unlawful acts that were the *product of a mental disease or defect.*

This "causation" test created a vast amount of controversy that led to its eventual rejection by the District of Columbia Circuit. The *Durham* test was seen as being too lenient in permitting insanity acquittals (and indeed the acquittal rate increased under this test) and as relying too heavily on the testimony of experts, such as psychiatrists, who were viewed as uniquely capable of deciding whether criminal deeds had been the product of a mental disease or defect. Moreover, the term *product* was characterized as ambiguous, sometimes viewed as a "but for" test that would excuse great numbers of offenders who should be held accountable for their misdeeds.

d. Model Penal Code (Substantial Capacity) Test

Model Penal Code § 4.01, which is widely accepted in federal courts and many state courts, combines *M'Naghten* and Irresistible Impulse, and provides:

A person is not responsible for criminal conduct if at the time of such conduct as a result of mental disease or defect he lacks substantial capacity either to appreciate the criminality [wrongfulness] of his conduct or to conform his conduct to the requirements of law.

Note that the MPC version tracks *M'Naghten* by including a cognitive prong. In order to give jurisdictions a choice between the knowledge-it-is-a-crime view and the knowledge-it-is-immoral approach (an issue raised by the vagueness in *M'Naghten's* test of knowing right from wrong), the MPC provides alternative words to describe what the defendant must "appreciate." One alternative asks whether the accused could appreciate the *criminality* of the conduct. This refers to whether the government prohibits the conduct through the criminal law. The alternate word, *wrongfulness*, focuses on awareness of society's moral disapproval of the behavior.

The MPC differs from *M'Naghten* by using the more generous term, *appreciate*, for *M'Naghten's* standard of "know." This suggests that more than intellectual knowledge of the criminality of conduct is necessary — the offender must have some level of understanding as well.

Another distinction is that *M'Naghten* and Irresistible Impulse seemed to require that the mental condition completely impaired or "utterly incapacitated" the defendant's self control, but the MPC only requires that it impair the accused's *substantial capacity* to appreciate criminality or conform conduct. The MPC explained this difference as justified by modern psychiatry that recognized gradations of incapacities. The term "substantial" refers to some "appreciable magnitude when measured by the standard of humanity in general." *MPC § 4.01, Explanatory Note.*

4. Procedural Issues in Insanity Defense

The unique features of the insanity defense have engendered some unique procedural rules.

a. Notice of Intent to Use Insanity Defense

The usual pattern is that the individual accused of a crime who plans on raising an insanity defense or plans to call an expert witness on a mental health issue, must provide the prosecution with notice of an intent to present this defense or call this witness. This triggers a process which authorizes the trial judge to order the defendant to be evaluated by mental health professionals. Each side gets a copy of the results of the court-ordered evaluation. The purposes of this unusual procedure are (1) to prevent the prosecution from being surprised by the defense's decision to rely on insanity, and (2) to allow the prosecution to have the defendant professionally evaluated prior to trial. Absent this notice, the defense could use the opening statement to announce its reliance on the insanity defense and on private mental health professionals who had, unbeknownst to the prosecution, evaluated the accused. If the state had neither notice of this defense nor an opportunity to have the defendant examined, the trial would be one-sided with the prosecution unable to prepare adequately to respond to the defendant's insanity defense.

b. Burden of Proof

The typical pattern is that the defendant is presumed sane and must raise an insanity defense if this defense is to be an issue. To raise the defense, ordinarily the defendant must put on some proof (sometimes called a *prima facie* case) that he or she is criminally insane. The next procedural step may involve one of two approaches. In the first model, in order to overcome the presumption of sanity, the defendant must satisfy the burden of persuasion by convincing the trier of fact, often the jury, that he or she meets the locale's insanity test. Sometimes the standard of proof on this issue is a preponderance of evidence, though a few jurisdictions use a higher one, such as by clear and convincing evidence.

The second approach, called burden-shifting, puts the burden on the prosecution after the defense has made its *prima facie* case. In this model, the presumption of sanity disappears once the accused offers a *prima facie* case of insanity. The government now must prove the negative—that the defendant was not insane at the time of the crime. This, too, could be by a preponderance of the evidence or even, as in Pennsylvania, beyond a reasonable doubt.

c. Jury Issues

Whether the defendant satisfies the jurisdiction's test of insanity is ordinarily a jury question. The typical state procedure submits this issue to the jury which decides the issue of insanity at the same time it decides guilt or innocence. Often the jury is given several options: Guilty, Not Guilty, Not Guilty by Reason of Insanity (NGRI), and, in some locales, Guilty But Mentally Ill (GBMI).

A GBMI verdict was created because of concern that some defendants were mentally ill and needed mental health treatment, but would not get it if found not guilty and released, or if found guilty and sent to prison where mental health facilities were often lacking. The alternate verdict, GBMI, essentially allows the defendant who is guilty of the crime to be held responsible and punished, yet also be able to receive mental health services that would not be available in prison or on probation. In some jurisdictions a GBMI verdict authorizes the court to have the defendant evaluated by mental health professionals to assess whether treatment is appropriate.

A defendant found GBMI is essentially found guilty and sentenced in the ordinary way to probation or incarceration. But the GBMI verdict dictates that the offender receive mental health services while on probation or in jail or, if medically necessary, in an inpatient or outpatient mental health facility. Once those services are no longer necessary, the defendant found GBMI will serve the remaining part of the sentence as an ordinary prisoner in jail, prison, or on probation, though mental health services could still be required. For example, if a robber is found GBMI and given a ten-year sentence, he or she could be sent to a mental hospital for treatment. If released from that facility before the ten-year sentence is served, the remaining years would be spent in prison.

d. Impact of Finding of Not Guilty By Reason of Insanity

Although a defendant found not guilty by reason of insanity technically is free from the burdens of being convicted of a crime, the defendant rarely will be allowed to return home after the verdict. Jurisdictions universally authorize the trial court to order the defendant to a mental hospital for a period of evaluation that may last several months. At the end of that evaluation, the government authorities may initiate civil commitment proceedings to keep the defendant involuntarily hospitalized if he or she is found to be dangerous to him or herself or others.

5. Abolition of the Insanity Defense

The insanity defense has generated a vast amount of criticism as some argue that it is easily abused and may bar punishment for people who ought to be held responsible for their actions. Accordingly, a few American jurisdictions have abolished the insanity defense. Idaho, for example, has enacted a statute that provides: "[m]ental condition shall not be a defense to any charge of criminal conduct." *Idaho Code § 18-207.*

In the few jurisdictions that have eliminated the insanity defense, a defendant's mental condition may still be relevant in several contexts. In some jurisdictions it may be a consideration on whether the defendant had a particular *mens rea*. It may also be important at the sentencing phase, especially in capital cases. For example, Utah's criminal code only allows one to use mental illness to show that the accused "lacked the mental state required as an element of the offense charged" or as mitigation evidence of the penalty in a capital case or to reduce the level of a criminal homicide or attempted homicide offense as specified by statute. *Utah St. § 76-2-305.*

D. Diminished Capacity

Diminished capacity can be approached in two different ways. It can be seen as something that negates the *mens rea* element of the crime. It can also be seen as a separate defense that offers the accused an excuse, but one that does not rise to the level of insanity. Oftentimes, the evidence used to support one of these approaches is the same, and thus they overlap.

1. Negating *Mens Rea*

In those cases where the defendant claims to have a mental disease or defect but cannot satisfy the jurisdiction's test of insanity, the mental condition may still be relevant and admissible for the defense on the issue of whether the accused had the necessary *mens rea* required for the crime. Just as each defendant is presumed sane, he or she is also presumed to have the capacity to form the *mens rea* necessary for the crime at issue. And just as the defendant may rebut the presumption of sanity with evidence of insanity, ordinarily the defendant may attempt to rebut the presumption of *mens rea* capacity by proof of a mental disease or defect. Some courts limit the use of a diminished capacity defense to specific intent crimes. *State v. Bourn*, 58 A.3d 236 (Vt. 2012).

For example, assume that a defendant is charged with intentional homicide. Since "intent to kill" is the *mens rea* for this particular category of homicide, the prosecution has the burden of proving beyond a reasonable doubt that the accused had the requisite intent to kill. The defendant would be entitled to an acquittal on this count if the state could not meet this high standard. One defense argument may be that the defendant's mental condition was such that he or she did not have the mental capacity to form the necessary intent. The defendant could even offer expert testimony from a psychiatrist on the issue and the state may call its own mental health experts to counter the defense proof. The defense evidence may be sufficient to cause the trier of fact to have a reasonable doubt whether the defendant had the intent to kill or may even be convincing enough to produce an acquittal for that charge.

Some jurisdictions, however, are reluctant to allow diminished capacity evidence when it is presented as negating the *mens rea* of the crime. For example, California, has specifically abolished the defense of diminished capacity and specifies by statute that evidence of a person's "intoxication, trauma, mental illness, disease, or defect shall not be admissible to show or negate capacity to form the particular purpose, intent, motive, malice aforethought, knowledge, or other mental state required for commission of the crime charged." *Cal. Penal Code § 25*. Such evidence is admissible, however, in ascertaining the sentence.

Arizona, similarly, has limited the diminished capacity defense by banning expert testimony on whether the defendant's mental incapacity had a bearing on the formation of a *mens rea* element. *See Clark v. Arizona*, 548 U.S. 2709 (2006) (the limit on defense expert testimony does not violate the Due Process Clause).

2. Diminished Capacity Defense

Diminished capacity, like insanity, can also be considered a separate defense. In this regard they are sometimes confused as they share common features. Diminished capacity and insanity are similar in that both routinely involve expert testimony that a particular defendant's abnormal mental condition rendered the defendant incapable of performing certain ordinary mental processes, such as knowing right from wrong (insanity) or intending a particular result (diminished responsibility).

On the other hand, the two concepts are markedly different in some respects. Diminished capacity is often referred to as a *partial defense* because it is relevant only to some crimes—those having a mental element that the defendant asserts was absent because of his or her mental condition. By way of contrast, insanity in most American jurisdictions is a total defense to any criminal charge. Thus, a defendant with a successful diminished capacity defense may be not guilty of intentional homicide, but still be liable for reckless homicide. On the other hand, the same defendant would be acquitted of all charges if found not guilty by reason of insanity.

Diminished capacity has been subject to the same criticisms as the insanity defense. A common argument is that it allows offenders to escape responsibility for their actions. Some jurisdictions reject diminished capacity unless the accused can show that it rises to the level of insanity. The Supreme Court in *Atkins v. Virginia*, 536 U.S. 304 (2002), however, held that it is a violation of the Eighth and Fourteenth Amendments to execute persons with intellectual disability. The Court has also rejected a Florida law that "define[d] intellectual disability to require an IQ test score of 70 or less." The Court found this "rigid rule" unconstitutional as it created "an unacceptable risk that persons with intellectual disability" would be executed. *Hall v. Florida*, 134 S.Ct. 1986 (2014).

Checkpoints

- An individual accused of a crime may not be subject to trial, sentencing or execution if mentally incompetent at the time of the proceeding.

- The test of mental competence to participate in a trial or other proceeding asks whether the accused understands the proceedings and can participate in the defense.

- A person found incompetent to stand trial may be sent to a mental hospital for treatment and evaluation, and may be kept hospitalized if he or she meets the jurisdiction's test for civil commitment purposes.

- Insanity is a complete defense to a criminal prosecution and measures the defendant's mental state at the time of the crime.

- American law has recognized four major tests of criminal insanity.

- The *M'Naghten* test is a cognitive test that asks whether at the time of the crime the accused had a mental disease that caused a lack of knowledge of the nature and quality of the criminal act or a lack of knowledge that the act was wrong.

- The irresistible impulse test focuses on whether the defendant could control behavior or lacked the will power to resist the criminal impulses.

- The *Durham* test, now rejected by its primary proponent, is broader than *M'Naghten* or irresistible impulse and asks whether the unlawful acts were the product of a mental disease or defect.

- The Model Penal Code test is a modernized version of *M'Naghten* and irresistible impulse. It measures whether the accused lacked substantial capacity to appreciate the criminality of the conduct or to conform the conduct to the requirements of the law.

- An insanity defense triggers application of several unique procedures including a defense notice to the prosecution of an intent to use the defense and mandatory mental evaluation ordered by the court.

- Every criminal defendant is presumed sane and the defendant has the burden of raising the insanity defense by putting on some evidence that he or she was insane at the time of the crime.

- Jurisdictions differ on who bears the burden of proving insanity and the standard of proof necessary.

- A jury in an insanity case may have three or four options: guilty, not guilty, not guilty by reason of insanity (NGRI), and guilty but mentally ill (GBMI).

- Guilty but mentally ill (GBMI) is a relatively recent option that recognizes that the defendant is guilty of the crime but needs mental health treatment.

- Diminished capacity can be used to negate the *mens rea* element of the crime or as a separate defense that may reduce the level of a crime because of a mental disease or defect.

Chapter 21

Intoxication

Roadmap

- States vary on how to treat intoxication
- The common law treatment of voluntary and involuntary intoxication
- The Model Penal Code's approach to intoxication

A. Overview

While it is commonly said that intoxication is no defense in a criminal case, this is an overstatement in most American jurisdictions since intoxication may serve as a defense in limited circumstances. Model Penal Code § 2.08 defines intoxication as "a disturbance of mental or physical capacities resulting from the introduction of substances into the body." Another definition is "the inability, resulting from the introduction of substances into the body, to exercise control over one's mental faculties." *Del. Code Ann. 11, § 424.*

There are many different types of intoxicants that can form the basis of a defense based on intoxication. A common statutory definition refers to the substances as "drugs, toxic vapors or intoxicating liquors." *Ariz. Rev. Stat. Ann. § 13-105(20).* Typical examples include alcohol, illegal drugs, and prescription medicines.

States vary on how and whether to allow an argument premised on intoxication. There are five different approaches that can be taken, although more than one may be used in the same case:

1. Some states will permit intoxication to be used to negate the *actus reus* of a crime. When presented this way the accused is arguing that he or she was extremely intoxicated and therefore did not commit a voluntary act.

2. Most states permit intoxication to be used as evidence to negate the *mens rea* of a crime. Under this approach, the accused is claiming to have

been so intoxicated that he or she did not have the *mens rea* (especially intent or knowledge) to commit the crime.

3. Another approach is that intoxication is presented as the underpinning of an insanity defense, with the accused arguing that he or she should not be criminally liable because the intoxication was part of a mental disease or defect.

4. Some states may specifically provide for a defense of intoxication similar to insanity.

5. Finally, some states totally reject intoxication as a defense.

When intoxication is asserted as a potential criminal defense, it is often necessary to distinguish between voluntary and involuntary intoxication. The crime involved can also make a difference. For example, intoxication may not be a viable defense if the crime is one of strict liability, but some states will allow intoxication to reduce a murder to a lesser homicide charge.

Intoxication can also be a factor in sentencing. A judge might increase the sentence if, as a result of voluntarily getting drunk, the defendant committed the offense. Alternatively, the sentence might be reduced if the court finds that alcohol influenced the accused in doing this offense and a recurrence is unlikely. Many jurisdictions also offer rehabilitative avenues if the crime involved drugs or alcohol. Thus, the accused may be placed in a drug treatment facility or provided alcohol counseling as a part of the sentence. Some jurisdictions have instituted drug courts, specialized courts to handle drug and alcohol cases from a problem-solving perspective.

B. Common Law

If using a common law approach to intoxication as a defense in a criminal case, it is first necessary to consider whether the intoxication was voluntary or involuntary. The mental element of the offense at issue is also critical. Does the offense have a specific intent or require knowledge of a fact, or is it one with only general criminal intent or strict liability?

1. Voluntary Intoxication

a. Defined

Voluntary intoxication (often called *self-induced intoxication* in the statutes) refers to intoxication caused by substances the defendant knowingly introduced into his or her body and which the defendant knew or should have known had a tendency to cause intoxication. Most intoxication cases involve voluntary intoxication, such as when a person gets drunk at a party or bar.

b. Negate an Element of the Crime

i. Actus Reus

An accused may be able to argue that due to intoxication there is insufficient evidence to prove the voluntary act or *actus reus* of the crime. For example, when the accused is so intoxicated that the act performed is no longer a voluntary act, but rather an act in a comatose state, it can be claimed that this element of the crime is not met. This argument, however, is seldom accepted.

The accused may also argue that he or she was incapable of performing a specified act because of the intoxication. For example, a person charged with obstruction of justice for destroying documents might argue that he or she was too intoxicated to run the shredder where the documents were destroyed.

ii. Omission to Act

On rare occasions intoxication may be a defense to criminal liability based on an omission. A person may be criminally liable for a failure to act when he or she had a duty to act under the circumstances. There is no liability if the person was unable to comply with the duty. It is arguable that in some, though not all, jurisdictions a person who is very intoxicated and perhaps unconscious cannot be convicted for a failure to act since he or she was unable to do so. On the other hand, some jurisdictions will deny a defense in this situation since the accused voluntarily became intoxicated and thereby placed him or herself in the position of being unable to comply with the duty.

iii. Mens Rea

More common are arguments that the intoxication negated the *mens rea* of the crime. At common law and in many jurisdictions today, voluntary intoxication is not considered a defense to a *general intent* or *strict liability* crime, but could serve to negate the *mens rea* associated with a specific intent crime. It might, for example, be used to negate intent, purpose, deliberation, premeditation, or knowledge. Thus, an individual who was intoxicated might have a viable defense to the crime of burglary, a breaking and entering of the dwelling of another, at nighttime, with the intent to commit a felony therein. The intoxication could have deprived the offender of the capacity to form the necessary specific intent. But this same person might still be convicted of the crime of trespassing, a general intent crime.

Some states may not explicitly recognize specific and general intent crimes in allowing an intoxication defense. New York, for example, provides that "evidence of intoxication may be offered by the defendant whenever it is relevant to negative an element of the crime charged." *N.Y. Penal Law § 15.25.*

2. Involuntary Intoxication

a. Defined

Often the term *involuntary intoxication* itself is not defined other than as intoxication that is not voluntary. Involuntary intoxication can come in many different forms. Most common illustrations of involuntary intoxication are situations when the accused consumes an intoxicant through force or duress, takes a prescribed medicine or other substance without knowing its intoxicating effect, or reaches a grossly excessive level of intoxication based on the amount of the intoxicant ingested (sometimes called *pathological intoxication*). In other situations, however, courts refuse to view the intoxication as involuntary, such as when the accused knowingly exceeds the prescribed quantity of medicine or knowingly mixes a prescribed drug with alcohol. Courts vary on whether intoxication is voluntary or involuntary when the accused takes a prescribed medication after having been warned of its intoxicating effect. Some courts will find it to be voluntary, as opposed to involuntary, intoxication if the individual failed to heed the warnings on the prescription label.

b. Negate an Element of the Crime

The law is more forgiving if the intoxication is involuntary. Like voluntary intoxication, involuntary intoxication may negate an element of the crime charged. This could be the *actus reus*, an omission to act, or the *mens rea*.

c. Insanity Defense

One approach, representing a minority position, is that involuntary intoxication is deemed to satisfy the "mental disease" requirement for the insanity defense. This view is often rejected on the theory that a "mental disease" refers to a condition that is *settled* rather than transient. But even if, as is usually the case, involuntary intoxication does not constitute a mental disease and therefore cannot be the basis for an insanity acquittal, the fact that the defendant was intoxicated at the time of the crime may be admissible as some proof that at that time he or she suffered from an alcohol-induced psychosis or other mental disease associated with intoxication and that does constitute a "disease" sufficient for the insanity defense.

d. Insanity-Like Defense

Even though involuntary intoxication will not suffice for an insanity defense in many jurisdictions, some jurisdictions recognize intoxication as a separate insanity-like defense that results in an acquittal for lack of criminal responsibility. In Alabama, for example, "involuntary intoxication is a defense to prosecution if as a result the actor lacks capacity either to appreciate the criminality of his conduct or to conform his conduct to the requirements of the law." *Ala. Code § 13A-3-2(c)*. Note that this defense is virtually identical to an insanity defense but is technically a separate one, excusing crimes committed because of involuntary intoxication as opposed to a mental disease or defect required for an insanity acquittal.

C. Rejecting or Limiting Intoxication

Some modern jurisdictions depart from the common law and limit or reject voluntary intoxication as a defense. A few states have gone so far as to totally eliminate a defense of intoxication and even bar evidence negating the *mens rea* element due to intoxication. Missouri, for example, specifically makes evidence of voluntary intoxication "in no event ... admissible for the purpose of negating a mental state which is an element of the offense." *Mo. Ann. Stat. § 562.076*.

These restrictions on proof of *mens rea* have been subject to constitutional challenges. In *Montana v. Egelhoff*, 518 U.S. 37 (1996), the defendant was charged with two counts of deliberate homicide, defined as "purposely" or "knowingly" causing death. Since the defendant was highly intoxicated at the time of the crime, he attempted to use the intoxication to establish that he did not purposely or knowingly kill. The trial judge followed Montana law and instructed the jury that it could not consider the defendant's intoxicated condition in assessing his *mens rea* at the time of the crime. The Montana statute provided, in part, that "[a] person who is in an intoxicated condition is criminally responsible for his conduct and an intoxicated condition is not a defense to any offense and may not be taken into consideration in determining the existence of a mental state which is an element of the offense" absent certain circumstances.

The defendant argued that barring him from presenting proof of his voluntary intoxication, violated his due process right to offer a full defense against the charge that he purposely and knowingly committed a killing. The Supreme Court disagreed, and in a closely divided opinion upheld the conviction. The Court upheld the Montana legislature's decision to ban use of intoxication as a defense or even allow it as evidence to show a lack of *mens rea*. The Court found that Montana's rules were supported by legitimate policies such as deterring drunkenness and irresponsible conduct while intoxicated and by moral precepts holding people responsible for their behavior while intoxicated.

Others jurisdictions severely limit the intoxication defense. Some allow intoxication to reduce a murder in the first degree to a murder in the second degree, but not to a lesser offense such as manslaughter or negligent homicide. Thus, a court might provide a jury instruction on intoxication when the accused faces a first degree murder charge, but find that intoxication is irrelevant if the charge were second degree murder. A related approach holds that voluntary intoxication may not be used as the basis for the heat of passion or extreme emotional disturbance that may reduce a murder to the lesser offense of voluntary manslaughter. *Del. Code Ann. 11, §641.*

Another limit is when the defendant, while drunk, kills or injures someone and raises a self-defense claim when charged with homicide or assault. Since the ordinary test of self-defense is whether the accused has a reasonable belief that harm is imminent and the force used to repel that harm is reasonable under the circumstances, the defendant's intoxication is of little help since the cases indicate the test is what a reasonable *sober* person would do. If the accused's intoxication affected his or her perceptions so that the conduct seemed reasonable to the accused, courts will nevertheless assess the reasonableness of the conduct from the perspective of an objective person whose perceptions were unaffected by intoxicants. Of course, the fact that the defendant was intoxicated does not preclude a claim of self-defense since the use of force may have been reasonable under the circumstances and may satisfy the objective test of self-defense.

D. Model Penal Code

The Model Penal Code allows intoxication to negative an element of the offense. The MPC and a large number of states, however, preclude the use of intoxication when the *mens rea* is recklessness (requiring awareness of and then ignoring a substantial risk of harm) and the accused claims that he or she did not act recklessly since he or she was unaware of the risk because of the voluntary intoxication. Thus, the accused charged with reckless homicide while driving drunk will be unsuccessful with the argument that he or she does not satisfy the test of recklessness because the defendant's intoxication caused the accused to be unaware of the serious risk being taken. For example, a Delaware statute states: "A person who creates such a risk but is unaware thereof solely by reason of voluntary intoxication also acts recklessly with respect" to the risk. *Del. Code Ann. 11, § 231(c)*.

Model Penal Code § 2.08(3) explicitly provides that intoxication is not a mental disease for purposes of insanity. This does not, however, preclude an insanity defense that may be an outgrowth of extensive use of alcohol. So an individual who suffers from a mental disease resulting from extensive use of alcohol may still argue insanity if he or she meets the elements of the insanity defense.

Finally the Model Penal Code does provide for an affirmative defense premised upon intoxication when the intoxication is not self-induced or when the intoxication is pathological. Pathological is defined as "intoxication grossly excessive in degree, given the amount of the intoxicant, to which the actor does not know he is susceptible." For example, the accused can present evidence to support a defense when he or she suffers an unexpected response to a prescribed medicine that causes an extreme reaction by the accused. The MPC characterized this intoxication defense as involving an incapacitation "as extreme as that which would establish irresponsibility had it resulted from mental disease." *MPC § 2.08, comment*.

Checkpoints

- States vary on how they approach an intoxication defense, with some states totally rejecting this defense.

- Intoxication might be allowed as evidence negating an element of the offense, such as the *actus reus* or *mens rea* of the crime. It may also be offered as a separate defense or as a form of insanity.

- At common law, voluntary intoxication could negate a specific intent, but not the general intent of a crime.

- Both the common law and Model Penal Code permit involuntary or pathological intoxication to constitute a defense.

- In some states, the degree of the homicide charge will be reduced when the accused was intoxicated.

Mastering Criminal Law
Master Checklist

The following reflects the topics covered in each chapter. A good understanding of the overall material would require a detailed knowledge of each of these topics.

Chapter 1 · Introduction to Criminal Law
- ❏ Basic principles of criminal law
- ❏ The structure of a crime
- ❏ The criminal process

Chapter 2 · Interpretation and Constitutionality
- ❏ Basic rules of statutory interpretation
- ❏ Interpretation of criminal statutes
- ❏ Constitutional considerations

Chapter 3 · Sentencing
- ❏ Punishment theories
- ❏ The sentencing process
- ❏ Different types of sentences

Chapter 4 · *Actus Reus*
- ❏ The requirement of an act
- ❏ What is an act?
- ❏ Different types of acts

Chapter 5 · *Mens Rea*
- ❏ The requirement of a mental state
- ❏ Different types of *mens rea*
- ❏ Exceptions to requiring a *mens rea*
- ❏ Negating the *mens rea*

Chapter 6 · Causation
- ❏ Rationale for requiring causation
- ❏ Different types of causation
- ❏ Negating causation

Chapter 7 · Burden of Proof
- ❏ Different burdens and presumptions
- ❏ Parties responsible for burden

Chapter 8 · Homicide and Related Crimes
- ❏ General principles related to homicide
- ❏ Different approaches to the law of homicide
- ❏ Classifications of different types of homicide

Chapter 9 · Rape and Other Sexual Offenses
- ❏ Elements of rape
- ❏ Different crimes related to rape
- ❏ Proving rape

Chapter 10 · Assault, Battery, and Related Offenses
- ❏ Different assault and battery crimes
- ❏ Defenses unique to these crimes

Chapter 11 · Theft, Property Offenses, and Burglary
- ❏ Source and elements of theft and property related crimes

Chapter 12 · Criminal Enterprises
- ❏ Different types of criminal enterprises
- ❏ Crimes applicable to criminal enterprises

Chapter 13 · Accomplice Liability
- ❏ Different approaches to accessory liability
- ❏ Attributes of accessory liability
- ❏ Negating accessory liability

Chapter 14 · Solicitation
- ❏ Elements of solicitation
- ❏ Unique rules related to solicitation
- ❏ Defenses related to solicitation

Chapter 15 · Attempt and Related Preparatory Crimes
- ❏ Elements of attempt

❏ Determining sufficient acts to forms attempt
❏ Negating claims of attempt

Chapter 16 · Conspiracy

❏ Policy rationale for the crime
❏ Elements of the crime
❏ Conspiracy and substantive offenses
❏ Negating conspiracy charges

Chapter 17 · Defenses in General, Alibi, and Entrapment

❏ What is a defense?
❏ Different types of defenses
❏ Factors that influence a defense
❏ The defenses of alibi and entrapment

Chapter 18 · Defending Self, Others, and Property

❏ Elements of self defense, property, and habitation
❏ Individuals entitled to claim self-defense, property, and habitation
❏ How to present a claim of self-defense, property, and habitation
❏ Rules that prohibit using self-defense

Chapter 19 · Necessity and Duress

❏ Principles for arguing duress and necessity defenses
❏ Civil disobedience arguments

Chapter 20 · Competency, Insanity, and Diminished Capacity

❏ Determining competency to stand trial
❏ Principles for arguing an insanity or diminished capacity defense
❏ Different approaches to the insanity and diminished capacity defense

Chapter 21 · Intoxication

❏ Differences between voluntary and involuntary intoxication
❏ Principles for arguing intoxication
❏ Different approaches to an intoxication defense

Index